WEST COAST COOKING

WEST COAST COOKING

GREG ATKINSON

SASQUATCH BOOKS
SEATTLE

DEDICATION

This book is dedicated to the generations of West Coast cooks, most of them mothers, who nourished our bodies and fed our souls with the care and attention that went into the meals they cooked. Their efforts brought us together around the table and laid the foundation of our culture.

Printed in Canada
Published by Sasquatch Books
Distributed by PGW/Perseus

15 14 13 12 11 10 09 08   10 9 8 7 6 5 4 3 2 1

Cover photograph: John Granen Photography
Cover and interior book design: Kate Basart/Union Pageworks
Illustrations: Jennifer Playford

Library of Congress Cataloging-in-Publication Data

Atkinson, Greg, 1959–

West coast cooking / Greg Atkinson.

p. cm.

Includes bibliographical references and index.

ISBN 10: 1-57061-472-5 / ISBN 13: 978-1-57061-472-9 (Hardcover)

ISBN 10: 1-57061-574-8 / ISBN 13: 978-1-57061-574-0 (Paperback)

1. Cookery, American--Western style. I. Title.

TX715.2.W47A85 2006

641.5979--dc22

2006044657

Sasquatch Books | 119 South Main Street, Suite 400 | Seattle, WA 98104

206.467.4300 | www.sasquatchbooks.com | custserv@sasquatchbooks.com

CONTENTS

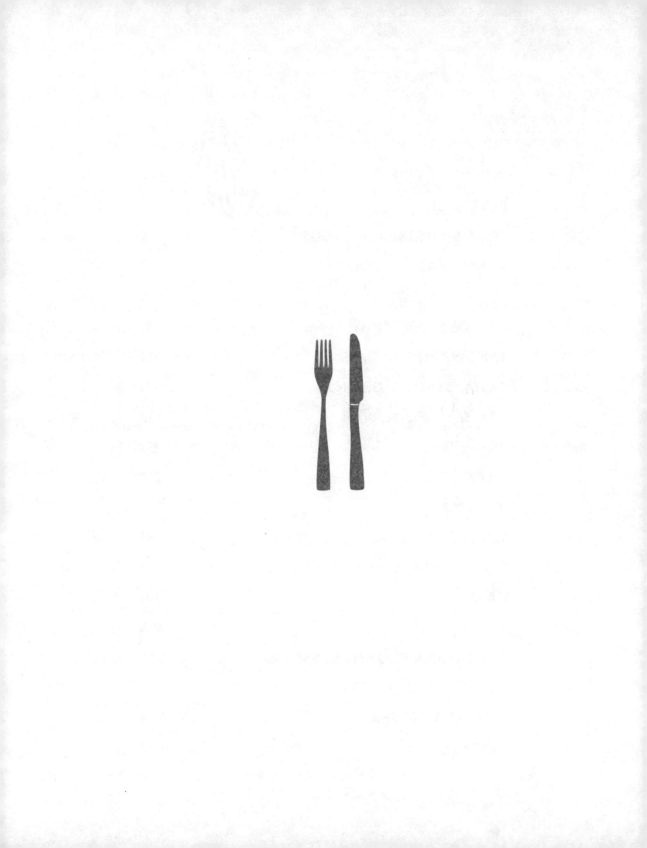

Acknowledgments

I am very grateful to my editor, Gary Luke, who persuaded me to write this book, our third book together.

Many of the recipes in this book have appeared on my web site, northwest-essentials. com. Visitors to the site have helped me improve the recipes by providing feedback, correcting simple errors, and questioning instructions when they were less than perfectly clear. I really appreciate that input.

Some material in this book appeared first in *Pacific Northwest* magazine, the Sunday newsmagazine of the *Seattle Times*. My editor there, Kathleen Triesch Saul, has contributed to this book in ways she might never have imagined—encouraging me to write about things I might not have considered, cheering me when the work seemed of limited importance, and demanding technical excellence all the while. Thanks Kathleen!

Most of all, I am grateful to my wife Betsy and to my sons Henry and Erich for sharing the great culinary adventure that is family life.

Introduction

As a relative newcomer to the West Coast (I came here in 1980), I have to wonder if I deserve the privilege of writing about West Coast cooking at all. Who am I to say what defines our regional cuisine? The "region," which runs roughly from Tijuana to Sitka, is vast and almost unbelievably diverse. The denizens of this region keep reinventing themselves, and what we eat is constantly changing, so how are we to pin it down?

In a lecture delivered to the International Association of Culinary Professionals in 2005, food historian Rachel Lauden pointed out that a cuisine is generally less ancient than we think it is. "We tend to think of a traditional cuisine as being what our grandmothers cooked," she said. "Now that I am a grandmother, I have to wonder just how authentic that notion really is. Essentially, it takes no more than about 25 years to redefine a national or regional cuisine."

I am not a grandmother, nor a mother of any kind. I am the father of two teenage boys, a devoted home cook, a professional chef and food writer, and, as a columnist for *The Seattle Times* and a contributing editor to *Food Arts* magazine, a fairly avid observer of cooking trends, especially the ones that originate or deeply affect the West Coast.

When I heard Lauden's lecture, I took heart. I was well on my way to cobbling together the collection of recipes that became this book, and I had begun to wonder for perhaps the hundredth time, with increasing urgency, exactly what defines West Coast cooking. Had I gotten it right?

I had as a point of reference the late Helen Brown's 1952 classic *West Coast Cookbook*. In many ways, her catalogue of recipes embracing pioneer, Mexican, and Chinese influences is still relevant, and I began to wonder if the collection of West Coast recipes I was compiling was equally "authentic." But thumbing through Brown's book did not make me particularly hungry, nor did I experience many flashes of recognition. It seemed clear to me that it was time for a new West Coast cookbook. Lauden's lecture reinforced that notion. What we cook now has grown out of what was cooked here when Helen Brown wrote her book, but it is not the same.

The parameters that define fine dining and home cooking alike have all shifted. In the fifties, restaurant chefs still tried to imitate the flavors and textures of good home cooking. But by the turn of this century, home cooks were emulating restaurant chefs. Between the time of Brown's untimely death and my own arrival on the West Coast, Alice Waters had launched the pivotal Chez Panisse in Berkeley, and her first chef, Jeremiah Tower, had gone on to open the late, great Stars restaurant in San Francisco. Chefs were no longer hidden in the back of the restaurant; they were celebrity role models.

Not only has West Coast cooking changed, but American food in general is also not what it was when Brown and her colleagues defined it for us in the mid-twentieth century. Brown was a member of a cabal of cooks and culinary experts that revolved around her good friend James Beard and grew to include fellow Californians Chuck Williams, M. F. K. Fisher, and Marion Cunningham. Faced with the emergence of fast food restaurants and the proliferation of processed "convenience" foods offered to home cooks in the wake of World War II, Brown and her associates sought to rescue American home cooking from the jaws of mass production and commerce that would have rendered it a mess of chemically altered stuff, barely recognizable but for the pictures attached to its disposable containers.

What exactly was this piece of Americana that Brown sought to rescue? The West Coast is, in many ways, just one part of a disturbingly homogeneous entity known as the United States. And since every denizen of this vast country is regularly exposed to the same stimuli in the form of national advertising, political campaigns, and national restaurant chains (not to mention the outpourings from Hollywood—global entertainments that are spawned here), it's difficult to say just what distinguishes this region of the country from any other part.

Of course, geography and climate play a role; certain things grow here that don't grow in other parts of the country and vice versa. California in particular produces far more than its share of the country's fruits and vegetables. The West Coast also has a unique history. It was—and is—subject to a different series of occupations and invasions than the ones inflicted on other regions of the country. But people here, for the most part, came from other areas of this same country.

More than the natural features of the land or its cultural history, the character of the region has, I believe, been defined by a certain attitude, an attitude that has influenced every aspect of life in these parts, from the way we educate our children to the way we relate to our elders, as well as the way we approach the stove. It's an attitude born of having come about as far as we could go. The history of America has, in a way, been a chronicle of our westward expansion, and having hit the western edge of the continent, Americans on the West Coast have had to face the end of that expansion. Of course, dreamers and idealists that we are, the "end" hasn't stopped us from expanding. Alaska, the last frontier, still beckons, and in myriad ways, ranging from the ridiculous to the sublime, we have turned to a sort of frontier within. It's no coincidence that the most far-out trends; the most cutting edge perspectives; the "weird, wacky stuff" to which the late, great Johnny Carson used to refer, originate here on the West Coast.

In the East, American food first emulated the food of the Old World, especially that of England. Throughout the colonial era, New England, the eastern seaboard, and the Deep South took on their own styles of cooking, nuanced by the local indigenous foods and driven by the crops that could be produced by the people who settled in those places. But all of those styles were essentially derivative of the English and European cooking from which they sprang.

By the time they reached the West Coast, Americans were less interested in trying to reproduce an Old World style. They had already incorporated many native North American ingredients—corn, beans, tomatoes, and chocolate—to the degree that they no longer thought of these foods as exotic, and were somewhat more open to outside and indigenous influences. Just as Creole cooking in the South became defined by the African and Native American cooks who determined what went on the table, so West Coast cooking took shape in the hands of the Mexican and Chinese cooks who kept the people fed.

Once they had established themselves and had begun to realize some of the potential of the land, West Coast cooks depended less on supplies brought in from the East and became almost defiantly self-reliant. Over the years, that sense of independence bordering on defiance came to define the attitude of the West Coast cook. Increasingly idiosyncratic and eclectic, cooks here became trailblazers. We took the best of what we knew about the old ways and integrated techniques and ingredients from the past with whatever we found at hand. West Coast cooks also looked increasingly at the influences from the other side of the Pacific Ocean, gradually incorporating Polynesian flavors here and Asian ingredients there.

East Coast observers sometimes shake their heads at our efforts. But increasingly, as the trailblazer cooks have found their bearings and have begun to discern what works and what doesn't, the rest of the world has come to acknowledge that West Coast cooks are on to something. And by the late twentieth century, there was no denying that food trends for the continent, and perhaps for the world, were being forged on the West Coast.

Finally, the criterion for what constitutes West Coast cooking became the simple question, "What do we eat?" The everyday foods that make up family meals, what we cook for company, and the special meals we prepare for holidays—these are the dishes that constitute our cuisine.

HOT DRINKS

COLD DRINKS

BEVERAGES

Beverages

"Tell me what you eat," wrote Brillat-Savarin, "and I will tell you who you are." Tell me what you drink, he might have said, and I will tell you where you come from. Folks on the West Coast drink all sorts of things, most notably some of the best wines in the world, which are produced here and happily enjoyed here as well. We also drink the "liquados" and "agua frescas" created in Mexico and modeled after the fruit- and flower-flavored beverages of Spain at the time of the European conquest. And like the conquered Aztecs, we drink beverages flavored with the native chocolate bean.

But like all Americans, most of us also drink a lot of coffee. And in this century coffee preferences and styles that evolved on the West Coast have gradually insinuated themselves across the country and into just about every place Americans go on this globe. At first our coffee habits were unique, radical even, a real departure from the norm established in other parts of North America. Here coffee was roasted darker and brewed not in the percolator or drip machine so popular in other parts of the country; here coffee was forced under pressure in the European style.

But iconoclasts are forever becoming icons. Just as the West Coast chefs and cooks exploring alternatives to the processed foods that were standard fare in most of the country during the last half of the twenti-

eth century gradually came to represent a new style of cooking that has become New American Cooking, so the coffee roasters of the West became standard bearers for what has become the prevailing way to enjoy a cup of coffee.

In 1971, at a tiny storefront in Seattle's Pike Place Market, partners Jerry Baldwin, Gordon Bowker, and Zev Sieg opened a coffee store. Motivated to find artisanal ways of selecting, roasting, and brewing coffee for more flavor and a deeper understanding of what makes a good cup of coffee, the partners were inspired by the success of their friend Alfred Peet who drew a loyal following to his coffee roaster and retailer in Berkeley. It was Peet who sold the guys their first green coffee beans for their new roasting operation.

Visitors to the store today would recognize instantly the trademark green and white logo of a mermaid and the name Starbucks, which has become the world's leading brand of coffee. But the founders never imagined that Starbucks, which took its name from a character in Herman Melville's *Moby Dick*, would become the giant corporate entity that it is today. Likewise, visitors to the massive yet somehow intimate Starbuck's headquarters a few blocks south of the original store would be hard pressed to fathom just how the tiny storefront spawned the giant company.

The link is Howard Schultz. When Starbucks was just beginning to expand—the company boasted just three stores—Schultz was working for the Swedish housewares maker Hammarplast, and he noticed that the Seattle coffee stores were ordering more coffee makers than the big department stores. According to an article by Dan Skeen on the web site MyPrimeTime.com, Schultz got very excited.

"It was just wonderful meeting people from a great young company . . . and I walked away from that meeting saying, 'God, what a great company, what a great city, I'd love to be part of that.'" But the company founders were slow to warm up to Schultz and his East Coast ambitions. "I was this East Coast person," Schultz said "and I had so much drive and energy, I think I might have scared them at first."

Eventually though, Schultz did join the company as director of retail operations and marketing, and according to press materials generated by the company, a business trip to Italy opened his eyes to "the rich tradition of the espresso beverage." By 1987, with the support of a group of local investors, Schultz purchased Starbucks and set into motion his vision of opening thousands of Starbucks cafés around the world.

"I tried to appeal to their sensibility about the company . . . hire people who have skills and experiences and perhaps competencies that are different than your own, and don't be afraid to change that mix, as long as there's a common goal and everyone leaves their ego at the door."

Meanwhile, original Starbucks founder Jerry Baldwin purchased Peet's and pursued his dream of a smaller company more focused on roasting coffee and selecting fine teas than on opening cafés. But the impact of these two companies on how Americans, and especially those of us on the West Coast, think about and experience coffee and perhaps beverages in general is immeasurable.

The story of Starbucks illustrates how entrepreneurial spirits enliven and re-inform the corporate culture, but it also sheds light on how big commercial efforts impact our individual lives. One of my oldest friends who lives back east and enjoys making disparaging remarks about our off-beat West Coast way of doing things likes to give me a hard time about Starbucks. "Charbucks," he calls it and claims that the company put smaller coffee houses out of business. On the contrary, I think Starbucks introduced millions of Americans to the pleasures of freshly roasted, carefully brewed coffee drinks and created opportunities for millions of independent entrepreneurs, paving the way for a whole new coffee culture.

What's more, Starbucks has led the way in responding to the needs of coffee growers by marketing specific, single-origin coffees. The efforts of this company and others have lifted coffee out of the realm of a generic commodity into a specialty that affords consumers opportunities to make choices about how our buying decisions will promote improved working conditions in coffee-growing countries. The company's involvement with organizations that promote environmentally sound and socially just farming practices reflect the culture out of which it emerged.

There is plenty of irony in the fact that the little company that set out to do things differently from the big boys ended up being the biggest boy of all. And like my East Coast friend, plenty of people are dubious about whether or not this is good for anyone other than the shareholders in the common stock. But for better or worse, Starbucks has been a major player with a profound impact on the West Coast table, and the American table in general.

Hot Drinks

★

HOW TO BREW A PERFECT POT OF COFFEE

These days, coffee is so often brewed in automatic drip makers that a recipe seems almost superfluous, but like the microwave oven, the almost ubiquitous coffee maker has not found a roost in my kitchen. We continue to make our coffee the old-fashioned way, pouring boiling water over the grounds. The coffee drips directly into a thermos bottle, which keeps the coffee hot, but we tend to drink it pretty quickly after it's made. Brewed coffee loses its charm if it is allowed to stand around for more than half an hour or so.

FOR ONE 4-CUP POT OF COFFEE

4 cups rapidly boiling water

4 rounded tablespoons freshly ground coffee beans

Sugar and half-and-half as accompaniments

1. Good water is essential to good coffee. If your tap delivers hard water or water with an "off" flavor, you might wish to use bottled spring water. Start with cold water in the kettle, and bring it to a boil over high heat. While the water is heating, fill your coffee pot or thermos with hot tap water to warm it up; discard the hot water.

2. Line a filter cone (Melitta makes the best ones) with an unbleached cone-shaped filter, and spoon 1 well-rounded tablespoon of freshly ground coffee beans for every cup of water your coffee pot holds into the filter.

3. As soon as the water boils, take it off the heat. (Boiling the water for too long reduces the amount of oxygen in the water and might make the coffee taste "flat.") Pour the boiling water over the ground coffee beans in a slow, steady stream, allowing the water to flow through the coffee grounds at about the same rate it is poured.

4. Serve the coffee very hot, directly from the container in which it was made. If you take sugar in your coffee, it is a good idea to put it in the cup before the coffee is

poured on; the motion of the incoming coffee will help it dissolve. As for half-and-half, add it or not, depending on your taste, after the coffee is in the cup.

HOMEMADE ESPRESSO

Characterized by brief, intense contact with coffee beans, preferably under pressure, true espresso can be made only with an espresso maker. At home, unless we have very expensive espresso makers, it's just not possible to match the efforts of the local barista. Nevertheless, for those who enjoy homemade espresso drinks, espresso can be thought of as double-strength dark-roasted coffee brewed in a French press or an Italian Moka pot. The brew—if it is to be taken straight—should be drunk from small cups within seconds after brewing. Many of the subtle nuances that make for a great cup of coffee are contained in volatile compounds that dissipate and are lost minutes after the coffee is brewed.

FOR EACH SMALL SERVING

2 tablespoons finely ground dark-roast coffee beans

½ cup water

Method 1 (using a French press)

If you are using a French press coffee maker, put the ground coffee in the pot. Bring the water to a boil, and pour it over the ground coffee. After 90 seconds, give the coffee a stir and press the plunger over the brew as far as it will go. It's sometimes necessary to lift the plunger after pushing

it down an inch or two and then finish pushing it down. Once the coffee is pressed, serve it immediately.

Method 2 (using an Italian Moka pot)

If you are using an Italian Moka pot, make the number of cups for which the pot was designed; don't try to make half a pot. Fill the bottom section of the pot with cold water up to the little round safety valve. Fill the basket with ground coffee and put it in place over the water-filled base. Secure the top half onto the base. Put the pot over high heat until the coffee begins to ooze through the shaft in the center of the pot. Reduce the heat to low, and when the pot is almost full, put down the lid. You will soon hear the sputter of air forced up from the empty lower chamber; this means the coffee is ready. Serve it at once.

CAPPUCCINO

With a crown of thick, creamy milk foam floated on top, and a good dose of espresso underneath, this Italian-style milk foam and coffee drink is the ultimate breakfast brew.

SERVES 2

1 cup whole milk or 2% milk

Two 2-ounce servings homemade espresso

Make the milk foam by heating the milk in a deep saucepan over high heat until it's steaming hot, almost boiling. Whisk vigorously until the milk takes on a layer of thick, creamy foam. Spoon the foam off the top onto cups of espresso. If it's made just right, the foam on top of a cappuccino will be about twice as thick as the coffee underneath, and the coffee itself will remain black, not milky.

Caffè Latte or Café au Lait

Typically made with more milk than espresso, this combination can be anywhere from equal parts to 3 parts milk and 1 part espresso. Prepare the milk as you would for cappuccino, but before you float the foam on top, pour some of the hot milk into the espresso below.

★

FISHERMAN'S WHARF IRISH COFFEE

Like many visitors to San Francisco, my father, in his navy days, discovered Irish coffee at the Buena Vista Bar on Fisherman's Wharf. Years later, when he learned how to make it from a local bartender, he earned a reputation for serving the drink after dinner parties in our home. Pop's Irish coffee was especially good because he caramelized the rim of each coffee mug by dipping it in honey and brown sugar and then browning the mixture over a dish of flaming whiskey. (Less restrictive than I am with my own sons, he generously allowed me to play the bartender, flaming the whiskey and burning the sugar for the party guests, so I have known how to make Irish coffee since I was a child.) Sweet and strong, the coffee seemed like a magical elixir to me, and I was always grateful when I was allowed to share a sip or two from

his mug. If it's served after dinner, as it should be, decaffeinated coffee makes sense here.

To Prepare the Cups

¼ cup honey

¼ cup brown sugar

¼ cup Irish whiskey

For the Irish Coffee

6 ounces (¾ cup) Irish whiskey

4 tablespoons brown sugar

24 ounces (3 cups) freshly brewed (preferably decaffeinated) coffee

1 cup whipped cream

1. Prepare the cups by putting the honey, brown sugar, and whiskey in separate dishes. (I use heatproof ceramic saucers.) Dip each of the 4 mugs first in the honey, then in the brown sugar. Ignite the whiskey and carefully roll the sugar-coated rim of each mug in the flame until the sugar is broiled to the surface of the mug.

2. To make the coffee, distribute the whiskey evenly among the mugs (1½ ounces per mug), then add a tablespoon of brown sugar to each one and stir in the coffee (6 ounces per serving).

3. Top each mug with whipped cream and serve hot.

★ CHAI OR SPICED TEA

One of the results of the proliferation of coffee bars has been the introduction of all sorts of alternatives to coffee that were little known in the days before our current coffee culture emerged. Many people enjoy the coffeehouse but don't particularly want the coffee. One company quick to capitalize on the need for an alternative to coffee was Oregon Chai, founded by a group of women in Portland, Oregon, in the mid-1990s, and inspired by the spiced tea that one of them discovered while trekking through the Himalayas. Their flagship product is a concentrate containing evaporated cane juice (organic sugar), honey, spices, black tea, and vanilla. Since I have never been to India, where chai is common, or the Himalayas, this spiced tea owes more to the American product than it does to the ages-old tradition that inspired it.

MAKES 8 SERVINGS

For the Spiced Tea Concentrate

⅔ cup organic sugar (evaporated cane juice)

¼ cup honey

3 cups water

8 teaspoons black tea leaves, or 6 teabags

2 cinnamon sticks

6 whole cloves

6 whole cardamom pods

To Serve

4 cups milk

1 teaspoon vanilla extract, or to taste

1. Make the concentrate. In a large, heavy-bottomed, nonreactive saucepan over medium-high heat, stir the sugar, honey, and water until the mixture begins to boil. Stir in the tea and spices, reduce the heat to low, and simmer the mixture until the spices and tea have infused the syrup with their essence, about 8 minutes.

2. Strain the syrup into a clean saucepan or 1-quart canning jar. The chai can be prepared up to this point and stored in a tightly sealed jar to be reheated later with milk, or it can be served at once.

3. To serve, combine equal parts of the prepared spiced tea concentrate, milk, and vanilla in a medium saucepan and stir over medium heat until the mixture is steaming hot. Ladle the hot chai into mugs and serve hot.

★ TRADITIONAL HOT CHOCOLATE

Real hot chocolate, made with whole chocolate containing cocoa butter, is naturally richer than hot cocoa made from dry cocoa powder, which contains little or no cocoa butter. This hot chocolate is more appropriate for dessert than for breakfast, but then again, it tastes just as good in the morning as it does in the evening.

MAKES 4 SERVINGS

½ cup water

¼ cup sugar

Pinch of salt

4 ounces (about ⅔ cup) bittersweet chocolate, chopped

3 cups milk

I teaspoon vanilla extract

Whipped cream or Homemade Marshmallows (optional; page 390)

I. Put the water, sugar, salt, and chocolate in a medium saucepan over medium heat and stir with a wooden spoon or a heatproof silicone spatula until the chocolate is melted.

2. Gradually stream in the milk, stirring all the while. While adding the milk, keep the mixture hot and steamy, just below the boil.

3. Take the saucepan off the stove and stir in the vanilla extract. Ladle into cups and serve right away, topped with whipped cream or marshmallows, if desired, or pour into a thermos to keep hot.

THICK HOT COCOA

This cocoa gains extra body from the addition of corn-starch. When you surprise your family with a thermos full of the stuff, you don't have to tell anyone what makes it so good. For an extra-rich treat, consider serving the cocoa with Homemade Marshmallows (page 390).

MAKES 4 SMALL SERVINGS

¼ cup dark (European-style) unsweetened cocoa powder

½ cup brown sugar

2 tablespoons cornstarch

Pinch of salt

½ cup water

2 cups milk

I teaspoon vanilla extract

I. Put the cocoa powder, brown sugar, cornstarch, and salt in a medium saucepan and stir with a whisk to mix. Add the water and whisk until smooth. Set the pot on a burner over high heat and continue whisking until the mixture comes to a full rolling boil.

2. Gradually stream in the milk, whisking all the while. While adding the milk, keep the mixture hot and steamy, just below the boil.

3. Reduce the heat to medium and stir gently just until the mixture is thickened and beginning to boil, 3 to 5 minutes. Remove the cocoa from the heat and stir in the vanilla extract. Ladle into cups and serve right away, or pour into a thermos to keep hot.

ATOLE CON CHOCOLATE

Pronounced "ah-TOH-leh," this Mexican beverage, which is served warm or hot, dates back to pre-Columbian times. Originally it was thickened with corn, but these days it is more likely to be made with rice flour. Instant mixes are available, but it's very easy to whip up a batch from scratch. I have had the best results with mochiko, a Japanese sweet rice flour made in California and readily found in the international aisles of West Coast super-markets. If mochiko is unavailable, a smaller amount of cornstarch is a reasonable substitute. For variety, omit the cocoa and use honey in place of sugar.

MAKES 2 LARGE SERVINGS

2 tablespoons mochiko (Japanese sweet rice flour), or 2 teaspoons cornstarch

¼ cup sugar

2 tablespoons unsweetened cocoa powder

1 teaspoon ground cinnamon

2 cups milk

1 teaspoon vanilla extract

1. Put the mochiko, sugar, cocoa powder, cinnamon, in a saucepan and stir with a whisk to mix. Add the milk and whisk over medium-high heat until the mixture comes to a gentle boil, then stir in the vanilla extract.

2. Transfer immediately to mugs or a ceramic pitcher and drink as soon as it cools to the desired temperature. Do not allow the beverage to cool completely to room temperature or it will become too thick.

★

GLÖGG OR HOT SPICED WINE

The Scandinavian influences on the cooking of the Pacific Northwest might go virtually unnoticed if it were not for Christmastime. In December, Danish, Norwegian, Finnish, and Swedish specialties appear in grocery stores, and home cooks descended from immigrants pull out their recipes for lutefisk, thin spice cookies, and the very potent, hot spiced wine known as glögg. Glögg can be made a month in advance and kept in bottles in the dark so that the flavor of the spices permeates the wine. It can also be made and served the same day. Be careful when adding the aquavit or brandy to the melted sugar, especially if you have a gas flame under the burner, because the brandy will boil furiously, and if it comes in contact with any flame, it will ignite. It is okay to burn off some of the alcohol—more will be added later—just be sure you don't burn off anything else.

MAKES ABOUT 2 QUARTS

1 cup sugar

2 cups anise-flavored aquavit or brandy

½ cup dark raisins

3 cinnamon sticks

12 whole cloves

12 whole cardamom pods

½ teaspoon anise or fennel seeds (optional)

1 bottle full-bodied red wine, such as zinfandel

1 bottle inexpensive ruby port wine

½ teaspoon almond extract (optional)

Strips of zest from 1 large navel orange, for garnish

1. In a large, heavy-bottomed, nonreactive saucepan over medium-high heat, warm the sugar until it becomes caramel colored; some of it will melt into a thick liquid. Stir in 1 cup of the aquavit. The caramelized sugar will seize up and solidify

at first, but as the brandy boils furiously around it, it will melt again. Reduce heat to low. Add the raisins and spices and simmer them in the brandy and sugar syrup until the spices are fragrant, about 2 minutes.

2. Stir in the wine and simmer gently without boiling until the wine is infused with the flavor of the spices. Strain out the spices, then stir in the port, remaining cup of aquavit, and almond extract, if desired. The wine can be prepared up to this point and stored in tightly sealed bottles to be reheated later, or it can be served at once.

3. Ladle the hot wine mixture into mugs. Use a vegetable peeler to remove strips of zest from a fresh navel orange, and garnish each serving with a strip of the zest.

HOT SPICED CIDER

Mulled or hot spiced cider is a comforting beverage in cold weather, but also a nice alternative to herbal infusions or decaffeinated coffee as an after-dinner drink. The essential flavors are cinnamon and clove, but you may wish to experiment with other spices such as cardamom, ginger, or allspice. I like to make spiced cider with the cloudy, unfiltered cider that's sold fresh in cartons in the produce department of most super-markets; it has more character than the clear, filtered stuff sold in bottles.

3 cinnamon sticks

10 whole cloves

4 cups natural apple cider

4 strips of orange or lemon zest (optional)

1. Put the cinnamon sticks and cloves in a medium-sized stainless steel or enameled saucepan over medium-high heat. (Aluminum or copper would give the cider a metallic taste.) Toss the spices in the pan until they release some of their aromatic oils into the air, 2 or 3 minutes. Add the cider and simmer, stirring, until the cider is heated through. The cider can be made ahead and held over very low heat for up to 1 hour, or moved to a thermal carafe to stay warm.

2. Ladle the cider into mugs and garnish each serving with a strip of fresh orange or lemon zest, if desired.

Cold Drinks

CLEAR ICED TEA

Tea that is brewed in the regular way, by pouring boiling water over tea leaves or bags, will turn cloudy when it's chilled. The cloudiness is harmless, but clear tea is more appealing. Crystal clear "sun tea" is made by steeping teabags in cold water in a glass jar in the sun for several hours. To make iced tea on a cloudy day, or when time is of the essence, gently simmer teabags in a saucepan of water. Always make iced tea extra strong to compensate for the melting ice with which it will be served.

MAKES 2 QUARTS

4 cups cold water

6 teabags

8 cups ice cubes

1. Put the cold water and teabags in a saucepan over medium heat and cook gently until the water is very hot, but not boiling, about 8 minutes. Take the pan off the heat and let it cool to room temperature.

2. Fill a 2-quart pitcher with ice cubes. Remove the teabags from the saucepan and pour the brew over the ice.

★ THEME PARK LEMONADE

Until I went to a theme park on a family vacation in the early 1970s, I had only had lemonade made from frozen concentrate or from a mix, and I had no idea how good the real thing could be. I watched, fascinated, as a kid not much older than I was squeezed a lemon into the cup, added a simple syrup made from sugar and water, and with a scoop of ice and a splash of water transformed that lemon into the most refreshing thing I had ever tasted. The real thing is always a revelation. Fresh lemons contain a host of subtle flavors that are diminished or lost entirely when the fruit juice is processed. One lemon will typically yield about ¼ cup juice. Superfine sugar, what English cooks call castor sugar, sometimes labeled baker's sugar, is ideal for lemonade because it dissolves more rapidly than regular granulated sugar.

MAKES ABOUT 2 QUARTS

1 cup freshly squeezed lemon juice

1 cup superfine (not powdered) sugar or granulated sugar

Water and ice to make 2 quarts

1. Put the lemon juice in a nonreactive pitcher or 2-quart canning jar. Stir in the sugar until it is completely dissolved.

2. Stir in cold water and ice to make 2 quarts. Serve cold.

★ CALISTOGA SPARKLING LEMONADE

It's hard to say if the present-day rage for bottled water moved from west to east or vice versa. But since it was founded in the 1860s, the town of Calistoga in California's upper Napa Valley has been among the places in the country where people go to "take the waters." And sparkling mineral water from Calistoga has been sold in bottles ever since Giuseppe Musante, who owned a soda fountain in the town, set up a bottling plant in the 1920s. These days, Calistoga is a division of Nestlé, the international food and beverage giant. Of course, other brands of bottled sparkling water will do.

½ cup sugar

½ cup freshly squeezed lemon juice

½ cup boiling water

About 3 cups chilled sparkling water

1. Put the sugar, lemon juice, and boiling water into a 1-quart canning jar and stir until the sugar is dissolved.

2. Slowly add the sparkling water. As soon as the jar is filled, serve at once or put the lid on tight to preserve the bubbles until the jar is opened.

★

WILD FENNEL LIMEADE

Wild fennel, with its extensive root systems, was planted all over the West Coast to prevent erosion of hillsides. But it serves other purposes as well. Fennel and other licorice-scented herbs have been used to flavor restorative drinks for centuries. The herb is the key flavoring ingredient in licorice-flavored aperitifs such as Pernod and pastis. Such beverages were originally devised as medicinal infusions of herbs, and one modern herbalist cites fennel as an "antispasmodic, diuretic, expectorant, galactagogue, stimulant, and stomachic," whatever all that means. I make no such claims about the simple formula for fennel limeade that follows, but it does seem to help people who are feeling disgruntled feel better.

MAKES ABOUT 2 QUARTS

2 cups water

1 cup chopped fresh wild fennel

2 tablespoons dried fennel seeds, crushed

1 cup sugar

1 cup freshly squeezed lime juice

6 cups ice water

Fennel sprigs, for garnish

1. Bring the water to a boil in a medium saucepan. Add the chopped fennel and fennel seeds and simmer gently for 5 minutes. Strain the infusion into a 2-quart canning jar or heatproof pitcher, discarding the solids.

2. Add the sugar and stir until it's completely dissolved. Stir in the lime juice and ice water. Put a sprig of fresh fennel in each serving glass before filling and serving.

★

LAVENDER LEMONADE

Lavender is an herb more associated with the bath than with the kitchen; its name is derived from the Latin word for "wash." Nevertheless, it has been used, albeit sparingly, for centuries to "clean up" the flavors of strong-tasting foods like lamb and some cheeses. When I first started cooking with lavender and writing about it in the 1980s, I thought it would never catch on, but over time it has become an increasingly popular flavor.

MAKES ABOUT 2 QUARTS

2 cups boiling water

½ cup fresh organically grown lavender flowers

1 cup sugar

1 cup freshly squeezed lemon juice

4 cups chilled sparkling water

Ice

1. In a medium bowl, pour the boiling water over the flowers and steep for 10 minutes.

2. Strain the liquid into a pitcher and discard the flowers.

3. Stir in the sugar and lemon juice, add the sparkling water, and serve the lemonade over ice.

HIBISCUS COOLER

In Mexico, hibiscus flowers (Hibiscus sabdariffa) *are sold as* flores de Jamaica, *and they are used as the base of one of the most popular* aguas frescas, *the cool drinks sold on the streets from large glass jars. The dried flowers are also a key ingredient in some popular herbal tea blends, and they can be found in bulk in the tea and herb sections of many grocery stores. They are rich in vitamin C and add not only a brilliant color and a piquant flavor to a beverage but also a certain density of texture, rendering it ever so slightly more viscous. This is one of my all-time favorite drinks.*

MAKES ABOUT 2 QUARTS

2 cups boiling water

½ cup dried hibiscus flowers

¾ cup sugar

¼ cup freshly squeezed lime juice

4 cups chilled water

Ice

1. In a medium bowl, pour the boiling water over the flowers and steep for 10 minutes.

2. Strain the liquid into a pitcher and discard the flowers.

3. Stir in the sugar and lime juice, add the water, and serve the cooler over ice.

HORCHATA DEL NORTE

This milky-looking beverage contains no dairy products; it is actually made from rice and almonds. Traditionally, it's made with white sugar and blanched almonds, but I like the slightly off-white color and added flavor of unrefined sugar and almonds with the skin on. The solids are finely ground while they're dry, and then mixed with water and strained out several times. The beverage is best when made the day before it's served.

MAKES ABOUT 2 QUARTS

⅓ cup uncooked white rice

1 cup whole almonds

1 cinnamon stick, about 3 inches long

¾ cup turbinado sugar or Sugar in the Raw

About 7 cups cold water

1. Put the rice, almonds, cinnamon stick, and sugar in a blender and pulse the motor off and on to grind the mixture very fine. Take the time to get the mixture as finely ground as possible.

2. Pour 2 cups of the water over the mixture and purée on high speed for 1 minute. Pass the liquid through a strainer into a clean 2-quart jar or pitcher. Put the solids back in the blender, add another 2 cups of water, and purée and strain again,

saving the solids for a third round. On the fourth and final go-round, you will add only 1 cup of water.

3. Chill the mixture for several hours or overnight in the refrigerator. Strain it one last time before serving.

TAMARINDO OR TAMARIND COOLER

The fruit of a tree native to Africa, tamarind pods are brown and simultaneously tart and sweet. The trees were brought to America in the 1500s and grow well in California. Up and down the West Coast, different people prize tamarind for different reasons. Southeast Asian cooks appreciate its tangy flavor for use in pad Thai and other savory dishes. Latin American cooks use tamarind for candies and drinks like this one. A cloudy, amber-colored drink, it looks and tastes something like unfiltered apple juice. Many Mexican and Asian markets stock both tamarind pods and ready-to-use tamarind purée.

MAKES ABOUT 2 QUARTS

8 ounces dried tamarind pods plus 1 cup boiling water, or 1 cup tamarind purée

⅔ cup sugar

About 6 cups ice-cold water

1. If using tamarind pods, make a purée by boiling a cup of dried tamarind pods in water for 10 minutes. Strain the juice through a fine-mesh sieve into a 2-quart pitcher or jar, pressing hard on the solids.

Discard the solids. If using tamarind purée, put it directly in a pitcher.

2. Stir the sugar into the purée until it is dissolved, and then stir in enough cold water to make 8 cups. Serve cold.

COFFEE FRAPPÉ

I like to spend one week every year working at an orphanage in Tijuana, where high school kids from my own town build homes for people on land developed by the local colonial government. I cook for the young people who come with me from the north, and while they are working at the house sites I work at the orphanage. One of the highlights of being there is working with the doñas who run the orphanage. They taught me to turn off the stove and the lights in the afternoon, and to honor the local siesta schedule, not necessarily with a nap but with a quiet time. During those times, I have found that leftover coffee from the morning brew, thoroughly sweetened and blended with crushed ice and half-and-half, becomes a pleasant afternoon pick-me-up. On market day one year, I bought a used blender to make coffee frappé for the doñas.

MAKES 4 SERVINGS

2 cups crushed ice

¼ cup sugar

1 cup strong brewed coffee or espresso, chilled

1 cups whole milk

1 teaspoon vanilla extract

Whipped cream (optional)

Pile the ice, sugar, coffee, milk, and vanilla in a blender and blend until smooth. Serve at once, with or without a dollop of whipped cream on top.

★
JADE GREEN TEA FRAPPÉ

I am not usually a fan of food and drink that is purely the product of corporate promotions, but when the Starbucks chain promoted a Green Tea Frappuccino on billboards and buses, I thought the drink looked pretty appealing. Although I resisted for as long as I could, eventually I ordered one. I was smitten and determined at once that I would learn to make it from scratch. The essential ingredients are the powdered Japanese green tea known as macha and melon-flavored syrup. Quite different from the green tea leaves that are steeped to make ordinary green tea, macha is a strong green tea that is ritualistically offered in tea ceremonies. Equally integral to the flavor of the drink is melon-flavored syrup. Made for Italian sodas, the syrup is somewhat hard to find. If your store doesn't stock it, try almond syrup.

MAKES 2 SERVINGS

2 cups crushed ice

2 tablespoons sugar

1 tablespoon macha green tea

1½ cups whole milk or 2% milk

2 tablespoons melon-flavored or almond syrup

Whipped cream (optional)

1. Put the ice, sugar, macha, milk, and syrup in a blender. Cover and purée until perfectly smooth.

2. Transfer the frappé to two 12-ounce glasses, top with whipped cream if desired, and serve at once.

★
CALIFORNIA DREAMIN' BREAKFAST SHAKE

This shake is easy enough for a kid to make, and on those mornings when breakfast seems like more of a hassle than it's worth, it is an appealing way to start the day. The flavor is reminiscent of a Dreamsicle. Since the acid in the orange juice causes the protein in the milk to solidify, the shake is delightfully thick, but as the ice melts, the beverage separates into curds and whey, so it's a good idea to drink it quickly.

MAKES 4 SERVINGS

2 cups crushed ice

1½ cups orange juice

1½ cups 2% milk

2 tablespoons sugar

1 teaspoon vanilla extract

Put all the ingredients in a blender. Cover and purée until perfectly smooth. Serve at once.

★

FROZEN STRAWBERRY SMOOTHIES

When strawberries are not at their peak season, they can be pale and insipid. Frozen berries are a much more flavorful option. Ironically, berries grown for the processors are typically varieties that are too sweet and soft and fragile for the fresh market; they are actually more flavorful than the berries we buy fresh, even at the peak of the season. With no ice cream, this shake is very low in fat.

MAKES 2 SERVINGS

One 10-ounce package (about 2 cups) frozen organic strawberries

1 cup milk

1 cup plain yogurt

¼ cup sugar

1 teaspoon vanilla extract

1. Put the frozen strawberries in a blender with the milk and yogurt and blend until the strawberries are crushed.

2. Add the sugar and vanilla extract and run the blender until the mixture is smooth. Pour into two 12-ounce glasses. Serve at once.

★

NORTHWEST BERRY SHAKES

In the Skagit Valley and a few other areas of western Washington and Oregon, farmers still grow the old varieties that made Pacific Northwest strawberries famous. These shakes can also be made with fresh or frozen blackberries, blueberries, or raspberries. Premium West Coast ice creams, like Double Rainbow brand from San Francisco, have less air churned in, so they are not as expensive as they look. A pint of the premium stuff weighs as much as a quart of the lesser brands, so it's worth the premium price, and the texture is much more satisfying.

MAKES 4 SERVINGS

2 cups frozen strawberries or other berries, preferably organic

2 cups whole milk

1 pint super-premium vanilla ice cream, such as Ben and Jerry's

1. Put the strawberries in a blender with the milk, and blend until smooth.

2. Add the ice cream to the blender and turn the motor on and off until the blender runs smoothly.

3. Run the blender until the mixture is smooth. Pour into 12-ounce glasses. Serve at once.

★

DATE SHAKES

As peculiar to someone from the East Coast as an egg cream would be to someone from the West Coast, a date shake is a regional classic. It's best made with the softest, freshest dates one can find. California produces 30 million pounds of dates every year, about 95 percent of the total U.S. production, but even in their home state, consumers seldom see fresh dates. Most of them are sold in a semidry form for snacking or baking. The solution is to soften the dates with a little boiling water before transforming them into a smooth paste to be whirred into milk and ice cream for the ultimate shake.

MAKES 2 GENEROUS SERVINGS

½ cup chopped dates

½ cup boiling water

2 large scoops (about ½ pint) premium vanilla ice cream

I cup milk

Whipped cream (optional)

1. Put the dates in a blender and pour the boiling water over them. Blend until the dates are very smooth. Scrape down the sides of the blender container with a rubber or silicone spatula.

2. Pile in the ice cream and milk and blend until smooth. Transfer to two 12-ounce glasses, top with whipped cream, if desired, and serve at once.

EGGS & BREAKFAST FOODS

Eggs & Breakfast Foods

The natural foods movement that paralleled the Great American Food Revolution, and perhaps a few other cultural revolutions along the way, was led by some of the most colorful characters in twentieth-century America. And—not surprisingly—they were from the West Coast.

When Chuck Kesey and his late brother, Ken, were boys, they often worked for their dad, who ran a dairy in Springfield, Oregon. "Ken liked to work the boiler, because that gave him a lot of time to write," says Chuck. "But I was more involved in the hands-on activities."

While Chuck studied dairy technology at Oregon State University, where he met his wife, Sue, a business major, the younger Kesey, Ken, graduated from high school, married his sweetheart Faye Haxby, and enrolled at the University of Oregon to pursue a degree in speech and communications. There he was awarded a scholarship to enroll in the creative writing program at Stanford. He earned money by working as an orderly at the psychiatric ward of the local VA hospital. He also was paid to participate in psychology department experiments with psilocybin, mescaline, and LSD.

The creative writing program, the hallucinogens, and the psychiatric ward provided the raw material for Kesey's first novel, *One Flew Over the Cuckoo's Nest*, published in 1962.

Almost immediately, he went to work on his next book, about a pair of brothers from a logging family: *Sometimes a Great Notion*.

Meanwhile, brother Chuck and his wife had purchased the Springfield Creamery in 1960. And while Kesey the younger performed culturally experimental parties known as acid tests and gathered a band of Merry Pranksters, the dairyman brother was quietly influencing another wing of the counterculture, the health food movement.

By 1969, the dairy business was becoming more and more centralized, and independent operators were disappearing. Chuck Kesey knew that to keep the dairy he would have to do something different.

"We needed something to niche us, so we could remain independent," recalls Sue. "We needed to create a brand of our own." As fate would have it, the inspiration for that brand had just moved into town.

Nancy Hamren had come to Oregon from the Haight-Ashbury district of San Francisco to help watch over Ken and Faye Kesey's farm, and when the other pranksters took off for the legendary pop festival at Woodstock, Nancy stayed behind. "I was not interested in piling into a Volkswagen van with the other hippies and their babies," she confided to me once in the kitchen at the Springfield Dairy. Before long, she was working as bookkeeper at the dairy, a job she continues to perform to this day.

"I had always loved yogurt because my grandmother was a natural foods enthusiast and she had introduced me to it," says Nancy. "With all that milk around, it seemed natural to try to make some." So she shared her yogurt recipe with the Keseys.

"I was very excited by this," Chuck Kesey told me. "I had been intrigued by living organisms in milk ever since college." At Oregon State, he had seen firsthand the results of feeding active cultures to animals. "I thought, why not put these things in our food?"

"It was the awakening of the counter-culture generation," says Nancy. "Everyone was open to new ideas and changing their eating habits, and the demand for natural food and yogurt had started to grow."

Nancy's Honey Yogurt was the first yogurt commercially made with live acidophilus and bifidum cultures. "It's tangier than most yogurts on the market," says Nancy, "but we don't test for pH or use timers to see when the yogurt's ready; we simply go in and sacrifice a pint and taste it." In fact, Chuck Kesey samples virtually every batch of yogurt that comes out of the plant. When Chuck deems it ready, he adjusts the thermostats to transform the warming rooms into coolers, thus checking the growth of the yogurt-making microbes and chilling the finished product before shipment.

The result is a yogurt with character. It's not sour, but it is sharp, with the kind of snap you'd find in a vintage cheddar. It makes the yogurt not only great for breakfast but also a versatile ingredient in salad dressings, dips, and other recipes. Like a lot of other cooks, I keep Nancy's yogurt around all the time, and I often use it instead of buttermilk in baking. (I never seem to have any buttermilk.) Perhaps this combination of character and versatility is what has earned Nancy's a national following.

The family has come a long way since 1972. That year the dairy was having such a hard time financially that Chuck Kesey was forced to get creative. "I decided to drive down to Marin County and ask Jerry Garcia if he and the band would come up to Eugene and do a benefit concert." Why turn to a rock band for help? "Well, you think about it," says Chuck. "Where else would I go?"

"We were part of this alternative culture," explains Nancy. "Music, natural foods, and natural living." It all went together. The performance was the first of ten legendary Grateful Dead concerts held at the creamery. And while no traditional marketing ploys were used, people spontaneously made connections between Ken Kesey, the Grateful Dead, and Nancy's Yogurt.

"It's kind of amazing that any natural food companies survived through that time," says Sue Kesey. "We were all just shoestring to shoestring." Still, demand for natural foods did grow. "We had a lot of conversations with our smaller natural food customers in the late seventies, not wanting us to sell to mass market stores," she recalls. "But when the Safeways and Fred Meyers of the world came knocking on our door and said we'd really like to stock your product, it completely blew us away . . . of course we said yes."

By 1987, Springfield Creamery had outgrown its old home and moved across Eugene to a larger plant on 10 acres. Then, in 1994, an electrical malfunction caused a fire, which destroyed most of the new building. Kit Kesey, son of Chuck and Sue and now operations manager, recalls the night of the fire. "I was so upset," he says. "The building was burning and the firemen looked like they were just going to let it burn down and try to keep it from spreading."

Then Uncle Ken showed up in his soccer coach shirt, with the whistle and all. He got up on the roof over there and started directing the firemen. 'Point the hoses over there!' he shouted. Thanks to him, we saved a lot of the most valuable equipment, and we were able to rebuild in a much shorter time than we would have." In fact, even though the fire was devastating, the creamery was back in production in just three weeks.

Now, in its latest incarnation, Springfield Creamery produces more than 80 different cultured dairy and soy products bearing the Nancy's label, including cream cheese, sour cream, and cottage cheese. It could be said that like his brother Ken, Chuck Kesey has made the transformation from iconoclast to icon.

★
HOMEMADE YOGURT

Making your own yogurt can be as simple as putting a spoonful of store-bought yogurt with live active cultures into warm milk and keeping the milk warm for a period of several hours, but the results can be hit or miss. Less-than-perfect conditions can render homemade yogurt too thin, and off-flavors can result from improper handling. But by paying close attention to the temperature and following a few careful steps, you can make a yogurt that is as good as any you can buy. Sterilizing the jars and using previously unopened plain yogurt as a starter will ensure that no uninvited bacteria set up camp in your yogurt. The process makes for a fun one-time science project, even if you don't make it a habit.

MAKES ABOUT 6 CUPS

5½ cups whole milk, preferably organic

½ cup plain (unflavored) yogurt from a brand new container

1. Sterilize 6 half-pint canning jars by simmering them in boiling water. Turn off the burner and let the jars stand in the water undisturbed while you prepare the yogurt. Preheat your oven to the lowest possible setting.

2. Stir the milk in a soup pot and heat until it just begins to boil. Remove the pot from the burner and cool the milk until it registers 115°F. Then stir in the yogurt.

3. Pour the milk-yogurt mixture into the sterilized jars, filling them to within ½ inch of the top, and seal the jars with new lids. Put the filled jars back into the pot in

which they were sterilized. There should be enough hot water around the jars to almost cover them. The water around the jars should be at 115°F. Put the pot with the jars into the warm oven; turn off the oven and close the door.

4. Check the temperature of the water every hour, and if necessary add a little hot water to bring the temperature back up. After 6 hours, move the jars from the pot in the oven to the refrigerator and chill the yogurt for several hours or overnight. The jars of yogurt will keep in the refrigerator for 10 days.

ORGANIC YOGURT PARFAITS

While developing recipes for a company called Organic to Go, I tested a lot of different versions of this grab-and-go breakfast, which is almost ubiquitous at Northwest coffee bars. Along the way, I discovered that stacked in a tall glass, the basic breakfast trinity of yogurt, fruit, and granola is transformed into something greater than the sum of its parts. If the granola is layered with the yogurt and fruit the night before, moisture from the yogurt softens the granola. The result is reminiscent of muesli, a Swiss dish of grains and fruit made tender by soaking overnight. If you prefer the yogurt crunchy, stack the ingredients just before serving. Very simple dishes like this one demand the most flavorful ingredients, and more often than not, organic tastes better than conventional. Using homemade granola and homemade yogurt makes this simple dish extraordinary.

2 cups organic plain or vanilla yogurt

2 cups granola (made with organic oats)

1 pint organic strawberries, sliced

1. Distribute half the yogurt among four 12-ounce parfait glasses or standard drinking glasses, putting ¼ cup in each glass.

2. Distribute half the strawberries over the yogurt, and then put ¼ cup of granola on top of the strawberries in each glass.

3. Top with the remaining yogurt, then the remaining fruit, and finally the remaining granola. Serve at once or, if a softer texture is desired, cover and refrigerate overnight.

HONEY-VANILLA GRANOLA

Dry cereal has a long and colorful history in America. A hundred years ago, Kellogg's Cornflakes and Post Grape Nuts were the health foods of their day. But their products spawned a plethora of packaged, ready-to-eat cereals that were loaded with sugar and synonymous with junk food. During the last quarter of the twentieth century, healthier homemade granola was so closely linked with the natural foods movement—with all its cultural and social implications—that "granola" became an adjective. This granola is easy to prepare, and it makes a wonderful breakfast or snack. Dress it up with toasted nuts or coconut and dried fruits if you like. Properly dried and cooled before it's packed, homemade granola will stay fresh for at least a week. Serve it with cold milk or yogurt.

8 cups organic rolled or quick-cooking oats

1 cup peanut or canola oil

1¾ cups honey

¼ cup water

1 tablespoon vanilla extract

1 tablespoon kosher salt

2 cups slivered almonds or coconut, lightly toasted (optional)

2 cups raisins, date pieces, or dried cranberries (optional)

1. Preheat the oven to 325°F and pile the oats into a large mixing bowl.

2. In a saucepan over medium-high heat, combine the canola oil, honey, water, vanilla extract, and salt. Bring the mixture to a boil, stirring to prevent it from boiling over. Pour the syrup over the oats and stir until the mixture is well combined.

3. Spread the granola onto 2 rimmed baking sheets and bake in the preheated oven for 10 minutes. Rotate the pans, exchanging the top for the bottom and the bottom for the top. Bake for 5 minutes more, then stir in the almonds, if desired.

4. Return the granola to the oven and after 5 minutes stir in the raisins, if desired, and turn the oven off. Allow the granola to dry out in the residual heat of the oven. This ensures that the cereal will be dry enough to keep. Transfer the cooled granola to an airtight container.

Eggs

FRIED EGGS

"I can make amazingly bad fried eggs," wrote the late M. F. K. Fisher in her wartime treatise on cooking, How to Cook a Wolf, *"tough, with edges like some kind of dirty starched lace, and a taste part sulphur and part singed newspaper." I think I have eaten fried eggs like those once or twice. But if they are handled very gently, fried eggs can be very good: tender and tasty. I believe that eggs fry better and taste better in oil than they do in butter. The whey in butter invariably browns and causes the eggs to stick to the pan. The oil should be fairly deep so that the eggs truly fry, but not so hot that they brown very much. Serve fried eggs as Mary Frances suggested, "with toast and coffee or with salad and white wine for supper."*

FOR EACH SERVING

Canola oil or (if you can find it) rice bran oil

2 eggs

Salt and freshly ground black pepper, to taste

1. Put enough oil in a small sauté pan to reach ½ inch up the sides of the pan. Warm the oil over medium-high heat until it is hot but not smoking.

2. Crack the eggs directly into the oil, taking care not to break the yolks. Let the eggs cook, undisturbed, until the whites are set on the underside but the yolks are still quite runny, about 3 minutes.

3. Using a flexible fish spatula, turn the eggs over only once, and cook just until they are firm enough to be lifted out of the oil, about 1 minute longer. Serve with salt and pepper, to taste.

★ BAKED EGGS

Whenever a crowd—and a "crowd" at breakfast means any more than two or three people—is joining me for breakfast, and eggs are on the menu, I like to bake them in the oven. These eggs are ideal to serve with Celia's Scrapple (pages 37-38) or with Browned Sausages (page 37) and toast.

MAKES 1 DOZEN EGGS

2 tablespoons unsalted butter

½ cup fine dried breadcrumbs

12 eggs

1. Preheat the oven to 350°F. Butter the insides of the 12 cups of a muffin tin, using about ½ teaspoon of butter in each cup. Sprinkle the buttered cups with breadcrumbs and shake the crumbs around to distribute them evenly over the buttered bottoms and sides of the cups.

2. Crack an egg into each buttered and breaded muffin cup and bake the eggs until the whites are perfectly set but the yolks are still slightly runny, about 12 minutes. Use a heatproof silicone spatula or rubber spatula to transfer the eggs from the cups to serving plates.

★ OVEN-SCRAMBLED EGGS

If you have one of those muffin tins with large, shallow cups designed for baking "muffin tops," it's fun to bake eggs in perfect discs to use in Breakfast Sandwiches (page 29) or Huevos Rancheros (page 30). These eggs can be "lightened" by using 2 ounces (¼ cup) egg white in place of each egg and by coating the tins with nonstick canola oil spray instead of butter.

MAKES 6 SERVINGS

1 tablespoon unsalted butter

6 eggs

2 teaspoons kosher salt

1 teaspoon freshly ground black pepper

1. Preheat the oven to 350°F. Butter the insides of 6 cups of a muffin tin, using about ½ teaspoon of butter in each cup.

2. Crack an egg into each buttered cup and bake the eggs until the whites are perfectly set but the yolks are still slightly runny, about 12 minutes. Use a heatproof silicone spatula or a rubber spatula to transfer the eggs from the cups to serving plates. Add salt and pepper, to taste.

★ GOAT CHEESE OMELET

Omelets can be filled with just about anything, but to my mind, a single delectable filling is often more appealing than a confusing array of savory fillings. Soft white goat cheese, like Montrachet, has a distinctive tang and a satisfying flavor, but a natural cream cheese such as

Nancy's brand organic cream cheese makes a delectable substitute.

MAKES 2 SERVINGS

4 fresh eggs, preferably from free-range chickens

3 tablespoons unsalted butter, less if using a nonstick pan

3 ounces fresh white goat cheese

Kosher salt and freshly ground black pepper, to taste

Toast as an accompaniment

1. Break the eggs into a bowl and give them 12 or 15 swift strokes with a fork to combine the egg and yolk, but don't overbeat them.

2. In a slope-sided frying pan over medium-high heat, melt 2 tablespoons of the butter and, when it sizzles, pour in the beaten eggs. Reduce the heat to medium and, with a heatproof spatula, gently push the cooked eggs toward the center of the pan, allowing the runnier middle of the omelet to flow out toward the edges of the pan.

3. Rub the additional tablespoon of butter around the inside edge of the pan, and use the spatula to lift the edges of the omelet and let the butter slip underneath. The whole omelet should slide easily around the inside of the pan.

4. Crumble the goat cheese over the surface of the eggs, which should be puffed but still slightly runny. Sprinkle the cheese

with salt and pepper and fold the omelet over the cheese. Rest a plate over the pan, then turn the whole affair over, depositing the omelet onto the plate. Cut the omelet in half and move half to another plate. Serve at once with hot, buttered toast.

★

JAPANESE-STYLE OMELET

Tamagoyaki, or Japanese omelet, is more a dinner food than a breakfast food. It is usually built layer by layer in a special rectangular pan, but a reasonable facsimile can be made in a well-seasoned cast-iron frying pan or a nonstick sauté pan. The key is to cook the egg in a series of thin layers, rolling one cooked layer out of the way to one side of the pan and then pouring in more egg to make the next layer. A building block in some forms of sushi, it is also a delightful thing-in-itself. This East-West version focuses less on authenticity than on simple goodness. I like to serve it with Sesame Spinach (pages 246–47) and short-grain rice for a quick supper. I also use eggs cooked in this manner to make Chinese Restaurant–Style Fried Rice (pages 135–36).

MAKES 4 SMALL SERVINGS

4 eggs

2 tablespoons water

1 tablespoon sake (optional)

1 tablespoon sugar

1 teaspoon salt

3 tablespoons unsalted butter or canola oil

1. Break the eggs into a bowl and give them 12 or 15 swift strokes with a fork

to combine the egg and yolk. Stir in the water, sake (if using), sugar, and salt.

2. In a special rectangular Japanese omelet pan or an 8-inch skillet over medium-high heat, melt 2 tablespoons of the butter or heat half the oil, and pour in about ¼ cup of the egg mixture. Reduce the heat to medium and, when the egg mixture is set, use a heatproof silicone spatula to gently roll the cooked eggs to one side of the pan. Add another teaspoon of butter or oil to the empty side of the pan and pour in another 3 tablespoons of the egg mixture, or just enough to coat the pan. When this layer has set, roll the first layer across it to the other side of the pan, incorporating it into the roll.

3. Continue adding more butter and oil and more layers of egg until all the egg is used up. You should get about 6 layers in all. Cut the roll into 4 short logs and serve hot or cold.

★

DOS PADRES-STYLE CHILES RELLENOS

Chiles rellenos, or stuffed chiles, take myriad forms. Most Mexican-American restaurants offer a simple and delectable fire-roasted green chile filled with cheese, which is dipped in egg batter and then fried. A friend and co-worker who hails from Oaxaca once brought me a version that his mother made when she was visiting him in Seattle. The large poblano chile was filled with apples, walnuts, breadcrumbs, and cheese. It was quite unlike

anything I have had before or since, a real eye-opener. But my initial introduction to chiles rellenos came in the 1980s when I was a dinner cook at Dos Padres restaurant in Bellingham, Washington, where, instead of being dipped in batter, cheese-filled green chiles were enclosed in a fluffy omelet topped with a quick red chile sauce. This dish is a nostalgic favorite, especially for a leisurely weekend brunch. Serve the chiles rellenos with warm corn or flour tortillas.

MAKES 2 SERVINGS

For the Chiles

2 large, fresh green chiles or whole canned fire-roasted green chiles

2 ounces Monterey Jack cheese, cut into sticks about ½ inch by 2 inches

3 eggs

½ teaspoon vinegar or lemon juice

½ teaspoon kosher salt, or ¼ teaspoon table salt

1 tablespoon olive or canola oil

For the Sauce

1 tablespoon olive or canola oil

1 tablespoon flour

1 teaspoon chili powder

One 7.75-ounce can Mexican tomato sauce, preferably Pato brand

1. If using fresh green chiles, roast and peel them. Preheat the broiler and put the peppers on a baking sheet. Heat the peppers under the broiler, about 6 inches from the element, until they are blackened

on one side, about 5 minutes. Turn the peppers over and broil until the other side is blackened as well, about 5 minutes more. Put the peppers in a brown paper bag and let them cool until they can be handled easily. Peel off the blistered skins, rinsing lightly if necessary to remove any blackened bits. Pull the cap off of each pepper and clean out the pith and the seeds. If using canned green chiles, simply remove them from the can.

2. Stuff the peppers by slipping a wedge of cheese into each pepper.

3. Separate the eggs into yolks and whites. Put the whites in the bowl of an electric mixer or in a large mixing bowl, and put the yolks in a medium mixing bowl. Whip the whites with the lemon juice and salt until they hold soft peaks, then lightly beat the egg yolks and fold them into the whites with a silicone or rubber spatula.

4. Heat 1 tablespoon oil in a large sauté pan over medium-high heat and transfer the egg mixture to the hot pan. Shimmy the pan on the burner for a moment to settle the eggs into a fairly uniform layer over the surface of the pan. As soon as the edges of the omelet begin to set, after about 2 minutes, lay the stuffed chiles side by side in the center. With the spatula, gently fold the omelet in half, lay a plate over the omelet, reduce the heat to the lowest possible setting, and let the omelet cook, undistured, until the cheese

inside the chiles is melted and the eggs are cooked through, about 5 minutes.

5. With a hot pad pressed against the plate, invert the pan so that the omelet is on the plate. Place the plate with the omelet near the stove while making the sauce. Raise the heat under the pan to high, and in the hot pan whisk together 1 tablespoon oil, the flour, and the chili powder. When the mixture is sizzling, whisk in the Mexican tomato sauce. Bring the sauce to a boil, pour it over the omelet, and serve at once.

★

NORTH BEACH SAUSAGE FRITTATA

Whenever I make an Italian-style open-faced omelet, I try to make it taste as good as one I had at Mama's on Washington Square, a casual eatery in San Francisco's Little Italy neighborhood. There, a number of restaurants offer delicious breakfasts where generous portions—big omelets and bigger cups of steaming coffee—are the norm. To streamline the assembly, you can cut up the red pepper and onion while the sausage browns. Serve the frittata with a crusty baguette warmed in the oven while the frittata bakes or with slices of toasted sourdough bread.

MAKES 4 SERVINGS

1 pound sweet or hot natural Italian sausage, cut into 1-inch pieces

4 tablespoons olive oil

1 medium sweet red bell pepper, cut into ½-inch pieces

1 medium onion, peeled and cut into ½-inch pieces

2 cloves garlic, grated on a Microplane grater or finely chopped

1 tablespoon fresh oregano leaves, or 1 teaspoon dried

6 eggs, lightly beaten

4 ounces pepper Jack cheese, grated

1. Preheat the oven to 400°F. In a large, oven-safe sauté pan over medium-high heat, cook the cut-up Italian sausage in 2 tablespoons of the olive oil until it is well browned and falling to bits. Lift the sausage out of the pan with a slotted spoon, reserving the fat in the pan. Keep the sausage on a plate beside the stove.

2. In the fat left in the pan, sauté the red pepper and onion with the garlic and oregano until the vegetables are soft, about 5 minutes. Take the vegetables out of the pan and add them to the sausages. Scrape the pan to remove any flavorful bits and add the bits to the sausage and vegetables.

3. Put the remaining 2 tablespoons olive oil in the pan and pour in the eggs. With a spatula, push the eggs gently away from the sides of the pan toward the center until they are about halfway cooked. Scatter the cooked sausage and vegetables over the half-cooked eggs and sprinkle the grated cheese over all.

4. Bake the assembled fritatta until it is well browned on the top and puffed in the center, about 8 minutes.

★
BREAKFAST SANDWICHES

I like the idea of eggs and ham in a tender roll for breakfast, but the actual experience is generally horrible. Made with fresh organic eggs and homemade hamburger buns, a sandwich of scrambled eggs and ham is delightful. The sandwiches are best made not with sliced ham from the deli section of the supermarket but with leftovers from a home-baked holiday ham (see Not My Grandfather's Ham, pages 233–34). In an ideal world, an enterprising parent could prepare these breakfast sandwiches ahead, keep them refrigerated overnight, and microwave them in the morning to send the kids off to school with a hot breakfast in hand. (In my house, there is no microwave.) In the real world, the sandwiches are great for a leisurely Sunday breakfast with a fat newspaper and a big pot of coffee.

MAKES 6 SERVINGS

6 Homemade Hamburger Buns (pages 272–73) or English muffins

6 Oven-Scrambled Eggs (page 25) or traditional scrambled eggs

6 slices natural applewood-smoked ham

1. Preheat the oven to 325°F and warm the hamburger buns or English muffins.

2. Prepare the scrambled eggs.

3. Assemble the sandwiches, using a slice of ham folded or cut to fit the shape of the bun and a mound of scrambled egg.

★
HUEVOS RANCHEROS

I suspect that there are as many ways to make hue-vos rancheros as there are cooks who make them. But simple is best. Crisp tortillas, still warm from the oil in which they were fried, are topped with fried eggs and warm salsa. The Home-Canned Tomato Salsa on page 405 works especially well. You can spread a thin layer of refried beans between the tortillas and the eggs, if you like.

MAKES 6 SERVINGS

Oil, for frying

6 corn tortillas

6 eggs

1½ cups Refried Pinto Beans (optional; page 143)

Home-Canned Tomato Salsa (page 405)

1. Line a baking sheet with a brown paper bag or with paper towels. Put enough oil in a small sauté pan to reach ½ inch up the sides of the pan. Warm the oil over medium-high heat until it is hot but not smoking. Fry the tortillas, one at a time, in the hot oil, pressing them into the oil with a spatula or swishing the oil over the surface of the tortilla so that it fries evenly. As the tortillas are fried, drain them on the lined baking sheet.

2. Fry the eggs in the same oil in which the tortillas were fried, following the method described in the Fried Eggs recipe on pages 24–25.

3. Assemble the huevos rancheros by spreading a few tablespoons of refried beans over the tortillas, if desired, and placing a fried egg on top. Spoon about ⅓ cup of the salsa over each egg.

★
PATTY'S BREAKFAST SOUFFLÉ

Like most American homemakers in the waning years of the twentieth century, my mother-in-law was juggling family and career duties and always had an eye out for cooking techniques that might make life easier. One recipe that made the rounds among the women in her set was a "breakfast soufflé," which was really a formula for a strata or savory bread pudding that the cook could assemble the night before and pop in the oven in the morning. She used to make this for gatherings at the family summer house in Washington's San Juan Islands. Serve the soufflé with fresh fruit or Vanilla Stewed Prunes (page 39).

MAKES 6 TO 8 SERVINGS

8 cups cubed French bread (1-inch cubes)

1 pound Browned Sausages (page 37)

12 ounces Monterey Jack or cheddar cheese, grated

6 eggs

1 cup milk

1 teaspoon kosher salt

½ teaspoon freshly ground black pepper

1. Butter a 3-quart casserole dish and pile in the bread cubes. Cut the cooked sausages into 1-inch lengths and distribute them evenly among the bread cubes.

Scatter the grated cheese over the bread and sausage.

2. Beat the eggs with the milk, salt, and pepper in a medium mixing bowl, and pour the mixture over the bread cubes, sausage, and cheese. Cover the dish and refrigerate overnight.

3. Preheat the oven to 400°F. Uncover the casserole dish and bake until the soufflé is well browned on the top and puffed in the center, about 30 minutes.

★

NOT REALLY BUTTERMILK PANCAKES

Since I never seem to have buttermilk in the house but I almost always have a container of plain yogurt, I often substitute yogurt for buttermilk in baking; the results are almost always an improvement over the standard form. These are the quintessential pancakes. Serve them hot on a Sunday morning with hot grilled sausages, and have a big newspaper within easy reach. Or consider planting a few fresh or frozen blueberries over the surface of the cakes before they get turned, and serve them with Blueberry Syrup (page 32) and Oven-Fried Bacon (page 36).

MAKES 8 TO 10 LARGE PANCAKES, SERVING 4

1¼ cups unbleached white flour

1 teaspoon baking powder

1 teaspoon baking soda

½ teaspoon salt

1 egg

¼ cup sugar

¼ cup canola oil

1¼ cups plain natural yogurt, such as Nancy's

2 cups fresh or frozen blueberries or huckleberries (optional)

Pure maple syrup or Blueberry Syrup (page 32) as an accompaniment

1. Preheat a griddle or a large cast-iron skillet over medium-high heat until a few drops of water bounce and sputter on the surface before evaporating.

2. While the griddle is heating, in a small mixing bowl, whisk together the flour, baking powder, baking soda, and salt.

3. In a medium mixing bowl, whisk the egg with the sugar and canola oil. Whisk in the yogurt, then whisk in the flour mixture, stirring just enough to bring the ingredients together. Do not overmix or the cakes will be tough.

4. If the griddle or skillet is not well seasoned, rub a little butter over the surface, or spray it with nonstick canola oil spray. Spoon the batter onto the hot griddle, and if using blueberries, sprinkle them immediately over the surface of the uncooked pancakes as soon as the batter is poured.

5. When the pancakes are puffed and golden brown on the undersides, after about 3 minutes, turn and cook until light and cooked through, about 2 minutes more. Serve with syrup.

BLUEBERRY SYRUP

My wife, Betsy, loves to camp. So as often as we can, we camp on her birthday, which comes late in June, just as the wild blueberries or huckleberries become ripe in the foothills of the Cascade Mountains. Now, even if I make these pancakes at home with frozen blueberries, I associate the flavor with camping in the woods, eating breakfast around the campfire, with the smell of wood smoke and bacon wafting through the tall trees. Pancakes with blueberry syrup constitute one of life's simple pleasures that no one should have to live without.

MAKES ABOUT 2 CUPS

½ cup sugar

½ cup water

2 cups fresh or frozen blueberries

I. Stir the sugar and water in a small saucepan over high heat until the sugar is dissolved and the simple syrup is boiling.

2. Add the blueberries, cover, and cook until they have all burst, about 5 minutes. Serve hot.

OATMEAL GRIDDLECAKES

Whole grain in the morning is almost always a good idea. But so is something completely appetizing and delicious. Some of us simply don't get excited about waking up to a bowl of hot mush. For us, oats are better served like this.

MAKES SIXTEEN 3-INCH CAKES, SERVING 4

2 cups rolled or quick-cooking oats (not instant)

½ cup unbleached white flour

I teaspoon baking soda

½ teaspoon salt

I egg

3 tablespoons brown sugar

¼ cup canola oil

1½ cups buttermilk or plain yogurt

Pure maple syrup as an accompaniment

I. Preheat a griddle or a large cast-iron skillet over medium-high heat until a few drops of water bounce and sputter on the surface before evaporating.

2. While the griddle is heating, put the oats, flour, baking soda, and salt in a food processor and process until the oats are roughly ground, but not as fine as flour, about 1 minute. (If no food processor is available, whir the oats in a blender to break them up and then whisk them with the flour, baking soda, and salt in a small mixing bowl.)

3. In a medium mixing bowl, whisk the egg with the brown sugar and canola oil. Whisk in the buttermilk, then whisk in the oatmeal-flour mixture, stirring just enough to bring the ingredients together. Do not overmix or the cakes will be tough.

4. If the griddle or skillet is not well seasoned, rub a little butter over the

surface, or spray it with nonstick canola oil spray. Spoon the batter onto the hot griddle and, when the pancakes are puffed and golden brown on the undersides, after about 3 minutes, turn and cook until light and cooked through, about 2 minutes more. Serve with syrup.

★

ÜBER PANCAKES

Heavily under the influence of the spell cast by Mollie Katzen's magical Sunlight Café, *a book of breakfast recipes, I started reworking some of our favorite family recipes for breakfast breads to incorporate more protein and whole grains. Sometimes the variations rendered our old favorites unrecognizable, but the results were nonetheless extremely good. Among the new breakfast dishes that emerged were these pancakes that one of our sons quickly dubbed Über Cakes. Leftover cakes freeze beautifully and can be reheated in the toaster for a quick, on-the-go breakfast another day.*

MAKES ABOUT SIXTEEN
4-INCH CAKES, SERVING 4

¾ cup unbleached white flour

½ cup whole wheat flour

¼ cup soy protein powder

I teaspoon baking soda

½ teaspoon salt

I egg

¼ cup canola oil

I tablespoon honey

I teaspoon vanilla extract

I ½ cups plain yogurt

Pure maple syrup or powdered sugar as an accompaniment

1. Preheat a griddle or a large cast-iron skillet over medium-high heat until a few drops of water bounce and sputter on the surface before evaporating.

2. While the griddle is heating, in a small mixing bowl, whisk together the white flour, whole wheat flour, soy protein powder, baking soda, and salt.

3. In a medium mixing bowl, whisk the egg with the canola oil, honey, and vanilla extract. Whisk in the yogurt, then whisk in the flour mixture, stirring just enough to bring the ingredients together. Do not overmix or the cakes will be tough.

4. If the griddle or skillet is not well seasoned, spray it with nonstick canola oil spray. Spoon the batter onto the hot griddle and, when the pancakes are puffed and golden brown on the undersides, after about 3 minutes, turn and cook until light and cooked through, about 2 minutes more. Serve with maple syrup or powdered sugar.

★ BUTTERY WAFFLES

Waffle batter from scratch takes less than five minutes to assemble, and the waffles cook very quickly, perfect for school or workday mornings. They are so rich that, if there is no time for a plate and some warm maple syrup, they can be eaten warm, right out of hand. If there is time to linger, serve the waffles with hot sausages and maple syrup.

MAKES 4 LARGE WAFFLES

I cup unbleached white flour

I teaspoon baking powder

½ teaspoon salt

I egg

2 tablespoons sugar

¼ cup (½ stick) unsalted butter, melted

I cup milk

I cup fresh or frozen blueberries (optional)

Pure maple syrup or Blueberry Syrup (page 32) as an accompaniment

I. Preheat a waffle iron. If you are planning to make several batches of waffles and serve them at the same time, preheat the oven to 200°F and line a baking sheet with baker's parchment.

2. While the waffle iron is heating, in a small mixing bowl, whisk together the flour, baking powder, and salt.

3. In a medium mixing bowl, whisk the egg with the sugar and, still whisking, stream in the melted butter. Whisk in the milk,

then whisk in the flour mixture, stirring just enough to bring the ingredients together. Do not overmix or the waffles will be tough. Fold in the blueberries.

4. If the waffle iron is not well seasoned, rub a little butter over the surface, or spray it with nonstick canola oil spray. Spoon the batter (about ½ cup per waffle) onto the hot iron and, when the waffles are puffed and golden brown, after about 5 minutes, remove them from the iron and keep warm or serve at once with syrup.

★ GOLDEN PUMPKIN WAFFLES

Even though I never had anything like these waffles as a child, they evoke a sense of nostalgia so keen that I feel wistful at the very thought of them; perhaps it's the warm scent of cinnamon and pumpkin reminiscent of the holidays. It's worth noting too that the pumpkin makes these decadent-tasting waffles considerably healthier than the average breakfast bread.

MAKES 6 LARGE WAFFLES

I ¼ cups unbleached white flour

I teaspoon ground cinnamon

I teaspoon baking powder

½ teaspoon salt

I egg

¼ cup brown sugar

¼ cup canola oil

1¼ cups homemade pumpkin purée (see page 256), or one 10-ounce package frozen winter squash purée, thawed

Pure maple syrup as an accompaniment

1. Preheat a waffle iron. If you are planning to make several batches of waffles and serve them at the same time, preheat the oven to 200°F and line a baking sheet with baker's parchment.

2. While the waffle iron is heating, in a small mixing bowl, whisk together the flour, cinnamon, baking powder, and salt.

3. In a medium mixing bowl, whisk the egg with the brown sugar and oil. Whisk in the pumpkin purée, then whisk in the flour mixture, stirring just enough to bring the ingredients together. Do not overmix or the waffles will be tough.

4. If the waffle iron is not well seasoned, rub a little butter over the surface, or spray it with nonstick canola oil spray. Spoon the batter (about ½ cup per waffle) onto the hot iron and, when the waffles are puffed and golden brown, after about 5 minutes, remove them from the iron and serve at once with syrup.

★
WEST COAST BREAKFAST BARS

Chock-full of flavor, these bars have enough complex carbohydrates and protein to provide a steady supply of energy for hours. Individually wrapped, they will keep for several days at room temperature or for as long as a month in the freezer. Grab one as you are walking out the door for an easy-to-eat breakfast on the go.

MAKES 16 BARS

2 eggs

¾ cup canola oil

¾ cup brown sugar

¼ cup molasses

1 cup unbleached white flour

1 cup quick-cooking rolled oats, plus ¼ cup for sprinkling

½ cup soy protein powder

1 teaspoon baking powder

½ teaspoon salt

1 cup walnuts, lightly toasted and chopped

1 cup raisins

1 cup chopped dates

¼ cup flax seeds

1 egg white, lightly beaten

1. Preheat the oven to 350°F and line a large baking sheet with a nonstick liner or baker's parchment.

2. Separate one of the eggs and set the white aside. In a large mixing bowl or the bowl of a stand mixer, combine the yolk, remaining whole egg, oil, brown sugar,

and molasses, and beat until smooth. In a separate bowl, whisk together the flour, 1 cup oats, soy protein powder, baking powder, and salt.

3. Pour the flour mixture into the oil and sugar mixture along with the walnuts, raisins, dates, and flax seeds. Stir just until the mixture comes together to form a sticky ball of dough.

4. Turn the dough out on a well-floured surface and divide it into 4 parts. Roll each piece of dough into a log about 8 inches long. Place the logs, side by side, on the lined baking sheet and score them with a dough cutter into 4 pieces each.

5. Slightly beat the reserved egg white. Brush the logs with the egg white and sprinkle with the remaining ¼ cup oats. Bake until the bars are cracked along the sides and browned on top, 18 to 20 minutes. Cool the bars on the pan before serving or storing.

Breakfast Meats

OVEN-FRIED BACON

Some of my favorite bacon comes from Niman Ranch, based in Marin County. Originally a single farm that provided meat for Alice Water's Berkeley restaurant, Chez Panisse, Niman Ranch is now a collective of more than 300 farms committed to raising animals in an ethical, biologically sustainable way where, according to founder Bill Niman, "the pigs have only one bad day."

The bacon from Niman Ranch is smoked with apple-wood. Cooking bacon in the oven may seem counter-intuitive, but if more than a few slices are needed, this method is the only way to go. With minimal attention, the strips come out flat and crisp. If you are baking more than one sheet of bacon at a time, rotate the pans in the oven from time to time so that the pans will cook evenly.

SERVES 4 TO 6

1 pound (about 16 slices) smoked, sliced bacon

1. Preheat the oven to 400°F. Line one rimmed baking sheet with a piece of aluminum foil (this saves time on cleanup), and line a second baking sheet with a brown paper bag or paper towels (to drain the finished bacon).

2. Lay the bacon strips out on the foil-lined baking sheet in a single layer and bake until the bacon becomes translucent and the fat in the bacon is beginning to render, about 10 minutes. Turn the slices over and continue baking until the bacon is well browned and crisp, about 8 minutes more.

3. Transfer the cooked bacon to the paper-lined baking sheet to drain.

★
BROWNED SAUSAGES

Browned sausages are one of the simple delights of the breakfast table, but I think it's a good idea to simmer the sausages in water before browning. This allows the sausage to cook through before it's browned so that the outside won't become overcooked before the inside is done. Sausages these days are made from leaner pork than they used to be. It might be necessary to add a tablespoon of oil in order to fry them properly. Choose organic or all-natural pork sausage for better flavor.

MAKES 4 SERVINGS

1 pound natural pork sausage breakfast links

1 cup water

2 teaspoons peanut, olive, or canola oil (optional)

1. Put the sausages and water in a large sauté pan or cast-iron skillet over high heat and bring the water to a full rolling boil.

2. When the water has boiled away, poke the sausages with a fork to release some of the fat. If no fat is forthcoming, drizzle the canola oil over the sausages.

3. Once the sausages have begun to fry, keep them in motion by moving the pan around on the burner or by rolling the sausages around in the pan with a fork. When they are browned, about 5 minutes after they have begun to fry, they're ready.

★
CELIA'S SCRAPPLE

On the East Coast, scrapple, in the Pennsylvania Dutch tradition, is a loaf made from odd (scrappy) cuts of pork cooked with cornmeal into a polentalike mush that is fashioned into a loaf and chilled. Slices of the loaf are browned in oil or lard for breakfast. In the early years of the twentieth century, Celia Robb Lucas, my wife's paternal grandmother, brought scrapple to the West Coast, where she adapted the formula to a simpler version using a pork shoulder roast. In my wife's family, a batch of scrapple is made every Christmastime, and the loaves are distributed far and near. This version uses boneless country-style pork ribs, a contemporary cut carved from pork shoulders. Serve scrapple fried in oil with Fried Eggs (pages 24–25) or Baked Eggs (page 25).

MAKES 2 LOAVES, SERVING 24

1½ pounds country-style pork ribs or pork shoulder meat

6 cups water

1 medium onion, peeled and finely chopped

1 tablespoon kosher salt

1 bay leaf

2 cups white cornmeal, preferably whole grain

3 tablespoons ground dried sage

2 teaspoons freshly ground black pepper

Flour and butter, for frying

1. In a large, heavy saucepan or a Dutch oven over high heat, combine the pork with the water, onion, salt, and bay leaf

and bring to a boil. Reduce the heat to low, cover the pan, and cook gently until the pork is tender enough to pull apart with a fork, about 3½ hours.

2. Butter 2 loaf pans, or spray them with nonstick canola oil spray. With a slotted spoon, lift the cooked pork out of the cooking liquid and set it aside to cool, reserving the cooking liquid in the pan. Remove the bay leaf from the cooking liquid and discard it. Turn the heat back up to high and whisk the cornmeal slowly into the boiling cooking liquid. Whisk in the sage and pepper. Cook steadily until the cornmeal is very tender, about 10 minutes, then take the pan off the heat. Shred the cooked pork and stir it into the cornmeal mush.

3. Divide the scrapple evenly between the loaf pans and chill for several hours or overnight.

4. To serve the scrapple, melt 1 teaspoon of butter for every serving in a large sauté pan or on a flat griddle over medium heat. Cut slices from the loaf of scrapple, roll the slices in flour, shaking off any excess, and fry them in butter until well browned and heated through, about 5 minutes on each side.

Breakfast Fruit

✴

ORANGE AND STRAWBERRY COMPOTE

I first discovered the pleasure of combining oranges and strawberries when I was pulling together a thank-you breakfast for the staff of a little restaurant where I cooked on San Juan Island in Friday Harbor in the mid-1980s. We had just gotten through a successful season that concluded with a blow-out dinner on New Year's Eve. We were about to close the restaurant for a couple of weeks, and the staff came in for a cleanup day on January 2. I wanted to use up as much of the fresh food as I could, and I had some of those white-shoul-dered winter strawberries. I grated some orange zest and segmented the oranges, combining them with the berries. The combination was so good that it has become a part of my standard repertoire.

MAKES ABOUT 4 SERVINGS

2 medium navel oranges, preferably organic

1 pint strawberries, preferably organic

1. With a zester, carefully remove the colorful outer rind from the orange. If no zester is available, use a potato peeler and cut the strips of zest with a paring knife into very thin strips. Put the citrus zest in a small bowl.

2. With a sharp paring knife, cut the tops and bottoms from the oranges, then cut away the white pith and discard it. Holding the fruit over the bowl containing the zest,

cut out the sections of pulp, leaving the membranes of each section behind.

3. Hull the strawberries and slice them lengthwise into 3 or 4 slices each. Toss with the cut oranges. Serve with breakfast.

<h2>★
VANILLA STEWED PRUNES</h2>

A public relations firm won an award from the International Association of Culinary Professionals when it helped the California Dried Plum Board reposition prunes in the marketplace as "dried plums," but there are some among us who always liked prunes. I am one of them. I especially like them cooked this way and served warm at breakfast. Vanilla bean paste is made from ground vanilla beans suspended in a sweet, starchy paste. If vanilla paste is unavailable, use half of a vanilla bean, split in half lengthwise and scraped to free up the seeds inside.

MAKES 4 SERVINGS

½ cup sugar

½ cup water

1 teaspoon vanilla bean paste, or half of a vanilla bean, split and scraped

1 cup (about 16 large) dried plums

1. Stir the sugar and water in a small saucepan over high heat until the sugar is dissolved and the syrup is boiling.

2. Add the vanilla bean and dried plums. Cover the pan, reduce the heat to low, and cook until the plums are very tender and have absorbed most of the syrup,

about 5 minutes. Serve warm or at room temperature.

<h2>★
BROILED GRAPEFRUIT</h2>

California grapefruit is wonderful, and even though the state is known for its sunshine, it's also the home of that famous San Francisco Bay fog. This is a perfect breakfast dish for chilly winter mornings when grapefruit is at its best.

MAKES 4 SERVINGS

2 large ruby red grapefruit

4 tablespoons raspberry jam or red currant jelly (optional)

1. Preheat the broiler. Cut each grapefruit in half through its equator. With a sharp knife, follow the outline of each segment, freeing the pulp and leaving it in its place.

2. Put the grapefruit on a cookie sheet and slide them under the preheated broiler. Cook 5 minutes or until the surface of the fruit is bubbling hot.

3. Put a dollop of jelly in the middle of each one and broil for 1 minute longer, or until the jelly is melting into the grapefruit. Serve hot.

chapter 3

James Beard's Sweet Onion Sandwiches
Grilled Rare Albacore with Ocean Salad and Wonton Crisps
Gulf Shrimp with Orange and Ginger Dipping Sauce
American Paddlefish Caviar on Buckwheat Blini
Very Cold Olympia Oysters with Frozen Verjus Mignonette
Steamed Pacific Oysters with Sweet Wine Butter
Fried Oysters
Fried Calamari with Lemon Aïoli
Asian-Style Stir-Fried Squid with Garlic and Ginger
Hom Bow (Chinese Barbecue Pork Buns)
Chinese Spring Rolls
Savory Meatballs
Finocchiona Pizzette
Chanterelle Mushrooms on Handmade Rye Crackers
Phyllo Triangles
Caponata
Hummus
Blue Corn Nachos with Homemade Salsa
Oregon Blue Cheese Dip
Dungeness Crab and Artichoke Dip
Chicken Liver Crostini
Olive Poppers
Pacific Northwest Fondue

APPETIZERS

Appetizers

James Beard has been called the father of American gastronomy, but in a way, this larger-than-life caterer, cooking instructor, food commentator, and West Coast native (he was born in Portland, Oregon, in 1903), was less a father to American food than its rebellious child. In fact, the rebellious generation of cooks that was forged in the sixties, the generation credited with creating the New American Style, owes a great deal to Beard.

Long before Alice Waters or Jeremiah Tower came on the scene, Beard was already there. In his late teens, he became interested in leftist political causes, and he was expelled from Reed College "for politics" and because of what he described in an interview with Barbara Kafka as "an attachment to one of the male professors." But the considerable force of his rebellious spirit was focused almost entirely on food. He spent a lifetime protesting an ill-defined but potent culinary trend that was threatening to obliterate some of the best ingredients and techniques of regional American cooking.

Throughout Beard's lifetime, tenets of the military-industrial complex were vehemently applied to food production. Even in the early years of the century, mechanized farming practices were employed to make farms more like factories. With the introduction of chemical fertilizers and pesticides and their widespread use in the wake of World War II, the patchwork of small family farms that had characterized the American landscape became a more uniform landscape of vast agricultural factories.

In spite of an ongoing countertrend that celebrates small and medium-size farms, the megatrend continues to this day. On acreage where several small farmers once raised various kinds of livestock and crops, a single farmer will now produce a single mono crop. Bulked up on chemical growth enhancers, foods grown on these vast factory farms are less nourishing and less flavorful than foods grown organically on farms where multiple crops are grown in a more sustainable manner. In turn, the factory farms feed processing plants where raw ingredients are rendered into prepared foods, prepackaged and ready for distribution to the American public.

Stripped of much of their nutritional value and tasting more like the artificial additives than their primary ingredients, most American foods in the middle of the last century were characterized less by their inherent goodness than by mass production and overprocessing. When Beard showed up on the scene to champion more simply prepared foods, served in season and as close as possible to their source, he brought a palate that was shaped by firsthand experience with more wholesome foods grown in a simpler time. He also brought to the table some of the discriminating sensibilities he inherited from his hotelier mother and her Chinese cook.

The cook, Jue Let, was originally the sous chef at Beard's mother's hotel in Portland, called The Gladstone. Late in life, when he was describing a restaurant that he enjoyed as a child to his friend Barbara Kafka, he said, "It had a Chinese chef, a very good one. Every good chef was Chinese." While Let cooked dishes that were based in French and English culinary traditions, his sensibilities were undoubtedly shaped by his Chinese heritage. Many of Beard's friends in childhood were Chinese and, curiously, he confided to Kafka that he often wished that he had been born Chinese too. Although he never cooked Chinese food per se, a certain Asian sensibility wound its way through much of Beard's awakening palate, and much of America's as well.

In the 1920s, Beard tried to establish a career in theater, but money allocated for acting classes in Europe was spent in restaurants, where the young Beard ate copious meals that he was later able to recall with uncanny precision. Though he had some promising performances on stage and a few bit parts in motion pictures, his acting career was not lucrative enough to support his considerable appetites. In the thirties, he launched a catering company and eventually a food shop called Hors d'Oeuvre, Inc. From then on, his professional efforts were entirely culinary in nature.

For four decades, from the mid-1940s until he died in 1985, Beard ran a cooking school out of his brownstone apartment at 167 West 12th Street in New York's Greenwich Village. A list of guest instructors and students from those years is a virtual Who's Who of American food, and from his cooking school and his ever-expanding circle of friends grew the understanding of what constitutes contemporary American food.

When Beard died, a group of his friends, prompted by the indomitable Julia Child and led by Beard protégé Peter Kump, decided to preserve his home as a center for the culinary arts, a gathering place for celebrating American food. Together they founded the James Beard Foundation. Now, every week, chefs from all over North America prepare meals at the old brownstone to showcase their talent and their favorite regional foods. In 1999, I cooked at the Beard House.

Months before the big night when we cooked for 72 discriminating New Yorkers, I planned the menu and determined how we would have Northwest food supplies and Washington wines shipped to the Big Apple. When the day of departure finally arrived, Chris Canlis, the owner of the restaurant where I worked in Seattle; Jeff Taton, my sous chef; and Betsy, my wife, stood on the sidewalk in front of the airport and inventoried our supplies. Copper River salmon from Alaska filled one huge cooler. Dungeness crab filled another. There was an enormous box of flowers and another enormous box filled with morel mushrooms.

Hours later, on the other side of the continent, as Westcott Bay oysters from San Juan Island received their dollop of frozen mignonette and the Dungeness crab legs were tucked into Belgian endive leaves with sections of red grapefruit, the guests arrived and the sparkling Oregon wine began to flow. Smoked salmon and paddlefish caviar on quail eggs along with the chilled oysters and crab legs were passed as hors d'oeuvres.

As soon as the guests were seated, I sent out a surprise course of a single hot oyster with sabayon, and our own handmade bread rolls were delivered hot to the tables. Then the meal began in earnest. Raspberries and hazelnuts tumbled down onto salad plates with mixed baby lettuces to be crowned with a hot hazelnut-crusted goat cheese fritter. Dungeness crab cakes were planted on pools of fragrant orange butter with colorful stripes of sweet red pepper purée. Then the rhubarb and ginger sorbet prepared everyone for the next course. Copper River salmon roasted in the Beard House oven was dressed with morel mushrooms in wine and cream. On the same plate, sautéed pea vines curled around the green pea flans punctuated with a few fat tips of Washington-grown asparagus. Dessert came in the form of horn-shaped nut cookies brushed inside with chocolate and spilling forth ripe strawberries, blueberries, and raspberries in profusion. I think James Beard would have liked it.

★

JAMES BEARD'S SWEET ONION SANDWICHES

Beard, according to his friend and biographer Evan Jones, was fond of tea sandwiches, especially watercress sandwiches like the ones he enjoyed on his first trip to London as a young man. But other friends, including Marion Cunningham, tell me that Beard liked these onion sandwiches served before dinner with cocktails. Slightly fussy, they serve, as Beard said all appetizers should, to "sharpen the appetite but not deaden it."

MAKES 16 BITE-SIZE SANDWICHES

8 slices Better Than Store-Bought White Bread (pages 267–68) or other white sandwich bread

8 tablespoons Homemade Mayonnaise (pages 115–16)

8 thin slices Walla Walla sweet onion or other sweet onion

Kosher salt and freshly ground black pepper, to taste

1 cup finely chopped fresh parsley

1. Spread each slice of bread with 1 tablespoon mayonnaise, and top half of the bread slices with 2 thin slices of onion. Season with the salt and pepper. Press a second slice of bread, mayonnaise side down, on top of the onions.

2. Use a small round cookie cutter to cut 4 rounds from each sandwich, or trim the crusts from each sandwich and cut it diagonally into wedges.

3. Press the edges of each mini-sandwich into the parsley, so that each is green on the sides and white on the bottom and top.

★

GRILLED RARE ALBACORE WITH OCEAN SALAD AND WONTON CRISPS

Sashimi-grade albacore loins, harvested off the coast of Washington, are usually flash frozen before they reach the market. The small loins, generally 16 to 18 inches long, are easy to handle on the grill and, when they are left very rare in the center, slice beautifully into neat portions. I like to serve the tuna on a mound of "ocean salad." Made from several kinds of seaweed in a sesame dressing, ocean salad is sold in the seafood sections of Asian markets and in some regular supermarkets. If ocean salad is unavailable, use shredded spinach tossed with a drizzle of sesame oil, a splash of rice vinegar, and a sprinkling of toasted sesame seeds. The "crisps" are made from fried wonton wrappers, which are sold in the produce section of most large supermarkets.

MAKES 2 DOZEN SMALL
APPETIZERS, SERVING 12

1 loin (about 1½ pounds) of albacore tuna

2 tablespoons soy sauce

2 tablespoons Madeira or sherry

1 tablespoon olive or canola oil

1 teaspoon toasted sesame oil

1½ cups ocean salad

1 teaspoon toasted sesame seeds (optional)

For the Crisps

Rice bran or canola oil, for frying

24 wonton wrappers

1. If the tuna is frozen, thaw it overnight in the refrigerator, or thaw it, still sealed in its packaging, in a sink full of cold water for about 3 hours.

2. In a small bowl, combine the soy sauce, Madeira, olive oil, and sesame oil. Add the thawed albacore loin and roll it in the marinade to coat it evenly. Allow the fish to marinate for 30 minutes at room temperature or for several hours in the refrigerator.

3. Preheat a gas or charcoal grill until the heat from the grill forces you to move your hand away when you hold it 5 inches above the grate. The charcoal should be burned down to white-hot coals. Grill the marinated albacore on one side without moving it until the edges closest to the grilling surface become opaque and cooked looking and dark brown marks are established underneath, about 3 minutes. (If you try to turn the fish too soon, it will stick to the grill and tear when you try to move it.)

4. Turn the albacore twice, grilling 3 sides of the loin and leaving the inside very rare, about 8 minutes in all. Take the loin off the heat and let it stand at room temperature while you make the crisps. Or, if you prefer to grill the loin a day

in advance, refrigerate until half an hour before serving time.

5. Line a baking sheet with a brown paper bag or paper towels. Put enough oil in a small sauté pan to reach ½ inch up the sides of the pan. Warm the oil over medium-high heat until it is hot but not smoking, then fry the wonton wrappers, 1 or 2 at a time, in the hot oil, pressing them into the oil with a spatula or swishing the oil over the surface so that each one fries evenly. As the crisps are fried, drain them on the lined baking sheet.

6. To assemble the appetizers, put a small mound, about a tablespoon, of ocean salad on top of each crisp, then top with a slice of grilled albacore. Sprinkle with sesame seeds, if desired.

★

GULF SHRIMP WITH ORANGE AND GINGER DIPPING SAUCE

Wild white shrimp from the Gulf of California (between Baja and the mainland of Mexico) or from the Gulf of Mexico are better than the more widely available tiger prawns that are farmed in environmentally hazardous ways. Extra-large 16-20 size shrimp are best for serving cold with a dipping sauce. If only smaller shrimp are available, don't cook them as long. Rinsing the shrimp in water to cool them down washes away some of the flavor; instead, spread them in a single layer on a baking sheet and blast-chill them in the refrigerator or freezer. Both the shrimp and the sauce can be prepared several hours before serving time.

For the Shrimp

2 pounds (about 3 dozen) large shrimp

12 cups water

3 tablespoons sea salt

For the Orange and Ginger Dipping Sauce

3 medium navel oranges

3 tablespoons rice vinegar

1 tablespoon sugar

½-inch piece ginger root, peeled

1 tablespoon cornstarch

1 teaspoon kosher salt

1. Butterfly the shrimp: Working with one shrimp at a time, use a very sharp knife to cut through the back side of the shell and about ⅛ inch into the meat without cutting the shrimp in half. Peel away the shell, leaving only the bit near the tail.

2. Place the water in a large (6-quart) pot and add the sea salt. Bring the salted water to a full, rolling boil and add the shrimp. Cook until the meat is white and the stripes are pink, about 3 minutes.

3. Drain the shrimp and spread them out in a single layer on a baking sheet or tray and put them immediately into the freezer until they are chilled, about 10 minutes; do not allow the shrimp to freeze.

4. Make the dipping sauce: With a zester, remove the colorful outer rind from the oranges, allowing this zest to land in a

small, nonreactive (stainless or enameled) saucepan. If no zester is available, use a vegetable peeler and then, with a sharp knife, cut the strips of zest into thin julienne strips. Juice the oranges and add the juice to the pan. In a blender, combine the vinegar, sugar, ginger, cornstarch, and salt and purée until the mixture is smooth. Stir the ginger mixture into the orange juice mixture and bring to a boil over medium-high heat. The sauce can be made ahead and served cold or at room temperature. Serve the shrimp cold with the dipping sauce.

★

AMERICAN PADDLEFISH CAVIAR ON BUCKWHEAT BLINI

American paddlefish populations are more stable and less threatened than sturgeon, so this is an environmentally friendly alternative to imported caviar. It also happens to taste fantastic. The little pancakes known as blini are easy to make; in fact, at parties, I often put my kids in charge of making them. The batter can be made ahead and kept in a squeeze bottle (like a ketchup bottle) for a few hours in the refrigerator. The crème fraîche can be kept in a second squeeze bottle and squeezed onto the finished pancakes just before you dollop the caviar on top. Lining the platter with shredded spinach makes for an eye-popping presentation, and it also makes picking the blini up off the platter easier. A clean white napkin will also work.

MAKES 2 DOZEN SMALL PANCAKES

1 egg, separated

2 tablespoons unsalted butter, melted

½ cup milk

¼ cup buckwheat flour

¼ cup unbleached white flour

½ teaspoon freshly squeezed lemon juice

½ teaspoon salt

Shredded spinach for lining the platter (optional)

½ cup crème fraîche

1 ounce American (Montana) paddlefish caviar

1. In a medium mixing bowl, whisk together the egg yolk and melted butter. Stir in the milk, then the buckwheat flour and white flour. In a small clean, dry bowl, whip the egg white with the lemon juice and salt until it holds stiff peaks. Fold the beaten egg white into the egg yolk–flour mixture, then transfer the batter to a squeeze bottle. The batter can be prepared several hours in advance and kept refrigerated.

2. Just before serving, squeeze quarter-size rounds of the batter onto a very hot griddle and cook, turning once, until browned, about 5 minutes.

3. Line a serving platter with shredded spinach or a clean napkin. Transfer the cooked blini to the serving platter. Spoon or pipe crème fraîche onto the cooked blini, and spoon caviar on top of the crème fraîche. Serve at once.

★ VERY COLD OLYMPIA OYSTERS WITH FROZEN VERJUS MIGNONETTE

The Olympia oyster (Ostrea lurida) *is the only oyster truly native to the West Coast. Pacific oysters* (Crassostrea gigas) *and Kumamoto oysters* (Crassostrea sikamea), *which are now farmed extensively up and down the coast, were originally imported from Japan. The diminutive Olympia is no larger than a grown man's thumbnail, but it packs as much flavor as European Flat oysters* (Ostrea edulis), *which are also farmed on the West Coast and are considered among the world's best oysters. If Olympias are not available, opt for Kumomotos. I like them served ice-cold on the half shell with a teaspoonful of frozen mignonette made from verjus. Verjus is the juice of green, unripened wine grapes. Not quite as sharp as lemon juice or vinegar, it is nevertheless fairly acidic. It can be used in salad dressings or to spike sauces with a tangy edge. Here, it's mixed with shallots and pepper and frozen into a kind of slush that serves to brighten oysters on the half shell. If no verjus is available, use 3 parts dry white wine and 1 part champagne vinegar.*

MAKES 4 SERVINGS

For the Oysters

4 dozen Olympia or other very small oysters, live in their shells

Crushed ice

Grape leaves, if available, for garnish

For the Mignonette

¼ cup verjus

¼ cup water

2 tablespoons finely chopped shallot

1 teaspoon coarsely ground black pepper

1. As soon as the oysters come into the kitchen, arrange them in a single layer in a baking dish, taking care to make sure they are right side up—that is, the bowl shape should be down and the flat "lid" should be up. Cover them with damp paper towels and put the pan in the refrigerator until just before serving time. Stored in this way, fresh, live oysters should keep for 3 days.

2. To make the mignonette, combine the verjus, water, shallot, and pepper. Put the mixture in a small ice cream maker such as a Donvier. If no ice cream maker is available, put the mixture in an ice cube tray. If using an ice cream maker, simply stir or crank until the mixture is uniformly soft-frozen. If using an ice cube tray, freeze the mixture undisturbed for half an hour, then stir to break up any crystals. Then freeze again, stirring every 15 minutes, until the mixture is smooth. Stored in the freezer, the mixture will become hard-frozen, but it can be broken up and stirred to make it soft-frozen once again.

3. Carefully shuck the oysters, one at a time. Using a towel to protect your hand from the sharp edges of the shell, hold the oyster firmly in one hand while you insert an oyster knife with the other. Push the

knife in a short way and slide it under the top shell to cut the adductor muscle that holds the shell shut. Remove the top shell, then slide the knife under the meat of the oyster to free it from the bottom shell.

4. Serve the shucked oysters, 1 dozen per serving, on a bed of crushed ice with a spoonful of the mignonette on top of each one. Garnish with fresh grape leaves, if desired.

★

STEAMED PACIFIC OYSTERS WITH SWEET WINE BUTTER

Oyster lovers are supposed to prefer their oysters as simply as possible, preferably dressed in nothing more than the drop of seawater inside their shells, and I do like oysters that way. But I am also a sucker for oysters in fancy attire, like this chi-chi arrangement of meaty-textured steamed oysters in a velvety chemise of sweet wine butter sauce with a ruffle of spinach leaves cut into ribbons. The combination of sweet wine and salty oysters is powerfully seductive.

MAKES 12 APPETIZER SERVINGS

3 dozen live medium Pacific oysters in the shell

1 cup water

One 375-milliliter (12.7 ounce) bottle late-harvest dessert wine

1 tablespoon sugar

Pinch of kosher salt

Generous grind of black pepper

2 cups (4 sticks) cold unsalted butter, cut into 1-inch bits

1 cup shredded spinach, for lining the platter

1. Scrub the oysters and put them in a large kettle with the water. Light the burner under the oysters and cook over high heat until most of the oysters have popped open, 8 to 10 minutes. (If the oysters are ready before the sauce is finished, turn off the burner and allow the oysters to stay warm in the pan.)

2. Put the sweet wine in a saucepan over high heat and cook until it has reduced to about one fourth of its original volume. Add the sugar, salt, and pepper. Whisk in the cold butter bits to make a smooth, creamy sauce.

3. Open the steamed oysters and arrange them on a platter lined with the shredded spinach. Spoon or ladle a tablespoon of sauce over each oyster. Serve at once.

★

FRIED OYSTERS

Properly fried, oysters are firm but moist, sealed in a soft-crisp coat. To ensure success, wait to apply the seasoned flour until just before you plunge the oysters into the oil. Make sure the oil is at the proper temperature and avoid overcrowding the pan. When I was asked to appear in an episode of Chefs A'Field, *an award-winning PBS series about chefs and farmers, I was paired with an oyster farmer, Bill Taylor of Taylor Shellfish. It was spring and the nettles were up, so I decided to prepare oysters fried* with a purée of nettles, and fried oysters do make a wonderful garnish for the Wild Nettle Soup on pages 74–75. They can also be served with Lemon Aïoli (pages 50–51) or a mixture of Homemade Mayonnaise (pages 115–16) or puréed chipotle peppers, to taste.

MAKES 1 DOZEN OYSTERS

12 oysters, shucked
½ cup unbleached white flour
½ teaspoon baking powder
½ teaspoon freshly ground black pepper
Oil, for frying

1. Line a baking sheet with a brown paper bag or some paper towels to receive the oysters as soon as they are fried. Rinse the shucked oysters in cold water to remove any bits of shell, then drain them in a single layer on paper towels.

2. In a small bowl, stir together the flour, baking powder, and pepper. Heat 1 inch oil in a cast-iron skillet over medium-high heat to 375°F, or until a cube of bread dropped in floats immediately to the surface and browns in 1 minute.

3. Roll the oysters in the flour mixture, shake off the excess flour, and fry them for 2 to 3 minutes, turning once with chopsticks or tongs. Drain on the prepared baking sheet.

★

FRIED CALAMARI WITH LEMON AÏOLI

Once relegated to small pockets of aficionados who knew more than the rest of us, squid became all the rage when it was dressed in a crispy coat of breadcrumbs (or Japanese panko) and served in Mediterranean restaurants with garlicky aïoli dipping sauces. Calamari has become such a standard on West Coast menus that it's hard to believe that a mere twenty years ago, it was almost impossible to find. In the hands of West Coast cooks, the Old World blend of egg yolks, garlic, and olive oil has become the starting point for myriad flavorful sauces from traditional garlic to fiery chipotle and Asian-tinged wasabi aïoli. Here the sauce becomes a conduit for the essence of lemon.

MAKES 6 SERVINGS

For the Lemon Aïoli

1 egg yolk
1 teaspoon freshly grated lemon zest
1 tablespoon freshly squeezed lemon juice
2 cloves garlic, finely chopped or grated
1 teaspoon kosher salt
¼ teaspoon ground white pepper
1 cup pure olive oil, not extra virgin

For the Calamari

1 pound cleaned squid, fresh or frozen
Kosher salt and freshly ground black pepper, to taste
¾ cup unbleached white flour

2 egg whites, beaten with 2 tablespoons water

2 cups panko (Japanese breadcrumbs)

Canola oil, for frying

1. Make the aioli. In a small mixing bowl, whisk the egg yolk with the lemon zest, lemon juice, garlic, salt, and white pepper for about 1 minute, or until mixture is very thoroughly combined. Keep the whisk in motion and slowly stream in the oil, starting with just a few drops at a time, then building to a slow but steady stream until all the oil is incorporated. The sauce should have the consistency of sour cream.

2. Line a baking sheet with baker's parchment. Cut the squid tubes into rings, about ½ inch wide. Toss the rings and the tentacles with salt and pepper. Roll the squid in the flour, shaking off any excess.

3. Dip the flour-coated squid in the mixture of egg white and water and allow the excess egg wash to run off. Roll the egg-dipped pieces in panko and spread them out in a single layer on the baking sheet.

4. Heat 1 inch oil in a large skillet to 375°F, or until a cube of bread dropped in floats immediately to the surface and browns in 1 minute. Fry the breaded squid rings and tentacles until crisp and lightly browned, 2 to 3 minutes. Serve with the aïoli.

★

ASIAN-STYLE STIR-FRIED SQUID WITH GARLIC AND GINGER

Stripped of its western-style coat of breadcrumbs, the simple white tubes and tentacles of cleaned squid are presented here in a flavorful blend of Asian pantry staples.

MAKES 4 SERVINGS

1 pound cleaned squid, fresh or frozen

About 12 cups water

1 tablespoon sea salt

3 or 4 cloves garlic

1-inch piece ginger root

1 tablespoon soy sauce

1 tablespoon rice vinegar

1 teaspoon Thai-style fish sauce (optional)

1 teaspoon sugar

2 tablespoons peanut or canola oil

1 tablespoon toasted sesame oil

1 teaspoon dried red chile flakes

1. Cut the squid tubes into rings, about ½ inch wide. Fill a large (6-quart) pot halfway with water and add the sea salt; bring the salted water to a full, rolling boil. Plunge the cut squid into the boiling salted water and stir just until the squid tightens up and turns white, about 6 seconds.

2. Drain the squid and spread it out in a single layer on a baking sheet or tray to halt the cooking. The squid can be

prepared ahead up to this point and kept chilled until just before serving.

3. Grate the garlic cloves and the ginger on a Microplane grater or chop them both very fine. In a small bowl, stir together the soy sauce, rice vinegar, fish sauce, if desired, and sugar.

4. In a large sauté pan or wok over medium-high heat, heat the peanut oil and sesame oil until hot but not smoking. Add the garlic, ginger, and chile flakes to the hot oil, then toss in the blanched squid and stir rapidly until the squid is cooked through, about 1 minute. Add the soy sauce mixture and stir to coat the squid. Serve at once.

★

HOM BOW (CHINESE BARBECUE PORK BUNS)

Hom bow are among the myriad buns and treats served from carts at restaurants that feature dim sum. The hours for dim sum correlate roughly to brunch service in Western restaurants, but the fare is completely different. Like the Chinese barbecue pork inside them, the buns can be purchased ready-made in the freezer sections of many Asian grocery stores, but they taste better when you make them at home. The yeast-raised buns are not too difficult to make. The only real challenge for most Western cooks is that cooking them requires a bamboo steamer basket to rest on top of a wok. If your town has a Chinatown or an international district, this should be easy to find.

MAKES 24 BUNS

For the Dough

1½ cups warm water

1 tablespoon (1 packet) active dry yeast

3 tablespoons sugar

4½ cups unbleached white flour

2 tablespoons peanut oil or canola oil

2 tablespoons toasted sesame oil

For the Filling

2 tablespoons water

2 tablespoons soy sauce

2 tablespoons oyster sauce

1 tablespoon sugar

1 tablespoon cornstarch

2 tablespoons peanut or canola oil

1 green onion, finely chopped

1 clove garlic, grated on a Microplane grater

8 ounces Chinese Barbecue Pork (page 230), cut into ½-inch bits

1. Make the dough. In the bowl of an electric mixer or in a large mixing bowl, stir together the warm water, yeast, and sugar. Allow the mixture to stand until the yeast is softened, about 5 minutes, then stir until the yeast is completely dissolved. If you are working with a stand mixer, pile in all the flour. With a paddle attachment, mix on low speed until everything comes together to make a thick, sticky batter. If you are mixing by hand, whisk in 1 cup of flour at a time until the batter is too thick to whisk, then switch to a wooden spoon

and stir in the remaining flour along with the peanut and sesame oils.

2. Use the dough hook on the mixer, or turn the dough out onto a well-floured countertop and knead it, pressing and folding it until it is very springy. Sprinkle the dough with additional flour if needed to keep it from sticking to the counter. Be careful not to add more flour than necessary or the dough will be stiff and the buns will be heavy. Leave the dough in the mixer bowl or return it to the regular mixing bowl. Cover the bowl with a damp, lint-free kitchen towel or with a piece of plastic wrap and put it in a warm place until the dough is doubled in size, about an hour.

3. While the dough is rising, make the filling. In a small bowl, stir the water, soy sauce, oyster sauce, sugar, and cornstarch and keep the bowl near the stove. Heat the oil in a wok or large sauté pan and sauté the green onion and garlic until fragrant, about 1 minute. Stir in the barbecue pork and the soy sauce mixture. Cook until the sauce is thickened and the pork is heated through, about 2 minutes. Spread the filling mixture over the surface of a large plate to cool.

4. Divide the risen dough into 2 pieces and roll each piece into a log about 12 inches long. Cut each log into 12 pieces to make 24 small balls of dough. Cut a large piece of baker's parchment or aluminum foil into 24 squares, each about 2 inches square.

5. Working with 1 ball of dough at a time, roll the dough out with a rolling pin on a well-floured surface into a 3-inch circle. Put 1 well-rounded tablespoon of pork filling in the center and gather the dough up and around the filling. Seal the bun by pinching the edges of the dough together.

6. As the buns are finished, place each one on a 2-inch square of parchment or foil. Let the buns rise until they are soft and almost doubled in bulk, about 35 minutes.

7. Arrange the buns, still on their parchment squares, in a single layer in a Chinese bamboo steaming-basket set over a wok with 2 inches of water. Cook over high heat until buns are cooked through, about 10 minutes.

CHINESE SPRING ROLLS

Spring rolls, also known as egg rolls, are more often enjoyed in restaurants than they are at home, but they are fun to make. Larger and more flexible than most supermarket egg roll wrappers, round, crêpelike lumpia wrappers from the Philippines are easier to handle; they're available at Asian grocery stores. If you are shopping in an Asian grocery store, look for rice bran oil too, which is the best oil for frying egg rolls, or just about anything. If no Asian market is nearby, don't despair: Regular egg roll wrappers and supermarket peanut oil will do. A mixture of Chinese barbecue pork (home-made or store-bought) and tiny wild shrimp from Oregon, which are sold already cooked and shelled, make a savory filling. A mandoline, or Japanese vegetable slicer, will make short work of cutting the carrots into superfine julienne strips.

MAKES 16 LARGE EGG ROLLS OR
24 MEDIUM-SIZE EGG ROLLS

2 tablespoons water

2 tablespoons soy sauce

2 tablespoons oyster sauce

1 tablespoon sugar

1 tablespoon cornstarch

2 tablespoons rice bran, peanut, or canola oil, plus more for frying

3 cups shredded napa cabbage

2 medium carrots, cut into very thin matchsticks

4 ounces fresh shiitake mushroom caps, thinly sliced

1 bunch green onions, thinly sliced

2 cloves garlic, grated on a Microplane grater

1-inch chunk ginger root, grated on a Microplane grater

8 ounces Chinese Barbecue Pork (page 230), cut into ½-inch bits

8 ounces small shrimp, cooked, peeled, and chopped

One 13-ounce package lumpia wrappers, or one 16-ounce package egg roll wrappers

1 large egg, lightly beaten

Rice bran oil or peanut oil, for frying

Chinese mustard or bottled Thai chili sauce as an accompaniment

1. Make the filling. In a small bowl, stir together the water, soy sauce, oyster sauce, sugar, and cornstarch and keep the bowl near the stove. Heat the 2 tablespoons oil in a wok or large sauté pan and sauté the cabbage, carrots, mushrooms, green onions, garlic, and ginger until fragrant and heated through, about 3 minutes. Stir in the barbecue pork, shrimp and water–soy sauce mixture. Cook until the sauce is thickened and the pork and shrimp are heated through, about 2 minutes. Spread the mixture over the surface of a baking dish to cool. (It is helpful to loosely mark portions of the filling with a dough scraper, visually dividing the filling into the number of portions it will take to fill the rolls.)

2. Fill the egg rolls. Work with one wrapper at a time and keep the remaining wrappers covered with a damp paper towel or a square of plastic wrap to prevent them from drying out. Brush a little of the lightly beaten egg around the top and side edges of the wrapper. Spread about 3 tablespoons of the cooked and cooled filling over the center of the wrapper. Fold the bottom of the wrapper up toward the center, over the filling, then fold in the sides. Roll the wrapper, pressing the filling as you go to make a snug packet. Repeat the process with the remaining filling and wrappers.

3. Fry the egg rolls. Preheat the oven to 250°F and line a baking sheet with a brown paper bag to receive the egg rolls as

they are fried. In a wok or large cast-iron skillet, heat 1 inch of oil until a pinch of egg roll wrapper sizzles immediately and floats to the top (a thermometer will register 350°F). Fry 3 or 4 egg rolls at a time without crowding. Turn them once with chopsticks or metal tongs and continue frying until the rolls are golden brown, about 4 minutes in all.

4. Transfer the fried egg rolls to the prepared baking sheet and keep them in the warm oven while you fry the remaining egg rolls. Serve hot with Chinese mustard or Thai chili sauce.

★

SAVORY MEATBALLS

At an hors d'oeuvres party, everyone seems to hone in on the protein and, as simple as they sound, meatballs rank high in the approval ratings. These meatballs are tender, but they hold together well and are easy to make. You can make them ahead, chill them, and then reheat them, but they are best served the same day they are made.

MAKES 32 BITE-SIZE MEATBALLS

3 tablespoons olive oil

1 pound ground beef

1 medium onion, peeled and coarsely chopped

1 egg

1 cup panko (Japanese breadcrumbs) or fresh white breadcrumbs

¼ cup finely chopped fresh parsley

1 tablespoon kosher salt

1 teaspoon freshly ground black pepper

½ teaspoon freshly ground nutmeg

1 cup unbleached white flour

4 cups beef broth

1 bay leaf

1. Preheat the oven to 375°F and spread the oil on a baking sheet with a ½-inch rim. Put the ground beef in a large mixing bowl.

2. Put the onion in a food processor and process, pulsing the motor on and off, until the onion is virtually puréed. Add the egg, panko, parsley, salt, pepper, and nutmeg and pulse the motor on and off a few times to incorporate all the ingredients.

3. Transfer the mixture from the food processor into the mixing bowl with the ground beef and, with a wooden spoon or clean hands, work the mixture until all the ingredients are thoroughly combined.

4. Divide the mixture into 4 equal parts and divide each of those pieces into 8 meatballs. All the meatballs should be the same size. If the mixture becomes sticky, dip your hands in cold water. Roll each ball in the flour, shake off the excess, and arrange the meatballs about ½ inch apart on the oiled baking sheet. Bake until the meatballs are browned and cooked through, about 20 minutes.

5. In a large, heavy soup pot or Dutch oven over medium heat, bring the beef broth and bay leaf to a boil. Transfer the browned meatballs to the boiling broth and simmer, uncovered, until the broth is reduced to half its original volume and the meatballs are very tender, about 45 minutes.

★
FINOCCHIONA PIZZETTE

Finocchiona is a form of salami. The best version in North America is handmade by Armondino Batali at his salumeria in Seattle. Batali is the father of Mario Batali of Food Network and New York restaurant fame. Here, slices of his salami, which are fragrant with fennel and pepper, are baked on top of little rounds of homemade bread dough for a fun and flavorful bite-size appetizer.

MAKES 36 BITE-SIZE SERVINGS

1 cup warm water

1 tablespoon (1 packet) active dry yeast

1 tablespoon sugar

2 cups unbleached white flour

1 tablespoon wine vinegar

1 tablespoon salt

5 ounces finocchiona or other salami, sliced paper-thin

Fennel flowers, for garnish

1. In the bowl of a stand mixer, or in a medium mixing bowl, stir together the warm water, yeast, and sugar. Add the flour, vinegar, and salt. Mix until ingredients are thoroughly combined, about 5 minutes. Then turn the dough out of the bowl onto a lightly floured countertop and knead until smooth and elastic. Return dough to the bowl.

2. Cover the mixing bowl with a damp towel or plastic wrap and allow the dough to rise until doubled in bulk, about 1 hour.

3. Preheat the oven to 400°F and spread the oil on a baking sheet with a ½-inch rim. Divide the dough into 3 equal pieces and roll each piece into a 12-inch log. Cut each log into 12 pieces and, working with one piece at a time, flatten the pieces to about the same size as a slice of finocchiona. Plant a piece of the salami on top of each dough round, and put the rounds on the baking sheet.

4. Bake until the dough is browned and the salami is sizzling hot, about 5 minutes. Serve at once on platters lined with fennel flowers.

★
CHANTERELLE MUSHROOMS ON HANDMADE RYE CRACKERS

When chanterelle season arrives in the Pacific North-west, it's as if the autumn light, filtered through big vine maple leaves and spiked with the scent of Douglas firs, is solidified on the forest floor in the form of these woodsy-tasting golden mushrooms. Every Northwest chef has a favorite way of preparing them. Jerry Traunfeld at the Herbfarm Restaurant in Woodinville, Washington, sometimes offers them in a savory tart with a rye flour crust. Christina Orchid of Christina's on Orcas Island serves them on toast. This simple appetizer pays homage to both of those wonderful chefs. If homemade rye crackers seem like too much fuss, opt instead for rounds or triangles of your favorite artisan rye bread, sliced thin and toasted crisp.

MAKES 3 DOZEN BITE-SIZED PORTIONS

1 pound fresh chanterelles or other forest mushrooms

3 tablespoons olive oil

2 teaspoons kosher salt, or to taste

1 teaspoon freshly ground black pepper, or to taste

2 tablespoons finely chopped shallot

2 tablespoons finely chopped parsley

Handmade Rye Crackers (page 299) or toasted artisan rye bread

1. Pick through the mushrooms, remove any debris or slimy bits, and then pull them apart lengthwise into shreds.

2. In a large sauté pan or cast-iron skillet over medium-high heat, warm the olive oil with the salt and pepper and, when the pepper begins to release its aromatic oils into the air, add the shallots. When the shallots are beginning to soften, after about 2 minutes, add the chanterelles and sauté until the mushrooms release their juices into the pan and are cooked through, about 5 minutes. Stir in the parsley.

3. Distribute the sautéed mushrooms evenly over the surface of the rye crackers or the toasts and serve hot.

★
PHYLLO TRIANGLES

Phyllo, sometimes spelled filo, is a Greek pastry dough that's widely available in frozen form. Traditionally, it's used in spinach pie or spanakopita and in baklava, a delectable nut dessert. It is popular with West Coast cooks because it makes a crispy container for all sorts of flavorful fillings. This filling is one I developed for Canlis restaurant to answer the call for a flavorful vegetarian hors d'oeuvre and to honor the owners' Middle Eastern heritage. The unlikely juxtaposition of cinnamon in a savory treat lends these bite-size packets an exotic air. If a convection oven is available, the fanned heat will help the triangles brown more evenly.

MAKES ABOUT 5 DOZEN PIECES

One 16-ounce package frozen phyllo dough

1 pound fresh spinach, washed and spun dry, or 12 ounces prewashed baby spinach, preferably organic

¼ cup extra virgin olive oil

¾ cup toasted pine nuts

1 tablespoon finely chopped garlic

1½ teaspoons freshly ground black pepper

¾ teaspoon ground cinnamon

¾ cup dried currants

12 ounces feta cheese

1 cup (2 sticks) unsalted butter, melted

1. At least ½ hour before you plan to make the triangles, thaw the phyllo dough at room temperature without removing it from the package. If using whole spinach, remove any stems from the leaves and cut them into ½-inch ribbons. If using prewashed baby spinach, cut the leaves into ribbons. Set aside.

2. Heat the olive oil in a large sauté pan over medium-high heat, then add the pine nuts. Keep the pan in motion until the nuts are golden brown. When the pine nuts are toasted, after about 2 minutes, add the garlic, pepper, and cinnamon. When the garlic is sizzling hot, add the spinach all at once. Cook briefly to wilt the spinach, then remove from the heat and stir in the currants. Transfer the mixture to a baking sheet or tray and let cool to room temperature. Crumble the feta cheese over the cooled spinach mixture and gently stir it in.

3. Cut the thawed phyllo dough into strips about 2 inches wide. Work with just a few strips at a time, and keep the remaining pastry covered in plastic so that it won't dry out. Lay 2 strips of the dough, one on top of the other, on a clean work surface. Brush each two-layered strip with melted butter, then place about 1 tablespoon of the spinach mixture near one end. Fold the end of the strip diagonally over the filling and continue folding the filled end of the strip, back and forth, into a triangle, like a flag, until you reach the other end. Place the finished triangle on a tray lined with baker's parchment and repeat with the remaining strips of pastry until all the filling is used. The triangles can be baked at once or prepared several days in advance and kept frozen until ready to serve.

4. Preheat a convection oven to 400°F or a conventional oven to 425°F. Bake the filled triangles until they are golden brown; room-temperature triangles will take 8 to 10 minutes, frozen ones will take 12 to 15 minutes. Serve hot.

★

CAPONATA

When it's made with small Japanese (ichiban) eggplants, this traditional Sicilian eggplant appetizer looks more appealing because each bit of eggplant has a little of the shiny, dark skin. It can be made with fresh Roma tomatoes or canned tomato paste, but I like to make it with a canned tomato sauce that's flavored with porcini mushrooms. The brand I use most often is from Trader Joe's, a California-based chain that contracts with processors of natural foods to produce their own proprietary brands. If the porcini tomato sauce is not available, use organic tomato purée.

MAKES ABOUT 4 CUPS

6 small Japanese eggplants

1 tablespoon kosher salt

1 medium onion

2 stalks celery

½ cup olive oil

2 tablespoons chopped garlic

1 tablespoon dried oregano

¼ cup balsamic vinegar

¼ cup capers

½ cup sliced pimento-stuffed green olives

1 cup canned tomato sauce with porcini or canned tomato purée

½ cup thinly sliced fresh basil leaves

Ak-Mak crackers or Sesame Crackers (page 300) as an accompaniment

1. Cut the eggplants into 1-inch cubes. In a medium saucepan, bring about 2 quarts of water to a rapid boil, add the salt, and cook the eggplant just until tender, about 3 minutes. Lift the eggplant out of the pan with a slotted spoon and spread it out on a baking sheet in a single layer to cool.

2. Peel and chop the onion, and dice the celery. Heat a large skillet over high heat and warm the olive oil. Immediately add the onion and celery, and cook until the onion begins to brown. Add the garlic and oregano and cook for 1 minute longer.

3. Transfer the sautéed vegetables to a large bowl and add the balsamic vinegar, capers, olives, and tomato sauce. Stir in the sliced basil. Allow the mixture to stand at room temperature for at least 10 minutes, or refrigerate for several hours before serving. Serve with crackers.

⭐

HUMMUS

Served with pita chips, this quintessential Middle Eastern spread makes an excellent appetizer for casual gatherings. Piled into half-moons of fresh Pita Breads (page 267), it also makes a delicious sandwich.

MAKE ½ BATCH

MAKES ABOUT 2½ CUPS

2 cups cooked garbanzo beans with their cooking liquid, or two 14.5-ounce cans garbanzo beans

½ cup tahini

½ cup lemon juice

1 teaspoon chopped garlic

4 tablespoons olive oil

1 tablespoon toasted sesame oil

1 teaspoon kosher salt, or to taste

⅛ teaspoon cayenne pepper (optional)

⅛ teaspoon ground cumin (optional)

Chopped parsley or paprika, for garnish (optional)

1. Drain the beans and save the liquid.

2. Put the beans in a food processor with the tahini, lemon juice, and garlic. Pulse the motor on and off until the mixture is roughly puréed. Add 3 tablespoons of the olive oil and the sesame oil and run the motor until the oils are incorporated into the purée. If the paste seems too thick, add some of the reserved cooking liquid from the beans. Motor in the salt, cayenne pepper, and cumin.

3. Transfer the hummus to a serving bowl, drizzle the remaining olive oil over the top, and garnish with chopped parsley or paprika.

★

BLUE CORN NACHOS WITH HOMEMADE SALSA

The term "nachos" can be traced to Piedras Negras, Coahuila, Mexico, where in 1943, one Ignacio "Nacho" Anaya put together a snack for customers at her taverna. These days, nachos, basically tortilla chips with cheese, are served virtually everywhere in North America, and they get topped with just about anything. I think they are best when they are simplest—just chips, cheese, and salsa. And like all simple recipes where technique is secondary to substance, this one demands that the ingredients themselves be the best. Colorful natural blue corn tortilla chips and soft, fresh Monterey Jack cheese with homemade salsa constitute the essential trinity.

MAKES 6 SERVINGS

For the Salsa

2 tablespoons water

1 tablespoon crushed red chiles, or to taste

1 fresh or canned jalepeño pepper, seeded and finely chopped

½ medium onion, peeled and roughly chopped

One 16-ounce can chopped fire-roasted tomatoes

One 2-ounce can chopped fire-roasted green chiles

1 tablespoon cilantro leaves, finely chopped (optional)

Salt, to taste

For the Nachos

One 9- or 10-ounce bag natural blue corn tortilla chips

8 ounces Monterey Jack cheese, grated

1. Preheat the oven to 425°F and lightly oil a baking sheet.

2. Make the salsa. Put the water in a saucepan and bring it to a full rolling boil. Add the red chiles and jalepeño and allow to soak for 5 minutes.

3. Meanwhile, put the onions in a food processor and process, pulsing the motor on and off until the onions are very finely chopped, almost puréed. Move the onions to a small mixing bowl.

4. Drain the tomato juice from the canned tomatoes into the bowl with the onions and put the drained tomatoes into the food processor. Pulse the motor on and off to finely chop the tomatoes. Add them to the bowl with the juice and the onions.

5. Process the green chiles in the same way and add them to the bowl. Stir in the presoaked red chiles and jalepeño and the cilantro, if desired. Season the salsa with salt to taste.

6. Scatter the chips in a single layer over the surface of the baking sheet and distribute the cheese evenly over the chips. Bake until the cheese is completely melted and bubbling hot. Serve at once with salsa.

OREGON BLUE CHEESE DIP

One of the best blue cheeses in the world comes from Rogue River Creamery in Oregon, where this artisan cheese has been made in the same way since the 1950s, when Thomas Villa traveled to Roquefort and smuggled back a piece of strategically moldy rye bread. For added zip, choose a tangy yogurt such as the nationally distributed Nancy's brand from Eugene, Oregon. Serve the dip with crisp, raw carrot and celery sticks and the best potato chips you can find.

MAKES 1 CUP

4 ounces Rogue River blue cheese

¼ cup plain natural yogurt

¼ cup Homemade Mayonnaise (pages 115–16) or quality purchased

Freshly ground black pepper, to taste

Carrot sticks and celery sticks as accompaniments (optional)

Ridged potato chips, preferably all-natural, as an accompaniment

Crumble the blue cheese into a small serving bowl. Stir in the yogurt and mayonnaise and grind black pepper over the surface of the dip. Serve with carrot and celery sticks and potato chips.

★

DUNGENESS CRAB AND ARTICHOKE DIP

Who can say where this cocktail party standard originated? Versions have sprung up all over North America, like mushrooms from some vast mycelium spread just beneath the surface of our consciousness. When we were writing a new bar menu for Canlis restaurant at the turn of this century, I asked all the lead cooks to brainstorm ideas for classic appetizers that could be shared, and Jeff Maxfield, who was sous chef at the time, devised this quintessential version of the classic American crab dip. Many versions rely on packaged seasoning blends for flavor; this one is delightfully natural.

MAKES ABOUT 4 CUPS

1 tablespoon olive oil

1 small leek, finely chopped

1 small onion, peeled and diced

1 tablespoon grated garlic

1 tablespoon minced ginger root

2 tablespoons riesling or other off-dry white wine

½ cup heavy cream

½ cup canned artichoke hearts, drained and chopped

8 ounces natural cream cheese

1 tablespoon Dijon mustard

1 tablespoon finely chopped fresh parsley

1 tablespoon finely chopped fresh fennel or dill leaves

½ teaspoon freshly ground black pepper

8 ounces fresh jumbo lump crab meat

Kosher salt, to taste

For the Crumb Topping

1 cup fresh breadcrumbs

½ cup grated Parmesan cheese

¼ cup (½ stick) unsalted butter, melted

½ teaspoon freshly ground black pepper

24 slices of French bread, lightly toasted

1. Preheat the oven to 425°F and lightly butter a 16-ounce gratin dish.

2. In a sauté pan, heat the oil and cook the leek, onion, garlic, and ginger over moderate heat, stirring until pale golden. Add the wine and cook, stirring, until the wine has evaporated. Add the cream and simmer, stirring, until it is thickened and slightly reduced, about 2 minutes. Then stir in the artichoke hearts.

3. Transfer the mixture to a medium mixing bowl and stir in the cream cheese. Mix until thoroughly incorporated, then stir in the mustard, parsley, fennel, and pepper. Stir in the crabmeat but do not overmix; some chunks of crabmeat should remain unincorporated. Taste the mixture and add salt, if desired. Transfer the mixture to the buttered gratin dish.

4. Combine the ingredients for the crumb topping and distribute the mixture over the surface of the crab dip. Bake until well browned on top and bubbling hot, 10 to 12 minutes. Serve with toasted French bread.

★
CHICKEN LIVER CROSTINI

Almost ubiquitous in and around Florence, Italy, crostini alla fegatini *is served as a complimentary appetizer in many restaurants there. In traditional formulas, the livers are often spiked with a salty bit of crushed anchovy or a sweetening touch of raisins. The classic Tuscan appetizer fits perfectly on the West Coast, where we like it made with caramelized onions and a splash of sweet wine. The livers can be chopped ahead, held in the refrigerator, and sautéed just before serving.*

MAKES 12 BITE-SIZE SERVINGS

1 pound (about 1¾ cups) chicken livers, preferably from free-range chickens

3 tablespoons olive oil

2 teaspoons kosher salt

½ teaspoon freshly ground black pepper

1 small onion, peeled and finely chopped

¼ cup marsala or Madeira

24 slices French bread, lightly toasted

1. Pick through the livers and remove any stringy or questionable-looking bits; then, with a chef's knife or with a dozen quick pulses in a food processor, chop the livers very fine.

2. In a large sauté pan or cast-iron skillet over medium-high heat, warm the olive oil with the salt and pepper. When the pepper begins to release its aromatic oils, add the chopped onion. When the onions are beginning to soften and color, after

about 4 minutes, add the chicken livers and sauté until the livers lose their dark red color and are almost cooked through, about 5 minutes.

3. Pour the wine into the pan, raise the heat to high, and cook until the wine is almost completely evaporated.

4. Distribute the cooked liver mixture evenly on top of the toasted bread rounds. Serve at once.

OLIVE POPPERS

Seattle's "culinary diva," Kathy Casey, introduced me to these tasty, bite-sized morsels, which she discovered in an old issue of Sunset *magazine, improved, and appropriated as her own. Once I became aware of them, I started seeing olive poppers everywhere. They can be made with all different sorts of olives and all different sorts of cheese. I like them best with a snappy cheddar from Oregon and a soft green olive from California. After making them for large parties, sometimes hundreds at a time, I've found a couple of timesavers. First, press the dough into the shape of a log and cut it into exactly the number of rounds you need to wrap your olives. To make short work of the wrapping job, use the thumb of one hand to press each round of dough into a flat pancake in the palm of the opposite hand, and then wrap the dough "pancake" around an olive.*

MAKES ABOUT 24 POPPERS

1 cup (4 ounces) finely grated sharp Tillamook cheddar cheese

2 tablespoons olive oil

½ cup sifted unbleached white flour

1 teaspoon smoked paprika

24 medium to large green olives, pitted

1. Preheat the oven to 400°F and line a baking sheet with baker's parchment.

2. In a food processor, or in a medium mixing bowl with a fork, combine the cheese and olive oil, then stir in the flour and smoked paprika.

3. Shape 1 heaping tablespoonful of dough around each olive, covering it well and shaping the dough into a ball.

4. Place the balls on the prepared baking sheet and bake until golden brown, about 15 minutes. Serve hot.

PACIFIC NORTHWEST FONDUE

At our house, cheese fondue is often a meal in itself. We like it best on Christmas Eve. The Swiss classic is made with white wine and Kirsch, a cherry brandy. But Matt Costello, a Pacific Northwest chef who rules the range at the Inn at Langley on Washington's Whidbey Island, taught me that fragrant apple cider, especially one of the increasingly available hard ciders from small producers, makes for an interesting regional adaptation. In addition to the standard chunks of artisanal bread, he serves his fondue with sliced apples and sweet pickles. The cider-based fondue is more kid-friendly than the authentic Swiss version we used to make, but it is sophisticated enough to please even the most discerning adults.

1 cup apple cider, preferably hard cider

2 tablespoons cornstarch

2 tablespoons water

1 pound Swiss cheese, grated

Salt and freshly ground black pepper, to taste

Freshly grated nutmeg, to taste

1 loaf country-style French bread, cut into 1-inch chunks

2 medium crisp apples, cored and sliced into 8 wedges each

Small sweet pickles

1. Put the apple cider in a saucepan or fondue pot over medium-high heat and bring it to a full, rolling boil to cook off some of the alcohol.

2. In a small bowl, stir the cornstarch into the water. Whisk the mixture into the boiling cider, and continue whisking until the mixture boils and thickens.

3. Add the cheese all at once and stir to melt. Season to taste with salt, pepper, and nutmeg. Keep the fondue warm in a fondue pot and serve with the bread cubes, apple slices, and pickles for dipping.

SOUPS & STEWS

Soups & Stews

In 1948, when Angelo Pellegrini published his classic work *The Unprejudiced Palate*, soup for most Americans came from a can. As early as 1869, when the Campbell Soup Company was founded on a handshake as the Joseph A. Campbell Preserve Company, mass-produced food products had begun to infiltrate American homes, hearts, and minds. Laura Shapiro's book *Something from the Oven* outlines the course of events that led American home cooks away from a cuisine based on cooking raw ingredients to one based largely on processed foods.

During the years after World War II, factories that had been set up to provide food for the "boys in uniform" who were "over there" continued to crank out processed food, even after the boys had come home. Promoters of the military-industrial food model set out to persuade Americans that cooking from scratch was simply outmoded. According to the Campbell's web site, it was during this era that Campbell's home economists started developing recipes like green bean casserole to make their product more of an ingredient than just a can of soup. The influence of their efforts, and the efforts of many other producers with the same goals, was profound.

But immigrant cooks like Angelo Pellegrini were not having any of it. His book did not provide any recipes per se. Instead, it provided an alternate perspective on cooking.

After a perusal of the cookbooks that were available at the time, he concluded, "What America needs is not another cookbook, but a book on bread and wine in relation to life."

"What the American Housewife needs, first of all," he continued, "is to formulate a sensible attitude toward food and drink; to see the dinner hour in perspective, as an element in the good life." Like a voice crying out in the wilderness, Pellegrini urged people to abandon their affair with the can opener in favor of good, old-fashioned home cooking, starting with a bowl of honest homemade broth with perhaps a few leaves of escarole and a grating of Parmesan cheese. Repent, he said, from the ruined and watery roast; try a simple grilled steak instead.

At a party at Serafina Restaurant in Seattle to celebrate the book's re-release in 2005, revelers reminisced and drank to Pellegrini's health. I sat with my mother-in-law, Patricia Lucas, who served as Pellegrini's secretary when he was a tenured professor at the University of Washington; she typed the original manuscript from his handwritten text. We ate reef net salmon from Lummi Island, a delectable pasta dish of orecchiette and broccoli rapini, and a main course of braised rabbit.

"Lest we get too reverent here," said Angela Pellegrini Owens, who was just three years old when her father wrote the original *Unprejudiced Palate*, "I'd like to share a story about my pet bunny." It seems that

Pellegrini persuaded his daughter that her pet should not have to live in a cage, and he sent the bunny to "a happier place," which for the bunny's corporeal form meant the dinner table. So for thirty years or so, Angela believed her little rabbit had gone to run free on a farm somewhere.

The influences that distinguish West Coast soups from soups served in any other part of the country are the same ones that characterize West Coast food in general. Geography and demographics help determine what foods we have on hand and how we decide to put them together. But my own repertoire of homemade soups has been shaped by my experience in restaurants.

In fact, my years in the restaurant business could be described as years in the soup business. The word "restaurant" is in fact a corruption of the French word for "restorative," an old name for soup. And the first restaurants licensed in France after the revolution were soup kitchens; the signs they hung outside their doors said, in effect, restoratives. Cafés, brasseries, and bistros can serve whatever they want, but any true restaurant must serve a true restorative or soup.

In the words of Angela Owens, "Lest we get too reverent here," a bit of disclosure: These days, as a restaurant consultant developing recipes for corporate clients, I formulate soup recipes to be mass-produced. The company that transforms my recipes uses all-natural and organic ingredients; it follows my recipes down to the smallest percentage of a gram to reproduce the small-batch soups I make into 500-gallon batches that are pumped into 5-pound bags, which are rapidly chilled, boxed, and shipped to my client. The company that makes my soups is a subsidiary of the giant Campbell Soup Company.

When I was working as a restaurant chef, I made soup—or supervised the making of soup—from scratch every day. Even on my days off, I made soup for my family. I enjoy the slow simmering of a stockpot on the back burner, or the sizzle of caramelizing onions on the front burner, a first step in the final assembly of most of the soups I make. Most of all, I enjoy amplifying the character of a soup by adding elements that lift it out of the bowl, garnishes that make it more than just a bowl of soup.

So my soups, even the ones I serve at home, often come with a touch of restaurant-style showmanship. When the occasion warrants it, I will spoon a flavored cream, drizzle a flavored oil, or pile on a heap of frizzled (quick-fried) leeks onto a soup to give it some panache. These little touches add more than visual flair; they provide contrast in the form of surprising textures and flavors. And the best garnishes reflect what's already in the soup. Corn chowder, built on a roux made with bacon drippings, is naturally garnished with crispy bacon bits. A purée of spinach and potatoes wears a little haystack of potato matchsticks on top of every bowl. Since the smell of just-sliced cucumber always reminds me of watermelon, a still pool of chilled cucumber soup gets an island of watermelon jelly in its center. The garnish sometimes makes the soup.

Among the descriptions of food so eloquently recorded in *The Unprejudiced Palate* a half century ago was one for a bowl of broth studded with tiny meatballs and bitter greens. That soup would still seem cutting edge if it were presented in a restaurant today. The juxtaposition of bitter greens beside comforting meatballs, both suspended in a clear, soothing homemade broth, captures, I think, the essence of what West Coast cooking is all about—combining the familiar with the unexpected in a casual context that makes it all seem incredibly alluring.

★

CHICKEN BROTH OR STOCK

Technically speaking, "broth" is the cooking liquid that surrounded a meat as it was boiled, and "stock" is a more deliberate preparation of liquid infused with the essence of meat and aromatic vegetables. For practical purposes, however, the two are almost interchangeable. Save the bones from cooked or raw chicken. If you don't have enough for a full batch of stock, store them in the freezer until you do. Alternately, poach a chicken in water for 1½ hours and remove the meat for use in sandwiches, salads, or enchiladas. Return the bones to the cooking liquid and proceed. Never put livers in the stockpot.

2 pounds chicken bones and giblets

1 carrot, coarsely chopped

1 onion, sliced, peel and all

1 head garlic, cut in half horizontally

1 stalk celery, sliced

1 teaspoon whole or cracked peppercorns (not ground)

1 bay leaf

6 sprigs parsley

4 whole cloves

1. Place all of the ingredients in a stockpot. Cover with water and bring to a boil.

2. Reduce the heat to a simmer and allow the stock to cook gently for 3½ hours, adding a little water if necessary to keep the ingredients covered. Strain the broth and discard the solids. Use the broth at once or store it, well chilled, for up to 1 week.

3. To prevent it from harboring bacteria, it is important to chill the broth as quickly as you can. If you don't have room in the refrigerator, or if you are afraid that the hot broth will warm other items in the refrigerator, make a bath of ice water in the sink and put the container of stock in the ice bath until it is cold.

⭐ TURKEY STOCK

A good basic stock for making soup and many sauces, turkey stock should be slightly gelatinous at refrigerator temperature. It's important to get the stock cooled down quickly so that it doesn't become a public swimming pool for wild bacteria. If it's been made from turkey that was brined, the stock will be well seasoned, so be careful when using the stock in recipes to avoid oversalting.

MAKES ABOUT 12 CUPS

About 4 pounds (about 4 quarts) turkey scraps and bones

About 4 quarts water

1 large onion, chopped, peel and all

4 stalks celery, chopped

2 medium carrots, chopped

6 sprigs parsley

1 bay leaf

2 or 3 sprigs thyme, or ½ teaspoon dried

1 teaspoon cracked peppercorns

½ teaspoon whole cloves

1. Pile the bones in a 6-quart stockpot with water to cover onions, celery, carrots, herbs, and spices. Bring the stock to a boil, and reduce the heat to low.

2. Skim off the grayish foam that floats to the top, and continue skimming off the foam every 15 minutes or so for the first hour. Let the stock simmer for 3 or 4 hours.

3. Strain the stock into a mixing bowl or another pot and discard the solids.

Chill the stock by standing the bowl or pot filled with stock in a larger container filled with ice water. If there's no room for the ice water bath, pour the broth into a shallow container and let it cool in the refrigerator. When the stock is well chilled, skim the fat off the surface.

⭐ POLPETTE EN BRODO OR MEATBALLS IN BROTH

"Tiny meatballs," wrote Angelo Pellegrini in The Unprejudiced Palate, *"will add character to clear broth." At the risk of becoming the "slavish plagiarist of untried recipes and perpetuator of culinary nonsense" that he rightfully disdained, I offer the following formula.*

MAKES 6 SERVINGS

For the Meatballs

1 pound ground beef (not too lean) or a combination of beef and pork

¼ cup grated Parmesan cheese, plus more as an accompaniment

1 egg

2 tablespoons finely chopped fresh basil leaves

1 tablespoon chopped fresh oregano leaves

2 teaspoons kosher salt, or 1 teaspoon table salt

½ teaspoon freshly ground black pepper

½ cup unbleached white flour

2 tablespoons olive oil or chicken fat

For the Soup

8 cups chicken broth, homemade (page 68), or store-bought, preferably organic; or turkey stock (page 69)

12 leaves escarole (curly endive), cut into fine ribbons

Crusty bread as an accompaniment

1. In a medium bowl, mix the ground beef with the cheese, egg, basil, oregano, salt, and pepper. Form the mixture into 36 balls, each one about the size of a plump cherry, and roll them in flour. Shake off any excess flour and brown the balls in the olive oil or chicken fat in a large skillet over medium heat.

2. Bring the broth to a gentle boil in a medium saucepan. Put the browned meatballs into the broth and let them cook through, about 10 minutes.

3. Lift the meatballs out of the broth with a slotted spoon and distribute them, along with the escarole, among 6 soup bowls. Ladle a cup of boiling broth into each bowl. Serve with crusty bread and grated Parmesan cheese passed separately.

★

MOM'S CHICKEN NOODLE SOUP

I always know I have made a successful batch of chicken soup when my sons award me their highest compliment: "This is almost as good as Mom's." Their mother doesn't cook as much as I do, but she is deeply in touch with their budding palates and knows exactly what they like. In fact, it seems to be in her very nature to know what each one of us likes.

MAKES 6 SERVINGS

2 tablespoons canola oil

1 medium onion, peeled and cut into small dice (about 1½ cups)

1 large organic carrot, peeled and cut into small dice

1 medium stalk organic celery, cut into small dice

2 tablespoons flour

2 cloves garlic, finely chopped or grated on a Microplane grater (about 1 teaspoon)

1½ teaspoons fresh thyme leaves, or ½ teaspoon dried

¼ teaspoon freshly ground black pepper

⅛ teaspoon ground nutmeg

8 cups homemade chicken broth, homemade (page 68), or store-bought organic broth

2 cups (about 4 ounces) egg noodles

1 pound organic free-range chicken breast meat, cooked and shredded into 1-inch pieces

¼ cup finely chopped fresh parsley

1 tablespoon kosher salt, or to taste

1. Heat the oil in a large stockpot and sauté the onion, carrot, and celery until soft and just beginning to color, about 5 minutes. Stir in the flour, garlic, thyme, pepper, and nutmeg and sauté for 1 minute longer.

2. Stir in the chicken broth and bring the soup to a boil. Cook until the vegetables are just tender, about 12 minutes.

3. Stir in the egg noodles and the cooked chicken meat, and cook until the noodles are tender, about 8 minutes. Just before serving, stir in the parsley and salt, to taste.

NANA'S CHICKEN SOUP

The Nana who created this chicken soup was not my own Grandma but the grandmother of a good friend of mine. When I was barely 20, I went with her to visit her Mexican grandmother, who served us chicken soup. Now, whenever I make it, I am transported back to the Mexican border, circa 1979. The soup is best when it's served with Homemade Flour Tortillas (pages 298–99).

MAKES ABOUT 6 SERVINGS

1 chicken, about 4 pounds

8 cups water

2 tablespoons salt

2 bay leaves

1 medium onion, peeled and thinly sliced

1 celery heart with leaves, sliced

2 carrots, peeled and sliced

1 large Anaheim chile, seeded and sliced

½ cup long-grain rice

1. In a soup pot over high heat, bring the chicken, water, salt, and bay leaves to a

boil. Reduce the heat to low, cover, and simmer for 45 minutes.

2. With a sturdy pair of tongs, pull the chicken out of the pot and put it in a pan or a bowl. Gently break the chicken into 3 or 4 pieces, and allow it to cool.

3. Meanwhile, put the onion, celery, carrots, chile, and rice into the broth in which the chicken was cooked. When the chicken is cool enough to handle, pull off all the meat and put it in the pot with the broth and vegetables. Simmer the soup gently until the grains of rice are fully cooked and very tender, 30 to 45 minutes.

QUICK TORTILLA SOUP

I love tortilla soup, but when I want it for lunch, I sometimes lack the time and patience to simmer a whole chicken, cool it, and pull the meat off the bones to produce the shredded chicken and chicken broth to make the soup from scratch. The process of searing tomatoes and chile peppers to remove their skins is also very time-consuming. Fortunately, good fire-roasted organic tomatoes and fire-roasted chiles come in cans, and so does reasonably good organic chicken broth. So I have developed a series of shortcuts that delivers a great-tasting tortilla soup in about a half an hour. Depth of flavor comes from the adobo sauce that surrounds canned chipotle peppers. Fresh avocado and cilantro and oven-crisp tortilla strips in each serving bowl make the soup a winner. I like to eat this soup when I feel a cold coming on.

For the Tortilla Strips

4 corn tortillas plus spray canola oil or 1 teaspoon corn oil or canola oil, or 4 ounces (about 36 pieces) packaged fried tortilla strips

For the Soup

2 tablespoons corn or canola oil

1 medium onion, peeled and thinly sliced

4 cloves garlic, thinly sliced

1 tablespoon dried oregano

2 boneless, skinless free-range chicken breast halves, about 6 ounces each

8 cups chicken broth, homemade (page 68) or store-bought, preferably organic

One 14.5-ounce can fire-roasted crushed tomatoes

One 4-ounce can diced green chiles

2 tablespoons adobo sauce from canned chipotle chiles

2 teaspoons kosher salt, or to taste

For the Garnish

4 ounces Monterey Jack cheese, grated or cut into ½-inch dice

1 medium avocado, peeled and cut into ½-inch dice

Several sprigs cilantro, to taste

1 lime, cut into wedges, as an accompaniment

1. Prepare the tortilla strips. Preheat the oven to 350°F and line a baking sheet with a nonstick silicone pan liner or a sheet of baker's parchment. Cut the tortillas into strips ½ inch wide, then cut the strips in half crosswise. Arrange the strips in a single layer on the lined baking sheet, and spray them with oil. (If spray oil is not available, rub them lightly with canola oil and spread them in a single layer on the baking sheet.) Bake until lightly browned and crisp, about 15 minutes. Alternatively, use fried tortilla strips from a bag.

2. In a heavy soup pot over medium-high heat, warm the oil and sauté the onion slices with the garlic and oregano until the onion is softened and beginning to brown, about 5 minutes. Meanwhile, cut the chicken into strips, about 1 inch long by ½ inch wide. Add the chicken to the pot with the onions and stir-fry until the strips are beginning to color.

3. Add the chicken broth, crushed tomatoes, green chiles, and adobo sauce and bring the soup to a full, rolling boil. Reduce the heat to medium and simmer, uncovered, until the chicken is cooked through and the onions are tender, about 15 minutes. Add salt to taste.

4. Allow the soup to simmer while you prepare the garnishes. Distribute half the tortilla strips in the bottom of each of 4 serving bowls, and put the rest in a separate bowl to be passed when the soup is served. Distribute the cheese and avocado

evenly among the bowls, arranging them in little mounds in the center of each bowl, and plant sprigs of cilantro on top of the mounds.

5. At the moment that everyone is ready to eat, ladle the hot soup over the garnishes in the bowls. Pass lime wedges and extra tortilla strips separately.

★

THAI-STYLE CHICKEN SOUP

I developed this soup for a cookbook published by Cancer Lifeline of Seattle that is both a fund-raiser and a tool for patients looking for healthy recipes. The version in the book does not contain red curry paste, and many people prefer the milder flavor of the resulting soup. For a more intensely flavored soup, add the optional red curry paste and brown sugar. If you like it, a dash of fish sauce is also good in this soup.

MAKES 4 SERVINGS

4 cloves garlic

2-inch piece ginger root

2 tablespoons vegetable oil

1 tablespoon red curry paste (optional)

1 tablespoon brown sugar (optional)

1 small onion, peeled and thinly sliced

1 medium red bell pepper, cored and sliced

1 medium carrot, peeled and sliced

1 boneless, skinless chicken breast half, about 6 ounces, thinly sliced

One 15-ounce can chicken broth

One 15-ounce can coconut milk

4 heads baby bok choy, sliced

Few leaves of fresh cilantro, for garnish

1 teaspoon dried red chile flakes, for garnish

1. Rub the garlic and ginger through a Microplane grater, or put them in the blender with a couple of tablespoons of water and purée until smooth. Put the vegetable oil in a medium heavy pot over medium-high heat and sauté the ginger and garlic until the aroma fills the air, about 1 minute. Add the red curry paste and brown sugar, if desired.

2. Add the onion, pepper, and carrot and sauté for 1 minute longer. Add the chicken and cook for 5 minutes, turning the chicken pieces 3 or 4 times as they begin to brown.

3. Pour in the chicken broth and coconut milk and bring the soup to a boil. Add the baby bok choy and cook until the bok choy is tender, about 2 minutes. Transfer the soup to serving bowls and top with cilantro leaves and chile flakes. Serve at once.

★

BROCCOLI AND CHEESE SOUP

This soup was sort of an "artist's sketch" that came out of developing soup recipes for a company called Organic to Go. From the very first test batch that eventually grew into a product that is now made in 500-gallon batches, I knew we were on to something. Aromatic vegetables are ground in the food processor and sautéed in butter, then broccoli is added, along with chicken broth and milk. Finally, the soup is thickened slightly with cornstarch and finished with grated cheese.

MAKES 6 SERVINGS

½ medium onion, peeled

4 stalks celery

1 medium carrot, peeled

½ cup (1 stick) unsalted butter

1½ teaspoons chopped garlic

1 head (1 pound) broccoli

2 cups milk

2 cups vegetable broth

1 teaspoon kosher salt

½ teaspoon freshly ground black pepper

2 tablespoons cornstarch

2 tablespoons water

4 ounces medium cheddar cheese, grated

1. Chop the onion and celery in the food processor, pulsing the motor on and off to get a uniform size of about ⅛ inch. Use the grater attachment on the carrots to get fine shreds. In a heavy soup pot, melt the butter over medium heat and sauté the onion, celery, carrot, and garlic until tender, about 5 minutes.

2. Peel the broccoli stems, cut them into chunks, then chop them in the food processor to get a uniform size of about ⅛ inch. Chop the florets in the same way.

3. Add the chopped broccoli, milk, and vegetable broth to the sautéed vegetables,

along with the salt and pepper. Increase the heat to high and bring the soup to a full, rolling boil.

4. In a small bowl, soften the cornstarch in the water and stir in a ladleful of the soup. Stir this mixture into the boiling soup and continue stirring until the soup is thickened and smooth. Take the soup off the heat and stir in the cheese. Serve the soup hot.

★

WILD NETTLE SOUP

Be sure to wear sturdy gloves when gathering or handling uncooked nettles. Like the month of March, which is when wild nettles are at their best, nettles come in like a lion but go out like a lamb. Before they're cooked, they have an irritating chemical in their leaves; once cooked, however, they are among the mildest-tasting greens imaginable. I used to thicken my nettle soup with potatoes, but the flavor of the potato almost overwhelmed the delicate flavor of the nettles themselves. Rice makes a better thickener—it's not only milder tasting, but it also has a smoother texture.

MAKES 6 SERVINGS

4 quarts stinging nettle tops, freshly picked

¼ cup (½ stick) unsalted butter

¼ cup olive oil

1 medium onion, peeled and thinly sliced

½ cup uncooked white rice

6 cups chicken broth, homemade (page 68) or purchased

1 teaspoon salt, or to taste

½ teaspoon freshly ground black pepper, or to taste

1. If the nettles have any foreign material in them, or if they were picked on a dusty day, you may need to wash them. Wearing sturdy rubber gloves, plunge them into a sink full of water and then lift them out, leaving any debris behind. Shake off the excess water.

2. In a soup pot over medium-high heat, melt the butter with the olive oil. Add the onion and sauté, stirring, until they begin to color, about 10 minutes. Add the rice and sauté just a moment to warm the grains.

3. Pile in the nettles and pour on the broth. Bring the soup to a boil, reduce the heat to low, and simmer until the rice is tender, about 15 minutes. Transfer the soup to a blender in small batches and purée. Pass the puréed soup through a strainer. Season to taste with salt and pepper and serve hot.

★

CORN CHOWDER WITH BACON

A trip to the farmer's market in late summer usually finds us coming home with an armload of bright, ripe golden corn. We like the taste of smoky bacon in our corn chowder, but if you want a vegetarian version, skip the bacon and use 3 tablespoons of butter or corn oil instead.

MAKES 8 SERVINGS

4 cups organic milk

2 cups organic chicken or vegetable broth

4 medium (about 2 pounds) Yukon Gold potatoes

4 ounces natural smoked bacon, cut into ¼-inch bits

1 medium organic onion, peeled and cut into ¼-inch dice

2 stalks celery, cut into ¼-inch dice

6 cloves garlic, grated on a Microplane grater or finely chopped

1 teaspoon fresh thyme leaves, or ½ teaspoon dried

2 tablespoons flour

6 ears fresh, organically grown corn, husked

2 teaspoons kosher salt

1 teaspoon freshly ground black pepper, or to taste

Chopped parsley for garnish (optional)

1. Put the milk and chicken broth in a large soup pot over medium-high heat and bring to a gentle boil. While the mixture is heating up, scrub the potatoes and cut them into 1-inch dice. Add the potatoes to the milk mixture, cover the pan, and reduce the heat to low. Simmer the potatoes until they are very tender, about 15 minutes.

2. Put the diced bacon in a large sauté pan over medium-high heat and cook until the bacon bits are crisp. With a slotted spoon,

lift the bacon bits out of the fat and set them aside. In the fat left behind, sauté the onion and celery until the vegetables are soft and just beginning to brown. Stir in the garlic and thyme, then add the flour.

3. Add a ladleful of the broth and milk mixture to the sautéed vegetables and stir until smooth. Stir in another ladleful of the milk and broth mixture, then transfer the vegetable mixture to the soup pot.

4. Scrape the kernels from the corn cobs and stir the corn into the soup. Simmer gently until the corn is tender, about 10 minutes. Season the soup to taste with salt and pepper. Serve hot, with the reserved bacon bits and chopped parsley on top of each serving.

★

FENNEL SOUP WITH PERNOD CREAM

Traci des Jardins is one of the most talented chefs working on the West Coast. When I dined at her restaurant, Jardinière, a few months after it opened in 1997, I was so favorably impressed that I asked Traci if I could work for a night in her kitchen just to get a closer look at what she was doing there. She graciously obliged, and her freewheeling staff kindly allowed me to observe what they were doing, as long as I kept my hands busy trimming artichokes or peeling celery roots. The first dish I ever ate there was a soup made with fresh fennel bulbs. Whenever I make that soup today, I think of Traci and her wonderful staff.

For the Soup

6 tablespoons (¾ stick) unsalted butter

1 medium onion, peeled and thinly sliced

1 large bulb fennel

1 large celery root (about 1 pound)

4 cups chicken broth, homemade (page 68) or store-bought, preferably organic

Kosher salt and ground white pepper, to taste

Fennel leaves, for garnish

For the Pernod Cream

2 tablespoons Pernod or any pastis-type liqueur

½ cup heavy cream

1. In a large soup pot over medium-high heat, melt the butter and sauté the sliced onion, stirring intermittently, until it is soft and golden, about 10 minutes.

2. While the onion is sautéing, cut the vegetables. Trim the feathery tops off the fennel bulb and set a few leaves aside for garnish. Cut the trimmed bulb in half lengthwise, then cut each hemisphere into ½-inch slices. With a sharp knife, peel the celery root and cut it into 1-inch cubes.

3. Add the sliced fennel and cubed celery root to the pot and pour the chicken broth over them. When the soup comes to a boil, reduce the heat to low and simmer until the celery root and fennel are very tender,

about 20 minutes. Purée the soup in small batches in the blender. Add salt and white pepper to taste, and keep warm.

4. Just before serving the soup, make the Pernod cream. In a saucepan over high heat, warm the Pernod, then light it and burn off some of the alcohol (caution—flames!). Pour in the cream and bring the liquid to a full rolling boil, stirring to prevent the cream from boiling over. Boil the cream for 1 or 2 minutes, or until it is slightly reduced and beginning to thicken. Drizzle some of the cream on top of each serving of soup and garnish with the reserved fennel leaves.

★

FRENCH-AMERICAN ONION SOUP

Even though it's made with clear beef broth (we use organic beef broth from a box when we don't have home-made beef stock on hand), the best onion soup should be so laden with onions that the broth becomes dense and almost custardlike in consistency. The secret is using a lot of onions and taking the time to truly caramelize them. After an entire soup pot full of onions has been cooked down to a fraction of their initial volume, the addition of beef broth "reconstitutes" the onions, bringing them back to their original bulk. Finishing the soup with the traditional topping of toast and cheese is superfluous, almost like gilding the lily, but do it anyway. I like this soup made with the fairly mild Swiss-style cheese from Sonoma Dairy.

MAKES 4 GENEROUS SERVINGS

¼ cup (½ stick) unsalted butter

6 cups peeled, thinly sliced onions

1 teaspoon sugar

2 tablespoons flour

½ cup port wine

1 teaspoon fresh thyme leaves, or ½ teaspoon dried

4 cups beef broth

Kosher salt and freshly ground black pepper, to taste

Eight ¼-inch-thick slices baguette

2 cups grated Swiss-style cheese, such as Sonoma Swiss

1. Melt the butter in a heavy 5- to 6-quart soup pot over medium heat. Cook the onions slowly for 15 minutes, stirring regularly to achieve a uniform golden brown. Add the sugar and continue to cook the onions until they soften and caramelize and turn a rich brown color. This will take at least 30 minutes; don't rush it, and don't let the onions burn.

2. When the onions are almost falling apart, stir in the flour, port wine, and thyme. Cook until the wine has boiled away and the mixture is beginning to sizzle again. Add the beef broth and check the seasoning.

3. Simmer the soup, uncovered, for 15 minutes. Meanwhile, toast the baguette slices under a broiler until they are golden

brown. Leave the broiler on. Ladle the soup into 4 oven-safe bowls, float 2 slices of toast on top of each, and cover the toast with the grated cheese. Put the filled soup bowls on a baking sheet and put them under the broiler until the cheese is melted and bubbling hot, about 4 minutes. Serve immediately.

★

FRESH PEA SOUP WITH BACON AND BREADCRUMBS

Some of the liquid in this soup comes from a head of lettuce, which melts as it cooks and intensifies the fresh, green taste of the peas. The technique is French but seems especially appropriate on the West Coast, where most of the lettuce for the entire continent is grown. Iceberg lettuce is often maligned, and when it is appreciated at all, it is generally only for its texture, but it actually has a wonderful—if delicate—flavor that becomes more pronounced when it is cooked.

MAKES 6 SERVINGS

¼ cup (½ stick) unsalted butter

1 medium onion, peeled and thinly sliced

1 small head iceberg lettuce, shredded

2 cups chicken broth, homemade (page 68) or purchased

1½ pounds fresh or frozen shelled green peas

Kosher salt and freshly ground black pepper, to taste

8 ounces bacon

½ cup fresh white breadcrumbs

1 teaspoon dried thyme

1. Put the butter in a large, heavy saucepan over medium-high heat and, when it has melted and begun to sizzle, add the sliced onion. Stir the onion until it is soft and transparent, but don't let it brown.

2. Add the shredded lettuce and stir until it is wilted, then add the chicken broth and, when the soup is boiling, add the peas. Cook just until the peas are tender, about 10 minutes, then transfer the soup in small batches to a blender and purée until smooth. Season to taste with salt and pepper. Keep the puréed soup hot until serving time.

3. While it is very cold from the refrigerator, cut the bacon across the slices into ¼-inch pieces. Cook the cut bacon in a frying pan over medium-high heat until it is crisp, then drain off the fat and mix in the breadcrumbs and thyme. Serve the crumb mixture on top of the hot pea soup.

★

FRESH TOMATO SOUP

This soup is so redolent with tomato flavor that you will wonder what the canned version has to do with tomatoes at all. It's best made with the oversized deep red tomatoes that come in at the end of summer. To set it off properly, a dollop of bright green pesto or a crumble of fresh white goat cheese is just the ticket.

MAKES ABOUT 4 SERVINGS

½ cup olive oil

1 large onion, peeled and thinly sliced

6 large tomatoes (about 3 pounds), cut into thin wedges

Kosher salt and freshly ground black pepper, to taste

Pesto, crumbled fresh chèvre, or olive oil, for garnish (optional)

1. Put the olive oil and onions in a heavy soup pot over medium-high heat and cook, stirring regularly with a wooden spatula or spoon, until the onions are soft and beginning to brown, about 5 minutes.

2. Add the tomatoes, cover the pan, and when the soup is boiling, reduce the heat to low. Simmer until the tomatoes are very tender and beginning to disintegrate, about 10 minutes.

3. Purée the soup with an immersion blender or, if no immersion blender is available, transfer the soup in small batches to a standard blender. (Put the lid on the blender, then drape a dish towel over the lid and, to prevent the hot soup from splashing out, hold the lid down with the dish towel while the motor is running.)

4. You might wish to strain the soup to remove the seeds. Season to taste with salt and pepper. Serve the soup hot with a dollop of pesto, a crumble of fresh chèvre, or a drizzle of olive oil.

★
SUNNY TOMATO ORANGE SOUP

"Brix" is a measure of the sugar in fruits and vegetables, but it is also a good indicator of flavor and nutritional value—the more brix, the more flavor and the more nutrients. The organic material (compost) in healthy soil allows tomato plants to convert sunlight into energy more effectively, so organic tomatoes typically have a significantly higher brix rating than tomatoes grown in the conventional way. This is true for all fruits and vegetables, but tomatoes especially seem to taste more vibrant when they are organically grown. This soup is an antidote to the winter blues. The color alone brightens a cloudy day, and the flavor is compelling.

MAKES 6 SERVINGS

⅓ cup olive oil

1 large onion, peeled and thinly sliced

1 tablespoon chopped garlic

1 teaspoon dried thyme

One 28-ounce can crushed tomatoes, preferably organic

4 large navel oranges

Kosher salt and freshly ground black pepper, to taste

1. Put the olive oil and onions in a heavy soup pot over medium heat and cook, stirring regularly with a wooden spatula or spoon, until the onions are soft and beginning to brown, about 10 minutes.

2. Add the garlic and thyme and sauté for 1 minute longer. Stir in the tomatoes, and simmer gently to blend the flavors, about 10 minutes. Meanwhile, use a zester or grater to take off the colorful outer rind of the oranges, and stir the zest into the soup. Squeeze the juice from the oranges and add the orange juice and pulp to the soup.

3. Transfer the soup in small batches to a blender. Put the lid on the blender, then drape a dish towel over the lid and, to prevent the hot soup from splashing out, hold the lid down with the dish towel while the motor is running.

ASPARAGUS SOUP

When asparagus stems are trimmed away, I find it hard to throw them out; there is so much flavor in them! The frugal peasant in me comes out and I save the stems to make soup. The secret to success is to strain the soup after it's cooked to remove the stringy fibers. A hand-cranked food mill comes in very handy here, but if you don't have one, pressing the soup through an ordinary mesh strainer will work.

MAKES 4 SERVINGS

2 tablespoons unsalted butter

1 medium onion, peeled and thinly sliced

½ cup rice

8 ounces asparagus stems (about 3 cups), chopped into 1-inch pieces

2 teaspoons chopped garlic

4 cups chicken broth, homemade (page 68) or store-bought organic

½ cup heavy cream (optional)

Kosher salt and freshly ground black pepper, to taste

1. Melt the butter over medium heat in a heavy soup pot or Dutch oven, add the onion, and cook, stirring now and then, until the onion is soft and translucent, about 5 minutes.

2. Stir in the rice, asparagus stems, garlic, and chicken broth. Bring the mixture to a boil, reduce the heat to low, and simmer until the rice is very tender, 20 to 25 minutes.

3. Transfer the soup in small batches to a blender, and blend until smooth. Force the purée through a food mill or a large strainer, pressing hard on the solids to extract the soup. Discard the tough fibers left in the strainer. Add cream, if desired, and season to taste with salt and pepper. Serve hot.

CARROT SOUP

Somehow, when the humble carrot is puréed in a savory broth spiked with caramelized onions, it takes on an entirely different character. Serve the soup hot with croutons or crusty bread.

MAKES 6 SERVINGS

¼ cup (½ stick) unsalted butter

1 medium yellow onion, peeled and thinly sliced

2 pounds fresh, sweet carrots, peeled and cut into ½-inch slices

4 cups chicken broth, homemade (page 68) or store-bought organic, or vegetable broth

2 teaspoons kosher salt, or to taste

1 teaspoon ground white pepper

½ teaspoon ground nutmeg

½ cup water or heavy whipping cream (optional)

1. Melt the butter in a heavy soup pot over medium-high heat. Add the onions and cook, stirring often, until the onions are tender and just beginning to brown, about 5 minutes. Add the carrots and broth and bring the mixture to a boil. Cover and reduce the heat to low. Let the soup simmer gently until the carrots are tender, about 15 minutes.

2. Purée the soup with an immersion blender. If no immersion blender is available, purée it in small batches in a standard blender. (Cover the top of the blender with a dish towel and hold down the lid so that the hot mixture does not splash out when you turn the machine on.)

3. Season to taste with salt, pepper, and nutmeg. If soup is too thick, thin it with water or cream.

★

KABOCHA SQUASH SOUP WITH ROASTED RED PEPPER PURÉE

Kabocha is Japanese for "pumpkin," and a Japanese pumpkin is a dark green winter squash, very similar to the Buttercup and Sweet Mama varieties. It has dense, sweet flesh that gives this soup a velvety texture. If kabocha is not available at your market, choose another variety that has similar qualities, such as hubbard or butternut. For a vibrant contrast, a purée of roasted red pepper and a sprinkling of green pumpkin seeds

(pepitas) are served on top of the soup. In most grocery stores, pepitas are sold already toasted.

MAKES 6 SERVINGS

For the Soup

One small to medium (about 3 pounds) kabocha squash

¼ cup (½ stick) unsalted butter

1 medium yellow onion, peeled and thinly sliced

4 cups chicken broth, homemade (page 68) or store-bought organic, or vegetable broth

½ cup water, as needed

2 teaspoons kosher salt, or to taste

1 teaspoon ground white pepper

½ cup toasted green pumpkin seeds (pepitas)

For the Pepper Purée

4 red bell peppers

1. Cut the squash into wedges, scrape out the seeds, then cut away the peel. Cut the peeled and seeded squash into 1-inch dice. You should have about 6 cups of cubed squash.

2. In a heavy soup pot or Dutch oven over medium-high heat, melt the butter and cook the onion, stirring often, until it is tender and golden brown, about 5 minutes. Add the squash and broth and bring the mixture to a boil. Cover and reduce the heat to low. Let the squash

simmer gently until tender, about 15 minutes.

3. In a blender, purée the soup in small batches. Cover the top of the machine with a kitchen towel, hold down the lid, and process, using short pulses at first so that the hot mixture does not splash out when you turn the machine on. Thin the soup, if desired, with water and season it to taste with salt and white pepper.

4. To make the pepper purée, preheat the broiler and put the peppers on a baking sheet. Broil the peppers, about 6 inches from the element, until they are blackened on one side, about 5 minutes. Turn them over and broil until the other side is blackened as well, about 5 minutes more. Put the peppers in a brown paper bag and let them cool until they can be handled easily. Peel off the blistered skins, rinsing lightly if necessary to remove any blackened bits, remove the cores and seeds, and then purée the peeled peppers in a blender.

5. Serve the soup with a dollop of red pepper purée in the center of each bowl and a sprinkling of toasted pumpkin seeds on top.

★

YUKON GOLD POTATO SOUP

Served cold, this would be vichyssoise; served hot it's sometimes called soupe bonne femme, *or "good housewife soup." Whatever it's called, it's easy, inexpen-*

sive, very satisfying, and very, very good. Thin-skinned Yukon Gold potatoes need not be peeled. In fact, the skins almost disappear when the soup is puréed, but their memory lends the soup more character. The most frugal (and authentic) versions use water; broth makes for a somewhat richer-tasting soup.

MAKES 6 SERVINGS

2 pounds (about 4 medium) Yukon Gold potatoes

2 large leeks (whiter ends only)

¼ cup (½ stick) unsalted butter

4 cups chicken broth, homemade (page 68) or store-bought organic, or vegetable broth

2 teaspoons kosher salt, or to taste

1 teaspoon ground white pepper

1 cup organic heavy cream

Snipped chives, for garnish

1. Cut the potatoes into 1-inch chunks. Split the leek ends in half lengthwise and rinse out any soil trapped between the layers; slice them crosswise into ¼-inch half-rounds.

2. In a heavy soup pot, melt the butter over medium heat and cook the sliced leeks, stirring often, until they are very tender but not brown, about 10 minutes. Add the cubed potatoes, broth, salt, and pepper and bring the soup to a boil. Cover and reduce the heat to low. Simmer gently until the potatoes are very tender, about 15 minutes. (The soup can be served as a rustic country soup at this point, but it is even better when puréed.)

3. In a blender, purée the soup in small batches. Cover the top of the machine with a kitchen towel, hold down the lid, and process, using short pulses at first so that the hot mixture does not splash out when you turn the machine on. Bring the heavy cream to a gentle simmer in the soup pot and stir in the puréed soup. Serve the soup hot with snipped chives on top.

⭐

HIPPIE SPLIT PEA SOUP

Like many members of my generation, I was a teenage vegetarian. The experience served me well, because in those days, in order to eat in the vegetarian style, one had to learn to cook. Most recipes for split pea soup call for ham, but this vegetarian version derives its deep flavor from an aromatic base of carrot, celery, and onion. The vegetables are slightly caramelized in oil while the peas boil in a separate pot.

MAKES 8 SERVINGS

7 cups water

1 bay leaf

1 tablespoon kosher salt

2 cups (1 pound) split green peas

3 medium carrots, peeled

1 medium onion, peeled

3 stalks celery

¼ cup olive or canola oil

Freshly ground black pepper, to taste

1. Put the water, bay leaf, and salt in a soup pot over high heat, and bring to a full,

rolling boil. Add the split peas, cover the pan, and reduce the heat to low.

2. Meanwhile, cut the carrots, onion, and celery into ¼-inch dice. Put the olive oil in a large sauté pan over medium-high heat and sauté the vegetables until they are soft and just beginning to brown, about 10 minutes.

3. Add the sautéed vegetables to the pot and continue to simmer, stirring occasionally to make sure the soup isn't sticking to the bottom of the pot, until the split peas are beginning to disintegrate, about 45 minutes.

4. Season the soup to taste with freshly ground black pepper. Remove the bay leaf and serve hot with cornbread or biscuits.

⭐

LENTIL SOUP WITH BACON, GARLIC, AND THYME

Unlike most other dried beans, lentils need no presoaking. This makes them ideal for a fairly quick supper. They can be used in place of split peas for an easy vegetarian soup, or they can be dressed up with bacon, garlic, and thyme for a sophisticated French country soup like this one. Our favorite lentils for this soup are the small green ones known as lentilles du Puy, which are widely grown in Washington state; they serve as a soil builder between crops of wheat.

MAKES 8 SERVINGS

7 cups water

1 bay leaf

1 tablespoon kosher salt

2 cups (1 pound) green lentils or other lentils

4 ounces bacon, cut into ¼-inch bits

1 medium onion, peeled and thinly sliced

6 cloves garlic, thinly sliced

1 tablespoon fresh thyme leaves

Freshly ground black pepper, to taste

1. Put the water, bay leaf, and salt in a soup pot over high heat and bring to a full, rolling boil. Add the lentils, cover the pot, and reduce the heat to low. Simmer the lentils until they are very tender, about 30 to 35 minutes.

2. While the lentils are cooking, put the diced bacon in a large sauté pan over medium-high heat and cook until the bacon bits are crisp. With a slotted spoon, lift the bacon bits out of the fat and set them aside. In the fat left behind, sauté the sliced onion until it is just beginning to brown, then add the garlic and thyme leaves, reduce the heat to low, and cook gently until the onions and garlic are very soft, about 10 minutes.

3. When the lentils are very tender and beginning to fall apart, remove the bay leaf and add the sautéed onion mixture.

4. Let the soup simmer until the flavors meld, about 15 minutes. Season the soup to taste with freshly ground black pepper and serve hot, with bacon bits on top of each serving.

Cold Soups

★

WEST COAST GAZPACHO WITH OREGANO

Half the vegetables for this cold soup are puréed and the other half are cut into small dice for texture. Fresh oregano gives the soup a scintillating bite. If fresh oregano is not available, use a teaspoon of dried oregano. When the tiny flowers are stripped from the stems, fresh oregano blossoms have an intriguing sweetness from the nectar. If you grow your own oregano, or know someone who does, try a few of the flowers on top of the soup.

MAKES 8 SERVINGS

6 medium (about 3 pounds) ripe tomatoes

2 medium (about 1 pound) red bell peppers, cored

1 medium cucumber, peeled

1 medium sweet onion such as Walla Walla, peeled

1 tablespoon kosher salt, or to taste

1 teaspoon freshly ground black pepper

⅓ cup sherry or red wine vinegar

2 cloves garlic, grated or finely chopped (about 2 teaspoons)

¼ cup extra virgin olive oil

2 tablespoons fresh oregano leaves, finely minced, or 2 teaspoons dried oregano leaves, crumbled

Oregano blossoms, or chives, for garnish

1. Roughly chop the tomatoes, one of the red bell peppers, half of the cucumber, and half of the onion, then puree them in a blender with the salt, pepper, vinegar, garlic, and olive oil.

2. Cut the remaining bell pepper into ¼-inch dice. Cut the second half of the cucumber and the remaining half of the onion into ¼-inch dice and pile the diced vegetables into a large bowl.

3. Pour the puréed vegetable mixture over the diced vegetables, stir in the oregano leaves, and chill the gazpacho for several hours or overnight. Serve the soup very cold with fresh oregano blossoms. If oregano flowers are not available, use fresh chives, snipped with scissors directly over each serving.

★

WASHINGTON WHITE GAZPACHO

According to the American Heritage Dictionary, *the word "gazpacho" is "Spanish, probably of Mozarabic origin; akin to Spanish* caspicias, remainders, worthless things." *Before it morphed into a tomato-based cocktail of a soup—before tomatoes were even known in the Old World, gazpacho was made with scraps of bread that were softened in water, tossed with garden vegetables, and dressed in oil and vinegar. This version harkens back to the soup's ancient origins, but tastes decidedly up to date.*

For the Soup

2 cups loosely packed French bread cubes, crusts removed

2 cups water

1 medium sweet onion, such as Walla Walla, peeled and chopped

2 medium cucumbers, peeled and coarsely chopped

½ cup champagne vinegar

¼ cup toasted almond oil

3 tablespoons sugar

2 teaspoons kosher salt

½ teaspoon white pepper

For the Garnish

8 ounces green grapes, stemmed and cut in half

½ cup sliced almonds, toasted

1. Put the bread and water in a blender with the onion, cucumber, vinegar, oil, sugar, salt, and white pepper. Purée until perfectly smooth.

2. Chill the soup for a couple of hours or until it is very cold. Serve it in cold bowls with split green grapes and toasted almonds for garnish.

★

CUCUMBER SOUP WITH WATERMELON JELLY

This soup, although it owes something to gazpacho, owes more to the kinship I have always sensed between cucumbers and watermelons. Slice one or the other, close your eyes, and take a whiff. Both vegetables evoke cool green lawns on warm summer days, which is exactly where and when this soup should be eaten.

MAKES 4 SERVINGS

For the Soup

2 medium cucumbers

½ sweet onion, such as Walla Walla

1 tablespoon rice wine vinegar

1 teaspoon sea salt

¼ teaspoon ground white pepper

For the Watermelon Jelly

3 cups (packed) seedless watermelon chunks

2 tablespoons sugar

2 teaspoons freshly squeezed lemon juice

One ½-ounce packet unflavored gelatin

4 pinches black sesame seeds

1. Peel the cucumbers and cut each one in half lengthwise. Use a spoon to carve out the seedy center section of each half cucumber. Discard the seeds and cut the cucumbers into 1-inch pieces. Pile the pieces into a blender.

2. Peel the half onion and cut into 1-inch pieces. Put the onion into the blender with the cucumber pieces and add the vinegar, salt, and white pepper. Purée the cucumber soup and chill it.

3. Make the watermelon jelly. Put the watermelon chunks in a blender with the sugar and lemon juice and purée. Strain the purée to yield 2 cups watermelon juice.

4. Put ½ cup of the watermelon juice in a small saucepan and sprinkle the gelatin over the surface. Allow the gelatin to soften for 5 minutes, then put the saucepan over high heat and stir until the gelatin is dissolved and the juice is beginning to boil.

5. Put a pinch of sesame seeds into each of 4 paper cups. Stir the hot gelatin mixture into the remaining watermelon juice and distribute the mixture evenly among the 4 cups, pouring the mixture over the sesame seeds.

6. Chill the jelly in the paper cups until it is firmly set, about an hour. To remove the jelly from the cups, dip the cups one at a time in hot water and then invert them into a serving bowl.

7. To serve, invert one watermelon jelly into the center of each of 4 wide-rimmed soup bowls, then ladle about ¾ cup of the cucumber soup around each watermelon jelly. Serve cold.

Stews

SAN FRANCISCO–STYLE SEAFOOD STEW

On parts of the globe where people and the sea come together, seafood stew is almost ubiquitous, and the West Coast of North America is no exception. Here, variations on the theme seem to revolve around the quintessential seafood stew known as cioppino, served at Fisherman's Wharf in San Francisco. Rather than try to reproduce yet another "authentic" version of that seafood stew, I offer here one of the many variations. This one evolved in a restaurant on San Juan Island, where I filleted whole fish every day for the evening menu. The carcasses were transformed into simple fish stock, and pieces of fillet that were too small to be served as an entrée were set aside for stew. We made the stew base early in the day and kept it chilled, to be reheated and larded with all the seafood just before serving. The same thing can be done at home. Serve it with plenty of crusty sourdough bread.

MAKES 6 VERY GENEROUS SERVINGS

For the Base

¼ cup olive oil

1 medium onion, peeled and thinly sliced

¼ cup fresh basil leaves, shredded, or 1 tablespoon dried

2 tablespoons fresh oregano leaves, shredded, or 2 teaspoons dried

1 teaspoon fresh thyme leaves, or ½ teaspoon dried

1 cup white wine

1 tablespoon grated or finely chopped garlic

1 tablespoon dried red chile flakes

1 teaspoon saffron threads

4 cups fish stock

One 28-ounce can diced tomatoes in their own juice, preferably organic

To Finish the Stew

1 bunch Swiss chard

1½ pounds salmon fillet, cut into 2-ounce chunks

1½ pounds halibut fillet, cut into 2-ounce chunks

12 oysters, preferably live, in their shells

36 mussels, live, in their shells

24 prawns, shelled and deveined

Lemon wedges and basil sprigs, for garnish

1. In a stainless steel or enameled soup pot, warm the olive oil over medium-high heat, then sauté the sliced onion until tender and just beginning to brown, about 5 minutes. Stir in the basil, oregano, and thyme, and when the herbs are sizzling hot, pour the wine over them. Stir in the garlic and chile flakes and boil until the wine has evaporated and the mixture is beginning to sizzle again.

2. Meanwhile, put the saffron threads and a cup of the fish stock in a small saucepan and cook over medium heat until the fish stock is just beginning to boil.

3. Add the saffron mixture, the remaining 3 cups fish stock, and the tomatoes to the

pot. (At this point, the base can be chilled until serving time.)

4. Roll the leaves of Swiss chard lengthwise into a cigar-shaped bundle and cut across the bundle to make thin ribbons of greens. Place the pot containing the stew base over high heat and add all of the seafood and chard. Cover and cook until the oyster and mussel shells have opened and the fish has turned opaque, about 15 minutes.

5. Use a slotted spoon to distribute the seafood evenly among 6 large serving bowls. Ladle the stew over the seafood. Garnish each serving with a wedge of lemon and a sprig of fresh basil, and serve at once.

★
PACIFIC NORTHWEST SEAFOOD STEW

Many seafood stews are modeled after Mediterranean ones with garlic and tomatoes. Developed in the 1980s to highlight Pacific Northwest ingredients, this seafood stew was drawn more from imagination than from any authentic tradition, but it does owe something to the traditional seafood soups from Normandy, a region with a climate and a slate of native ingredients similar to those found here. It's flavored with sweet apple cider and cream. Saffron, leeks, and licorice-scented fennel provide savory background flavors and a conceptual tip of the hat to the stew's Mediterranean cousins.

MAKES 6 SERVINGS

For the Base

¼ cup (½ stick) unsalted butter

¼ cup flour

1 medium leek, split lengthwise and thinly sliced

1 medium bulb fennel, split lengthwise and thinly sliced (reserve the leaves for garnish)

2 cups heavy cream

For the Seafood

3 cups apple cider

1 generous pinch saffron threads

12 oysters, preferably live, in their shells

36 mussels, live in their shells

1½ pounds salmon or halibut fillet, cut into 2-ounce chunks

12 large prawns, shelled and deveined

1. In a large saucepan, warm the butter over medium-high heat until it is melted and bubbling hot, but not browned. Stir in the flour and whisk the mixture to make a light, golden-colored roux. Sauté the sliced leek and fennel in the roux until it is beginning to color, about 5 minutes. Whisk in the heavy cream. When the soup base comes to a boil, cover the pot and reduce the heat to a simmer.

2. In a soup pot over high heat, bring the apple cider and saffron and to a full, rolling boil. Meanwhile, scrub the oysters and pluck the "beards" off the mussels. Add the seafood to the boiling cider.

Cover and cook until the oyster and mussel shells have opened and the shellfish have turned opaque, about 15 minutes.

3. Use a slotted spoon to distribute the seafood evenly among 6 large serving bowls, whisk the cider in which the seafood was cooked into the soup base, and ladle the stew over the seafood. Garnish each serving with a sprig of fennel leaves, and serve at once.

★

PIONEER BEEF AND VEGETABLE STEW

When folks made beef stew before World War II, all the ingredients were organic by default; agricultural chemicals were rare and expensive. Now, older folks complain that modern foods don't have the flavor of the stuff they remember from childhood. It's important when selecting the vegetables for this stew to choose the darkest, most colorful carrots and the sweetest peas. Organic ingredients are your best bet.

MAKES 4 SERVINGS

¼ cup olive oil

2 tablespoons unsalted butter

6 tablespoons flour

I pound naturally raised stew beef, cut into I-inch chunks

2 cups peeled and sliced carrots

2 cups sliced celery

I medium onion, peeled and chopped

4 cups organic beef broth

2 tablespoons finely chopped garlic

2 teaspoons kosher salt, or to taste

I teaspoon freshly ground black pepper

I pound red potatoes

2 cups (about 4 ounces) sliced mushrooms

1½ cups frozen sweet peas

¼ cup finely chopped parsley

I. Put the olive oil and butter in a heavy soup pot over medium-high heat and stir until the butter is melted and sizzling hot. Stir in the flour and continue stirring as the mixture foams up. Keep stirring the roux over medium-high heat until the foam subsides and the mixture is uniformly nut-brown colored. This will take about 15 minutes.

2. Stir the beef into the roux and cook, stirring regularly, until the beef is browned on every side, about 5 minutes. Stir in the carrots, celery, and onion and cook for I or 2 minutes longer to heat the vegetables through. Stir in the beef broth and the garlic and cook the stew over medium heat, stirring every few minutes to prevent sticking, for 45 minutes. Season with salt and pepper.

3. Wash and cut the potatoes into I-inch cubes and stir them into the stew. Continue cooking until the potatoes and beef are tender, about 30 minutes. Stir the mushrooms into the stew.

4. When the mushrooms have taken up enough of the broth to sink into the stew, turn off the heat and stir in the peas and parsley. As soon as the peas are heated through, the stew is ready to serve.

⭐

FRONTIER-STYLE CHILI

In my neighborhood, the local deer population, unchecked by predators, has swelled to unhealthy proportions. While they remain beautiful, even majestic, the animals are also voracious pests, and our gardens have become their foraging grounds. Every spring, our neighbors gather for a plant exchange, and every fall we gather for a pumpkin-carving potluck. One neighbor always brings a big crockpot full of his venison chili. The chili is equally good made with grass-fed beef. Slow simmering in the spicy broth renders the meat meltingly tender.

MAKES 6 SERVINGS

2 tablespoons vegetable oil

2 pounds boneless venison or lean grass-fed beef, cut into 1-inch pieces

2 stalks celery, chopped

1 medium onion, peeled and chopped

4 cloves garlic, chopped

2 tablespoons chili powder

1 teaspoon dried oregano

4 cups cooked pinto beans with cooking liquid (page 145), or two 15.5-ounce cans pinto beans

One 18-ounce can chopped tomatoes

One 4-ounce can chopped green chiles

Salt to taste

Chopped onion as an accompaniment (optional)

Grated cheese as an accompaniment (optional)

1. Heat the oil in a heavy soup pot over medium-high heat, and brown half of the beef, turning to make sure it is browned on all sides, about 5 minutes. Transfer to a large bowl, using a slotted spoon or pair of tongs, and in the oil left behind, cook the remaining beef in the same way. When the second round of beef is browned, add it to the bowl with the first batch.

2. In the oil left behind, sauté the celery and onion and cook until the vegetables are soft and translucent. Add the garlic, chili powder, and oregano, and cook for 1 minute longer.

3. Return the beef to the pot along with any accumulated juices. Stir in the beans, tomatoes, and green chiles, and bring to a boil.

4. Reduce the heat to low, cover, and simmer until the beef is very tender, about 2 hours, stirring occasionally to make sure the chili is not sticking to the bottom of the pan. Season to taste with salt and serve hot with chopped onion and grated cheese, if desired.

SALADS & DRESSINGS

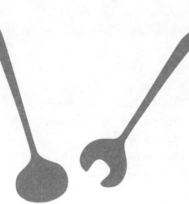

Salads & Dressings

The tradition of great West Coast salads probably began with wild miner's lettuce and other edible greens gathered by the first settlers and continued through a century or more of refined growing and shipping techniques that made California's Central Valley the salad bowl of North America. From the gloriously crunchy and ubiquitous iceberg lettuce that made its way across the continent to the dark green leafy romaine that spawned the Tijuana-born Caesar salad, leafy greens have always been at home in West Coast kitchens.

When I started cooking professionally here in the early 1980s, the distinctive mixture of young salad greens known as mesclun was not sold in stores. Nor, for that matter, was the soft white goat cheese known as Montrachet. But seeds for mixed salad greens were available by mail order, and so, in the garden space behind my derelict rental in Bellingham, Washington, I started growing my own greens. At the Food Co-op, I found goat cheese and thought I had discovered a pretty wonderful combination. Little did I know I was stepping onto a bandwagon; thousands of other West Coast cooks, Jeremiah Tower and Alice Waters of Chez Panisse in Berkeley among them, were doing the same thing. Had I known that they were there, doing what they were doing, I might have dropped out of college and joined them.

Instead, I stayed where I was, cooking one way at home and another way at work as a dinner cook at a Mexican restaurant called Dos Padres, where we served hundreds of taco salads every week. These were composed of shredded iceberg lettuce, topped with a mixture of grated Monterey Jack and cheddar-style cheese (both made by the great Tillamook Cheese Factory on the Oregon coast), ground tortilla chips, and a scoop of spicy ground beef. The whole arrangement was drizzled with an egg-based lemon and oil dressing that the restaurant owner, Bill Martinez, said was his adaptation of the famous Canlis salad dressing. I had never heard of Canlis salad, and I had no idea what he was talking about. Years later, when Martinez was no longer alive, I became executive chef at Canlis restaurant, and I wished I had some way of reconnecting with the late, great Martinez.

Even without running off to join the circus that was the California food scene in the last quarter of the twentieth century, sooner or later I was caught up in it. The waves of influence from Chez Panisse flowed out in an ever-widening circle. No one—with the possible exception of her one-time business partner Jeremiah Tower—is more closely associated with what became known as the new West Coast cooking than Alice Waters, doyenne of the California restaurant scene.

Even in the hamlet of Friday Harbor on Washington's San Juan Island, where I was cooking in a tiny French café, the name Alice Waters had an almost mystical resonance. In the 1980s, I would call Chez Panisse from time to time and ask them to fax me a menu, just so I could see what sort of food they were serving. When I carefully cut and washed tiny lettuces grown for me by a local farmer, I thought of the cooks at Chez Panisse, who I imagined were doing the same thing.

I was fascinated with Alice and her restaurant, not because they were famous, although they were, but because of what they were famous for. Alice was radical; she never lost her rebellious, youthful spirit. She wasn't doing French food by the book, she was doing it by intuition. She had heart.

Shortly after the turn of the century, I left my job as executive chef at Canlis restaurant to develop the food and beverage programs at IslandWood, an environmental learning center for school-age kids that opened near my home on Bainbridge Island. I prepared meals and tried to teach by example and experience how the choices we make at the table affect the world we all share. It seemed to me that the work I was doing echoed some of what Alice Waters had done at the Edible Schoolyard Project, a garden at Martin Luther King Jr. Middle School near her home in Berkeley. More than ever, I felt an affinity for this woman's life and work that went deeper than our shared love of great food. I tried unsuccessfully to get Alice to visit IslandWood and lend her influence to its success.

I finally met Alice, almost by chance, a few months after completing my work at Island-Wood, at a peach orchard in Brentwood, California. The iconoclast had become a verified icon. Diminutive in person, she was nevertheless formidable in her hat and sundress. The dinner, which was in her honor, was served family style at a single long, white-clothed table laid between the rows of peach trees and set for a hundred. The first words Alice spoke to me after we were introduced were, "Please pass the salad."

★

BERKELEY MESCLUN SALAD WITH BAKED GOAT CHEESE

In the last quarter of the twentieth century, when young cooks first started localizing elements of French country cooking, finding good salad greens presented an almost insurmountable hurdle. These days, the mixed baby greens known as mesclun are available ready to eat in most supermarkets, making what was once a labor of love into an easy-to-prepare element of any weeknight dinner. This French-American salad may be the quintessential West Coast salad.

MAKES 4 SERVINGS

For the Salad

8 ounces organically grown prewashed mixed baby greens

2 tablespoons olive oil

1 small (4-ounce or 6-ounce) log fresh white goat cheese, or two 2-ounce crotins cut into 4 rounds

For the Vinaigrette

1 shallot, finely chopped

2 tablespoons white or red wine vinegar

1 tablespoon Dijon mustard

6 tablespoons fruity green olive oil

Kosher salt and freshly ground black pepper, to taste

1. Put the greens in a salad bowl, cover with a damp paper towel, and refrigerate until serving time.

2. Preheat the oven to 450°F. Drizzle the olive oil onto a small baking sheet or an oven-safe sauté pan, set the cheese rounds on the oil, and turn them once so that each round of cheese is coated top and bottom with the oil. Pop the cheese rounds into the oven and bake until they are heated through, about 8 minutes.

3. While the cheese is baking, make the vinaigrette. In a medium bowl, whisk together the shallot, vinegar, and mustard; then, still whisking, drizzle in the olive oil. Toss the salad greens with the vinaigrette. Sprinkle kosher salt and freshly ground black pepper over the dressed greens and distribute them evenly among 4 salad plates.

4. With a spatula, carefully transfer a round of hot goat cheese to the center of each salad, and serve at once.

★

SPINACH SALAD WITH DRIED TART CHERRIES AND GOAT CHEESE FRITTERS

Flavorful goat cheese fritters in a crispy breadcrumb coat are the stars of this salad, but the supporting cast of tender baby spinach leaves and tart red cherries in balsamic vinegar could stand on their own. If the fritters are too much fuss, simply crumble some goat cheese over the salad. Like mixed salad greens, fresh spinach for salads used to require careful trimming and washing of the greens. I think we did not eat spinach as often as we should have because it was so labor intensive. Prewashed greens have become almost ubiquitous.

MAKES 4 SERVINGS

For the Salad and Vinaigrette

1 head (about 1 pound) tender young spinach, or one 10-ounce bag baby spinach leaves

½ cup dried tart cherries

3 tablespoons water

3 tablespoons balsamic vinegar

6 tablespoons olive oil

Kosher salt and freshly ground black pepper, to taste

For the Goat Cheese Fritters

1 small (4-ounce or 6-ounce) log soft white goat cheese

¼ cup flour

1 egg

½ teaspoon salt

½ cup coarse fresh breadcrumbs or panko

Olive or canola oil, for deep-frying

1. Pluck the leaves from the stems of the spinach, allowing them to fall into a clean sink filled with cold water. Swish the leaves around to loosen any clinging soil, then lift the leaves out of the water, leaving any soil behind. If you opt for prewashed spinach leaves, rinse the spinach in cold water and spin it dry. (Even if you buy prewashed spinach, it will benefit from a revitalizing bath in cool water.) Put the spinach in a salad bowl and lay damp paper towels on top to keep it fresh.

2. Put the dried cherries in a small saucepan over medium heat with the water and balsamic vinegar. Bring the liquid to a boil, reduce the heat to low, and simmer gently until the cherries are plumped and tender, about 3 minutes. Remove the pan from the heat and stir in the olive oil to make a vinaigrette. Let cool to room temperature.

3. Make the fritters. With a sharp knife dipped in hot water, cut the cheese log into 4 rounds, each about 1 inch thick. Put the flour in one bowl; beat the egg with the salt in a second bowl, and put the breadcrumbs in a third bowl.

4. Roll each portion of cheese in the flour, and shake off the excess. Dip each flour-coated round of cheese into the egg mixture, then roll in breadcrumbs to coat, and set aside. The fritters can be prepared ahead up to this point and refrigerated for several hours or overnight.

5. Just before serving, heat ½ inch of the oil in a medium sauté pan until a cube of bread floats immediately to the top and sizzles; an instant-read thermometer should read 375°F. Fry the breaded cheese rounds, turning once, until golden on both sides, about 4 minutes altogether. Drain on paper towels.

6. While the goat cheese fritters are frying, toss the spinach with the cherry vinaigrette. Sprinkle with a little salt and pepper. Distribute the salad evenly among 4 salad plates, and plant a hot goat cheese fritter in the center of each salad. Serve at once.

★

ROAST BEET SALAD WITH GOAT CHEESE AND WALNUTS

Variations on this quintessential West Coast salad range from the inspired to the absurd. In her book Chez Panisse Vegetables, *Alice Waters uses three or four kinds of beets and the zest and juice of oranges to make the salad her own. Corporate interests have distributed angst-inducing versions that include canned beets and bottled dressing. It seems to me that, pared down to its, er, roots, the salad needs no tweaking to ring true and clear. It's important to toast the walnuts ahead of time and let them cool to room temperature before assembling the salad.*

For the Salad

2 bunches watercress, or two 5-ounce bags baby arugula or baby spinach

1 pound (4 small or 2 medium to large) beets

One 4-ounce log fresh white goat cheese

1 cup walnuts, lightly toasted

Kosher salt and freshly ground black pepper, to taste

For the Vinaigrette

1 shallot, finely chopped

2 tablespoons raspberry vinegar

6 tablespoons walnut oil

1. If using watercress, trim the base from the bundles, give the greens a quick bath in a sink full of cold water, and spin them dry. Hold the greens in the refrigerator until just before serving.

2. Preheat the oven to 375°F. Wrap the beets in foil and roast them until they are fork-tender. Depending on the size and freshness of the beets, this will take anywhere from 30 minutes to an hour. When they are cool enough to handle, peel the beets; the skins should slip off easily. Cut the cooked, peeled beets into large matchsticks about ½ inch wide by 2 inches long, and set aside.

3. Make the vinaigrette. In a salad bowl, whisk together the shallot and vinegar and

then, still whisking, drizzle in the walnut oil. Toss the cut beets with the dressing.

4. Distribute the watercress evenly among 4 salad plates, and arrange the dressed beet matchsticks on top. Drizzle any dressing left in the bowl over the greens. Crumble the goat cheese over the vegetables, then scatter the walnuts over all, and sprinkle each serving with salt and pepper to taste.

★

CALIFORNIA COBB SALAD

This salad originated at Robert Cobb's Brown Derby Restaurant in Hollywood in 1937. It may well have been the creation of executive chef Robert Kreis, but legend has it that Bob Cobb himself came up with the combination of greens, avocado, cold chicken, bacon, hard-cooked eggs, and crumbled blue cheese that has become a classic. I think the best time to make Cobb salad is when leftover cold roast turkey or chicken is on hand, but the salad is so good that it warrants roasting or grilling some chicken just to make the salad. Arranging the ingredients in neat stripes prevents the salad from looking too chaotic.

MAKES 4 ENTRÉE SERVINGS

For the Salad

1 head romaine lettuce, or one 10-ounce bag prewashed romaine lettuce leaves

1 pound (about 3 cups) cooked breast of turkey or chicken

2 firm, ripe California (Hass) avocados

2 hard-cooked eggs

8 thick slices (about 8 ounces) bacon, cooked, drained, and chopped

12 grape or small supersweet tomatoes (about ½ pint), rinsed

¾ cup crumbled Roquefort or other blue-veined cheese

For the Dressing

3 tablespoons red wine vinegar

I tablespoon Dijon mustard

I clove garlic, finely minced or grated on a Microplane grater

I teaspoon sugar

I teaspoon kosher salt

½ teaspoon freshly ground black pepper

½ cup olive oil

I. If you're using a head of romaine, clean it first. Cut off the base, pull off any browned or damaged leaves, and cut off any brown edges. Lay the head on a cutting board and cut it lengthwise into strips, about I inch wide, and then cut across the strips to make I- by 2-inch rectangles. Plunge the cut lettuce into a sink full of cold water, swish it around, and then lift it out, leaving any soil or debris behind. Spin the cut and washed lettuce until it's dry, then put it on a platter or in a wide-open salad bowl, cover with a damp paper towel, and refrigerate until just before serving time.

2. Peel any skin off the cold roast chicken or turkey, and cut the meat into neat ½-inch cubes.

3. Cut the avocados in half lengthwise and remove the pits. Using a large metal cooking spoon, scoop out the half avocados in a single piece and lay them on the cutting board. Cut into I-inch dice.

4. Peel the hard-cooked eggs and force them through the largest holes of a cheese grater.

5. Arrange the chicken, avocados, eggs, bacon, tomatoes, and blue cheese in stripes across the platter of lettuce.

6. To make the dressing, whisk together the vinegar, mustard, garlic, sugar, salt, and pepper in a small mixing bowl and keep whisking until the ingredients are very well combined, about 30 seconds. Whisking all the while, stream in the olive oil to make a smooth dressing.

7. Just as it's being served, drizzle the dressing over the salad and toss gently. The dressing can also be passed separately.

TIJUANA CAESAR SALAD

Conflicting stories about the origins of this classic salad abound, but a certain consensus maintains that Caesar salad was created in 1924 by restaurateur Caesar Cardini at Hotel Caesar in Tijuana, Mexico. (Some even add that Cardini was improvising because he had run out of ingredients as a result of a rush of business in the wake of a horse race featuring the legendary Seabiscuit, but it should be noted that this embellishment to the story became popular only after the award-winning movie about Seabiscuit was released in 2003.) Julia Child, in her cookbook From

Julia Child's Kitchen, wrote that she enjoyed the salad with her parents at Hotel Caesar in 1925 or 1926. If Julia was convinced that his was the original, then I am too. I am, however, inclined, like thousands before me, to tweak that original just a bit. I like to make a smooth emulsion of the dressing ingredients in the blender instead of whisking them together in the salad bowl; I also replace the original Worcestershire sauce with a few anchovies and an unorthodox splash of balsamic vinegar, which has become almost as much a staple in West Coast kitchens as Worcestershire sauce used to be.

MAKES 4 ENTRÉE SERVINGS OR 8
FIRST-COURSE SERVINGS

For the Salad

2 large heads romaine lettuce

¾ cup olive oil (not extra virgin)

2 cups cubed French bread (1-inch cubes)

1 teaspoon kosher salt, or to taste

¾ cup freshly grated Parmesan cheese

Freshly ground black pepper, to taste

For the Dressing

Juice of 1 lemon (about ¼ cup)

1 tablespoon balsamic vinegar

1 egg, preferably from a cage-free chicken

4 anchovies from a freshly opened jar or can

2 cloves garlic

1 cup olive oil (not extra virgin)

1. Cut the base off each head of romaine. Pull off any browned or damaged leaves and cut off any brown edges. Lay the heads on a cutting board and cut them lengthwise into strips, about 1 inch wide, then cut across the strips to make 1- by 2-inch rectangles. Plunge the cut lettuce into a sink full of cold water, swish it around, and then lift it out, leaving any soil or debris behind. Spin the cut and washed lettuce until it's dry, then put it in a wooden salad bowl, cover it with a damp paper towel, and refrigerate until just before serving time.

2. Make the croutons. Heat the olive oil in a medium skillet over medium heat until it is hot and just beginning to smoke. Fry the bread cubes in batches until deep golden, 15 to 20 seconds per side. With a slotted spoon, transfer the croutons to a plate, sprinkle with the salt, and set aside.

3. Make the dressing. Put the lemon juice, vinegar, egg, anchovies, and garlic in a blender and blend until the mixture is smooth. With the motor running on low speed, gradually stream in the olive oil to make a smooth dressing.

4. At serving time, toss the lettuce with the croutons, half of the cheese, and the dressing. Distribute the salad evenly among the salad plates and sprinkle additional cheese over each serving. Top each salad with freshly ground black pepper to taste.

★ CANLIS SALAD

In 1945, when he opened his first Canlis Broiler on Waikiki Beach, West Coast restaurateur Peter Canlis drew on his own Greek heritage and his intuitive understanding of what his upper-class clientele liked to eat to devise a salad that would be the next Caesar. By the time he opened Canlis in Seattle in 1950, the salad was a classic.

MAKES 6 GENEROUS SERVINGS

For the Salad

2 heads romaine lettuce

1 pound bacon, chopped, cooked, and drained

3 Roma tomatoes, each cut into 6 wedges

1 small bunch green onions, thinly sliced

1 tablespoon dried oregano, crumbled

1 cup (loosely packed) freshly grated Romano cheese

½ cup finely chopped fresh mint leaves, or to taste

Seasoned Croutons (page 112)

Kosher salt and freshly ground black pepper, to taste

For the Dressing

1 coddled egg

¼ cup freshly squeezed lemon juice

1 teaspoon freshly ground black pepper

⅔ cup olive oil

1. Cut the base off each head of romaine. Pull off any browned or damaged leaves and cut off any brown edges. Lay the heads on a cutting board and cut them lengthwise into strips, about 1 inch wide, then cut across the strips to make 1- by 2-inch rectangles. Plunge the cut lettuce into a sink full of cold water, swish it around, then lift it out, leaving any soil or debris behind. Spin the cut and washed lettuce until it's dry, then put it in a wooden salad bowl, cover it with a damp paper towel, and refrigerate until just before serving time.

2. Make the salad dressing. In a small bowl, beat the egg with the lemon juice and pepper. Still beating, stream in the olive oil and continue beating for a few seconds to create a smooth dressing.

3. At serving time, toss the lettuce with the bacon, tomatoes, green onions, oregano, half of the cheese, mint, croutons, and a generous sprinkling of salt and pepper. Then toss with the dressing, starting with ¾ cup and adding more to taste. Add more salt and pepper if desired. Distribute the salad evenly among the salad plates and sprinkle additional cheese over each serving.

STEAKHOUSE-STYLE TOMATO SALAD

California grows some of the best tomatoes in the world, but it is only fair to say that it also grows some of the worst. Too often, growers select varieties and growing practices designed to produce tomatoes that will tolerate rough handling and long periods of storage. Tomatoes that are fully ripened would perish before they reached the market by conventional factory-farming routes, so sometimes it seems that only tomatoes grown on small farms and destined for farmer's markets are really suited for eating fresh. As unlikely as it may sound, a good second choice for farmer's market tomatoes are the ones grown in greenhouses in southern British Columbia, the widely distributed B.C. Hothouse brand.

MAKES 4 SERVINGS

2 pounds (about 4 medium) ripe tomatoes

½ medium red onion, peeled

I small bunch fresh basil

½ cup Balsamic Vinaigrette (page III)

Kosher salt and freshly ground black pepper, to taste

I. Cut the cores from the tomatoes, then cut them into I-inch-wide wedges, about 8 per tomato, and pile the tomato slices into a salad bowl.

2. Slice the onion lengthwise into thin strips no more than ⅛ inch thick, and toss with the tomatoes.

3. Remove the stems from the basil leaves and stack the leaves into short stacks of 6

or 7, then roll the stacks like little cigars and slice across the cigars to make very thin ribbons or a chiffonade of basil. Toss the basil chiffonade with the tomatoes and onions and the vinaigrette.

4. Season to taste with salt and pepper and distribute the salad evenly among 4 serving plates.

RAINBOW GARDEN SALAD WITH CLASSIC RANCH DRESSING

Green-leaf lettuce, with its frilled edges and straight-forward flavor, is a workhorse of a lettuce, perfect for casual family salads like this one. I like to cut the leaves of green leaf with scissors to get bite-size pieces that include some of the crunchy base of the leaf and some of the tender tip in each bite. It's easier than it sounds, and the cut lettuce holds up well in the refrigerator. Here it becomes the foundation for a colorful salad with a dreamy homemade ranch-style dressing.

MAKES 4 SERVINGS

I head green-leaf lettuce

4 small blue or purple potatoes, cooked whole in boiling water until tender

2 medium carrots, peeled and cut into curls with a vegetable peeler

I bunch (about 5) medium radishes, thinly sliced

I bunch green onions, thinly sliced

I pint cherry tomatoes

Ranch Dressing (page IIO)

1. Pull the leaves off the head of lettuce, discarding any that are wilted or damaged. Working over a sink full of cold water, cut each leaf with scissors into bite-sized pieces, working from the base of the leaf outward. Smaller leaves from the center of the head may be left whole. Swish the cut leaves around in the water to loosen any soil, then lift them out of the sink, leaving any soil or debris behind. Spin the cut and washed lettuce until it's dry, then put it in a zipper-lock bag or a wooden salad bowl covered with a damp paper towel, and refrigerate until just before serving time.

2. Peel the cooked potatoes and cut them into 1-inch cubes.

3. At serving time, toss the lettuce with the diced potato, carrot curls, radish slices, and green onions. Scatter the cherry tomatoes on top. Serve the salad directly from the salad bowl, passing the dressing separately.

★

ALASKA SCALLOP SALAD

Sizzling in a crisp coat of Asian breadcrumbs, sweet Alaska scallops are superimposed against a bed of slightly bitter greens tossed in an Asian-style oil-free dressing. The flavors, the textures, and the contrast between tasty fried food and healthy salad greens make for a lively salad indeed. In summer use fresh arugula from a farmer's market; in winter opt for a head of crispy frisée.

For the Salad

1 head frisée (curly endive), or 1 bunch arugula

8 very large Alaska scallops (about 12 ounces total)

1 teaspoon kosher salt

½ teaspoon freshly ground black pepper

1 egg

2 tablespoons water

½ cup unbleached white flour

1 cup panko (Japanese breadcrumbs)

1 cup canola oil

⅓ cup julienned papaya

1 medium tomato, quartered, seeded, and cut into ¼-inch strips

For the Vinaigrette

¼ cup crystallized ginger, cut into fine julienne strips

¼ cup boiling water

1 cup rice vinegar

½ cup corn syrup

1 tablespoon salt

1. Cut the base off the head of frisée and tear the leaves into bite-size pieces. If using arugula, pick through the bunch to remove any damaged or yellow leaves. Plunge the torn greens into a sink full of cold water, swish them around, then lift them out, leaving any soil or debris

behind. Spin the washed greens until they're dry, then put them in a salad bowl, cover with a damp paper towel, and refrigerate until just before serving time.

2. Cut each scallop horizontally across the grain into 3 slices to make 24 "coins." Sprinkle the scallop coins with the salt and pepper. Crack the egg into a small bowl, beat it with a fork, and stir in the water. Put the flour in a second bowl and the panko breadcrumbs in a third. Roll the cut scallops in the flour and shake off the excess; then dip them in the egg mixture, making sure the whole surface is covered. Roll the flour-and-egg-coated scallops in panko to coat, and lay them in a single layer on a baking sheet lined with baker's parchment. (The scallops can be prepared ahead up to this point and held, refrigerated, for several hours. If you prepare them ahead, make sure they do not touch or the coating will come off when they are moved.)

3. Make the vinaigrette. In a small bowl, cover the sliced ginger with the boiling water and set aside to stand for 5 minutes, or until the ginger is slightly softened. Stir in the vinegar, corn syrup and salt.

4. In a heavy skillet, heat the oil until a cube of bread floats immediately to the surface and begins to sizzle, or until a deep-fat thermometer registers 375°F. Fry the scallops, no more than 6 at a time, in the hot oil until crisp and golden, about 1 minute on each side. Set the fried scallops on a baking sheet lined with paper towels.

5. As soon as the scallops are fried, toss the greens with the vinaigrette and distribute them evenly among 4 serving plates. Top each salad with papaya strips and slivered tomatoes. Arrange the scallops on top of the dressed greens and serve at once.

★

DOS PADRES TACO SALAD

Bill Martinez founded Dos Padres restaurant in the Fairhaven neighborhood of Bellingham when he grew weary of campus politics at Western Washington University, where he worked in the engineering department. I worked for Bill when I was a college student during the 1980s. He said he wanted to re-create the "California-style" Mexican food of his Mexican-Irish-American heritage. What he created was something more, a family-owned restaurant that treated all its employees and customers like family too. The salad dressing for Bill's taco salad was based on the dressing that he had seen whisked table-side at the Canlis restaurant that used to occupy the ground floor of the grand old Fairmont Hotel on Nob Hill in San Francisco. Ubiquitous in the States, taco salad is unheard of in Mexico. We served freshly fried tortilla chips, and extra chips were ground up to top the salad. To make your own tortilla chip crumbs, pulverize plain tortilla chips in a food processor.

MAKES 6 SERVINGS

For the Salad

1 small head iceberg lettuce, finely shredded, not chopped

1 cup crushed tortilla chips

1½ cups (about 6 ounces) grated Monterey Jack cheese

2 medium tomatoes, sliced into wedges

About 2 cups Taco Beef (pages 223–24)

For the Dressing

1 coddled egg

¼ cup white wine vinegar

½ cup canola oil

Kosher salt and freshly ground pepper, to taste

1. To make the salad dressing, crack the egg into a small mixing bowl and whisk in the vinegar. Add the oil in a thin stream while continuing to whisk constantly. Add salt and pepper, to taste. Serve the dressing as soon as it's made, or keep it refrigerated for up to 1 day.

2. Distribute the shredded lettuce evenly among 6 salad plates and, with your hands, press it into a mound. Sprinkle crushed tortilla chips over each mound of lettuce. Distribute the grated cheese evenly over the salads and garnish each salad with a couple of tomato wedges.

3. Drizzle the salad dressing over the salads and, just before serving, top each salad with a generous ¼ cup of hot Taco Beef. Serve at once.

★
DUCK AND APPLE SALAD

Substantial enough to constitute a meal in itself, this salad was born in the kind of restaurant kitchen where a salted and roasted leg of duckling is pretty easy to come by. Very often, chefs buy whole ducklings and serve the breasts grilled and the legs roasted or preserved in their own fat. There's no reason why home cooks should not do the same thing. Of course, it's also possible to buy duck leg confit that is ready to heat and serve.

MAKES 4 SERVINGS

1 head frisée (curly endive)

4 Quick "Preserved" Duck Legs (page 210)

1 medium onion

2 medium tart apples

¼ cup duck fat or olive oil, or a combination

2 tablespoons Calvados or other brandy

1 tablespoon apple cider vinegar

3 tablespoons fresh sweet apple cider

1 teaspoon freshly ground black pepper, or to taste

1. Tear the head of frisée into bite-size leaves, rinse them in cool water, and spin them dry. Store the washed and dried leaves in a zipper-lock bag and refrigerate. Just before serving time, distribute the leaves evenly among 4 large salad plates.

2. Pull the preserved duck meat off the bones and cut it into thin slices. Cut the onion in half lengthwise, and cut off the top and bottom of each half. Pull

off the peel. Cut the half onions into thin slices vertically. Cut the sides from the apples, leaving the cores behind. Rest the apple pieces, flat side down, on the cutting board and cut into thin slices.

3. Melt the duck fat in a sauté pan over medium-high heat. Add the sliced onion and sauté until it is soft and just beginning to brown, about 5 minutes. Add the sliced duck and apple and sauté until heated through, about 2 minutes.

4. Pour the Calvados or brandy into the pan and tilt the pan toward the flame or light it with a match to burn off the alcohol. Pour in the cider vinegar, apple cider, and pepper, and boil rapidly to reduce the liquid slightly, about 2 minutes.

5. Distribute the apple and duck mixture evenly among the plates on the bed of frisée and serve at once, with additional freshly ground black pepper to taste.

★

DUNGENESS CRAB LOUIS

This salad, which has become an American classic, probably originated at the Olympic Club in Seattle. Certainly in 1904, when the Metropolitan Opera Company played Seattle, the great tenor Enrico Caruso enjoyed a salad there by the same name. But the salad is more often associated with San Francisco, where it appeared on the menu at Solari's restaurant in 1910. By 1919 a recognizable version was published in The Hotel St. Francis Cookbook. My version is an amalgam *of a half dozen or so "authentic" recipes. It's closest to one I found in Helen Brown's* West Coast Cookbook *(but I left out the green pepper that hers and hers alone contained). The delicate leaves of B.C. Hothouse—brand Bibb lettuce from British Columbia, sold in special packs with its roots still attached, make an excellent base for the salad.*

MAKES 2 ENTRÉE SERVINGS OR 4
FIRST-COURSE SERVINGS

For the Salad

1 head Bibb lettuce

Meat from 1 large (2-pound) Dungeness crab (about 1½ cups)

2 hard-cooked eggs, peeled and quartered

2 Roma tomatoes, quartered

For the Dressing

½ cup mayonnaise

¼ cup chili sauce (homemade or Heinz)

¼ cup crème fraîche or natural sour cream

¼ cup chopped green onion

2 tablespoons thinly sliced green olives

1. The fragile leaves of Bibb lettuce are easily bruised, so handle them with care. Gently break the head of lettuce into individual leaves, rinse them in cool water, and spin them dry. Store the washed and dried lettuce in a zipper-lock bag and refrigerate until just before serving time.

2. In a small bowl, whisk together the mayonnaise, chili sauce, crème fraîche,

green onion, and olives. Stir in the chilled crabmeat.

3. Arrange the chilled lettuce leaves on 2 dinner plates and divide the dressed crab mixture evenly between them. Arrange the wedges of hard-cooked egg and tomato on top. Serve at once.

★

APPLE ORCHARD SALAD WITH LEMON AND HONEY VINAIGRETTE

Indian summer rolls easily into fall when the first fall apples are sliced over a bed of late-summer greens from the farmer's market. Cool blue cheese and warm toasted walnuts round out the plate, and a creamy lemon and honey vinaigrette ties everything together. Based on a salad that I developed for Organic to Go, which offers it for sale in locations from Seattle to Los Angeles, this has become one of my all-time favorites.

MAKES 2 SERVINGS

For the Salad

4 ounces (about 3 cups packed) organic mixed baby greens

1 medium apple, preferably organic, cored and sliced but not peeled

½ cup toasted walnuts

2 ounces (about ½ cup) crumbled blue cheese

For the Dressing

2 tablespoons freshly squeezed lemon juice

2 tablespoons clover honey

¼ cup Homemade Mayonnaise (pages 115–16) or purchased all-natural

Kosher salt and freshly ground black pepper, to taste

1. If you're using unwashed greens from a farmer's market or your own garden, clean them first. Remove any browned or damaged leaves. Plunge the leaves into a sink full of cold water, swish them around, and then lift them out, leaving any soil or debris behind. Spin the cut and washed greens until they're dry, then pile them in an airtight container and refrigerate until just before serving time. If using prewashed salad greens, simply divide them between 2 serving plates.

2. Arrange the apple slices attractively over the salad greens, scatter the toasted walnuts on top, and pile the crumbled cheese in the center.

3. Make the dressing. In a small bowl, whisk the lemon and honey until thoroughly combined, then whisk in the mayonnaise and salt and pepper to taste, stirring until the dressing is perfectly smooth.

4. Drizzle the dressing over the salad and serve, with freshly ground black pepper passed separately.

★

MANGO AND AVOCADO SALAD

I originally encountered the juxtaposition of mango and avocado in a cookbook called Ten Talents. *Revised in 1985, this peculiar little volume was once a standard at health food stores all over North America. The original recipe was simply mango and avocado, sliced and served together. The combination struck a chord with me and with thousands of diners who ordered it off the various menus on which I have planted the combination over the years. I like it best as it is presented here, on a bed of lamb's lettuce drizzled with raspberry mustard vinaigrette.*

MAKES 6 SERVINGS

For the Salad

3 ripe mangoes

3 ripe avocados

3 cups cleaned and dried lamb's lettuce (mâche) or baby spinach

½ pint fresh raspberries

For the Dressing

2 tablespoons smooth Dijon mustard

¼ cup raspberry vinegar

¾ cup grapeseed or canola oil

I. With a sharp knife, cut the flat halves from the side of each mango, leaving the central section of the fruit attached to the pit. With a large spoon, free the pulp from each half mango in a single piece from the skin. Lay the skinned and pitted mango sections flat side down on a cutting board

and slice them into 6 vertical slices; set aside.

2. Cut each avocado in half and discard the pits. Remove the peel from each half avocado and place flat side down on the cutting board. Cut each half avocado into 6 vertical slices. For each salad, arrange half a sliced mango in a fan design on a chilled salad plate, and lay a slice of avocado beside each slice of mango, creating a striped fan design. At the "handle" of the fan, place ½ cup lamb's lettuce leaves.

3. Make the dressing. In a small mixing bowl with a wire whisk, thoroughly combine the mustard and vinegar. Whisking rapidly, add the oil in a very thin stream to create a smooth emulsion. Drizzle about 2 tablespoons of the dressing over the intersection of the lamb's lettuce and the fan of avocado and mango on each plate. Distribute the berries evenly among the salads. Serve at once.

★

POTATO SALAD, AFTER HELEN BROWN

In the original West Coast Cookbook, *the late Helen Brown dressed "barely tender" potatoes for her California Potato Salad with white wine and melted butter. (No mayonnaise!) Brown was an acolyte of James Beard (the two of them corresponded extensively) and a prescient cook who helped herald an awakening culinary sensibility that she never lived to see. I think she* would have enjoyed the diversity of potatoes available at twenty-first-century farmer's markets. With names like Russian Banana, Ruby Crescent, and Rose Finn Apple, numerous varieties of long, finger-shaped potatoes are lumped together into the category of "fingerlings." I based this recipe on Brown's, but instead of the red potatoes called for in her recipe, I opted for fingerling potatoes. I also abandoned Brown's butter in favor of extra virgin olive oil.

MAKES 8 SERVINGS

3 pounds (about 48) small fingerling potatoes, red or white

1 tablespoon kosher salt

⅓ cup white wine

2 tablespoons white wine vinegar

½ cup extra virgin olive oil

1 bunch green onions, white and green parts, thinly sliced

¼ cup chopped fresh parsley, preferably Italian flat-leaf

2 tablespoons chopped fresh tarragon leaves

Kosher salt and freshly ground black pepper, to taste

1. Put the potatoes in a 4-quart saucepan with the salt and just enough water to cover them (about 6 cups). Bring to a boil over high heat, reduce the heat to medium-low, and simmer until the potatoes are fork-tender, about 8 minutes.

2. Drain the potatoes and spread them in a single layer on a baking sheet until they are cool enough to handle. Cut each potato in half lengthwise.

3. In a smaller saucepan, boil the white wine for 1 minute to cook off most of the alcohol. Whisk in the wine vinegar and olive oil to make a simple dressing. Pour the warm dressing over the cooked and cooled potatoes and allow them to soak up the dressing. The salad can be finished and served at once or refrigerated for several hours before serving.

4. Transfer the dressed potatoes to a large (preferably wooden) salad bowl and toss with the green onions, parsley, and tarragon. Season to taste with salt and pepper.

★

JAPANESE POTATO SALAD

My friend Hiroko Sugiyama makes this potato salad for her family, and when I was visiting her with my son to prepare him for an exchange student trip to Japan, she served us this salad. I wanted to know what gave the salad its unique flavor. A purist who uses only the finest ingredients, most of them made from scratch, Hiroko seemed embarrassed to admit that she used Kewpie Brand mayonnaise, a popular and inexpensive Japanese brand that contains MSG. The mayonnaise is widely distributed on the West Coast and, like the cucumber pickles, which are brighter green than Western-style pickles, it can be found in Asian groceries and in most large supermarkets with international food sections.

3 pounds Red Rose or Yukon Gold potatoes

2 teaspoons kosher salt, plus more to taste

½ cup Homemade Mayonnaise (pages 115–16) with ½ teaspoon MSG, or Kewpie brand mayonnaise

3 or 4 Japanese cucumber pickles, sliced into ½-inch rounds

Freshly ground black pepper, to taste

1. Put the whole potatoes in a 4-quart saucepan with the salt and just enough cold water to cover them. Bring to a boil over high heat, reduce the heat to low, and simmer until the potatoes are fork-tender, about 15 minutes.

2. Drain the potatoes and spread them in a single layer on a baking sheet until they are cool enough to handle. Peel the skin from the cooked and cooled potatoes; it should pull off quite easily.

3. While the potatoes are still warm, cut them into 1-inch chunks and toss them with the mayonnaise and pickles. Season with salt and pepper to taste. Keep the salad well chilled until serving time.

★

WEST COAST COLE SLAW

The dark leaves of kale and red chard give this version of cole slaw an exotic look, and the perfume of sesame oil reinforces the notion that this is no ordinary slaw. The greens should marinate in the dressing for at least 20 minutes before you serve the salad.

For the Salad

½ medium head green cabbage (about 1 pound)

1 bunch red chard, rinsed and shaken dry

1 bunch Tuscan ("black") kale, rinsed and shaken dry

2 medium carrots, peeled and grated

For the Dressing

½ medium sweet onion, peeled

¼ cup rice wine vinegar

2 tablespoons sugar

2 teaspoons toasted sesame oil

2 teaspoons kosher salt

1 teaspoon freshly ground black pepper

¾ cup Homemade Mayonnaise (pages 115–16) or store-bought

1. Cut the half head of cabbage in half to make 2 wedges, then cut out the core from each wedge. Working with one wedge at a time, press the wedge cut side down onto the cutting board and, using a very sharp knife, cut the wedges into shreds no more than ⅛ inch thick.

2. Trim the stems from the bunch of red chard, bundle the leaves in a tight roll, like a big cigar, then cut across the bundle to make very fine ribbons. Repeat this process with the bunch of kale.

3. Toss the cabbage, chard, kale, and carrots in a large bowl.

4. Pile the ingredients for the dressing into a food processor and process until smooth. (If no food processor is available, grate the onion and whisk together all the ingredients for the dressing.)

5. Pour the dressing over the vegetables and toss to coat. Allow the greens to marinate in the dressing for at least 20 minutes or for several hours, refrigerated, before serving time.

★

CHINESE PEANUT NOODLE SALAD

It seems crazy that my criterion for West Coast–style Asian noodle salad is based on a dish prepared by a white man from Delaware, but it is. Tom Douglas, the larger-than-life Seattle restaurant mogul who helped set the standard for what constitutes Pacific Northwest cooking, introduced a lot of northwesterners to Asian dishes in a context that made them taste new. And he prepares them in a way that makes it easy for Western cooks to grasp what's going on. I can never make noodle salad without thinking of Tom.

MAKES 4 TO 6 SERVINGS

For the Noodles

8 cups water

2 tablespoons kosher salt

12 ounces dried Chinese egg noodles

1 pound broccoli florets, cut into 2-inch pieces

1 medium red bell pepper

½ cup chopped dry-roasted peanuts

1 bunch cilantro, coarsely chopped

1 bunch green onions

For the Peanut Sauce

⅓ cup water

2 tablespoons rice vinegar

1-inch piece ginger root, grated on a Microplane grater

2 or 3 cloves garlic

1 tablespoon soy sauce

1 tablespoon brown sugar

1 teaspoon toasted sesame oil

⅔ cup smooth natural peanut butter

1. Bring the water and salt to a boil in a heavy, 6- to 8-quart pot. Add the noodles. When the noodles have been cooking for 5 minutes, add the broccoli florets. By the time the noodles are tender, the broccoli should be bright green and almost tender too. Drain the noodles and broccoli through a colander and spread them out on a baking sheet to cool.

2. Make the peanut sauce. Put the water, vinegar, ginger, and garlic in a blender and purée until the ginger and garlic are liquefied, about 2 minutes. Add the soy sauce, brown sugar, sesame oil, and peanut butter and blend again until smooth and creamy.

3. Transfer the cooled noodles and broccoli to a large salad bowl. Cut the red pepper into julienne strips and toss with

the noodles. Toss the salad with the peanut sauce and top the salad with the chopped peanuts, cilantro, and green onions. Serve cold or at room temperature.

★

RANCH DRESSING

As proudly reported on the company's web site, the original ranch dressing came from Hidden Valley Guest Ranch near Santa Barbara. It was created in the late 1950s by ranch owner Steve Hanson, who used buttermilk, mayonnaise, and his own mixture of dry spices to make a creamy dressing that ranch guests often took home in canning jars. In a revisionist effort to make the stuff using fresh ingredients, I stumbled upon this combination that is a revelation. Any cook willing to chop some parsley and snip a few chives will agree: fresh is better. Yogurt in place of buttermilk makes the dressing creamier and tangier.

MAKES ABOUT 2 CUPS

I cup plain, natural yogurt such as Nancy's, with active cultures

I cup Homemade Mayonnaise (pages 115–16) or quality purchased

2 tablespoons snipped chives

I tablespoon chopped fresh parsley

I clove garlic, grated on a Microplane grater

I tablespoon apple cider vinegar

I teaspoon sugar

½ teaspoon salt

½ teaspoon freshly ground black pepper

Stir all the ingredients together. The dressing keeps, covered and refrigerated, for up to I week. Stir it just before serving.

★

BASIC FRENCH DRESSING

While I try not to condemn anyone else's food choices and do not consider myself a "food snob," I do sometimes shudder at the sight of bottled salad dressing. It's so expensive, so unnecessary, and generally so unfortunate in flavor that I can't help wishing everyone would just stop buying it and make their own. Basic French dressing should be in every good cook's repertoire. Use it with greens, with cold pasta and vegetables, or with potato salad.

MAKES ABOUT ⅔ CUP

2 tablespoons red wine vinegar

I tablespoon Dijon mustard

I shallot, peeled and finely chopped

2 teaspoons kosher salt

½ teaspoon freshly ground black pepper

6 tablespoons olive oil

Whisk the vinegar, mustard, shallot, salt, and pepper in a small mixing bowl until thoroughly combined. Whisking constantly, stream in the oil, a spoonful at a time, to make a smooth dressing.

★
BALSAMIC VINAIGRETTE

This dressing took the West Coast by storm in the 1980s, when balsamic vinegar, once a hard-to-find specialty product from Modena, Italy, became widely available. It has become something of a standard, as familiar to most Americans as last century's Thousand Island dressing.

MAKES A LITTLE MORE THAN 1 CUP

¼ cup balsamic vinegar

2 tablespoons Dijon mustard

1 tablespoon organic sugar (evaporated cane juice) or brown sugar

2 teaspoons kosher salt, or 1 teaspoon table salt

½ teaspoon freshly ground black pepper

¾ cup olive oil

Whisk the vinegar, mustard, sugar, salt, and pepper in a small mixing bowl until thoroughly combined. Whisking constantly, stream in the oil, a spoonful at a time, to make a smooth dressing.

★
GREEN GODDESS DRESSING

Introduced during the 1920s by the chef at the opulent Palace Hotel in San Francisco to honor an English actor named George Arliss, who was starring in a play called The Green Goddess, *this dressing is served at the hotel's Garden Court restaurant to this day. It became increasingly popular through the middle of the twentieth century, when it could be found on menus all over the country. Serve with tender leaves of butter lettuce.*

MAKES ABOUT 2 CUPS

One 2-ounce tin anchovy fillets

¼ cup chopped fresh parsley

¼ cup chopped chives or green onions

¼ cup tarragon vinegar

1 egg

¼ teaspoon freshly ground black pepper

1½ cups refined (not extra virgin) olive oil, canola oil, or a combination

½ cup sour cream

1. In a food processor or blender, whir the anchovies, parsley, chives, and vinegar with the egg and pepper for about 1 minute, or until the mixture is thoroughly combined.

2. With the motor running, slowly stream in the oil, starting with just a few drops at a time and building to a slow but steady stream until all of the oil is incorporated.

3. Finish the dressing by folding in the sour cream. The dressing keeps, refrigerated, for up to 1 week, but it's really best the day it's made.

★
SEASONED CROUTONS

Croutons are mandatory for the Tijuana Caesar Salad (pages 97–98) and Canlis Salad (page 99), but they're great on other salads too. Serve them as soon as they are made, or seal in an airtight container and store for several days.

MAKES 3 CUPS

¼ cup (½ stick) unsalted butter

I tablespoon finely chopped garlic

I tablespoon Italian seasoning (dried herb blend)

2 teaspoons salt

2 teaspoons dried oregano

I teaspoon granulated garlic (optional)

3 cups cubed bread

I. Preheat the oven to 325°F. Melt the butter and stir in the chopped garlic, Italian seasoning, salt, dried oregano, and granulated garlic. Toss the bread cubes with the butter mixture and spread the cubes in a single layer on a baking sheet.

2. Bake the croutons, stirring them around the baking sheet every 5 minutes, until they are golden brown, about 15 minutes. Let cool completely.

chapter 6

SANDWICHES

Homemade Mayonnaise
Reduced-Fat Mayonnaise
Twenty-First-Century Hamburgers
I-5 Grilled Chicken Sandwiches
Alaska Beer-Battered Halibut Sandwiches
BLT and Avocado Sandwiches
Phouvy's Sandwiches, or Banh Mi

TACOS

Norte Americano–Style Beef Tacos
Surfer-Style Fish Tacos

BURRITOS AND WRAPS

Crispy Bean and Cheese Burritos
Vegetarian Mediterranean Wraps
Grilled Chicken Caesar Salad Wraps
California Rolls

PIZZA

Family-Style Pizza
Individual Pizza Crusts
Pissaladière
Goat Cheese and Roasted Red Pepper Pizzas
Hollywood Smoked Salmon Pizzas, after Wolfgang Puck
Pacific-Style Tartes Flambés

Sandwiches, Etc.

"Let's grab a bite to eat," my father would say, and somehow that expression, one of my father's favorites, summed up his whole attitude toward food: Make it fast, and make it now. Don't skip it, but don't let it get in the way of anything else.

My father was not alone in wanting to be able to eat on the run. His generation was the one that gave us McDonald's restaurants. Originally a single operation founded by two brothers, Richard "Dick" and Maurice "Mac" McDonald in San Bernardino, California, the concept was co-opted by Ray Kroc, a 52-year-old mixer salesman who persuaded the brothers first to let him open franchises of McDonald's and eventually to sell him the company.

In a tribute to Kroc, published in *Time* magazine, the French-American chef Jacques Pepin writes, "Instead of a structured, ritualistic restaurant with codes and routine, he gave them a simple, casual and identifiable restaurant with friendly service, low prices, no waiting and no reservations. The system eulogized the sandwich—no tableware to wash. One goes to McDonald's to eat, not to dine."

This last phrase could have come from Kroc himself. A master of the aphorism, Kroc gave us such gems as, "If there's time to lean, there's time to clean," and "None of us is as good as all of us." The ideas are not original, nor were the ideas that shaped Kroc's borrowed idea for the fast food system that grew into McDonald's as we know it today—drive-in restaurants and franchises were already in existence—but Kroc's ability to summarize thoughts into pithy and easily remembered phrases, and his knack for turning a burger factory into an American icon amounted to a formidable power.

In the wake of *Fast Food Nation: The Dark Side of the All-American Meal*, a stunning exposé by Eric Schlosser, and the documentary film *Supersize Me*, Americans' attitudes toward fast food have begun to change. Nevertheless, love it or hate it, the influence Kroc and McDonald's have had on the way Americans eat and drink has been one of the most profound legacies of West Coast cooking.

This all came back to me while I was poring over *Nancy Silverton's Sandwich Book: The Best Sandwiches Ever—from Thursday Nights at Campanile*. Silverton, who along with her husband, Mark Peel, owns and operates La Brea Bakery in Los Angeles, decided to write the book when, at the end of a weeklong "food junket" in Tuscany, she vowed that she would never eat again.

"Our final stop on the tour was a small neighborhood crostini bar in Florence, Fuori Porta, where locals come in the evening to eat a simple meal of toasted bread with toppings." In the presence of those simple Italian sandwiches, her appetite revived, and "before I knew it, I too was drinking red wine and eating grilled bread rubbed with garlic and layered with prosciutto, arugula, and Parmesan."

Back home in Los Angeles, she was determined to re-create that experience for her guests, but the restaurant wasn't really about sandwiches. So on Thursday nights, the bar at Campanile became the scene of Sandwich Night, and a new collection of great sandwich recipes was born.

"Too often," she writes, "American sandwiches are just a quick and easy meal that rarely transcend their generic coffee-shop incarnation."

Like Silverton's crostini in Florence, my first ham sandwich in Paris was a revelation. Who knew that bread with a crust as thin and crackly as glass could be soft as marshmallows inside? Who knew that the bread's yeasty aroma could marry the smoky scent of the ham, and that together the two smells could rise like a prayer on a cloud of incense? No butter, no mayonnaise, nothing stood to interfere with the naked coupling of ham and bread.

Later came my first *croque monsieur*, a relatively complex edifice of ham and bread and Gruyère cheese topped with a thick white Mornay sauce bound with more Gruyère, all browned under the red and blue flames of a gas-burning salamander. That sandwich, eaten off a plate with a knife and fork while seated across the table from my wife at a café in Chartres, tasted like a coming of age. The Gruyère cheese masked the scent of the yeast and smoke, the soft *pain de mie* yielding more readily than a crusty baguette, all lying under the thick blanket of Mornay sauce, demanding a slow, savoring

approach quite unlike the paper-wrapped ham sandwich eaten standing up.

Sandwiches

★

HOMEMADE MAYONNAISE

Making a sandwich on homemade bread is best if the sandwich fillings, including the mayonnaise, are homemade as well. Homemade mayonnaise is easy to make, especially if you own a food processor. If you make mayonnaise without a food processor, it helps to have a second pair of hands; one person handles the whisk while the other person slowly dribbles in the oil.

MAKES ABOUT 2½ CUPS

1 whole egg or 2 egg yolks

2 tablespoons white vinegar

1 tablespoon Dijon mustard

1 teaspoon kosher salt

¼ teaspoon ground white pepper

2 cups canola oil

1. In a food processor or a medium mixing bowl, whip the egg with the vinegar, mustard, salt, and white pepper for about 1 minute, or until mixture is light and fluffy.

2. With the motor running, or while whisking rapidly, slowly stream in the oil, starting with just a few drops of oil at a time, then building to a slow but steady stream until all the oil is incorporated. As the sauce comes together to make a stable emulsion, the last of it can be added

somewhat more steadily than the first few tentative dribbles.

⭐
REDUCED-FAT MAYONNAISE

While working to develop recipes for a company that specializes in grab-and-go foods, I came to realize that the demand for lower-fat spreads was greater than I had ever imagined. Rather than resort to one with unwanted additives, I decided to develop our own. The key was replacing half the oil with a "slurry" of cornstarch and water, which is cooked and cooled before it's added to the mayonnaise. The finished spread was noticeably lighter, but every bit as delicious as regular mayonnaise.

MAKES ABOUT 2½ CUPS

1 cup water

2 tablespoons cornstarch

2 egg whites

2 tablespoons white vinegar

1 tablespoon Dijon mustard

1 teaspoon kosher salt

¼ teaspoon ground white pepper

1 cup canola oil

1. Whisk the water and cornstarch in a small saucepan over high heat until the mixture boils and becomes thick. Remove the slurry from the heat and let it cool to room temperature.

2. In a food processor or in a medium mixing bowl, whip the egg whites with the vinegar, mustard, salt, and white pepper

for about 1 minute, or until mixture is light and fluffy.

3. With the motor running, or while whisking rapidly, slowly stream in the oil, starting with just a few drops of oil at a time, then building to a slow but steady stream until all the oil is incorporated. Still whisking or motoring, stream in the cooked and cooled cornstarch slurry.

⭐
TWENTY-FIRST-CENTURY HAMBURGERS

No sandwich, and perhaps no foodstuff of any kind, has had more impact on the eating habits of Americans in general and denizens of the West Coast in particular than the hamburger. Even before the first McDonald's opened in the mid-1950s, the coast was the site of several fast food chains, and all of them featured hamburgers. It's hard to imagine, tasting a hamburger from a fast food place today, what made the sandwich so appealing to begin with. But the key to great hamburgers is simple; it's all about paying attention—first to the source of the beef, then to the quality of the bun, and finally to the way it's all prepared and assembled. The best burgers are grilled, but very good results can also be achieved on an old-fashioned griddle, a flat, preferably cast-iron cooking surface that fits over two standard burners. Even a free-standing griddle, like the ones used for pancakes, or one of the popular new indoor grills will work.

MAKES 4 HAMBURGERS

1½ pounds naturally raised ground beef

2 teaspoons kosher salt

½ teaspoon freshly ground black pepper

Homemade Hamburger Buns (pages 272–73)

Homemade Mayonnaise (pages 115–16) or other favorite condiments

1 large, red-ripe tomato, sliced

4 leaves butter lettuce, rinsed and patted dry

1. Build a charcoal fire in an outdoor grill or preheat a griddle over medium-high heat. When the coals are white-hot, or when the griddle is up to temperature, rub the cooking surface with canola oil.

2. While the grill or griddle is heating, divide the hamburger meat into 4 equal portions, and flatten each piece into a disc about 5 inches in diameter. Do not knead the meat or otherwise overhandle it, but do take care to form neat edges on the discs by pressing the rim between thumb and forefinger to make tall sides. This will prevent the patties from shrinking too much and will give them a nice, flat shape. The center of the patties should be a little thinner than the edges. (Without this edge, the burgers would be much thicker in the center than they are on the edges, more like a flattened meatball than a true burger.)

3. Season the patties generously with salt and pepper, and grill them or cook them on the griddle until they are well browned on one side and beginning to ooze on top, 2 to 3 minutes. Turn the patties and cook on the other side until they are just cooked through, about 2 minutes more.

4. While the burgers are grilling, split the hamburger buns into top and bottom halves. Spread the bottom of each bun with mayonnaise or whatever condiments you like, pile on tomato slices and lettuce leaves, and then plant the cooked hamburger patties on top and finish each hamburger with a top bun.

★
I-5 GRILLED CHICKEN SANDWICHES

Interstate Highway 5 stretches from Tijuana to the Canadian border, and so does the appeal of the grilled chicken sandwich, which is almost as popular at drive-in restaurants as the hamburger. Like the burger, this sandwich is infinitely better when it's made with the care and attention that only a dedicated home cook can afford. Brining the chicken makes it moister, more tender, and more flavorful.

MAKES 4 SANDWICHES

Homemade Hamburger Buns (pages 272–73)

Lemon Aïoli (pages 50–51)

4 leaves butter lettuce, rinsed, patted dry, and shredded

1 large red-ripe tomato, sliced

Honey-Lemon Grilled Breasts of Chicken (pages 197–98)

Split the hamburger buns into top and bottom halves. Spread the bottom of each bun with lemon aïoli, pile on shredded lettuce and tomato, then plant a grilled chicken breast on top and finish each sandwich with a top bun.

★

ALASKA BEER-BATTERED HALIBUT SANDWICHES

Right up there with burgers and grilled chicken sandwiches is the third member of the holy trinity of fast food, the fish sandwich, a fried fillet of white fish served on a soft white roll, with tartar sauce and shredded lettuce. At fast food restaurants, the sandwich can be a disappointment; made with care, though, a sandwich like this can be a wonderful thing. I've enjoyed mahi mahi tempura sandwiches at drive-ins in Hawaii and fried ling cod in Washington state, but my favorite is Alaska halibut fried in beer batter modeled after one I ate at a tiny hole in the wall in Sitka. Serve the sandwich with ice-cold bottles of the same beer used to make the batter.

MAKES 6 SANDWICHES

For the Tartar Sauce

1 soft-boiled egg yolk

1 teaspoon dry mustard powder

1 tablespoon fresh lemon juice

¾ cup light olive oil or vegetable oil

1 small kosher dill pickle, grated

1 tablespoon fresh dill, chopped

1 tablespoon fresh parsley, chopped

Salt and freshly ground black pepper

For the Sandwiches

Beer-Battered Alaska Halibut (page 166)

6 Homemade Hamburger Buns (pages 272–73)

2 cups shredded iceberg lettuce

1. Make the tartar sauce. In a food processor, combine the egg yolk, mustard, and lemon juice. With the motor running, add a few drops of oil, and when they are incorporated, add a few more. Stream in the remaining oil very slowly to make a thick emulsion.

2. Stir in the pickle, dill, and parsley. Add salt and pepper to taste. Serve at once or transfer to a clean glass jar and store, refrigerated for up to 1 week.

3. When all the fish has been fried, split the hamburger buns into top and bottom halves. Spread the bottom of each bun with Tartar Sauce, pile on shredded lettuce, then plant the fried fish fillets on top and finish each sandwich with a top bun.

★

BLT AND AVOCADO SANDWICHES

Bacon from sustainably raised pork can be counted as one of life's great simple pleasures. Tucked into a sandwich made on homemade bread, spread with homemade mayonnaise, and piled high with ripe tomato and perfect leaves of butter lettuce, it becomes the focal point of an American classic. Add slabs of buttery green avocado, and it moves into the realm of the sublime.

8 slices Whole Wheat Sandwich Bread (pages 270–71) or Better than Store-Bought White Bread (pages 267–68)

2 tablespoons Homemade Mayonnaise (pages 115–16)

1 pound Oven-Fried Bacon (page 36)

8 leaves butter lettuce, rinsed and patted dry

1 large, red-ripe tomato

1 ripe, medium avocado

½ teaspoon kosher salt

¼ teaspoon freshly ground black pepper

1. Spread 4 slices of bread with mayonnaise and top each one with bacon. Distribute the lettuce leaves evenly over the bacon, then slice the tomato and distribute the slices evenly over the lettuce.

2. Cut the avocado into halves lengthwise and remove the pit. Using a large metal cooking spoon, scoop out the half avocados in a single piece and lay them on a cutting board. Cut them into ½-inch slices. Lay the avocado over the tomato slices and sprinkle with the salt and pepper.

3. Put the remaining bread slices on top of the seasoned avocado and press the bread together to make 4 large sandwiches. Wrap and chill for a picnic, or serve at once.

★

PHOUVY'S SANDWICHES, OR BANH MI

I first encountered Vietnamese-style sandwiches when Phouvy Sylimanathum, one of my co-workers at Canlis restaurant, brought me one from a Vietnamese grocery store in the Seattle neighborhood known as Little Saigon. Phouvy spent his childhood in Laos, and on his way to the United States in the wake of "The American War" in Southeast Asia, he spent some time in Vietnam. He said these sandwiches helped him recapture his youth. Even though I had never tasted the sandwiches before, I developed an immediate attachment to them, with feelings that border on nostalgia. When I started baking our own rolls at the restaurant, Phouvy started making these sandwiches for the crew at the restaurant. One of the secrets to the elusive flavor is Vietnamese soy sauce, which has a yeasty scent reminiscent of Vegemite. Maggi seasoning sauce, a kind of soy sauce used widely in Asia and Central America, has the same flavor.

For the Spread

¼ cup chicken liver pâté, homemade or from a delicatessen

¼ cup Homemade Mayonnaise (pages 115–16) or quality purchased

For the Sandwiches

4 hoagie-style sandwich rolls

8 slices (about 8 ounces) cooked turkey or ham

1 medium red bell pepper, seeded and cut into fine julienne strips

1 medium carrot, peeled and cut into fine julienne strips

1 small hot (jalepeño) chile, seeded and cut into fine julienne strips

8 sprigs cilantro

8 dashes (about 4 teaspoons) Vietnamese soy sauce or Maggi seasoning sauce

1. Make the spread. In a small bowl, mash the pâté into the mayonnaise and stir with a fork until smooth.

2. Split the rolls into top and bottom halves. Spread the bottom of each roll with the spread, layer on the sliced ham or turkey, and top with a mixture of julienne-cut vegetables, a couple of sprigs of cilantro, and a dash or two of Vietnamese soy sauce. Finish each sandwich with a top bun.

Tacos

★

NORTE AMERICANO-STYLE BEEF TACOS

No food has become more ubiquitous on the West Coast than the taco. A slang word that basically means "snack," "taco" on the West Coast usually means a corn tortilla filled with meat, cheese, lettuce, and tomato. My favorite taqueria in Tijuana serves tacos made with everything from tongue to tripe. At the eatery, which is open to the street, speedy cooks sear the various meats and assemble the tacos before the diners' eyes. This version, with the cheese melted onto the beef filling, perfectly captures the messy joy that characterizes the North American taco.

And this technique ensures that all the tacos are ready at once, perfect for a casual family meal.

MAKES 12 TACOS, SERVING 4 TO 6

Taco Beef (pages 223–24)

Corn or canola oil, for frying

12 corn tortillas

3 cups (about 12 ounces) grated Monterey Jack cheese

6 cups shredded iceberg lettuce

2 large tomatoes, chopped

Homemade Salsa (page 60)

1. Prepare the taco beef and keep it warm in the skillet. Preheat the oven to 300°F. Line a baking sheet with a brown paper bag so it will be ready to receive the tortillas when they're fried.

2. Heat about an inch of oil in a cast-iron skillet or heavy sauté pan over high heat. When it reaches 375°F on a thermometer, or when a pinch of tortilla floats immediately to the surface and swims across the surface of the oil, bubbling all the way, it's ready.

3. Fry the tortillas one at a time in the hot oil, folding them in half with a fork to make half-moon shapes. As they are fried, balance the folded, fried tortillas, fold side up, on the paper-lined baking sheet to drain.

4. To assemble the tacos, put 2 rounded tablespoons full of beef in the fold of each fried tortilla. Tuck a generous pinch of

grated cheese over the beef. Lay the filled tacos out in a single layer on a baking sheet and bake them in the preheated oven until the cheese is melted and oozing out of the tacos, about 8 minutes.

5. While the tacos are baking, put the shredded lettuce, chopped tomatoes, and salsa in separate bowls, ready for each person to garnish the tacos. Serve the tacos hot.

★

SURFER-STYLE FISH TACOS

San Diego–style fish tacos have been codified into a kind of West Coast staple that transcends the regional origins of the dish. Fish tacos are served in all sorts of places, from funky to swank, up and down the entire coast. Some of the best fish tacos I have ever eaten were served on blue corn tortillas at the Fiddlehead Café in Juneau, Alaska. The fish can be grilled, broiled, or batter-fried. The tortillas are most often soft corn, but crisp corn tortillas or flour tortillas are also commonly used. For the classic San Diego–style fish taco, the fish should be fried and the corn tortillas served soft.

MAKES 6 TACOS

For the Tacos

12 corn tortillas

1½ cups shredded red cabbage

2 large tomatoes, chopped

6 lime wedges

For the Sauce

⅓ cup mayonnaise

⅓ cup crema Mexicana (available in Hispanic markets) or sour cream

2 tablespoons North American–style chili sauce (such as Heinz)

For the Fish

1 cup all-purpose flour

1 teaspoon fine sea salt

½ teaspoon freshly ground black pepper

1 cup dark beer

Peanut or canola oil, for deep-frying

1 pound halibut fillet, cut into 12 rectangular strips

1. Preheat the oven to 250°F. Line a baking sheet with baker's parchment and put 6 stacks of 2 tortillas each on top. Lay another piece of parchment on top, then cover the pan with aluminum foil, crimping the edges to create a seal. Warm the tortillas in the oven while the fish is fried. Line another baking sheet with a brown paper bag or some paper towels so it will be ready to receive the fish when it's fried.

2. Put the shredded cabbage, chopped tomatoes, lime wedges, and taco sauce in separate bowls, ready to assemble the tacos when the fish is fried.

3. In a large bowl, whisk together the flour, sea salt, and pepper and then whisk in the beer. Heat about 2 inches of oil in a cast-iron skillet or deep, heavy saucepan over high heat. When it reaches 375°F on a thermometer, or when a drop of the beer batter floats immediately to the

surface and swims across the surface of the oil, bubbling all the way, it's ready.

4. Dip the halibut in the beer batter and gently lower the strips into the oil, 3 or 4 at a time, and cook until the batter is golden brown, about 3 minutes. Lift the fish out of the oil with a slotted spoon and put it on the paper-lined baking sheet. Hold it in the warm oven while you fry the rest of the fish. Stir together the ingredients for the sauce.

5. To assemble the tacos, put 2 fish strips and a generous pinch of cabbage in the center of each warm stack of tortillas (2 tortillas per taco). Spoon chopped tomatoes over the taco and garnish with a lime wedge. Let each person add the sauce to taste.

Burritos and Wraps

★

CRISPY BEAN AND CHEESE BURRITOS

Cooking my way through college as a dinner cook at a family-owned Mexican restaurant in Bellingham, Washington, I became something of an authority on burritos. The burritos we served were not "soft"; instead, they were fried in oil until they were crisp. The style is known in some parts of the country as chimichanga. The frying took place either on top of the griddle or in a shallow pan of oil (depending on which of us cooks was in charge that night), and instead of simply turning the burritos over once to fry the second side, we developed

a technique for rolling the filled burritos as they fried so that they took on a three-sided log shape, something like the famous Toblerone chocolate bars. A quarter century later, the restaurant, which is still in operation under new owners, has long abandoned the three-sided burrito, but I've continued to follow the procedure when I make burritos at home.

MAKES 4 BURRITOS

For the Burritos

4 Homemade Flour Tortillas (pages 298–99) or quality store-bought tortillas

2 cups Refried Pinto Beans (page 143)

2 cups (about 4 ounces) grated Monterey Jack cheese

¼ cup canola oil

For the Garnish

4 cups shredded green-leaf lettuce

1 cup Home-Canned Tomato Salsa (page 405)

Natural sour cream (optional)

1. Lay a large piece of baker's parchment on the countertop and lay the tortillas on top of the parchment. Spread ½ cup of refried beans in a mound down the center of each tortilla, then distribute the grated cheese evenly over the refried beans.

2. Roll each tortilla, pressing the filling together as you roll. After the first turn, fold the sides of the tortilla in toward the center and finish rolling.

3. Heat the oil on a griddle or in a cast-iron skillet over medium-high heat. When it reaches 375°F on a thermometer, or when a pinch off the edge of a tortilla floats immediately to the top and swims across the surface of the oil, bubbling all the way, it's ready.

4. Lay the burritos in the shallow hot oil and fry until the bottoms are crisp and golden brown, about 2 minutes. Roll them about a third of the way over and fry until the second side is crisp and golden brown, about 2 minutes more. Give the burritos a final turn and fry the third side.

5. Serve the burritos hot on a bed of shredded lettuce, with salsa and sour cream passed separately.

★

VEGETARIAN MEDITERRANEAN WRAPS

Shortly after I went to work as a creative consultant for a promising start-up company called Organic to Go, the CEO asked me to develop a few wraps or sandwiches rolled inside tortillas for the "grab and go" business. He thought that, made with mostly organic, all-natural ingredients, our wraps would taste better than any offered by our competition. He was right. Easy to eat at a desk, and more fun than a traditional sandwich, our wraps quickly became one of our best sellers, from Seattle to Los Angeles. This recipe is based on one of the first wraps we offered.

MAKES 4 SANDWICHES

4 large sun-dried tomato tortillas

1 cup Hummus (pages 59–60)

1 cup (about 4 ounces) sun-dried tomatoes in oil, cut into julienne strips

32 kalamata olives or other black olives, pitted and chopped

4 cups (about 6 ounces) prewashed baby spinach leaves

1 cup (about 6 ounces) crumbled feta cheese

1. Lay a large piece of baker's parchment on the countertop and lay the tortillas on top of the parchment. Spread ¼ cup of hummus over each of the tortillas.

2. Distribute the sun-dried tomatoes evenly over the hummus, then put one fourth of the olives on top of the tomatoes on each sandwich.

3. Distribute the spinach among the tortillas, then put the crumbled feta on top of the spinach.

4. Roll each tortilla, pressing the filling together as you roll. After the first turn, fold the sides of the tortilla in toward the center and finish rolling. Wrap each rolled and filled tortilla in a piece of baker's parchment.

5. Cut each parchment-wrapped roll in half at a 45-degree angle and serve the wraps at once, or place each pair side by side on a square of plastic wrap, wrap tightly, and keep chilled until serving time.

⭐

GRILLED CHICKEN CAESAR
SALAD WRAPS

Traditionalists who insist that Caesar salad must be made one way and one way only shudder at the expanding proliferation of Caesar-style salads, topped with all sorts of nontraditional elements, like grilled chicken. But in the lexicon of casual West Coast cooking, Caesar has become a basic form on which variations are myriad. One of the more bizarre forms is the Caesar salad wrap, in which the salad ingredients and the heretical toppings are bundled inside colorful tortillas. Since this form allows the salad to be enjoyed sans fork at a desk or picnic, it has become tremendously popular. The fact that it is really delicious also helps.

MAKES 4 SANDWICHES

4 large spinach tortillas

¾ cup Caesar Dressing (page 98)

4 cups shredded romaine lettuce

2 pieces Honey-Lemon Grilled Breasts of Chicken, sliced (pages 197–98)

I cup (about 4 ounces) grated Asiago or Parmesan cheese

I. Lay a large piece of baker's parchment on the countertop and lay the tortillas on top of the parchment. Spread 3 tablespoons of Caesar dressing over each of the tortillas.

2. Put I cup of shredded romaine on top of the dressing, then lay the sliced chicken on top of the lettuce. Sprinkle the grated cheese over the chicken.

3. Roll each tortilla, pressing the filling together as you roll. After the first turn, fold the sides of the tortilla in toward the center and finish rolling. Wrap each rolled and filled tortilla in a piece of baker's parchment.

4. Cut each parchment-wrapped roll in half at a 45-degree angle and serve the wraps at once, or place each pair side by side on a square of plastic wrap, wrap tightly, and keep chilled until serving time.

⭐

CALIFORNIA ROLLS

A kind of norimaki, or sushi wrapped in nori seaweed, the California roll is not only one of the most approachable ways of preparing sushi, but it is also a perfect way to introduce someone to the pleasures of eating sushi. Cooked crabmeat, avocado, cucumbers, and sushi rice are wrapped in nori, and the roll is then cut into bite-sized rounds, which are served with pickled ginger and wasabi. The combination varies slightly from maker to maker but is almost universally available on the West Coast. I like it best with Alaska king crab leg, but faux crabmeat or surimi, made from Alaskan haddock, is a far more typical choice for the filling. You will need an inexpensive bamboo mat for rolling the sushi.

MAKES 4 ROLLS, SERVING 4

For the Sushi

2 medium avocados

I medium cucumber

4 sheets nori (Japanese pressed seaweed)

4 cups Sushi Rice (pages 136–37)

1 cup cooked crabmeat or surimi

2 tablespoons toasted sesame seeds

For the Accompaniments

4 tablespoons pickled ginger

4 teaspoons prepared wasabi (Japanese horseradish)

Japanese soy sauce, to taste

1. Cut the avocados in half lengthwise and remove the pits. Using a large metal cooking spoon, scoop out the half avocados in a single piece and lay them on the cutting board. Cut them into 1-inch dice.

2. Peel the cucumber, cut it in half lengthwise, and use a spoon to scoop out the seedy centers from each half. Cut the seeded cucumber into 1-inch sticks.

3. Lay a sheet of nori, shiny side down, on a bamboo sushi-rolling mat. Use about 1 cup of the sushi rice to lightly cover the surface of the nori sheet, leaving a 1-inch border uncovered.

4. Layer one fourth of the crabmeat, one fourth of the cucumber, and one fourth of the avocado on top of the rice in a straight line running from one side of the roll to the other. Sprinkle with one fourth of the toasted sesame seeds and then, starting at the end closest to you, gently roll and press the rice and the nori around the filling to form a fairly firm log.

5. Repeat the process with the remaining sheets of nori and the fillings to make 4 logs. The logs can be prepared a couple of hours ahead, but the texture is adversely affected by refrigeration and the fillings are perishable, so don't keep any leftovers overnight. Just before serving, cut each log into 6 slices and serve with the pickled ginger, wasabi, and soy sauce.

Pizza

FAMILY-STYLE PIZZA

According to the pollsters, Americans' favorite take-out food is pizza, and people on the West Coast are certainly no exception to the rule: We eat as much pizza as anyone. I started making pizza like this to serve once a week at staff meals in restaurants where I worked. And when I took a leave from the world of fine dining to launch the food and beverage program at IslandWood, an environmental learning center for school-age kids, I made this pizza the centerpiece of one of the regularly rotating menus. We prepared the dough in huge batches to make 36 pizzas at a time. When I polled the young people at the end of each week to learn their favorite meals, the groups overwhelmingly picked pizza as their first choice.

MAKES ONE 8- BY 16-INCH PIZZA

For the Crust

1 cup warm water

1 tablespoon (1 packet) active dry yeast

1 tablespoon sugar

2½ cups unbleached white flour

1 tablespoon kosher salt, or 1½ teaspoons table salt

2 tablespoons olive oil for the pan

For the Toppings

1½ cups pizza sauce, homemade or quality store-bought

1 pound (about 4 cups) mozzarella cheese, shredded

4 ounces (about 1 cup) Parmesan cheese, grated

1. In the bowl of an electric mixer or in a large mixing bowl, stir together the warm water, yeast, and sugar. Allow the mixture to stand until the yeast is softened, about 5 minutes, then stir until the yeast is completely dissolved.

2. If you are working with a stand mixer, pile in all the flour, along with the salt. With a paddle attachment, mix on low speed until everything comes together to make a thick, sticky batter. (If you are mixing by hand, whisk in 1 cup of flour, then switch to a wooden spoon and stir in the second cup of flour along with the salt.)

3. Use the dough hook on the mixer to knead the dough. (If you are working by hand, turn the dough out onto a countertop sprinkled with the remaining ½ cup of flour and knead the dough, pressing it and folding it until it is very springy, sprinkling with additional flour

if needed to keep the dough from sticking to the counter. Be careful not to add more flour than necessary or the dough will be stiff and the crust will be heavy.)

4. Leave the dough in the electric mixer bowl or return it to the regular mixing bowl and cover the bowl with a damp, lint-free kitchen towel or a piece of plastic wrap and put it in a warm place until the dough is doubled in size, about an hour.

5. Heat the oven to 425°F. Rub a half sheet pan (17 by 9 inches) with the olive oil. Turn the dough out of the mixing bowl onto a lightly floured surface and roll it into a rectangle about the same size as the pan.

6. Spread the pizza sauce on top of the crust and sprinkle the mozzarella and Parmesan cheese over it.

7. Bake on the bottom rack of the oven until the crust is brown and the cheese is bubbling hot, about 20 minutes. Move the pizza from the pan to a cutting board and cut into 12 pieces. Put the cut pizza back on the baking sheet and serve hot.

★

INDIVIDUAL PIZZA CRUSTS

Jeremiah Tower, the first chef at Alice Waters' famed Chez Panisse restaurant in Berkeley, claims that he was the first West Coast chef to make individual pizzas with innovative toppings. In Jeremiah Tower Cooks, *he describes a party at which the turnout was larger than expected. When the original topping ran out, he started* topping the little pizzas with whatever they had on hand. Meanwhile, in Los Angeles, Wolfgang Puck was launching his own line of individual serving-size pizzas, including the famed smoked salmon pizza that became a signature dish at Spago, which he opened in 1982. Unaware of any of this, I was cooking in the mid-1980s on an island off the coast of Washington, where we made individual pizzas for appetizers, varying the toppings every day according to our own caprice. We parbaked the individual crusts, then topped them with whatever seemed appropriate to the season. The recipes that follow use individual pizza crusts in various ways. Also try them topped with Bright Green Basil Pesto (see pages 146–47) or a scattering of fresh pears and crumbled Gorgonzola cheese.

MAKES 6 INDIVIDUAL PIZZA CRUSTS

1 tablespoon (1 packet) active dry yeast

1 tablespoon sugar

1 cup warm water

2½ cups unbleached white flour

1 tablespoon kosher salt, or 1½ teaspoons table salt

2 tablespoons olive oil

1. In a large measuring cup, sprinkle the yeast and sugar over the warm water and stir to dissolve. Allow the mixture to stand until the yeast is softened, about 5 minutes, and then stir until the yeast is completely dissolved.

2. Put the flour and salt in the work bowl of a food processor and, with the motor running, pour in the water and yeast mixture and the olive oil.

3. Process until the dough is smooth and pulls away from the sides of the work bowl, about 2 minutes.

4. Allow the dough to rise in the machine until it is doubled in bulk, about 1 hour. (If the machine is needed for another purpose, the dough can be transferred to a mixing bowl lightly rubbed with olive oil.)

5. When the dough has risen, pulse the motor on and off a few times to drive out the air and collapse the dough back into a ball. Turn the dough out onto a well-floured surface and divide it into 6 golf ball–sized pieces. Allow the pieces to rest until they are no longer springy but soft and pliable, about 5 minutes.

6. Preheat the oven to 425°F and put a pizza stone on the lowest rack. If no pizza stone is available, put a rack in the lowest position and preheat a heavy aluminum baking sheet on the rack.

7. Roll each piece of dough into a circle about 8 inches in diameter. Bake the circles of dough, one or two at a time, until they are puffed and lightly browned, about 5 minutes. The partially baked crusts can be prepared several hours or up to 1 day in advance, then topped and baked just before serving.

PISSALADIÈRE

Cheese-free pissaladière, with its characteristic layer of caramelized, thyme-scented onions and scattering of anchovies, pine nuts, and olives, originated in the south of France, where the Italian influence is strong and French pride is stronger still. But this style of pizza has found a new spiritual home on the West Coast, where it sits very well with our laid-back attitudes and even better with our wines, from the clearest and simplest sauvignon blanc to the boldest old vine zinfandels. When I first started making this style of pizza in 1985, I prided myself on using Washington's famous Walla Walla sweet onions. Since then, however, I have learned that sweet onions are best reserved for use in dishes in which they are served raw. Regular yellow onions contain less water and caramelize more easily.

MAKES 6 INDIVIDUAL PIZZAS

¼ cup extra virgin olive oil

2 medium yellow onions, peeled and thinly sliced

1 tablespoon sugar

1 tablespoon fresh thyme leaves, or 1 teaspoon dried

Individual Pizza Crusts (pages 126–27)

½ cup pitted small olives, such as niçoise olives

¼ cup pine nuts

6 anchovy fillets, cut into thin strips

12 sprigs thyme

1. Heat the olive oil in a heavy saucepan over medium heat. Add the onions and cook them slowly for 15 minutes, stirring regularly to achieve a uniform golden brown. Add the sugar and thyme leaves and continue to cook the onions until they soften and caramelize and turn a rich brown color. This will take at least 30 minutes; don't rush it, and don't let the onions burn.

2. Preheat the oven to 450°F and put a rack in the lowest position.

3. Distribute the caramelized onion mixture evenly over the surface of the partially baked crusts. Scatter the olives, pine nuts, anchovies, and thyme sprigs over the onions and the cheese. Bake until the crusts are well browned and the topping is bubbling hot, 12 to 15 minutes. Serve hot.

GOAT CHEESE AND ROASTED RED PEPPER PIZZAS

When we made various styles of individual pizzas for the appetizer section of our menus in the 1980s, a number of West Coast chefs settled on some combination of roasted red peppers, goat cheese, and garlic. All these flavors seemed so straightforward and of the moment then—and somehow, even twenty years later, they still do. Don't succumb to the urge to buy already roasted red peppers in a jar; they never taste as good as they look.

4 medium sweet red bell peppers

6 cloves garlic, sliced into paper-thin rounds

6 tablespoons (about ⅓ cup) extra virgin olive oil

Individual Pizza Crusts (pages 126–27)

8 ounces (about 1½ cups) goat cheese, crumbled

1. Roast the peppers. Preheat the broiler and position an oven rack 6 inches below the broiler element. Put the peppers on a baking sheet and broil until the skin on the side of the peppers closest to the hot element is blistered and blackened, about 4 minutes. Give the peppers a turn, positioning the blackened side not on the bottom, but to one side, and broil until another side is blackened. Turn the peppers once more to blacken the third surface of the peppers. Transfer the peppers to a brown paper bag and let them stand at room temperature until they have cooled to room temperature, about 15 minutes.

2. Switch the oven from broil to bake at 450°F. While the peppers are cooling, cook the sliced garlic cloves in the olive oil in a small saucepan over medium heat until they are very lightly browned. Take the pan off the heat and let the garlic cool in the oil.

3. Peel the peppers by hand; the skin should pull right off. Under running water, briefly rinse off most of the clinging, blackened bits of skin. Don't rinse too vigorously or you'll wash away the flavor. Pull the peppers open and remove the seeds and any remaining cores.

4. Tear the peppers into rough strips and distribute them evenly over the surface of the partially baked crusts. Crumble the goat cheese over the pepper strips and drizzle the garlic and olive oil over the cheese. Bake until the crusts are well browned and the topping is bubbling hot, 12 to 15 minutes. Serve hot.

★

HOLLYWOOD SMOKED SALMON PIZZAS, AFTER WOLFGANG PUCK

The Austrian-born Wolfgang Puck captured America's heart partly because he is one of the best chefs of his generation and partly because his former wife and business partner, Barbara Lazaroff, is a brilliant restaurant designer and promoter of her ex-husband. Her design for the original Spago Hollywood perfected the display kitchen, which has become a hallmark of West Coast dining. By tailoring his classical European training to precisely fit American tastes, he struck a chord with dishes like "gourmet pizza," a seeming contradiction in terms when it was first used. His smoked salmon pizza, which we heard about in Washington state through the restaurant grapevine almost as soon as it appeared, was quickly copied in versions like this one, which can be cut into individual wedges and served as an hors d'oeuvre.

Individual Pizza Crusts (pages 126–27)

1 cup crème fraîche or natural cream cheese

2 tablespoons chopped fresh fennel leaves or dill, plus sprigs for garnish

1 small red onion, peeled and very thinly sliced

6 ounces cold-smoked salmon (lox), sliced paper-thin

1 ounce Montana paddlefish or farm-raised California sturgeon caviar (optional)

1. Instead of partially baking the individual crusts, bake them until they are golden brown and crisp, about 10 minutes in all. Allow the crusts to cool for 5 minutes before applying the toppings.

2. Stir together the crème fraîche and fennel leaves and spread the mixture evenly over the warm crusts. Arrange the sliced red onion and smoked salmon over the surface and garnish the pizzas with sprigs of fennel or dill. Top the pizzas with caviar, if desired.

★

PACIFIC-STYLE TARTES FLAMBÉS

Alsatian in derivation, a platter of these pizzas cut into wedges is a perfect hors d'oeuvre with cocktails or chilled wine. But the pizzas are also substantial enough to con-stitute a light meal in themselves, especially when they're served one per person with a green salad. I've eaten these savory pizza-style tarts in France, but ironically I like them best made with Nancy's natural cottage cheese

from Eugene, Oregon, and Niman Ranch applewood-smoked bacon from a company based in Marin County, California.

½ cup natural cottage cheese, such as Nancy's, or fromage blanc

½ cup crème fraîche or sour cream

1 tablespoon flour

4 ounces natural bacon, such as Niman Ranch brand, cut into ¼-inch bits

1 small onion, peeled and very thinly sliced

Individual Pizza Crusts (pages 126–27)

Kosher salt and freshly ground black pepper, to taste

1. In the food processor, combine the fromage blanc, crème fraîche, and flour. Process until smooth.

2. Cook the bacon in a skillet over medium heat until some of the fat is released, then add the sliced onion and cook for 2 or 3 minutes, or until the onion is barely softened.

3. Distribute the cheese mixture evenly among the partially baked crusts, spreading it right up to the edges. Sprinkle the bacon and onions and salt and pepper on top. Bake until the crusts are well browned and the topping is bubbling hot, 12 to 15 minutes. Serve hot.

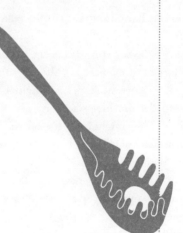

RICE

BEANS

NOODLES AND PASTA

PASTA, BEANS & GRAINS

Pasta, Beans & Grains

Like every other category of American food, the world of rice and pasta has been deeply influenced by the ministrations of corporate food processing giants. But on the West Coast, the effects have been mitigated by a trend toward increasingly homemade and handmade pasta, noodles, and side dishes.

Choose a day when there is a noticeable chill in the air. It's best if the sun is shining and the leaves are turning red, or golden, or even brown. Find yourself a green kabocha squash by eleven o'clock in the morning so you can have pumpkin risotto ready in time for lunch. Kabocha is Japanese for "pumpkin." Maybe you've never noticed them before, but chances are they're sold at your local grocery store. They might be underneath the produce stand, in a basket on the floor. They might be at the farmer's market, or in your neighbor's backyard. Somewhere, one is waiting for you.

If you already have another kind of winter squash or pumpkin, take a good, long look at it. Maybe it can pretend to be kabocha long enough for you to make risotto. Buttercup squash and so-called Sweet Mama squash are almost identical to kabocha; they will do. Hard, dense-fleshed sugar pumpkins, red kuri squash, and Gold Nugget squash will work too. A butternut squash will do the trick if it isn't too intent on being a butternut. Watery, stringy, or thin-skinned squashes are out.

When you get the squash home, think about how it felt to stay home from school on a fall day, when the house was quiet and the light was pouring in and you had all your thoughts to yourself. Think about your grandmother. If you can't remember her, think about mine. She wore dresses even on weekdays. She had pointy glasses and wore sensible shoes that wouldn't hurt her bunions. She laughed a lot, but she usually tried to hide it, acting straight so that we would take her seriously. She cooked things up in her kitchen that she liked to eat, and if you had sense enough to know what was good, you liked them too. The light used to pour into her kitchen sideways through the leaves of the trees, and it was quiet in there. She never bothered with the radio or any kind of music when she was cooking.

Put the squash on a solid wood cutting board on top of a sturdy countertop and approach it with your biggest knife in one hand and a serious look on your face. These squash have a skin as hard as life itself, and you have to cut right through it. Cut about halfway in and, if you're feeling strong and the squash seems compliant, push all the way through to cut it in half. If you're feeling weak or timid, and the knife is wedged deep in the squash like the sword in the stone, pick them up together and whack them down together to break the squash in half; you'll feel stronger then.

Once you've cut the squash in half, the rest is easy. Lay the cut side down so that the thing is stable, then cut the half squash in half again to make two quarters. Don't worry about the other half squash for now; you won't need it. Use a soup spoon to carve out the seedy middle and then, using your knife again, cut the skin off the squash and cut the peeled and seeded flesh into 1-inch cubes, or shapes as close to cubes as you can get. You should have a generous 2 cups of diced squash.

Measure yourself a cup of rice. For now, forget what Marcella Hazan and Lynne Rosetto Kasper have said. They don't know who you are or where you live, and you don't need Arborio or Carnaroli rice. Use ordinary short-grain rice from Japan. You can use the kind from Louisiana or California if you want, but I like to use plain white, unwashed pearly-shaped grains from Asia. And I like to imagine that I'm high above the earth looking down at the Pacific Ocean: I'm on one side, raising my cup of rice in a kind of salute, and Asia's on the other side, where the sun is barely rising. Far off on the other side of the globe is Italy, where the sun has already set.

Now light two burners and put a small saucepan on the back one and a nice, heavy-bottomed 3-quart stew pot on the front one. I have a stainless steel pan with sloped sides that works nicely. Put a can of chicken broth and half a can of water in the back pot; don't put anything in the front one yet. Instead, chop half an onion while the

pan gets hot. Now put a tablespoon of oil in the front pan and a tablespoon of butter. The butter will sizzle and melt in the oil. Sauté the onion until it is soft. Peel a few cloves of garlic and slice them paper-thin; add them to the onion.

Add the cubed squash and stir for a minute or two to warm it up. Add the rice and stir for another couple of minutes, until the rice is translucent. Think about translucent. Think about light passing partway through and not coming out the other side. Where did it go?

Stir in a cup of white wine. If there is no wine, stir in a cup of apple juice. No one will know. When the wine has hissed and boiled and evaporated, stir in half a cup of the hot broth from the back burner. And keep stirring until the rice is crying out for more liquid, until the pan begins to sizzle every time you stir and the risotto sounds like it's trying to fry again. Lower the heat a little, add another half-cup of broth, and think about the salad you will serve with the risotto.

It may be composed of lettuce or spinach, but it should be simply dressed with nothing but 3 tablespoons of olive oil and 1 tablespoon of balsamic vinegar with salt and pepper. You can think about my grandmother's great-grandfather if you like. Desiderio Chini came over from Bologna, Italy, in 1809. Think of how he must have missed his home, the food there, the balsamic vinegar that his mother kept in a barrel in the rafters of the house. Think of how he missed the Parmigiano-Reggiano that was rubbed in his time with crushed grape seeds and ashes so that the big 40-pound wheels stood in black stacks in the open markets there.

Sneak a short break from the constant stirring to grate some Reggiano cheese and think of how my old Italian ancestor must have missed the patter of his own language in his mother's kitchen. He married a twenty-five-year-old woman named Margarita Bauve from New Orleans in late September of 1813 and lived with her until he died in 1830. She was 42 when he died, and she would live to be 75. My own grandmother was widowed when she was 55 and would live to be 93.

After 10 or 15 minutes, the pumpkin cubes will soften and their corners will disappear. The rice will swell and the broth will grow creamy and smooth. Keep adding broth as the rice demands it.

There was an African-American girl who lived in the Chini household. According to family tradition, she came with my thrice-great grandmother from Louisiana and stayed in the house next door with the older children, who slept there when the family outgrew the tiny house where they began. The kitchen was in a third structure, behind the two houses. The whole complex is still standing on a quiet street in Pensacola, Florida. Some of my family's old things are still there.

Rice

★

JAPANESE-STYLE SHORT-GRAIN RICE

Short-grain Japanese-style rice calls for a different cooking technique than long-grain Indian-style rice. The short-grain varieties absorb slightly less water and benefit from presoaking, or at least a very thorough rinse in several changes of water. My favorite rice is called Tamaki Haiga. Haiga has a double meaning in Japanese. It literally means "rice bran," but it is also the word for a traditional Japanese brush work. Characterized by the juxtaposition of rustic simplicity and ethereal refinement, Haiga used in this way can be thought of as a visual form of haiku poetry. Tamaki Haiga rice is less than fully refined; lingering traces of the rough outer bran give it more flavor and texture than white rice, but it is quicker and easier to cook than truly brown rice. Williams Rice Milling Company in the Sacramento Valley of Northern California produces this rice, which is widely distributed to Asian markets and better Japanese restaurants all over the West Coast. Leftover cooked rice can be chilled and reused for Chinese Restaurant—Style Fried Rice (pages 135–36).

MAKES 6 TO 8 SERVINGS

2 cups short-grain rice, preferably Tamaki Haiga

3 cups water

1. Put the rice in a large mixing bowl and cover it with several inches of tap water. Swish the rice around in the water to release any clinging residue from the

milling process. Pour off the water and repeat the process 2 or 3 times, until the water that comes off the rice is no longer cloudy but almost perfectly clear.

2. Pour the washed rice through a large strainer and allow all the water to run off.

3. Put the washed and drained rice in a rice cooker or heavy 4-quart saucepan with a close-fitting lid, and pour 3 cups of cold tap water over it.

4. Use the instructions that came with your rice cooker to cook the rice, or put the covered saucepan over high heat until the water is boiling and steam is escaping from under the lid. Immediately reduce the heat to low and allow it to simmer, tightly covered and undisturbed, for 20 minutes.

5. If you did not use a rice cooker, take the cooked rice off the stove and let it stand at room temperature, still covered, for 10 minutes before serving.

★

CHINESE RESTAURANT-STYLE FRIED RICE

I never paid too much attention to fried rice until I was the chef at Canlis restaurant in Seattle, where fried rice was a regularly featured item on the rotating menu of "family meals" prepared for the crew. There, once a week or so, one of the cooks would swiftly but painstakingly prepare the omelet, cut the carrots and ham, and, using cold rice left over from the five o'clock meal, toss together a batch of fried rice for the second family meal

of the night, served just after closing time. Ever since, I have made the dish for my family at home. It makes for a great lunch or a side dish for a casual family supper. Rice bran oil, available in Japanese groceries and in some supermarkets, adds a touch of authenticity; if it's not available, canola oil will do.

MAKES 4 SERVINGS

Ingredients for Japanese-Style Omelet (pages 26–27)

3 tablespoons rice bran or canola oil

2 medium carrots, peeled and cut into ½-inch dice

1 cup fresh shelled or frozen green peas

8 ounces cold ham

3 cups leftover cooked rice, long or short grain

3 tablespoons Chinese-style soy sauce

1 bunch green onions, both green and white parts, sliced thin

1. Prepare the omelet and let it cool to room temperature on a cutting board. If the procedure for making the omelet seems too involved, simply cook the egg mixture in butter or oil in a large skillet over medium-high heat without stirring it too much (the cooked eggs should be in sheets rather than scrambled bits), then roll the cooked eggs into a log. Cool the cooked egg mixture on a cutting board.

2. In a large skillet or frying pan over medium-high heat, heat the oil and sauté the carrots until they are barely soft, about 3 minutes. Add the peas and ham and

cook until the ham begins to color on the edges, about 2 minutes. Add the rice, breaking it up with a wooden spoon or spatula, and stir-fry until the rice is heated through, about 5 minutes.

3. Add the soy sauce and green onions, tossing and stir-frying until the sauce is evenly distributed over the rice, about 1 minute. Serve the rice immediately while it is steaming hot.

★

SUSHI RICE

The very words make me tremble. But they shouldn't. Preparing rice for sushi can be intimidating to a Western cook, not because the process is particularly difficult, but because it is so extremely simple and the finished product so utterly naked that any imperfections will be impossible to hide. Most Japanese cooks use highly polished short-grain rice for sushi. I like to use the barely polished Tamaki Haiga rice described in the recipe for Japanese-Style Short-Grain Rice (pages 134–35), but this same procedure can be followed using the more polished rice produced by the same company, or with any short-grain rice. Rice for sushi is prepared in almost exactly the same way as regular short-grain rice, with the addition of a small piece of dried seaweed (kombu) and a splash of sake. After the rice is cooked, a sweet and salty vinegar dressing is applied and the rice is fanned as it cools to form a shiny surface. Use the rice to make California Rolls (pages 124–25) or Mixed Sushi (page 137), or serve it with Grilled or Seared Rare Ahi (pages 169–70).

For the Rice

2 cups short-grain rice, preferably Tamaki Haiga

3 cups water

1-inch square piece of kombu

2 tablespoons sake (rice wine)

For the Vinegar Dressing

⅓ cup rice vinegar

2 tablespoons sugar

1 tablespoon salt

1. Put the rice in a large mixing bowl and cover it with several inches of tap water. Swish the rice around in the water to release any clinging residue from the milling process. Pour off the water and repeat the process 2 or 3 times, until the water that comes off the rice is no longer cloudy, but almost perfectly clear.

2. Pour the washed rice through a large strainer and allow all the water to run off. For the best texture, let the rice stand in the colander for an hour before cooking.

3. Put the washed and drained rice in a rice cooker or heavy 4-quart saucepan with a close-fitting lid, and pour 3 cups of cold tap water over it. Add the piece of kombu and the sake.

4. Use the instructions that came with your rice cooker to cook the rice, or put the

covered saucepan over high heat until the water is boiling and steam is escaping from under the lid. Immediately reduce the heat to low and allow it to simmer, tightly closed and undisturbed, for 20 minutes.

5. While the rice is cooking, in a small bowl whisk together the vinegar, sugar, and salt. If you have a *hangiri*, the round wooden tub made specifically for cooling sushi rice, soak it in cold water. If no *hangiri* is available, use a large wooden salad bowl or a cold crockery bowl.

6. If you did not use a rice cooker, take the cooked rice off the stove and let it stand at room temperature, still covered, for 10 minutes before proceeding.

7. Transfer the cooked rice to the *hangiri* and toss it with the rice vinegar dressing, fanning it lightly with a fan or piece of cardboard.

Mixed Sushi

Chirashizushi or mixed sushi (*chirashi* means "scattered") is perfect for a casual family supper. Cooked vegetables or seafood are scattered over the surface or tossed with the finished sushi rice before serving. The secret to this dish is selecting harmonious colors, textures, and flavors of ingredients. Select a trio or quintet of ingredients that reflect the best of the season. In the spring, garnish the rice with strips of Japanese-style Omelet (pages 26–27) and freshly shelled green peas. In summer, use a mixture of garden vegetables, including strips of red

pepper and tender young green beans. In the fall, opt for shiitake mushrooms and chunks of cooked kabocha squash.

★

PACIFIC PUMPKIN RISOTTO

This simple formula for risotto, built upon a foundation of sautéed winter squash, owes less allegiance to its mixed cultural origins than it does to its place of origin, the West Coast. California-grown short-grain rice and Japanese pumpkin marry happily with a technique (and some cheese) born in Italy. When the last of the broth is almost absorbed, stir in a handful of grated Reggiano, and demand that everyone who is eating with you come at once. There is a moment when risotto is at its peak, and it must not be allowed to pass. If the cheese makes the grains look flat, stir in another tablespoon of butter to make them shine, and ask someone else to toss the salad. The light will sparkle off the surface of the risotto as you spoon it into shallow bowls.

MAKES 4 SERVINGS

1 tablespoon olive oil

1 to 2 tablespoons unsalted butter

1 medium onion, peeled and cut into ¼-inch dice

3 or 4 cloves garlic, thinly sliced

2 cups diced kabocha or other dense, sweet squash

1 cup short-grain rice, such as Tamaki Haiga

½ cup white wine

3 cups light chicken broth, boiling hot

½ cup grated Parmigiano-Reggiano

1. In a large, heavy saucepan or Dutch oven over medium-high heat, warm the olive oil and 1 tablespoon butter. When the butter is melted and sizzling, add the onion and sauté until it is soft and clear, about 5 minutes. Stir in the garlic and diced squash and cook until the squash is hot and just beginning to brown, another 5 minutes or so.

2. Stir in the rice and cook until the rice is translucent, about 1 minute.

3. Stir in the wine, and when it has boiled off, add ½ cup of the chicken broth. Stir until the broth is absorbed, then add another ½ cup broth. Continue stirring and slowly adding broth for 20 minutes, or until the rice and the pumpkin are tender.

4. When the last of the broth has been added, stir in the cheese and, if desired, the extra tablespoon of butter. Serve the risotto hot.

★

FENNEL RISOTTO

This risotto was conceived as a side dish for fish. I like to serve it with the Halibut Baked with a Glaze of Herbs on page 167. But the risotto also makes a lovely, clean, vegan main dish. Cheese seems superfluous. It is especially appealing in the early summer.

MAKES 4 SERVINGS

2 or 3 tablespoons olive oil

1 medium onion, peeled and cut into ¼-inch dice

1 fennel bulb

3 or 4 cloves garlic, thinly sliced

1 cup short-grain rice, such as Tamaki Haiga

½ cup white wine

2 tablespoons Pernod (optional)

3 cups vegetable broth or light chicken broth, boiling hot

1 tablespoon unsalted butter (optional)

1. In a large, heavy saucepan or Dutch oven over medium-high heat, warm 2 tablespoons olive oil. Add the onion and sauté until it is soft and clear, about 5 minutes.

2. While the onion is sautéing, cut the fennel bulb in half lengthwise, lay the two halves cut side down on the cutting board, and cut them into ¼-inch crescent-shaped slices. (Save the green fennel tops to make Fennel and Caper Aïoli [page 163] and to garnish the finished dish.) Stir the sliced fennel and garlic into the sautéed onion and cook until the fennel is hot and slightly translucent, about 3 minutes.

3. Stir in the rice and cook until the rice is translucent, about 1 minute.

4. Stir in the wine and the Pernod, if using, and when it has boiled off, add ½ cup of the broth. Stir until the broth is absorbed, then add another ½ cup.

Continue stirring and slowly adding broth until the rice is tender, about 20 minutes.

5. When the last of the broth has been added, stir in the last tablespoon of olive oil or the butter, if desired. Serve hot.

COCONUT RICE

Long-grain rice is less exacting than short-grain rice, at least the way I cook. I never wash it as vigorously as I do short-grain rice, and it seems to turn out fine nonetheless. And while I use short-grain rice almost exclusively as "plain rice," I often tweak long-grain rice by using broth or other liquids instead of water. I buy large bags of jasmine rice and use it for pilaf, Spanish rice, and various other rice dishes. This recipe is a favorite with Honey-Lemon Grilled Breasts of Chicken (pages 197–98) or Smoky Vanilla Pork Roast (pages 230–31).

MAKES 6 SERVINGS

2 cups basmati, jasmine, or other fragrant long-grain white rice

One 14-ounce can coconut milk

2 cups water

1. In a medium, heavy saucepan over medium-high heat, stir the rice with the coconut milk and water and bring the liquid to a boil. Cover the pan, reduce the heat to low, and simmer until the rice has absorbed the cooking liquid, about 30 minutes.

2. Stir the rice, re-cover the pan, and let the rice stand for at least 5 minutes before serving.

DOS PADRES-STYLE SPANISH RICE

At the Martinez family—owned Dos Padres restaurant in Bellingham, Washington, in the 1980s, we made this delectable Spanish rice, reminiscent of rice pilaf. Part of what made it so good was the homemade chicken broth that we made almost daily at the restaurant. If you use homemade broth, you will need to add salt to the dish; if you use canned broth, you probably won't.

MAKES 6 SERVINGS

2 cups jasmine or basmati rice

4 ounces (4 thick-sliced strips) good bacon

½ medium onion, peeled and finely chopped

2 cups puréed tomatoes

2 cups chicken broth

1 clove garlic, chopped

1 teaspoon dried oregano

1 teaspoon salt, or to taste

½ teaspoon freshly ground black pepper, or to taste

1. Preheat the oven to 350°F.

2. Rinse the rice in three changes of water, swishing it around in every rinse to remove as much starch as possible. Allow the rice to drain for 10 minutes.

3. Cut the raw bacon across the slices to make ¼-inch bits. Put the bacon bits in a heavy pan and place the pan over medium heat. Stir until the bacon bits are browned, about 5 minutes. Add the chopped onion and cook until the onion

is soft and translucent, about 5 minutes longer.

4. Add the puréed tomatoes, chicken broth, garlic, and oregano and stir until the mixture is boiling, then add the rice.

5. Transfer the mixture to a 2-quart casserole. Cover the dish with baker's parchment then with aluminum foil and bake for 30 minutes. Remove the foil and parchment and stir the rice to fluff it up. Serve at once or re-cover the rice and hold it in a warm (250°F) oven for up to one hour before serving.

⭐
ALCELMO'S SPANISH RICE

This incredibly fresh-tasting Spanish rice Alcelmo Gar-cía, one of my co-workers at Seattle's Canlis restaurant, used to make for restaurant family meals or crew chow. What made his Spanish rice so good was a purée of fresh tomatoes and onion that stood in for most of the water. When I saw the women who worked in the kitchen of an orphanage in Tijuana making Spanish rice in the same way as Alcelmo, I knew I had hit upon the authentic ver-sion of this quintessential Mexican dish.

MAKES 6 SERVINGS

2 cups basmati, jasmine, or other fragrant long-grain white rice

1 medium onion, peeled and coarsely chopped

1 tablespoon grated garlic

1 tablespoon dried oregano, crushed

3 medium (about 1 pound) ripe tomatoes

2 teaspoons kosher salt

1 bay leaf

½ cup finely chopped fresh parsley

1. Rinse the rice in several changes of cold water to wash off some of the starch. Let the rice drain in a strainer or a colander while you prepare the other ingredients.

2. Pile the onion, garlic, oregano, and tomatoes in a blender and purée until the vegetables are liquefied. Add enough water to bring the volume of the purée to 4 cups.

3. Pour the puréed tomato mixture into a heavy 3-quart saucepan with the salt and bay leaf and bring the liquid to a boil. Stir in the rinsed rice, cover the pan, reduce the heat to low, and simmer until the rice has absorbed the cooking liquid, about 30 minutes.

4. When the rice is cooked, stir in the chopped parsley, re-cover the pan, and let the rice stand for 5 minutes before serving.

⭐
FRAGRANT PINE NUT, CURRANT, AND SAFFRON PILAF

Pilaf is distinguished from other rice dishes by the tech-nique of sautéing the grains in oil or melted butter before any liquid is added. In this version, the oil is infused with the fragrance of toasted pine nuts. The rice itself has a warm popcorn fragrance. Onions, garlic, and white wine add their own aromatic notes, and the harmonizing presence of saffron pulls it all together. This dish leaves your home smelling like heaven on earth, and since it is completely vegan, it makes a wonderful dish for a dinner party where some guests might have aversions to foods containing animal products. Since the dish is assembled as it cooks, make sure all the ingredients are ready to go before you start cooking.

MAKES 6 SERVINGS

¼ cup olive oil

½ cup pine nuts

2 cups basmati, jasmine, or other fragrant long-grain white rice

I medium onion, peeled and finely chopped

I tablespoon chopped garlic

I cup dry white wine, sake, or vermouth

3 cups water

I tablespoon kosher salt

½ teaspoon saffron threads

½ cup dried currants

I. Warm the oil in a heavy 3-quart saucepan over medium heat and add the pine nuts. Stir until they release some of their fragrance and become lightly toasted. As soon as the pine nuts are golden brown, stir in the rice and sauté briefly, just until it is translucent. Add the onion and garlic and sauté until the vegetables are soft, about 5 minutes.

2. Pour in the white wine, water, and salt and bring the liquid to a boil. Sprinkle the saffron threads over the surface of the liquid and gently stir them in. Cover the pan, reduce the heat to low, and simmer until the rice has absorbed the cooking liquid, about 30 minutes.

3. Stir the currants into the cooked pilaf, re-cover the pan, and let the rice stand for at least 5 minutes so that the currants will soften.

SAN FRANCISCO–STYLE RICE PILAF

Like millions of other Americans of my generation, I was a victim of the myriad advertising campaigns that ran on national television during the 1960s. Their brain-numbing jingles continue to resound in my mind decades later. Among the many inane tunes is the one for Rice-a-Roni. According to the company's web site, the San Francisco treat was created by the DeDomenico family, who opened a pasta factory in San Francisco's Mission District in 1912. They changed the name to Golden Grain Macaroni Company in 1934 and intro-duced Rice-a-Roni in 1958, inspired by an Armenian neighbor's recipe for rice pilaf. The Quaker Oats Com-pany purchased Golden Grain in 1986. I loved the stuff when I was a child, but determined as a young adult that I could make a better version from scratch; I was right.

MAKES 6 SERVINGS

2 tablespoons unsalted butter

2 tablespoons olive oil

½ cup slivered almonds

1½ cups basmati, jasmine, or other fragrant long-grain white rice

4 ounces dried angel hair pasta or thin
spaghetti noodles

1 tablespoon chopped garlic

1 teaspoon dried thyme

1 cup dry white wine, sake, or vermouth

3 cups chicken broth, homemade (page 68)
or purchased

1 teaspoon kosher salt, or to taste

1 teaspoon freshly ground black pepper, or
to taste

1 bunch green onions, both white and green
parts, trimmed and chopped

¼ cup chopped fresh parsley

1. Melt the butter in the olive oil in a
large, heavy saucepan over medium-high
heat and add the slivered almonds. Stir
until they release some of their fragrance
and become lightly toasted. As soon as
the nuts are golden brown, stir in the
rice and sauté briefly, just until the rice is
translucent. Break the noodles into short
pieces, about 2 inches long, and stir them
into the rice mixture to sauté until they are
golden brown.

2. Add the garlic and thyme and sauté
until very fragrant, about 2 minutes.

3. Stir in the white wine and broth and
season to taste with salt and pepper. Bring
the liquid to a boil, then reduce the heat
to low and cover the pan. Simmer until
the rice has absorbed the cooking liquid,
about 30 minutes.

4. Stir the green onions and parsley into
the cooked pilaf and serve hot.

★

GOLD RUSH CORN MUSH

*Ever since chefs discovered polenta, the Italian name for
cornmeal mush, the old pioneer staple that had nearly
gone the way of the Conestoga wagons has been back
and better than ever. We should all be glad; polenta is
a delightful side dish. Serve it with browned sausages for
an easy family supper or with Ragoût of Duckling with
Fried Sage Leaves (page 211) for company.*

MAKES 6 SERVINGS

3 cups water

1 tablespoon kosher salt

1 cup stone-ground yellow cornmeal,
preferably whole grain

½ cup (1 stick) unsalted butter, cut into 2-
inch bits

1. Put the water and salt in a medium,
heavy saucepan over high heat, and when
the water is rapidly boiling, slowly stream
in the cornmeal, stirring all the while with
a wire whisk.

2. Reduce the heat to medium and
continue stirring, switching to a wooden
spoon as the mixture thickens, until the
grains have swelled and become tender,
about 15 minutes. Stir in the butter, cover
the pan, and keep the polenta warm until
serving time.

Beans

★

HOW TO COOK DRIED BEANS

Almost any dried beans, including kidney beans and garbanzo beans, can be cooked following this basic formula. White beans cooked in this manner can stand in favorably for rice or potatoes. Their interesting texture and subtle flavor make them a welcome change. Serve them as a side dish with pork, as a foundation for grilled fish, or as a main dish with Southern-Style Greens (page 246) and Skillet Cornbread (page 294).

MAKES 6 CUPS

6 cups water, plus more if needed

2 cups dried beans

1 or 2 bay leaves

1 tablespoon salt

1 ham bone or ham hock (optional)

1. In a large kettle over high heat, bring the water to a boil. Add the beans, bay leaves, and salt, and as soon as the water returns to a boil, turn off the heat. Cover the pan and leave undisturbed for 1 hour.

2. When the hour has passed, turn the burner on high and bring the beans to a boil. Add a ham bone or ham hock if you wish, then reduce the heat to medium-low.

3. Cook, stirring occasionally, for 1½ to 2 hours. Check the beans occasionally and add just enough water to keep them barely covered. When the beans are tender, serve them hot with their accompanying broth.

★

REFRIED PINTO BEANS

Refried beans have always been one of my favorite comfort foods, and I sometimes say that I could eat them every day and never get tired of them. When I was volunteering at an orphanage in Tijuana, I discovered that there, refried beans are indeed eaten every day, and no one ever seems to tire of them. Use the beans for Crispy Bean and Cheese Burritos (pages 122–23) or build a meal around the beans with Alcelmo's Spanish Rice (page 140) and Homemade Flour Tortillas (pages 298–99).

MAKES 6 SERVINGS

6 cups water, plus more if needed

1 tablespoon kosher salt

1 bay leaf

2 cups dried pinto beans

2 tablespoons unsalted butter or canola oil

1. Put the water, salt, and bay leaves in a large pot over high heat, and when the water is boiling hard, add the beans. Turn off the burner, cover the pot, and allow the beans to stand, undisturbed, for 1 hour.

2. Turn the heat on again, and when the liquid is boiling, reduce the heat to low. Simmer the beans until they are very tender, 1½ to 2 hours. If the beans begin to dry up, add more water.

3. In a large mixing bowl or right in the cooking pot, mash the beans with the butter or oil until they are smooth.

⭐

SAVORY GREEN LENTILS WITH AROMATIC VEGETABLES

Home cooks tend to think of lentils as the foundation for soup, but in restaurants, chefs are using lentils—and other beans—in place of other starches. The flavor and texture of these lentils go very well with Bronzed King Salmon (pages 161–62) or Wine Country Pan-Seared Breasts of Duckling with Peppered Zinfandel (pages 209–10).

MAKES 8 SERVINGS

6 cups water

1 bay leaf

1 tablespoon kosher salt

2 cups (1 pound) green lentils

¼ cup extra virgin olive oil

1 medium onion, peeled and cut into ¼-inch dice

2 carrots, peeled and cut into ¼-inch dice

2 stalks celery, cut into ¼-inch dice

½ cup finely chopped fresh parsley

Freshly ground black pepper, to taste

1. Put the water, bay leaf, and salt in a large soup pot over high heat and bring to a full, rolling boil. Add the lentils, cover the pan, and reduce the heat to low. Simmer the lentils until they are very tender, about 25 minutes.

2. Warm the olive oil in a large sauté pan over medium-high heat and sauté the onion, carrot, and celery until the vegetables are soft and beginning to brown, about 10 minutes.

3. When the lentils are tender, but not so tender that they are starting to fall apart, remove the bay leaf and stir in the sautéed vegetables. Simmer until the vegetables and lentils are very tender, about 10 minutes more.

4. Just before serving, stir in the parsley and season the lentils to taste with freshly ground black pepper.

Noodles and Pasta

⭐

HOMEMADE NOODLES

When I first started making homemade pasta, in the late 1970s, I learned by reading Marcella Hazan's instructions in More Classic Italian Cooking. *At the time, I had never seen real Parmigiano-Reggiano cheese, I had never tasted fresh basil or balsamic vinegar, and the only olive oil I had ever used was an occasional drizzle of the Pompeian brand classic that lived in my mother's spice cabinet. If I had heard the term "extra virgin," I probably would have laughed; I was, after all, still a teenager. But armed with Hazan's cookbook, I had the homemade pasta thing down. I like to imagine that I have streamlined the method somewhat, but it is basically the same as when I first started making it.*

For the Pasta

2 cups unbleached white flour

3 eggs, lightly beaten

For the Cooking Liquid

1 gallon water

2 tablespoons kosher salt

1. Pour the flour into the work bowl of a food processor and, with the motor running, add the lightly beaten eggs and pulse the motor off and on until the mixture comes together to form a fairly firm dough. If no food processor is available, simply pile the flour in a mound on a clean kitchen counter. Press a depression in the center of the mound to create a small "well." Pour the lightly beaten eggs into the well, then beat the eggs with a fork, gradually working in the surrounding flour to create a fairly firm dough.

2. On a lightly floured surface, knead the dough until it is very smooth and very elastic, about 8 minutes. Wrap the dough in plastic wrap or a damp, lint-free towel and set aside for at least 10 minutes; this will allow the gluten in the dough to relax.

3. Clean and dry the work surface, then sprinkle with flour. Roll the pasta into a large circle about ⅛ inch thick. Working quickly, to prevent the pasta from drying out, elongate the circle of dough into a rectangle by stretching it as you roll. Continue rolling and stretching the pasta until it is as thin as you can get it. You should have a rectangular sheet of pasta about 24 by 18 inches.

4. To make tagliatelle, or flat noodles, roll up the sheet of pasta, jelly roll style, and cut across the roll to make ribbons about ¼ inch wide.

5. To cook the pasta, put the water and salt in a large stockpot over high heat, and when the water comes to a full, rolling boil, stir in the noodles. Stir attentively to prevent the noodles from sticking together, and cook until just tender: As soon as the water returns to a boil, count to 10 and the noodles should be ready.

GREG'S BUTTERED NOODLES

When I asked Ruth Reichl to provide a menu based on recipes from her monumental Gourmet Cookbook, she suggested buttered noodles as an accompaniment to her oven-braised beef. I tried to find a recipe in The Gourmet Cookbook and discovered every other kind of noodle dish I could imagine, but not one for simple buttered noodles. Perhaps the dish is too simple to warrant a recipe, but whenever I used to offer buttered noodles as a complimentary entrée to young children who were intimidated by the very "grown-up" food I served at fine dining restaurants, their parents asked for the recipe. Stirring in a little of the water in which the noodles were cooked brings the butter and the residual starch left on the noodles together into a creamy sauce. Serve this noodle dish by itself with a pinch of chopped parsley or as a side dish with Versatile Baked Chicken (pages 185–86) or any grilled or roast meat.

1 gallon water

1 tablespoon kosher salt, plus more to taste

Homemade Noodles (pages 144–45), or 1 pound dried egg noodles

¼ cup (½ stick) unsalted butter

Freshly ground black pepper, to taste

2 tablespoons fresh parsley, chopped (optional)

Grated Parmesan cheese as an accompaniment (optional)

1. Bring the water and 1 tablespoon salt to a boil in a heavy, 6- to 8-quart pot. If you are using homemade egg noodles, cook according to the instructions on pages 144–45. If you are using dried noodles, stir them into the water and boil until they are just tender, about 10 minutes, depending on the brand. (Start checking the noodles for doneness after 7 or 8 minutes; some brands cook very quickly.) Drain the noodles, saving a little of the cooking water to toss with the noodles later.

2. Put the butter into the empty pot in which the noodles were boiled, and stir it around until it is melted. Toss the cooked noodles with the hot butter and stir in enough of the cooking liquid, a tablespoon at a time, to make a creamy sauce around the noodles.

3. Season to taste with salt and pepper and, if desired, fresh parsley. Pass the grated Parmesan separately.

★

MARIN COUNTY PASTA WITH BRIGHT GREEN BASIL PESTO

Quickly scanning a recipe for pesto that directed the cook to blanch the garlic in boiling water before adding it to the food processor, I mistakenly believed that the recipe instructed the cook to blanch the basil. "What a good idea!" I thought. I knew that a blast of heat destroys the enzyme that causes basil to turn black when it's cut or chopped, yielding a brighter green pesto. I was a little afraid that I might lose a lot of flavor, but I decided to give it a try anyway. To my surprise, the loss of flavor was minimal; in fact, without the vegetal smell of the black-ening leaves (think day-old grass clippings), the true aroma of fresh basil was better preserved than ever. I am now convinced that it's the best pesto I have ever eaten.

For the Pesto

4 ounces (¾ cup) pine nuts

4 ounces (1 cup packed) freshly grated Parmigiano-Reggiano cheese

1 (4-ounce) bunch fresh basil, preferably organic

1 tablespoon chopped garlic

1 teaspoon kosher salt, or to taste

½ teaspoon freshly ground black pepper, or to taste

½ cup extra virgin olive oil

For the Pasta

1 gallon water

1 tablespoon kosher salt, plus more to taste

Homemade Noodles (pages 144–45), or 1 pound dried egg noodles

Freshly ground black pepper, to taste

Grated Parmesan cheese as an accompaniment (optional)

1. Make the pesto. In a food processor, or a mortar and pestle, pulverize the pine nuts into fine powder, but don't grind them all the way into paste. Add the Parmigiano-Reggiano cheese to the pine nuts and continue to process the mixture until it becomes a crumbly mass.

2. Put a medium saucepan of water to boil on high heat. Pluck the leaves from the basil and discard the large stems. When the water is rapidly boiling, drop in the basil leaves. Give the leaves a quick stir and as soon as they are wilted, after about 30 seconds, drain the leaves and pile them into the food processor. Process to incorporate the basil into the pine nut mixture.

3. Add the garlic, salt, and pepper, and with the motor running, stream in the olive oil.

4. Bring the water and 1 tablespoon salt to a boil in a heavy, 6- to 8-quart pot. If you are using homemade egg noodles, cook according to the instructions on pages 144–45. If you are using dried noodles, stir them into the water and boil until they are just tender, about 10 minutes, depending on the brand. (Start checking the noodles for doneness after 7 or 8 minutes; some brands cook very quickly.) Drain the noodles and save a little of the cooking water to toss with the noodles later.

5. Put the pasta back into the pot in which it was boiled and stir in the pesto. Stir in enough of the cooking liquid, a tablespoon at a time, to make a creamy sauce around the noodles. Continue stirring until the pesto melts.

6. Season to taste with salt and pepper and serve hot. Pass the grated Parmesan separately.

PUMPKIN RAVIOLI

If you go to the trouble of making homemade pasta, you might as well make ravioli. This version is popular up and down the West Coast in the fall, especially in the small, unpretentious, owner-operated Italian restaurants that still somehow hold their own against the chain restaurants. All of us cooks who serve this dish think we "discovered" it, but it originated in the Emilia Romagna region of northern Italy, and it belongs to the collective unconscious. I don't know anyone who doesn't like it.

**MAKES 54 SMALL RAVIOLI, SERVING 4
AS AN ENTRÉE OR 6 AS AN APPETIZER**

2 pounds fresh pumpkin

1 tablespoon oil

1 cup grated Parmigiano-Reggiano cheese

1 teaspoon kosher salt

½ teaspoon freshly ground black pepper

¼ teaspoon freshly grated nutmeg

Homemade Noodles (pages 144–45), rolled out but not cut

½ cup (1 stick) unsalted butter

24 fresh sage leaves

1. Preheat the oven to 375°F. Cut the pumpkin into wedges, scoop out the seeds, and brush the inside of each wedge with oil. Bake until the flesh is easily pierced with a fork, about 50 minutes.

2. Scoop the cooked pumpkin out of its shell and stir or process it to make a smooth paste. Stir in the cheese, salt, pepper, and nutmeg. Chill the filling while you make the pasta.

3. Divide the sheet of pasta in half to get 2 rectangles, each measuring 12 by 18 inches. On one sheet of pasta, place rounded teaspoonfuls of the filling on every 2-inch square. You should have 6 rows of 9.

4. Use a damp finger or a pastry brush to moisten the pasta between the mounds of filling, then lay the second sheet of pasta over the filling and press firmly between the mounds to seal the little pillows of pasta. Use a pizza cutter or pastry wheel to cut between the rows.

5. Boil the ravioli in plenty of boiling salted water until it's just tender, about 4 minutes. Lift the cooked ravioli out of the boiling water with a large strainer. (If a two-part pasta cooking pot is available, cook the ravioli in the inside perforated pot.)

6. To serve the ravioli, melt the butter in a large sauté pan over medium-high heat. Fry the sage leaves in the melted butter and lift them out of the sizzling butter with a slotted spoon. Toss the hot ravioli with the butter, then garnish every serving with fried sage leaves.

★

OLYMPIC PASTA PRIMAVERA

This is a refreshing take on that old workhorse of the Italian restaurant known as pasta primavera, or spring-time pasta. For a quarter of a century or so, the term has referred almost exclusively to spaghetti with a mixture of fresh vegetables in a reduced cream sauce. This is because Craig Claiborne, the late restaurant critic for the New York Times, *codified a particular formula for a dish spontaneously thrown together by Sirio Maccioni, owner of Le Cirque restaurant in the mid-1970s. Before that, the term was nonspecific. In typically rebellious West Coast fashion, here's a bid to make the term "pasta primavera" nonspecific once again. With no cream, the pure, unadulterated flavors of fresh spring asparagus and wild morel mushrooms come through loud and clear. Since the cheese is passed separately, this dish is a good option if a vegan is at the table.*

MAKES 8 SERVINGS

1 gallon boiling water

2 tablespoons plus 2 teaspoons kosher salt

1 pound dried penne

1 pound fresh morel mushrooms, or 1 ounce dried

½ cup olive oil

1 bunch (1 pound) organically grown asparagus, trimmed

1 teaspoon freshly ground black pepper

4 cloves garlic, chopped

Grated Parmigiano-Reggiano cheese as an accompaniment

1. Put the water and 2 tablespoons salt in a large stockpot over high heat, and when the water comes to a full, rolling boil, add the pasta. Cook until the pasta is just tender, about 10 minutes. While the pasta is cooking, put a large strainer or colander over a large mixing bowl in the sink. When the pasta is cooked, drain it through the strainer or colander, saving some of the cooking water. Spread the drained penne out on a lightly oiled baking sheet and allow to cool for a few minutes while you prepare the other ingredients.

2. If you are using dried morels, put them in a heatproof measuring cup or a small mixing bowl and pour enough of the reserved cooking liquid over them to cover; press the mushrooms down with the back of a slotted spoon to help them absorb the liquid. Let them stand in the water to soften while you prepare the other ingredients.

3. Preheat the oven to 400°F. Put ¼ cup of the oil in a large mixing bowl; toss

the asparagus with the oil, then sprinkle it with the remaining 2 teaspoons salt and the pepper. Spread the asparagus in a single layer on a baking sheet lined with a nonstick liner and roast until the asparagus is hot and barely tender, about 5 minutes.

4. If you are using dried morels, drain them and lift them out of the soaking liquid, allowing any soil to sink to the bottom. Slice the morels into rings. (If you are using fresh mushrooms, simply slice them into rings without soaking.) In a large skillet over medium heat, sauté the sliced mushrooms with the remaining ¼ cup olive oil and the garlic until the mushrooms are heated through, about 5 minutes, then pour about ½ cup of the reserved pasta cooking liquid over them. (If you used dried morels, pour most of the soaking liquid into the skillet, being careful to leave any soil in the bottom of the cup.)

5. Toss the cooked pasta with the baked asparagus and sautéed morels. Serve hot, passing the grated Parmesan separately.

★

HIPPIE FARFALLE WITH PINE NUTS, CURRANTS, AND KALE

The Encarta World English Dictionary defines a hippie as "a young person, especially in the 1960s, who rejected accepted social and political values and proclaimed a belief in universal peace and love." This dish recalls the kinds of foods I ate during my own hippie days, when I rejected the unwritten law that real Americans were meat eaters and became a vegetarian. Farfalle is Italian for "butterfly," and the name refers to the pasta shape sometimes called bow tie noodles in English. The Italian name reminds me of the pretty white moths that wreak havoc on my cabbage plants but seem to leave the kale alone. This is a good pasta dish for midsummer, perfect for a vegetarian respite from too many meals based on meat. The cheese, passed separately, is optional. Serve the pasta with a green salad and Focaccia (pages 273–74).

MAKES 6 SERVINGS

1 gallon boiling water

2 tablespoons plus 2 teaspoons kosher salt, or to taste

1 pound dried penne

½ cup dried currants

1 bunch (1 pound) kale, preferably organically grown

½ cup olive oil

½ cup pine nuts

4 cloves garlic, peeled and thinly sliced

1 teaspoon freshly ground black pepper, or to taste

Grated Parmesan cheese as an accompaniment (optional)

1. Put the water and 2 tablespoons salt in a large stockpot over high heat, and when the water comes to a full, rolling boil, add the pasta. Cook until the pasta is just tender, about 10 minutes, then drain it through a large strainer or a colander, saving a cup of the cooking water to pour over the dried currants. Spread the drained penne out on a lightly oiled baking sheet and allow to cool for a few minutes while you prepare the other ingredients. The pasta can be prepared ahead up to this point and finished later.

2. In a small bowl, pour the reserved cup of pasta water over the dried currants; let them stand in the water to soften while you prepare the other ingredients.

3. Cut the kale into a chiffonade. Roll the leaves into a cigarlike bundle, and with a large, sharp knife cut across the bundle in a rocking motion to produce ribbons about ⅛ inch wide.

4. Put the oil in a large sauté pan over medium-high heat and cook the pine nuts in the oil until they are fragrant and just beginning to brown, about 2 minutes. (Watch closely; pine nuts burn quickly.) Add the sliced garlic and sauté until it is bubbling hot but not browned. Add the kale and sauté for 2 minutes, or until it is wilted.

5. Drain the currants and add them to the sautéed kale mixture, then toss the hot greens with the cooked pasta, season to taste with salt and pepper, and serve, passing the grated Parmesan separately.

★
FETTUCCINE WITH CHICKEN, CREAM, AND TARRAGON

With a salad and some good, crusty bread, this pasta makes a great main dish that comes together in under a half an hour. I originally prepared it as a restaurant family meal for the staff at a small café where I worked in Friday Harbor on Washington's San Juan Island, but the crew there convinced me that the dish was too good for the back of the house, and eventually it found its way onto the menu in the dining room. The owner of the restaurant had a sort of "farm," really just a couple of pretty acres devoted to raising a cow and some vegetables. That rich cow's milk yielded wonderful cream, which I used in dishes like this one. Pasteurized organic cream is a good alternative.

MAKES 6 SERVINGS

I gallon boiling water

I tablespoon plus 2 teaspoons kosher salt

I pound dried fettuccine

3 boneless, skinless free-range chicken breast halves, 6 ounces each

3 tablespoons unsalted butter

4 cloves garlic, chopped

I teaspoon freshly ground black pepper

I tablespoon fresh tarragon leaves, or I teaspoon dried

I½ cups heavy cream, preferably organic

Tarragon sprigs, for garnish (optional)

Grated Parmigiano-Reggiano cheese as an accompaniment

I. Put the water and I tablespoon salt in a large stockpot over high heat, and when the water comes to a full, rolling boil, add the pasta. Cook until it is just tender, about 10 minutes, then drain. Spread the drained pasta on a lightly oiled baking sheet large enough to accommodate the cooked pasta in a single layer, and allow it to air-dry for a few minutes while you prepare the other ingredients. (The pasta can be cooked several hours ahead and held on the baking sheet, refrigerated, under plastic wrap.)

2. Cut the chicken into I-inch pieces. Melt the butter in a large sauté pan over medium-high heat, add the chicken, and sauté it, moving the pieces around, until they are no longer visibly pink and are just beginning to brown, about 5 minutes.

3. Stir in the garlic, remaining 2 teaspoons salt, and pepper and cook for about I minute longer, but don't let the garlic brown. Add the tarragon leaves and cream and boil until the cream is reduced to about half of its original volume and is slightly thickened.

4. Toss the cooked pasta with the hot sauce. Serve hot, garnished with tarragon sprigs, and pass the grated Parmigiano-Reggiano separately.

TURKEY TETRAZZINI

According to the wisdom of the web and Gourmet *magazine editor Ruth Reichl, chicken Tetrazzini was created by the chef at the Palace Hotel in San Francisco in 1908 and was named for the Italian soprano Luisa Tetrazzini. But the century-old dish has taken a beating over the years, especially when it was tweaked during the mid-twentieth century to become a vehicle for canned mushroom soup. Tetrazzini has become the quintessential way to use up leftover Thanksgiving turkey. Made from scratch, the dish is delectable and worthy of its popularity and of some rehabilitation.*

MAKES 6 SERVINGS

¼ cup (½ stick) unsalted butter

1 pound fresh mushrooms, sliced

2 tablespoons flour

2 cups chicken broth, homemade (page 68) or purchased

½ cup heavy cream

¼ cup dry sherry

2 teaspoons kosher salt, or to taste

1 teaspoon freshly ground black pepper, or to taste

¼ teaspoon freshly grated nutmeg

¼ cup chopped fresh parsley

3 cups cooked turkey chunks (tear skinned, boned turkey into bite-size pieces)

8 ounces dried spaghetti, cooked until tender in salted water

For the Topping

1 cup fresh breadcrumbs

½ cup grated Parmesan cheese

¼ cup (½ stick) unsalted butter, melted

1. Preheat the oven to 350°F and butter a 2-quart baking dish. (The casserole looks best in a ceramic oval.)

2. Melt the butter in a large sauté pan over medium-high heat and cook the mushrooms until they are just tender, about 4 minutes. Sprinkle the flour over the mushrooms and stir in the chicken broth, cream, and sherry. Cook and stir until the mixture boils and starts to thicken.

3. Stir in the salt and pepper, and taste for seasoning. Then stir in the nutmeg and parsley. Stir the turkey and cooked spaghetti into the mushroom sauce and transfer the mixture to the buttered baking dish.

4. For the topping, combine the breadcrumbs with the Parmesan cheese and butter and scatter the mixture over the noodles. Bake until the topping is golden brown and the filling is bubbling around the edges, 30 to 35 minutes.

CHINESE NOODLES WITH SHIITAKE MUSHROOMS

Chow mein, Chinese for "stir-fried noodles," is a dish that has been a part of West Coast cooking for more than a century. *Basically a dish of fried noodles with seasonal vegetables and sometimes meat, it has led, for most of its tenure here, a kind of double life. In* Easy Family Recipes from a Chinese-American Childhood, *San Francisco–based food writer Ken Hom writes, "In the American version the noodles are deep-fried in advance into crispy morsels, which are then allowed to dry." In the Chinese version, served only on the "secret menu" at most Chinese restaurants, egg noodles are first cooked in boiling water and then tossed in hot oil with vegetables. While not particularly authentic to any one version, this noodle dish pays a certain homage to Chinese home cooking. Rose brand Chinese noodles, which I buy from Tsue Chong Company in Seattle's international district, are sold both fresh and dried and are widely distributed on the West Coast.*

MAKES 6 SERVINGS

1 gallon water

2 tablespoons kosher salt

12 ounces fine-cut Chinese wheat noodles, fresh or dried

2 ounces (about 2 cups) dried sliced shiitake mushrooms, or 1 pound fresh shiitake mushrooms

1 medium onion

3 tablespoons peanut or canola oil

1 tablespoon toasted sesame oil

1-inch piece ginger root, grated on a Microplane grater

4 cloves garlic, grated on a Microplane grater

⅓ cup soy sauce

1 bunch green onions, cut into ⅛-inch slices

1. Put the water and salt in a large stockpot over high heat, and when the water comes to a full, rolling boil, add the Chinese noodles. Cook until the noodles are just tender, about 5 minutes (Chinese noodles cook more quickly than Italian-style pasta noodles). While the noodles are cooking, put a large strainer or colander over a large mixing bowl in the sink, and when the noodles are cooked, drain them through the strainer or colander, saving some of the cooking water. Spread the drained noodles out on a lightly oiled baking sheet and allow them to cool for a few minutes while you prepare the other ingredients.

2. If you are using dried mushrooms, put them in a heatproof measuring cup or small mixing bowl and pour enough of the reserved cooking liquid over them to cover; press the mushrooms down with the back of a slotted spoon to help them absorb the liquid. Let them stand in the water to soften while you prepare the other ingredients. (If you are using fresh shiitake, remove the stems and cut the caps into ½-inch-thick slices; discard the stems.) Dried shiitake will soak up almost all the water in which they are soaked in about 5 minutes.

3. Peel the onion, cut it in half lengthwise, and cut each half into ¼-inch slices.

4. Warm the peanut oil and sesame oil in a wok or a large sauté pan over high heat, and stir-fry the ginger and garlic until very fragrant, about 30 seconds. Add the sliced onion and stir-fry until it is soft and beginning to brown, about 3 minutes. Add the mushrooms and stir-fry until they are heated through. Toss in the cooked noodles and the soy sauce, and when the noodles are lightly coated with the sauce and heated through, toss in the green onions. Serve hot.

★

DEAD HEAD PAD THAI

Before he settled down and became a stockbroker and financial planner, my wife's cousin Bob, who stood up for me as a groom's man at our wedding, worked at various odd and colorful jobs. For years, he was a housepainter. And for a while, during the early 1980s, he used to follow the Grateful Dead concert tours, pulling a trailer equipped with a rudimentary kitchen. In the trailer, he made and sold pad thai, which he served with Bob's Hot Habanero Shake. Bob's noodles were my introduction to the phenomenon that is Thai food. I never got his recipe, but after years of carefully dissecting the dish and studying other recipes, I have finally developed one that comes close. I decided to forgo the habanero shake in favor of a few dried red chile flakes.

MAKES 4 SERVINGS

For the Noodles

8 ounces dried rice stick noodles

4 cups hot tap water

For the Sauce

⅔ cup tamarind purée (page 14), or ⅓ cup lime juice plus ⅓ cup water

3 tablespoons brown sugar

3 tablespoons fish sauce

1 tablespoon rice vinegar

2 teaspoons dried red chile flakes

2 tablespoons peanut or canola oil

For the Omelet

3 large eggs

½ teaspoon kosher salt

2 tablespoons peanut or canola oil

4 cloves garlic, grated on a Microplane grater

1-inch piece ginger root, grated on a Microplane grater

For the Garnish

3 cups bean sprouts

½ cup chopped roasted, salted peanuts

1 bunch green onions, white and green parts only, cut into ⅛-inch slices

¼ cup loosely packed cilantro leaves

Lime wedges

1. Cover the rice sticks with the hot tap water in a large bowl; soak until the noodles are barely tender, about 20 minutes. Drain the noodles and keep them close to the stove.

2. In a measuring cup or small mixing bowl, whisk together the ingredients for the sauce and keep it near the stove.

3. Make the omelet. In a small bowl, beat the eggs with the salt. Preheat a large sauté pan over medium-high heat. Put the oil in the pan and swirl the pan to coat it with the oil. Sauté the garlic and ginger until fragrant, about 1 minute, then pour in the eggs. When the eggs begin to set, stir gently with a heatproof silicone or wooden spatula until they are cooked through, about 2 minutes.

4. Add the drained noodles to the eggs and toss with a heatproof silicone or wooden spatula until the noodles and eggs are evenly distributed. Pour the sauce mixture over the noodles and eggs, increase the heat to high, and cook, tossing constantly, until the noodles are evenly coated.

5. Add the bean sprouts, half the peanuts, and half the green onions. Continue to cook, tossing constantly, until the sprouts are heated through and the noodles are tender, about 3 minutes.

6. Transfer to a serving platter, and sprinkle with the remaining peanuts and green onions and the cilantro. Serve hot, passing the lime wedges separately.

chapter 8

Grilled Copper River Salmon with Rhubarb and Ginger Chutney
Bronzed King Salmon with Apple Cider Butter Sauce
Pacific Ponzu Salmon
Cedar Planked Salmon with Fennel and Caper Aïoli
Pan-Seared Alaska Halibut with Shiitake and Lemon
Slow-Cooked Alaska Halibut with Spring Vegetables
Beer-Battered Alaska Halibut
Halibut Baked with a Glaze of Herbs
Alaska Halibut Baked with Stone-Ground Mustard Glaze on a Bed of
  Spring Greens
Halibut Baked in Parchment with Fresh Fennel
Grilled or Seared Rare Ahi
Grilled Tuna Steaks with Papaya Lime Panache
Crisp Petrale Sole with Caper and Shallot Sauce
Pioneer Pan-Fried Trout with Sautéed Mustard Greens
Portland Pan-Fried Trout in Hazelnut Crust with Apple Cider Sauce
Pescado à la Vera Cruz
Scallops with Artichokes and Orange Butter Sauce
Canlis Dungeness Crab Cakes
Gulf Prawns, Pan-Sautéed with Red Chiles and Lime
Grilled Australian Lobster Tails with Tamarind Butter

FISH & SEAFOOD

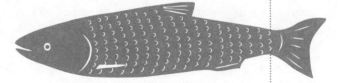

Fish & Seafood

It is impossible for me to think about West Coast seafood without thinking about seafood guru Jon Rowley. I first learned about Jon when he was promoting Copper River salmon some years ago, single-handedly generating enough hype to create a bona fide regional cultural event, "The Return of the Copper River Kings," generating a national buzz that continues to this day, some twenty years after it began. I first wrote about him when he helped a Seattle supermarket secure the first truly tree-ripened peaches I had ever seen in a grocery store. And once, a few years after I started paying attention to his projects, I joined forces with our mutual friend Jerry Traunfeld, the chef at the Herbfarm restaurant, to cook at one of Jon's legendary Umami luncheons.

Before the word became inextricably linked with the "fifth" taste, a meaty taste associated with glutamates, Jon promoted a broader understanding of *umami* to mean something closer to its Japanese roots. The characters in Japanese that form the word mean literally "beautiful" and "taste," but the term is used in Japanese to describe anything that is at its moment of ripeness and perfection; a potentially profitable stock option, for instance, can be said to have great *umami*. At the event at the Herbfarm, we gathered ingredients at the height of their season and prepared a lunch. We started by picking strawberries in a strawberry field; four hours and four courses later we served strawberry shortcakes.

These days, Jon provides scrutiny of seafood-related articles and recipes for *Gourmet* magazine, so I asked Ruth Reichl, the editor-in-chief at *Gourmet*, to share a few thoughts about my friend. She fired back an e-mail that said, in part, "I have so much to say about Jon that it's hard to do . . . Julia Child used to call him the fish missionary, and he's taught me so much about buying, cooking and eating fish that I hardly know where to begin. He's incredibly passionate, knowledgeable and smart—not to mention endearing—and he's part of the reason why people in this country eat more fish than they used to."

I have known Jon Rowley for a good long time now, and though I count him and his wife, Kate, among my very best friends, I'm sometimes frustrated with him. He is so very thorough and methodical about everything he does, so exacting, that I sometimes feel not just spontaneous beside him, but reckless and crazy.

Jon is more than a seafood expert; he is a passionate connoisseur. An old-fashioned polymath, he is as obsessive about produce and, for that matter, books and compost as he is about salmon. It's hard to imagine anyone so laid back, so completely relaxed in his own skin as Jon is, as being obsessive about anything. But he is.

For a while, his passions were directed mainly at the composting bins at a community garden known locally as a pea patch near his home in Seattle. He experimented and refined his methods of composting until he earned himself a master composter certification. (Since 1986, the Seattle Tilth Community Composting Education Program has trained more than 200 master composters.) Then he promoted his efforts by offering food writers and community leaders an opportunity to have a compost bin named after themselves at the pea patch. If the wooden boards surrounding it have not disintegrated, there's one there named after me.

He and Kate were married at about that time, and they asked that in lieu of more traditional gifts, invitees send elements to be added to their compost pile. Among the "2 cubic yards of carefully selected garbage" that they accumulated were a case of "inadequate peaches," sent by *Vogue* food columnist Jeffrey Steingarten, and 25 pounds of fresh buffalo dung from Colorado. Along with her best wishes, Julia Child sent a nicely wrapped banana peel.

When Seattleites spontaneously decided to deposit a ton of flowers, one small bouquet at a time, at a fountain at Seattle Center in response to the terrorist attacks on the World Trade Center in the fall of 2001, it was Jon Rowley who came along afterward and unwrapped the dead flowers, separated them from the ribbons and plastic, and turned them into compost for the garden at the pea patch.

Jon is a kind of frontier bon vivant, a Johnny Appleseed of sorts who spreads seeds of understanding wherever he goes. He shows up now and then at my kitchen door with mussels or leeks or wine and stays for dinner. He insists that mussels be cooked first in a dry pan, for instance, so that the first of their juices will escape, caramelize, and evaporate before they eventually release enough juice to steam themselves open. Once one has witnessed Jon perform one of these unnervingly exacting and fussy stunts, and tasted the results, it is impossible ever to go back to doing things the old, easy, less flavorful way.

In Reichl's e-mail, she went on, "Years ago, when I was at the *L. A. Times*, I got him to come lead us on a tour of supermarkets and show us how to buy fish. I thought it would be a couple of hours; 9 hours later, I cried uncle. But it was an amazing day, and one of my favorite articles, ever, came out of it." Days with Jon are like that. I end up crying uncle, but good things always come out of the experience.

★

GRILLED COPPER RIVER SALMON WITH RHUBARB AND GINGER CHUTNEY

Very often, West Coast chefs forgo the usual dicta of tradition. Instead of relying on the arsenal of sauces developed over hundreds of years in France and codified a century ago by August Escoffier, we make up our own sauces as the seasons and our own caprice dictate. This can be silly and unfortunate at times, but it can also be revelatory. In one of my fits of regional loyalty, I decided to forgo lemons on my menu because lemons did not grow within a hundred miles of where I lived. To get a tangy counterpoint to rich salmon, I reached instead for the rhubarb growing in my own backyard. Rhubarb, which comes into season at the same time as the coveted Copper River kings, has a refreshing astringent quality that complements this rich seafood beautifully. It has since become something of a tradition—at least in the kitchens upon which I have had some influence—to serve rhubarb with Copper River salmon. If you have a bumper crop of rhubarb, make the chutney on page 401 and enjoy this dish any time you like. Grilled asparagus and M. F. K. Fisher's "Shook" Potatoes (pages 238–39) are good accompaniments.

MAKES 4 SERVINGS

For the Chutney

2 stalks (about 2 cups) rhubarb, chopped

½ cup chopped crystallized ginger

¼ cup sugar

¼ cup raspberry vinegar

I teaspoon salt

For the Salmon

4 fillets Copper River salmon or other wild king salmon, 7 ounces each, skin removed

2 teaspoons kosher salt

I teaspoon freshly ground black pepper

2 tablespoons light olive oil or corn oil

I. Preheat a gas or charcoal grill until the heat from the grill forces you to move your hand away when you hold it 5 inches above the grate. The charcoal should be burned down to white-hot coals.

2. While the coals are getting hot, make the chutney. In a nonreactive (stainless steel or enameled) saucepan over medium-high heat, stir together the rhubarb, crystallized ginger, sugar, raspberry vinegar, and salt. Cook, stirring, until the sugar is dissolved and the mixture is beginning to boil. Cover, reduce the heat to low, and cook until the rhubarb is very tender and beginning to disintegrate, 6 to 8 minutes. Serve the chutney at once or keep it, covered and refrigerated, for several days.

3. Grill the salmon. Wipe the grill with a cloth dipped in olive oil, or spray it with an oil mister. Position the grill 4 inches above the bed of the glowing coals and wipe it with an oily cloth. Sprinkle the fillets with the salt and pepper and rub with the oil.

4. Place the fillets, skinned side up, on the rack and grill for 5 minutes. If the oil ignites, cool the flames with a little water splashed from a cup or streamed from a squirt gun. With a long spatula, turn the fillets once and grill for 5 minutes more. Transfer to a warm platter or serving plates, and serve with the chutney.

⭐

BRONZED KING SALMON WITH APPLE CIDER BUTTER SAUCE

A "dry brine" of salt, sugar, and pepper, rinsed off before the salmon is cooked, gives salmon a crisp and flavorful edge. The cooking is a two-step process of searing and then baking, and if a cook wants to get as much done in advance as possible, the process can be interrupted halfway through. Apple cider butter sauce, a variation on the classic beurre blanc, is the ideal accent. Serve this salmon over a bed of Savory Green Lentils with Aromatic Vegetables (page 144).

MAKES 4 SERVINGS

For the Salmon

4 fillets wild king salmon, 7 ounces each, with skin

2 tablespoons sugar

1 tablespoon kosher salt

1 teaspoon freshly ground black pepper

2 tablespoons canola oil

For the Sauce

¼ cup apple cider

¼ cup apple cider vinegar

1 tablespoon sugar

2 tablespoons heavy cream

1 cup (2 sticks) cold unsalted butter, cut into ½-inch bits

1. Use a pair of tweezers or hemostats to remove any pin bones in the salmon. Mix the sugar, salt, and pepper and rub this mixture over the top surface of each piece of salmon. Allow the salmon to sit with this coating in the refrigerator for at least 1 hour or for as long as 3 hours.

2. Rinse the dry brine off the salmon and pat each portion dry with paper towels. Warm the oil in a large sauté pan over medium-high heat and cook the salmon, skin side up, in the oil until it forms a bronze crust and slips easily from the bottom of the pan, about 5 minutes. Transfer the salmon from the sauté pan to a baking sheet with a ½-inch rim. When all the salmon pieces are "bronzed," they can be finished at once, held at room temperature for up to half an hour, or kept in the refrigerator for several hours.

3. Make the sauce. In a saucepan over high heat, boil the apple cider with the cider vinegar and sugar until most of the liquid has evaporated and only a couple of tablespoons of syrupy essence remain. Add the cream to the reduced mixture, and when it is boiling rapidly, start adding the butter, a few bits at a time, whisking well after each addition. When all the butter is added, remove the pan from the burner and keep the sauce warm until serving time.

4. To finish the fillets, preheat the oven to 450°F and bake the salmon until it's sizzling and just cooked through, about 5 minutes.

5. To serve, slip a spatula between the salmon fillet and the skin, which should be stuck fast to the baking sheet. If some of

the skin comes off the pan with the salmon, pull it gently from the fillet. Serve hot.

★

PACIFIC PONZU SALMON

Ponzu is a light Japanese sauce made from dashi, the classic broth made with kombu and bonito flakes, and yuzu, a citrus fruit that is almost impossible to find in the United States. Bottled yuzu juice is available, but it tastes and smells more like the sodium benzoate with which it is preserved than anything else. This sauce is more concentrated and far more intense than a classic Japanese ponzu, which is quite delicate; a little, in fact, goes a long way. But I think it matches the bold style of West Coast cooking. Serve the salmon with Japanese-Style Short-Grain Rice (pages 134–35) and Baby Bok Choy (page 251).

MAKES 6 SERVINGS

For the Ponzu Sauce

1 grapefruit

1 orange

1 lime

¼ cup sugar

¼ cup soy sauce

¼ cup rice vinegar

For the Fish

6 salmon fillets, 7 ounces each

1 teaspoon fine sea salt

2 tablespoons vegetable oil

1. Make the ponzu sauce. Use a zester (a special tool for removing the outer rind of citrus fruits) to remove the colorful outer rind from the grapefruit, orange, and lime; set the zest aside. If you don't have a zester, use a vegetable peeler to remove the zest, then cut it into julienne strips with a sharp knife. Juice the fruits and combine the juices.

2. Put the sugar in a dry pan over medium-high heat and swirl the pan until the sugar has dissolved. It will be caramel colored. Pour in the fruit juice and step back; the mixture will boil and steam rapidly, then settle into a steady boil. Boil for about 2 minutes, swirling the pan now and then to dissolve the caramelized sugar.

3. When the caramelized sugar has dissolved, add the soy sauce and vinegar. Drop in half of the citrus zest that you set aside, and continue boiling the sauce until it is slightly thickened, 1 or 2 minutes. Save the remaining citrus zest for garnish.

4. Pat the salmon fillets dry and sprinkle with the sea salt. Put a large, nonstick skillet over medium-high heat and allow the pan to preheat for 1 minute. Put the oil in the pan; it should be almost smoking hot.

5. Put 2 or 3 of the salmon fillets into the pan, skin side up, and allow the salmon to cook, undisturbed, until a crisp brown crust has formed on the fleshy side of the fish, 4 to 5 minutes. With a fish spatula, lift the fillets out of the pan and set them

skin side down on an ungreased baking sheet. Repeat with the remaining fillets. The salmon and sauce can be prepared ahead up to this point and finished just before serving.

6. Preheat the oven to 400°F and bake the seared salmon fillets until the fish is heated through and the fillets slip easily off their skins, about 5 minutes.

7. Make a puddle of ponzu sauce in the center of each of 6 plates and set a fillet on top of each. Garnish with the reserved zest from the grapefruit, orange, and lime.

★

CEDAR PLANKED SALMON WITH FENNEL AND CAPER AÏOLI

Even though it's something of a West Coast tradition, especially in western Washington, where I live, I thought salmon cooked on a cedar plank was gimmicky until I tried it for myself. When I first started cooking at the environmental learning center known as IslandWood, I came into a surplus of cedar shakes left over from the construction of the buildings. I discovered that aromatic cedar shakes or planks do indeed make ideal baking and serving trays for salmon. The skin sticks to the plank, and when the salmon is fully cooked, a spatula slips easily between the salmon and its skin. Look for cedar shakes or planks at a building supply store; they cost a lot less than the fancy planks sold at cooking supply stores. Serve the salmon with the Fennel Risotto (pages 138–39).

For the Fennel and Caper Aïoli

2 egg yolks

1 tablespoon freshly grated lemon zest

2 tablespoons lemon juice

1 tablespoon garlic, finely chopped or grated

1 teaspoon kosher salt

¼ teaspoon ground white pepper

2 cups pure olive oil, not extra-virgin

2 tablespoons fresh fennel leaves, finely chopped

2 tablespoons capers, drained and chopped

For the Salmon

4 sockeye salmon fillets, about 6 ounces each, with skin

1 teaspoon fine sea salt

1. Make the aïoli. In a food processor, whip egg yolks, lemon zest, lemon juice, garlic, salt, and white pepper for about 1 minute, or until mixture is very thoroughly combined.

2. With the motor running, slowly stream in the oil, starting with just a few drops of oil at a time, then building to a slow but steady stream until all the oil is incorporated.

3. Stir the fennel leaves and capers into the sauce and transfer the sauce to a serving dish.

4. Preheat the oven to 400°F. Rinse the salmon fillets, pat them dry, and place them skin side down on a cedar plank or shingle. Sprinkle with sea salt.

5. Put the cedar plank on the top rack in the oven and set a baking sheet on a lower rack to catch any drips. Roast until a pale brown crust has formed on the surface of the fish and white spots have begun to appear on the sides of the fillets, about 10 minutes.

6. Serve the salmon directly from the plank, passing a bowl of Fennel and Caper Aïoli separately.

★

PAN-SEARED ALASKA HALIBUT WITH SHIITAKE AND LEMON

Although it's not heralded with the same hysteria that accompanies salmon season, halibut season is a time of quiet rejoicing in professional kitchens around the Pacific Northwest. Halibut is so easy to cook! Simply grilled and garnished with a squeeze of lemon, it sells like crazy in restaurants, and guests never complain, because spring halibut has a certain texture and flavor that always pleases people. One of my sons claims not to like fish, but even he likes halibut. My other son, who loves all things from the sea, devours halibut with an enthusiasm that most kids reserve for sweets. When I posted this recipe on my web site, it received a record number of hits. Serve it with Japanese-Style Short-Grain Rice (pages 134–35) and any green vegetable.

4 halibut fillets, 7 to 8 ounces each and about ½ inch thick

2 teaspoons sea salt

1 teaspoon ground white pepper

¼ cup olive oil

8 ounces fresh shiitake mushrooms

2 tablespoons naturally brewed soy sauce

2 tablespoons freshly squeezed lemon juice

1. Sprinkle the halibut with the sea salt and white pepper. Put a skillet large enough to accommodate the 4 fillets in a single layer over medium-high heat and add the olive oil. When the oil is hot, lay the halibut fillets in the oil with their good-looking side down. Cook without disturbing for 3 minutes, or until the fillets are golden brown on the underside. Flip them over, reduce the heat to medium, and cook until the fish is just cooked through, about 4 minutes more.

2. While the halibut is cooking, pull the stems off the shiitake caps and cut the caps into ½-inch slices; discard the stems. Transfer the cooked halibut to 4 dinner plates and briefly brown the sliced shiitake caps in the oil left behind.

3. Add the soy sauce and lemon juice and stir for 30 seconds or so to pick up any flavorful bits clinging to the pan. Pour the shiitakes with the surrounding sauce over the fillets, and serve hot.

SLOW-COOKED ALASKA HALIBUT WITH SPRING VEGETABLES

Typically, halibut is cooked quickly—pan-seared, broiled, or baked in a very hot oven—but slowing things down can bring on some interesting results. My friend Sharon Kramis taught me the trick I use here, in which the halibut is packed into an oven-safe dish just large enough to hold it and then covered in olive oil and slowly brought up to temperature. In a slow (300°F) oven, it takes about half an hour for the fish to cook through, but watch it closely because if the oven is hotter than that, the fish could overcook. The oil used to bake the fish becomes an aïoli-like sauce.

MAKES 4 SERVINGS

For the Halibut

4 halibut fillets, 7 to 8 ounces each

3 teaspoons sea salt

1 teaspoon ground white pepper

¾ cup olive oil

For the Vegetables

4 blue potatoes, peeled and cut into ½-inch slices

2 carrots, peeled and cut into large julienne strips

1 medium yellow beet, peeled and cut into 1-inch cubes

8 ounces snap peas

Pea vines, for garnish, if available

For the Sauce

1 egg yolk

4 cloves garlic, finely grated

1 tablespoon freshly squeezed lemon juice

1. Preheat the oven to 300°F. Sprinkle the halibut fillets with 2 teaspoons of the sea salt and the white pepper and place them in a baking dish just large enough to hold them in a single layer (a 1-quart oval works well). Pour the olive oil over the fish and bake until the fish registers 145°F on an instant-read thermometer, about 30 minutes. When the fish is ready, transfer it to a warm platter and tent with parchment or foil to keep it warm.

2. While the fish is baking, cook the potatoes, carrots, and beets in batches in a large pot of boiling salted water, just until they are fork-tender, about 8 minutes for the potatoes, 10 minutes for the beets, and 5 minutes for the carrots. Cook the peas in the same water for 3 minutes. As the vegetables are cooked, lift them out of the water and hold them on a baking sheet.

3. Put the egg yolk, garlic, lemon juice, and remaining 1 teaspoon sea salt in a blender and run the motor until the mixture is light and smooth. With the motor running, slowly stream in the oil in which the halibut was baked.

4. If the vegetables are cold, pop them in the oven for a moment to warm them up. Distribute them evenly among 4 plates, then set a halibut fillet in the center of

each plate and spoon a dollop of the sauce on top of each fillet. Garnish with pea vines and serve at once.

⭐

BEER-BATTERED ALASKA HALIBUT

Because it contains bubbles of carbon dioxide that expand in the heat of the fryer, beer makes an excellent frying batter that cooks up light and crisp. The residual flavors of hops and malt lend the fried food character. I like to use a beer that has a pronounced flavor, such as the slightly sweet Alaskan Amber Ale. Made with pure water from the 1,200-square-mile Juneau ice fields, the beer is based on a hundred-year-old recipe; it's richly malted and well balanced with bitter hops. It almost seems wasteful to put this beer into a batter, but it's not. Serve the fried fish with Sweet Potato Home Fries (page 244) and West Coast Cole Slaw (pages 108–9), and some of the same beer to drink, or use the fish fillets in the sandwiches described on page 118.

MAKES 6 SERVINGS

For the Halibut

Rice bran or canola oil, for frying

2 pounds halibut fillet, cut into 6 pieces

1 teaspoon sea salt, or 2 teaspoons kosher salt

½ teaspoon freshly ground black pepper

For the Beer Batter

2 eggs

One 12-ounce bottle beer or ale such as Alaskan Amber

2 cups unbleached white flour

1½ teaspoons baking powder

½ teaspoon sea salt, or 1 teaspoon kosher salt

1. Preheat the oven to 250°F. Line a baking sheet with a brown paper bag or some paper towels so it will be ready to receive the fish when it's fried. Put about 3 inches of oil in a medium cast-iron skillet or deep, heavy saucepan over high heat to get hot. When the oil reaches 375°F on a thermometer, or when a drop of the beer batter floats immediately to the surface and swims across the surface of the oil, bubbling all the way, it's ready.

2. While the oil is heating, make the beer batter. In a large bowl, whisk together the eggs and beer. In a separate bowl, combine the flour, baking powder, and salt. Add the flour mixture to the egg mixture and whisk until well combined.

3. Sprinkle the fish fillets with the salt and pepper, then dip them in the beer batter and fry, 2 at a time, until they are well browned and cooked through, about 7 minutes. Transfer the first fish fillets to the paper-lined baking sheet, and put them in the warm oven while frying the remaining fillets.

★

HALIBUT BAKED WITH
A GLAZE OF HERBS

A mayonnaise–like glaze adds an elegant finish to baked halibut. My friend Christina Orchid, who owns Christina's restaurant on Orcas Island, taught me a simple trick of combining a fresh herb with bottled mayonnaise to make an easy sauce for fish. I took it one step further with a homemade sauce spiked with several herbs. The green herbs turn outrageously bright in the heat of the oven, and the piquant, velvety sauce suggests something far more refined than its humble origins.

MAKES 4 SERVINGS

For the Herb Glaze

1 egg yolk

1 tablespoon rice vinegar

2 tablespoons fresh dill, roughly chopped

2 sprigs tarragon, stemmed

2 sprigs basil, stemmed, finely shredded

½ teaspoon sea salt

¼ teaspoon white pepper

½ cup refined olive or canola oil

For the Halibut

4 halibut fillets, 8 ounces each

Salt and pepper, to taste

Extra sprigs of tarragon, basil, and dill, for garnish

1. In a small mixing bowl, whisk together the egg yolk, rice vinegar, dill, tarragon, basil, salt, and white pepper. Add a few drops of the oil, whisking very thoroughly after each addition. When half the oil has been added, a very small amount at a time, begin adding the remaining oil in a thin stream, whisking all the while. Pouring very slowly, allowing each addition to become thoroughly incorporated, stream in the remaining oil to create a thick, smooth emulsion. Transfer to a self-sealing food storage bag and cut ½ inch off one corner to create an impromptu pastry bag.

2. Preheat oven to 400°F. Season the halibut fillets with salt and pepper. Arrange seasoned fillets on a buttered baking sheet and bake 10 minutes.

3. Remove from oven and pipe about 2 tablespoons herb glaze on top of each portion. Return to oven for 1 minute, or until glaze is bubbling hot. Transfer to plates and garnish with bouquets of herbs.

★

ALASKA HALIBUT BAKED WITH
STONE-GROUND MUSTARD GLAZE
ON A BED OF SPRING GREENS

Often, in springtime, when the fields lie bare and newly turned, weeks before the seeds for the first crops have even sprouted, mustard plants, having overwintered on the edges of the field, are already beginning to bloom. The mustard flowers are often the first assurance that winter has indeed passed and summer is coming. This same time of year often marks the arrival of the first fresh halibut from Alaska. I like to serve the halibut with a sauce made from stone-ground mustard over a bed of spring greens, garnished with those wild yellow mustard flowers or similar flowers from any vegetables in the brassica family, such as kale, that may have been left over the winter to go to seed.

For the Mustard Glaze

2 egg yolks

2 tablespoons stone-ground mustard

1 tablespoon freshly squeezed lemon juice

1 teaspoon kosher salt, or ½ teaspoon table salt

1 cup olive oil (not extra virgin)

For the Halibut

2 pounds fresh Alaska halibut fillets, cut into 6 pieces

2 tablespoons olive oil or canola oil

1 teaspoon sea salt, or 2 teaspoons kosher salt

To Finish the Plates

12 ounces (about 6 cups) mixed spring greens

Yellow mustard flowers, for garnish, if available

1. Preheat the oven to 400°F and make the glaze. In a small mixing bowl, combine the egg yolks, mustard, lemon juice, and salt. Whisk until very well combined. With the whisk moving rapidly through the sauce, add a few drops of oil, then a few more, making sure the oil is very well incorporated after each addition. Gradually stream in the remaining oil in a pencil-thin stream to make a thick emulsion. Transfer to a zipper-lock plastic bag and cut ½ inch off one corner to create an impromptu pastry bag.

2. Coat the halibut fillets with the oil and sprinkle them with the salt. Arrange the seasoned fillets in a single layer on a lightly oiled baking sheet and bake until the juices around the fish have congealed and the fish is slightly firm to the touch, about 7 minutes.

3. While the halibut is baking, distribute the greens among 6 dinner plates. Remove the halibut from the oven, and pipe 2 tablespoons of the glaze in a neat stripe on top of each portion. Return to the oven and bake until the glaze is bubbling hot, another 30 seconds or so. Transfer to the plates and garnish with yellow mustard flowers.

★

HALIBUT BAKED IN PARCHMENT WITH FRESH FENNEL

At the restaurant where I worked in Friday Harbor, we used to get very excited about the first spring halibut every year, and we would bake the fish in parchment with a bouquet of fresh, newly sprouting herbs from the kitchen garden. When the parchment is opened at the table, a blast of herb-scented steam issues forth. Alaska halibut, frozen at sea, also works beautifully in this easy, make-ahead dish. Even on frosty pre-spring mornings, fresh wild fennel is already sprouting. If you don't have fennel in the garden, use the leaves from a bulb of fennel in the produce section of the store, or opt for another herb such as fresh basil or dill.

MAKES 4 SERVINGS

4 fillets Alaska halibut, 6 to 7 ounces each

4 teaspoons kosher salt

2 teaspoons freshly ground black pepper

¼ cup (½ stick) unsalted butter, melted

4 bushy fennel sprigs

1. Rinse the halibut fillets under cold running water, then pat them dry with paper towels. Lay the fillets on a plate and sprinkle them with the salt and pepper. Preheat the oven to 450°F.

2. Cut 4 large squares of baker's parchment, each about 12 inches square, and fold them in half. Cut a half circle so that when the squares are unfolded each will form a heart-shaped piece. Butter the parchment hearts and place a seasoned fillet of halibut on one side. Lay a sprig of fennel on top of each fillet. Fold the parchment over and, starting at the pointed end of the half circle, fold about an inch of the parchment in toward the center; then continue folding, making a series of folds in the paper to seal in the fish. Repeat this process with each parchment square to make 4 packets.

3. Put the parchment packets on a baking sheet and bake them in the preheated oven for 12 minutes. Transfer to serving plates and open the packets at the table.

★

GRILLED OR SEARED RARE AHI

I often worry about the ethics of serving large game fish when I know that the stocks have been dramatically reduced in my own lifetime. But according to the experts at the Monterey Bay Aquarium, who publish Seafood Watch *(www.seafoodwatch.org), ahi, also known as yellowfin or bigeye tuna, gets a green light as long as it's troll caught. (Ask your fishmonger how the fish was caught and avoid it if it's caught on a long line; the method produces a lot of wasted by-catch.) I am very happy that ahi is still plentiful because it is one of my all-time favorite foods, especially when it's cooked like this. After you sear the fish, serve it sliced around a mound of hot Japanese-Style Short-Grain Rice (pages 134–35). Top it off with Sesame Spinach (pages 246–47).*

MAKES 4 SERVINGS

2 pounds troll-caught ahi tuna, in one piece

1 teaspoon sea salt, or 2 teaspoons kosher salt

1 teaspoon freshly ground black pepper

1 tablespoon soy sauce, plus more as an accompaniment

1 tablespoon Madeira or off-dry sherry

1 tablespoon olive oil

1 teaspoon toasted sesame seeds

4 tablespoons pickled ginger for garnish

Wasabi (Japanese horseradish) as an accompaniment

1. Don't buy the fish already cut into steaks; instead, buy one big piece and cut it lengthwise, with the grain, into 4 rectangular "logs," each about 2 by 2 by 4 inches.

2. In a small bowl, combine the salt, pepper, 1 tablespoon soy sauce, Madeira, olive oil, and sesame seeds. Roll the fish in this marinade to coat the pieces evenly, and marinate for 30 minutes at room temperature or several hours in the refrigerator.

3. In a backyard barbecue, build a fire with wood or charcoal, and when the heat from the grill forces you to move your hand away when you hold it 5 inches above the grate, or when the flames settle into white-hot coals, grill the fish. You may opt to forgo the grill and pan-sear the fish in a dry skillet over high heat. Cook the fish on the grill or in the skillet, turning as soon as the fish is cooked about ⅛ inch inward, about 1 minute on each of its 4 sides.

4. Garnish each serving with a bit of pickled ginger and serve with a small dish of soy sauce and a mound of prepared wasabi. Serve hot or warm.

★

GRILLED TUNA STEAKS WITH PAPAYA LIME PANACHE

A long time ago, I used to serve Pacific swordfish steaks with this same papaya panache. I was under the impression that, unlike Atlantic swordfish, Pacific swordfish stocks were in good shape. I was wrong. Unfortunately, the fish have been widely overharvested, and I no longer feel comfortable cooking, serving, or ordering swordfish, at least until the fish has had some time to make a comeback. Fortunately, the preparation goes well with other game fish, like troll-caught ahi tuna, whose stocks are not considered depleted. Better still are the small steaks cut from troll-caught albacore off the coast of Washington. Smaller and shorter-lived albacore are far less likely to contain lead than larger species of tuna.

MAKES 4 SERVINGS

For the Panache

1 tablespoon dried green peppercorns

1 tablespoon boiling water

1 large, ripe papaya

1 tablespoon grated lime zest

1 tablespoon freshly squeezed lime juice

1 tablespoon sugar

½ teaspoon sea salt, or 1 teaspoon kosher salt

¼ medium red onion, peeled and thinly sliced

For the Tuna

4 ahi steaks, about 8 ounces each, or 8 albacore steaks, about 4 ounces each

I teaspoon sea salt, or 2 teaspoons kosher salt

I teaspoon freshly ground black pepper

2 tablespoons olive or canola oil

I. Make the panache. In a small mixing bowl, cover the green peppercorns with the boiling water and allow them to soften.

2. Cut the papaya in half lengthwise, scoop out and discard the seeds, then peel the halves and cut them across into strips about ⅛ inch thick.

3. Stir the lime zest, lime juice, sugar, and salt into the softened green peppercorns and their soaking liquid, then add the sliced papaya and sliced red onion and toss to coat.

4. In a backyard barbecue, build a fire with wood or charcoal, and burn until the flames settle into white-hot coals, or preheat a gas grill.

5. Sprinkle the tuna steaks with salt and pepper. Put the olive oil on a plate and, just before grilling, dip the seasoned steaks in the oil to lightly coat each side. Grill the fish, turning it once, as soon as it is cooked about ¼ inch inward, about 2 minutes on each side. Serve the panache at room temperature over the hot grilled fish.

★
CRISP PETRALE SOLE WITH CAPER AND SHALLOT SAUCE

*Really a type of Pacific flounder (*Eopsetta jordani*) and not a true sole at all, petrale is prized for its tender and versatile fillets, which respond well to almost any method of cooking. At my house, we like them best coated in seasoned breadcrumbs and pan-fried in a shallow pool of butter and oil. Ends of loaves and slices that have lost the first blush of freshness are perfect candidates for seasoned breadcrumbs. The crumbs are useful for frying everything from rounds of goat cheese to breasts of chicken and fillets of fish. They are also good sprinkled over fish that's destined to be baked. If no day-old bread is available, use panko (Japanese breadcrumbs) instead.*

MAKES 4 SERVINGS

For the Seasoned Breadcrumbs

6 or 7 slices day-old bread, or 1½ cups panko

I tablespoon mild (Hungarian) paprika

2 teaspoons kosher salt

I teaspoon freshly ground black pepper

I teaspoon dried thyme

2 tablespoons refined olive or canola oil

For the Sole

4 fillets petrale sole, 6 ounces each

2 teaspoons kosher salt

½ cup unbleached white flour

2 eggs

2 tablespoons water

3 tablespoons unsalted butter

3 tablespoons olive oil

For the Sauce

2 tablespoons butter and oil from the frying pan

2 tablespoons finely chopped shallot

2 tablespoons capers, drained

1 cup chicken or vegetable broth

¼ cup chopped fresh parsley

1. Make the breadcrumbs. Preheat the oven to 200°F, or the lowest setting. Cut the bread, crusts and all, into 1- or 2-inch cubes and pile the bread cubes into the work bowl of a food processor. Process until the cubes are all cut into uniform crumbs. With the motor running, add the paprika, salt, pepper, thyme, and oil and pulse until everything is well combined. Spread the seasoned crumbs on a baking sheet and bake in the warm oven for about an hour to dry the crumbs.

2. Bread the fillets. Rinse the fillets and pat them dry. Sprinkle with the salt. Line up 3 soup bowls, and put flour in one bowl. Beat the eggs with the water in the second bowl, and put the seasoned breadcrumbs in the third bowl. Dredge each fillet in flour, shaking off the excess. Dip each flour-coated fillet into the egg mixture, allow any excess egg to run off, then roll in the breadcrumbs to coat, and arrange the coated fillets in a single layer

on a parchment-lined baking sheet. The fillets can be prepared ahead up to this point and refrigerated for several hours.

3. Twenty minutes before serving time, preheat the oven to 200°F. Put 2 tablespoons of the butter and 2 tablespoons of the oil in a frying pan over medium heat, and when the butter is melted and sizzling, fry 2 of the breaded fillets until they are golden brown. Turn and cook the other side, about 5 minutes in all. Put the fried fillets on a baking sheet and hold them in the warm oven while you make the sauce.

4. From the pan in which the fish fillets were fried, pour off all but 2 tablespoons of the oil and butter. Over medium-high heat, cook the shallots until they are slightly browned. Add the capers and chicken broth and turn the heat up to high. Boil until the broth is reduced to half its original volume. Swirl in the parsley, and serve the sauce hot with the pan-fried fish.

★

PIONEER PAN-FRIED TROUT WITH SAUTÉED MUSTARD GREENS

In the mountain streams that run into the Pacific Ocean are myriad forms of trout; most popular are the rainbow and cutthroat varieties. My father-in-law, who was born in the early 1920s, grew up trout fishing, hiking miles to find the best streams. He passed his love of hiking and fishing on to his five daughters, and my wife has carried on the tradition to some extent, dragging me occasionally into the woods, where I have savored wild trout fresh from the stream. Most trout served in West Coast homes and restaurants is rainbow trout from the Idaho Trout Company, a sustainable fish farming operation established in 1948.

MAKES 4 SERVINGS

4 trout fillets, 6 to 8 ounces each, with skin

2 teaspoons sea salt, or to taste

1 teaspoon freshly ground black pepper, or to taste

½ cup stone-ground cornmeal

Olive oil, for frying

1 bunch mustard greens, rinsed and shaken dry

2 tablespoons apple cider vinegar

1. Preheat the oven to 250°F and line a baking sheet with a brown paper bag or a few paper towels to receive the fish as soon as it's fried. Season the trout fillets with salt and pepper. Dredge each fillet, flesh side down, in the cornmeal, shaking off the excess. (There is no need to coat the skin side.)

2. Put a ½-inch layer of olive oil in a cast-iron skillet over medium-high heat. When the oil is hot, fry 2 of the fillets, cornmeal side down, until they are golden brown, then turn and cook the other side, about 5 minutes in all. Put the fried fillets on the paper-lined baking sheet and hold them in the warm oven while you fry the other fillets. Keep the second round of fillets warm while you prepare the mustard greens.

3. Cut the mustard greens across the stems into ribbons 1 to 2 inches wide. Pour all but about 2 tablespoons of the oil from the pan in which the fish were fried and sauté the cut greens in the remaining oil until they are wilted, about 2 minutes. Splash the apple cider vinegar over the greens, toss to coat, then distribute the cooked greens evenly among 4 dinner plates.

4. Lay one fried trout fillet, skin side down, over each pile of greens and serve at once.

★

PORTLAND PAN-FRIED TROUT IN HAZELNUT CRUST WITH APPLE CIDER SAUCE

A Pacific Northwest slant on the classic trout amandine, this recipe evolved out of a dish I once served at a gathering for members of Chef's Collaborative in Oregon. Oregon grows more hazelnuts than any other state, and it also grows some of the best apples in the country. I was invited to cook with tilapia, a sustainably raised freshwater fish native to Lake Victoria in Africa, and of course the technique outlined here will work with tilapia. I think it's even better with trout.

MAKES 4 SERVINGS

4 trout fillets, 6 to 8 ounces each, with skin

2 teaspoons sea salt, or to taste

1 teaspoon freshly ground black pepper, or to taste

½ cup unbleached white flour

2 eggs

2 tablespoons water

½ cup hazelnuts, toasted, skinned, and finely chopped

½ cup crumbs made from day-old white bread or panko (Japanese breadcrumbs)

Hazelnut, rice bran, or canola oil, for frying

1 small onion, peeled and finely chopped

¾ cup apple cider

2 tablespoons apple cider vinegar

1. Preheat the oven to 250°F and line a baking sheet with a brown paper bag or a few paper towels to receive the fish as soon as it's fried. Rinse the fillets and pat them dry. Sprinkle them with salt and pepper.

2. Prepare the fish fillets for frying. The goal is to apply a three-layered coat of flour, egg wash, and hazelnut/breadcrumb mixture on the flesh side while leaving the skin side uncoated. Line up 3 soup bowls, and put the flour in one bowl. Beat the eggs with the water in the second bowl, and put the hazelnuts and breadcrumbs in the third bowl. Dredge each fillet, flesh side down, in the flour, shaking off the excess. Dip each flour-coated fillet into the egg mixture, allow any excess egg to run off, and then cover the fillets, one at a time, with the mixture of hazelnuts and breadcrumbs. The fillets can be

prepared ahead up to this point, arranged in a single layer on a baking sheet, and refrigerated for several hours.

3. Put a ½-inch layer of oil in a cast-iron skillet over medium-high heat. When the oil is hot, fry 2 of the fillets, crumb side down, until they are golden brown, then turn and cook the other side, about 5 minutes in all. Put the fried fillets on the paper-lined baking sheet and hold them in the warm oven while you fry the other fillets. Keep the second round of fillets warm while you prepare the sauce.

4. Pour all but about 2 tablespoons of the oil from the pan in which the fish were fried and sauté the onion in the remaining oil until softened, about 2 minutes. Pour the apple cider and apple cider vinegar over the onion and cook until the liquid is reduced to one third of its original volume. Serve the trout fillets hot, surrounded by the apple cider sauce.

★

PESCADO À LA VERA CRUZ

One of our signature dishes at Dos Padres Mexican restaurant when I cooked there in the 1980s was this take on a Mexican classic. After onions, tomatoes, and olives were sautéed in a cast-iron skillet, they were pushed to one side of the pan to make room for two small fillets of Alaska cod, which was seared in the same olive oil. After the fish was turned over, a spoonful of Spanish rice was tucked into the pan and the dish was served right in the pan. Most of the guests thought this was pretty cute, except for one Alaska fisherman just back from a fishing trip, who begged the waitress to take it out of the pan. "I've been cooking for myself and eating out of the pan for a month. Could you please take this out of the pan and put it on a plate for me?" Serve the fish with Dos Padres–Style Spanish Rice (pages 139–40).

MAKES 2 SERVINGS

I pound Alaska cod or farm-raised tilapia fillets, cut into 4 pieces

½ teaspoon sea salt, or I teaspoon kosher salt

½ teaspoon freshly ground black pepper

3 tablespoons extra virgin olive oil

I medium onion, peeled and thinly sliced

3 large garlic cloves, very thinly sliced

2 small tomatoes, cut into 6 wedges each

6 green olives, sliced

2 tablespoons very finely chopped parsley

⅛ teaspoon dried red chile flakes, or to taste

¼ cup white wine

I. Sprinkle the cod fillets with the salt and pepper and keep them on a plate near the stove.

2. Warm 2 tablespoons of the olive oil in a 10-inch sauté pan or cast-iron skillet over medium-high heat. Sauté the onion and garlic until the vegetables are soft and beginning to color. Stir in the tomato wedges, sliced olives, chopped parsley, and chile flakes and, with a spatula, push the vegetables to one side of the pan.

3. Add the third tablespoonful of olive oil to the pan and lay the fish fillets in the oil. Cook them on one side without moving them until a light brown crust forms on the underside, about 3 minutes. With a fish spatula, shimmy the fish off the bottom of the pan—it may stick a little— turn it over, and pour in the white wine.

4. Cover the pan and reduce the heat to low. Simmer until the fish flakes when pressed gently with the spatula, about 5 minutes more. Serve the fish directly from the pan, if desired, or transfer to serving plates.

★

SCALLOPS WITH ARTICHOKES AND ORANGE BUTTER SAUCE

When I was the chef at Canlis from 1996 to 2002, I worked closely with Shayne Bjornholm, the sommelier, to create food and wine pairings for a monthly tasting menu. One month I presented Bjornholm with the peculiar challenge of artichoke and citrus on the same plate, two foods notoriously difficult for pairing with wine. He rallied with a Washington sauvignon blanc. And although several years and many food and wine pairings have come and gone, the flavors of that particular pairing still resonate with me.

MAKES 4 SERVINGS

For the Artichokes

4 large artichokes

8 cups water

2 tablespoons kosher salt

For the Sauce

1 medium orange

1 teaspoon sugar

½ teaspoon kosher salt

¼ teaspoon ground white pepper

⅓ cup cold unsalted butter, cut into bits

For the Scallops

1 tablespoon canola oil

1 pound large sea scallops

Sea salt and freshly ground black pepper, to taste

1. Precook the artichokes. In a large stockpot, bring the water and salt to a full, rolling boil. Cook the artichokes in the boiling salted water until tender, about 20 minutes. Remove the leaves from each artichoke with a sharp knife, then use a teaspoon to scrape away the hairy centers to produce artichoke bottoms. Cut each artichoke bottom in half.

2. Make the orange sauce. Use a citrus zester to remove long curls of zest from the orange, then juice the orange. Put the zest, juice, sugar, salt, and pepper in a small saucepan over high heat and boil until the mixture is reduced to about one third of its original volume. Whisk in the butter bits and keep warm until ready to serve. (The sauce can be held in a warm spot for 15 minutes before serving, or in a thermos bottle for several hours.)

3. Cook the scallops. Put the canola oil in a sauté pan large enough to accommodate the scallops in a single layer and warm the pan over medium heat. Sprinkle the scallops with salt and pepper and arrange them carefully in the pan with one of their flat sides down. Allow them to cook, undisturbed, until the undersides are well browned and the scallops are cooked halfway through, about 3 minutes. Turn and cook for 1 or 2 minutes longer.

4. Put one split artichoke bottom on each of 4 salad plates. Distribute the scallops evenly among the plates and drizzle about 2 tablespoons of the orange butter sauce over each plate.

★

CANLIS DUNGENESS CRAB CAKES

Predictably made with blue crab, cracker crumbs, and that delectable commercial blend of salt and spices known as Old Bay Seasoning, East Coast crab cakes have their following. They are reliable and honest. On the West Coast, no tradition guides us when we make crab cakes; instead, we somewhat self-consciously assemble ingredients that try to "say something." At one point during my tenure at Canlis restaurant, I was working with my friend Sharon Kramis to revitalize the menu. I wanted our crab cakes to "say" that Canlis was looking west to the Pacific, not back East, that we were of the moment, not caught in the past. Sharon added a little pickled ginger and some green onions to give the cakes a subtle Asian flair, and I planted them in pool of orange butter sauce with a vibrant streak of red pepper purée, which, I thought anchored them securely on the West Coast.

These crab cakes are one of the all-time great dishes that I have been involved with.

MAKES 8 SERVINGS AS AN APPETIZER
OR 4 AS A MAIN COURSE

3 cups panko (Japanese breadcrumbs)

¼ cup water

1 pound Dungeness crabmeat

2 tablespoons finely chopped red bell pepper

2 tablespoons finely chopped green onions

2 tablespoons finely chopped pickled ginger

½ cup Homemade Mayonnaise (pages 115–16) or quality purchased

1 egg, lightly beaten

1 teaspoon kosher salt

½ teaspoon freshly ground black pepper

¼ cup olive oil

1 cup shredded spinach leaves, for garnish

2 tablespoons freshly grated orange zest, for garnish

For the Sauce

1 cup freshly squeezed orange juice

½ teaspoon sea salt, or to taste

½ teaspoon ground white pepper, or to taste

¾ cup (1½ sticks) cold unsalted butter, cut into 1-inch chunks

For the Red Pepper Purée

2 large red bell peppers

1 tablespoon balsamic vinegar

2 tablespoons olive oil

1. Put ½ cup of the panko in a large bowl with the water. Stir in the crabmeat, red pepper, green onions, and pickled ginger. Then stir in the mayonnaise, beaten egg, and salt and pepper. Work the crabmeat into this mixture to make a kind of crab slaw or salad.

2. Put half of the remaining panko onto a plate and set the other half within reach. Using a 4-ounce scoop or a ½-cup measuring cup, scoop up some crab mixture and put it on the panko-covered plate. Press additional panko onto the top of the cake. Repeat with the remaining crab mixture; you should have 8 cakes. The crab cakes can be prepared ahead up to this point and kept refrigerated for several hours or overnight.

3. Make the sauce. In a nonreactive saucepan over high heat, boil the orange juice with the salt and white pepper until it is reduced to ⅓ cup. (The sauce base can be made ahead up to this point and kept refrigerated for several days. Return to a boil before adding the butter.) Whisk the butter into the boiling reduced orange juice mixture to make a smooth, emulsified sauce. Season to taste with additonal sea salt and white pepper. Don't let the sauce cool down, because if you try to reheat it, it will separate. (The sauce can be kept in a warm spot for 15 minutes before serving, or in a thermos bottle for several hours.)

4. Make the red pepper purée. Preheat the oven to 425°F. Arrange the peppers in a single layer on a sheet pan and bake until the skin is blistered and blackened, about 15 minutes. Remove from the oven, and transfer the peppers to a brown paper bag. Allow them to stand undisturbed until cool enough to handle, 10 to 12 minutes. Peel the peppers—the skin should slip off easily. If any blackened bits remain stuck to the peppers, they can be rinsed away, but avoid rinsing away the flavorful juices. Remove the stems, then gently split and seed each pepper. In a blender, purée the roasted peppers with the vinegar and olive oil.

5. Twenty minutes before serving time, preheat the oven to 425°F. Heat the olive oil in a large skillet over medium-high heat. Refresh the panko breading on the cakes and sauté them, four at a time, until golden brown on each side, about 5 minutes. Transfer the browned cakes to a baking sheet.

6. Finish the browned cakes in the oven for 5 minutes. Spoon about 3 tablespoons of the orange butter sauce onto each serving plate, and plant a pair of sizzling hot crab cakes onto the pool of sauce. Garnish each serving with some shredded spinach, a dollop of red pepper purée, and a pinch of orange zest.

⋆
GULF PRAWNS, PAN-SAUTÉED WITH RED CHILES AND LIME

Buying shrimp and prawns is fraught with moral challenges. On the one hand, farmed shrimp often come from operations that compromise mangrove ecosystems in the tropical world. On the other hand, wild shrimp are sometimes harvested using methods that inadvertently kill sea turtles, which are endangered. Fortunately, trap-caught shrimp are environmentally friendly. Ask your fishmonger where your shrimp come from and how they were harvested. Opt for the 16–20 size; each one weighs about 1 ounce.

MAKES 12 APPETIZER SERVINGS
OR 4 ENTRÉE SERVINGS

1½ pounds extra-large prawns (16–20 size)

3 tablespoons olive oil

Pinch of dried red chile flakes

Pinch of chopped fresh garlic

3 tablespoons freshly squeezed lime juice

3 tablespoons white wine

6 tablespoons (¾ stick) cold unsalted butter, cut into 1-inch bits

1. Cut the prawns down the length of their shell on the backside without cutting all the way through. Rinse the cut prawns to remove any dark bits.

2. Pour the oil into a hot sauté pan. When it begins to smoke, add the prawns and cook until the shells are turning pink, 1 to 2 minutes on each side. Stir in the chile flakes and garlic.

3. Add the lime juice and white wine, and when the liquid is almost boiled away, add the butter. Swirl the pan to allow the butter to become emulsified with the pan juices. Serve at once.

★

GRILLED AUSTRALIAN LOBSTER TAILS WITH TAMARIND BUTTER

Spiny or rock lobsters thrive in the warm waters off the coast of California and the Baja Peninsula, but the vast majority of Pacific lobster tails served in West Coast restaurants come from the carefully managed Western Australia Fishery, which was the first recipient of the Marine Stewardship certification. According to the Seafood Watch program at the Monterey Bay Aquarium, it's a good idea to make sure that the lobster you buy comes from these waters, since rock lobster harvested in Central America or the Caribbean is likely to be overfished or illegally caught before they reach reproductive age. At Canlis restaurant in Seattle, we used to serve meaty Australian lobster tails grilled with lemon butter. Then we discovered that they were even better with tangy tamarind in place of the lemon. The tails are sold frozen, so plan to thaw them overnight in the refrigerator before grilling. Serve the grilled lobster tails with Garlic Mashed Potatoes with Cheese (page 240) and Sesame Spinach (pages 246–47).

MAKES 4 SERVINGS

For the Tamarind Butter

2 ounces dried tamarind pods plus ½ cup boiling water, or ½ cup tamarind purée

1 tablespoon sugar

½ teaspoon sea salt

½ cup (1 stick) cold unsalted butter, cut into 1-inch chunks

For the Lobster

½ cup white vermouth

4 large Australian lobster tails, 8 ounces each, thawed, in the shell

2 tablespoons canola oil

Sea salt and freshly ground black pepper, to taste

1. In a backyard barbecue, build a fire with wood or charcoal and allow the flames to settle into white-hot coals. While the coals are heating, allow the lobster tails to come to room temperature.

2. Make the butter. Boil the tamarind pulp in the boiling water until it is soft, then force it through a strainer into a small saucepan, or start with prepared tamarind purée. Boil the tamarind purée with the sugar and sea salt until it is reduced to half its original volume, then whisk in the butter. Keep the sauce warm, but do not allow it to boil, or it will separate.

3. Grill the lobster tails. Put a pour spout on the bottle of vermouth, or transfer it to a squirt bottle. Start the tails shell side down on the hot grill, splashing them regularly with vermouth to keep the meat moist. Grill until the meat is no longer translucent but creamy white, about 8 minutes. Brush the white meat with canola oil and turn the tails over to get brown

grill marks on top. Use tongs or grill forks to loosen the meat inside the shells before serving.

4. Serve one lobster tail per person, with a judicious sprinkle of sea salt, a grind of pepper, and a generous coating of tamarind butter.

Poultry

Behind the scenes at every great restaurant, the cooks make certain meals that customers never see. These are staff meals, family meals, or, as we like to say in my kitchen, "crew chow." By any name, these are the meals that keep the restaurant going. Every restaurant is different, and each one has its own policies about feeding the staff, but far and away, at least among the better houses, a family meal at least once a day is the norm. When I was executive chef at Canlis restaurant in Seattle there was a staff of about 60 people, and every day at 5 o'clock we had dinner, and then at 11 or so we have a substantial snack.

This is how it's been at most of the places I've worked. In Friday Harbor, when I was chef at a small café, the entire crew sat down after service every night with bread and wine, and chicken or fish, and salad, or whatever we needed to use up before the next day's service. There were never more than six or seven of us, and the meals were fairly intimate.

Mealtime was an opportunity to meet and go over the fine points of service, and a chance to share news of our lives outside the restaurant. We worked and ate together like one big, dysfunctional family. Sometimes one of the employees would bring a boyfriend or girlfriend to the family meal, and it was just like bringing a date home to meet the family, only worse. None of us was

shy about asking probing personal questions. Some of us, in fact, were bold and rude. Still, a good time was generally had by all.

In his runaway best seller, *Kitchen Confidential*, Anthony Bourdain describes the perfunctory family meals that were presented in the various restaurant kitchens where he worked in New York City. Crew chow in Bourdain's book ranged from the ordinary to the hideous. Most common was the ubiquitous chicken leg, noodles, and salad. Worst was the awful thing called a raft, a mishmash of solids strained out of the stockpot. Most restaurants discard this stuff, but Bourdain insists that at some places, that is all there is for the staff to eat.

When I went to New York some years ago to spend time as a guest cook in three different four-star restaurants, I saw plenty of that famous trinity of chicken, noodles, and salad. But I also saw roast beef, baked fish, sandwiches, hot dogs, all kinds of ordinary foods that would never have been served in the dining room, and all of these foods were consumed with gusto by the hungry cooks and waiters. "We eat really good here," said Daniel Boulud's sous chef, as we served ourselves chicken legs, noodles, and salad, and I had to agree.

The meals in New York's great French restaurants were not quite as interesting as the staff meals in France, however. When I worked for a too-brief time at Moulin de Mougins in Provence, then rated three stars by the Michelin guide, crew chow gave me an intriguing glimpse into the stratified world of the French. Perhaps it was because my senses were heightened by the excitement of being in a foreign country, or perhaps it was because the food really was extraordinary, but the meals I had there were not only the most memorable crew meals of my life, they were some of the most memorable meals I've had—period.

Mealtimes at Moulin de Mougins were segregated into three levels of sophistication. The management ate the finest food, virtually as good as what the guests ate, and they drank good wine. The waiters and cooks drank modest wine and ordinary food. The dishwashers ate mysterious things, pots of lentils and polenta with rejected parts of animals butchered for the restaurant, and they drank very plain, barely fermented wine from collapsible plastic jugs.

On my first afternoon at the restaurant, I was led into the dining room and seated at a table with a half-dozen well-dressed sophisticates who were introduced to me as the *direction*, or management. I smiled weakly. I was uncomfortable with my French and unable to understand much of what was said.

We were presented with tiny plates of smoked salmon, and I ate as politely as I could while the *direction* practiced obscure idioms in their brilliant native tongue and asked me very slowly if, since I lived Washington, did I live with the president? "No, no," one of them answered for me, "He's from the West Coast, where they've only just recently chased out the savages." No one spoke a word of English.

I sat quietly and allowed the smoked salmon to be exchanged for a neat packet of veal, tied with strings and stuffed with sausage. My glass was filled with a deep red wine. I struggled with the strings around my veal and glanced nervously at the others, who managed to remove their strings with the same fluid ease with which they spoke. My strings wouldn't budge, and my tongue would not form a single word in French.

Finally came the cheese course, smooth white Camembert and bottles of chilled spring water. It was soothing, and I felt fortified enough to look the others in the eye, but I was far too humbled to practice anything I had learned from the *Jiffy French Phrase Book*.

The next day, after shucking two cases of live scallops, I ate with the cooks. We had lamb's brains in browned butter with capers. The meat was pale and soft, and not very appetizing, but the bread and cheese were abundant and so was the wine. Everyone ate quickly so there would be time for cards. The food was pushed aside and out came the deck. The cooks pounded the table with their fists as they lost and stood triumphant, with chairs tumbling behind them, when they won. I was incapable of following the games.

On the third day, I was assigned to work in the *laboratoire*, a prep kitchen in a separate building behind the main restaurant, where all the basic foods were brought in and broken down before they went into the main kitchen. There, whole birds were eviscerated and plucked. Rabbits and deer were butchered. Fresh mushrooms and berries were made into duxelles and sorbets.

In charge of the lab was one of the few honored master chefs of France. He was in semiretirement and worked at the restaurant, he said, "just to keep from rotting away." We spent the morning chopping huge bones on a stump outside the *laboratoire*, where he would later transform them first into rich broth and eventually into a rich concentrate known as demi-glace for use by the other chefs. By lunchtime, the stump had been sprayed down with a garden hose and the bones were roasting with aromatic vegetables.

We ate at a bare table in an attic room, from mismatched plates. With the tattered sleeves of his monogrammed chef's jacket pushed unceremoniously up to his elbow, the grandfatherly chef served spaghetti with meat and tomato sauce. We drank country wine from jelly jars and broke bread directly over the table without bread plates. There was no butter, no cheese, and no pretense. "This, you must understand," he told me instructively in very plain, precise French, "is real food, simple food."

Made with beef from a steer he had butchered himself, handmade pork sausage, and fresh tomatoes, the sauce was seasoned unpretentiously with dried herbs, fresh ground pepper, and a sprinkling of commercial chicken bouillon granules. It was

the quintessential spaghetti sauce. A gentle wind came through the open windows from the herb garden outside and, more than at any other time since I had been in France, I felt at home. "This is good," I said. "It reminds me of home."

"Of course it does," the old man said, as if he knew me, as if he knew my grandmother's kitchen with its peculiar smells and sounds. "It is real food." Without referring directly to the haute cuisine served in the dining room 50 meters from where we sat, the old master managed to imply that the food served there at hundreds of francs per plate was something less than real. So I came to France to learn the secrets of haute cuisine and learned instead what I had always known, that simple food is the best food.

"This is the way to live, isn't it?" he asked me.

"Yes sir, I think so," I said.

Most of the best family meals at restaurants are like the best family meals at home: simple, familiar foods served without a lot of fuss and fanfare. People in my crew often cook the traditional comfort foods they grew up with, and since they come from Laos, Mexico, Japan, and the Philippines, crew chow can be pretty interesting. At Canlis, my favorite staff meal revolved around Jeff Taton's chicken adobo, with steamed rice and salad. Even after eating it two or three times a month for several years, I looked forward to the dish every time it was offered.

HOW TO CUT UP A CHICKEN

Some people shy away from cutting up a chicken because the process seems messy and intimidating. But once you know how, it's easy. Whole chickens cost less per pound, and since you get better-shaped pieces with less waste, it is worth the effort to cut up a chicken yourself. And an added bonus is that when you cut your own chicken, you have parts for making your own chicken stock (page 68).

MAKES 8 PIECES, SERVING 4

One 3- to 4-pound free-range chicken

I. If the chicken has any giblets, set them aside for stock. Reserve the liver for another use. Put the chicken breast side up on a stable cutting board, with the legs pointing toward you. (Professional chefs always put a kitchen towel under the cutting board to keep it from sliding or wobbling.) Using a sharp chef's knife, cut into the top of the breast plate and cut through the cartilage all the way to the bottom. You will have split the top half of the bird butterfly style and left the underside intact.

2. Spread the split carcass open to gain access to the backbone. Placing the blade along one side of the backbone, press firmly and rock until the blade is all the way through. Repeat on the other side of the spine. You should have 2 half-chickens and a backbone. Set the backbone aside.

3. Find the natural division between the breast and the thigh and cut each half-chicken in half again to get 4 quarters.

4. Divide the legs into drumstick and thigh. With the chicken leg lying skin side down on the cutting board, wedge the base of knife blade into the joint and rock the blade to separate the leg. Trim the "knuckle" off the bottom of each leg and set these aside with the backbone.

5. Cut the wings off. It's best to include a little of the breast with the upper section of the wing; this makes the wings into a more substantial piece at serving time. Cut the wing with about an inch of breast meat away from each breast. Then snip off the last joint from each wing and put those aside with the backbone for stock.

6. To prevent any bacteria from getting on other foods, wash the knife and cutting board in hot, soapy water and use a light bleach solution (I tablespoon in 2 quarts of water) to sanitize the countertop.

VERSATILE BAKED CHICKEN

This is the way chicken is often prepared in restaurants to feed the hungry crew. Simpler to cook and serve than a whole roast chicken, chicken baked in individual pieces is a perfect weeknight meal for families—be they nuclear or extended. Very often, chicken is a vehicle for other flavors, and only rarely do we enjoy the taste of the bird itself. Since chicken is so straightforward, in this preparation, it is important to choose one that has great flavor on its own. If you compare a factory farmed bird with a free-range or organic bird, the difference will be profound. Serve this baked chicken with Greg's Buttered Noodles (pages 145–46) and a green salad. Flavorful condiments such as regular soy sauce, Mexican hot sauce, and Southeast Asian sweet chili sauce can be offered on the side.

MAKES 4 SERVINGS

1 chicken (about 4 pounds) preferably free-range, cut into 8 pieces (see page 185)

Nonstick canola oil spray, or 1 tablespoon canola oil

1 tablespoon kosher salt

1½ teaspoons freshly ground black pepper

1. Preheat the oven to 450°F and spray or rub a baking sheet with canola oil.

2. Sprinkle the chicken pieces all over with salt and pepper, and arrange them in a single layer on the oiled baking sheet. Bake until they are well browned and crispy and cooked through, about 25 minutes. An instant-read thermometer inserted into the thickest part of a thigh or leg should read 165°F.

★

GERALD'S LEMON CHICKEN

The late Gerald Knight came to the West Coast from the South American country of Guyana via New York City. I was still in my twenties when I went to work in Gerald's kitchen, and he was one of the first chefs who had a serious influence on my cooking. He used to direct me to make this dish for the "family meal" or staff meal at a restaurant called Café Bissett in Friday Harbor, Washington. He thought it was too simple for the dining room. When he moved on and I was promoted to chef, I put the dish on the menu, where it became one of our most requested items. Lemon zest, garlic, and herbs lend the chicken a bright, fresh flavor, while a bath of lemon juice and white wine tenderizes the meat. Like Versatile Baked Chicken (pages 185–86), this chicken should be served with Greg's Buttered Noodles (pages 145–46) or Japanese-Style Short-Grain Rice (pages 134–35) and a green salad for a casual supper.

MAKES 4 SERVINGS

2 whole lemons

½ cup off-dry white wine, such as riesling or semillon

4 cloves garlic, grated on a Microplane grater or finely chopped

1 tablespoon fresh thyme leaves, or 1 teaspoon dried

1 tablespoon fresh tarragon leaves, or 1 teaspoon dried

2 teaspoons kosher salt

1 teaspoon freshly ground black pepper

1 free-range chicken, 3½ to 4 pounds, cut into 8 pieces (see page 185)

1. Preheat the oven to 400°F.

2. Use a special zesting tool to remove the colorful outer rind of the lemons. If no zester tool is available, peel off sections of the lemon zest with a vegetable peeler and then cut them into 1/16-inch strips with a sharp knife. Put the lemon rind into a

2-quart, nonreactive (glass or ceramic) baking dish.

3. After the zest has been removed, juice the lemons and strain the juice into the baking dish. Stir in the wine, garlic, thyme, tarragon, salt, and pepper.

4. Roll the chicken pieces in the lemon juice mixture in the baking dish. Arrange the pieces in the dish skin side up and bake until they are well browned on top and an instant-read thermometer inserted into the thickest piece registers 180°F, about 30 minutes.

5. To make a sauce, tilt the baking dish over a saucepan to collect all the pan juices. (While pouring off the juices, hold the chicken pieces in the pan with a slotted spoon.) Boil the juices down over high heat until they are reduced to about half their original volume.

6. Pour the juices back over the chicken pieces and serve the chicken family style from the baking dish, or distribute the chicken pieces evenly among 4 serving plates and pass the sauce separately.

★
JEFF'S CHICKEN ADOBO

Adobo, the unofficial national dish of the Philippine Islands, was served frequently for "family meal" when I was the chef at Canlis restaurant in Seattle, where my sous chef, Jeff Taton, often made his version for the crew. But the dish is popular up and down the West Coast, with myriad variations. Some people like to marinate the chicken overnight in the same seasoned soy and vinegar mixture outlined here, then grill it over hot coals and boil the marinade to serve as a sauce on the side. The dish is also quite popular made with pork instead of chicken. Serve chicken adobo hot in wide open bowls with Japanese-Style Short-Grain Rice (pages 134–35) and a green vegetable such as Jade Green Broccoli (page 252).

MAKES 8 SERVINGS

2 naturally raised chickens, 4 pounds each, cut into 8 pieces each (see page 185)

2 cups soy sauce

2 cups vinegar

2 cups water

5 cloves garlic, grated on a Microplane grater or finely chopped

1 tablespoon cracked black pepper

2 bay leaves

Steamed white rice as an accompaniment

1. Put the chicken pieces in a large, heavy saucepan or Dutch oven with the soy sauce, vinegar, water, garlic, pepper, and bay leaves. Bring the mixture to a boil and reduce the heat to medium-low.

2. Keep the chicken simmering gently until the meat is very tender and pulls easily away from the bone, about 45 minutes. Serve it in wide open bowls with plenty of steamed rice and the pan juices.

★
MOM'S CHICKEN WITH RICE

Like many West Coast cooks, I arrived from another place bringing my family recipes with me. This recipe would be at home anywhere in the world, but I like it best the way I make it here on the West Coast with short-grain California-grown rice and local, organically raised chicken. Unlike so many things that are not as good as they used to be, this dish seems even better than it was when I was a kid. It is so easy to enjoy, so thoroughly satisfying, and so completely free of pretense that we find ourselves returning to it again and again. Serve with Mom's Buttered Carrots (page 243).

MAKES 4 TO 6 SERVINGS

1 free-range (3½ to 4 pounds) chicken, preferably organic, or 6 boneless chicken thighs

1 tablespoon kosher salt

1 teaspoon freshly ground black pepper

¼ cup olive oil

1 medium onion, peeled and thinly sliced

2 cups long-grain white rice, such as jasmine or basmati

4 cloves garlic, grated on a Microplane grater or finely chopped

1 bay leaf

1 tablespoon fresh thyme leaves, or 1 teaspoon dried

1 cup white wine

3 cups chicken broth, homemade (page 68) or purchased

1. If using a whole chicken, cut it into 8 pieces (see page 185). Sprinkle the chicken pieces or boneless thighs with the salt and pepper.

2. In a Dutch oven over medium-high heat, brown the chicken pieces in the oil, turning them several times to brown on all sides, about 7 minutes in all.

3. Pull the chicken out of the pan, and in the oil, sauté the onion until it is soft and slightly browned. Stir in the rice, garlic, bay leaf, and thyme, then pour in the white wine and chicken broth and bring the liquid to a boil.

4. Put the chicken pieces back in the pot, reduce the heat to low, and cover. Simmer until the rice has absorbed the cooking liquid and the chicken is cooked through, about 35 minutes. Serve hot.

★
ARROZ CON POLLO

This traditional Latin American dish is made following the same basic technique for making Mom's Chicken with Rice, but the colorful and flavorful addition of sausages, red peppers, smoked paprika, and saffron make this version worthy of company. The dish is really a meal in itself, but it might be preceded by a Caesar salad or the Mango and Avocado Salad on page 106. Serve Flan (pages 350–51) or Mexican Chocolate Cake (pages 318–19) for dessert.

1 pound chorizo or hot Italian sausages, sliced ½ inch thick

2 tablespoons olive oil

6 boneless chicken thighs

1 tablespoon kosher salt

1 teaspoon freshly ground black pepper

1 medium onion, peeled and chopped into ½-inch pieces

1 medium red bell pepper, cut into ½-inch pieces

2 cups long-grain white rice, such as jasmine or basmati

4 cloves garlic, grated on a Microplane grater or finely chopped

1 tablespoon smoked paprika or chili powder

One 12-ounce bottle beer

One 14.5-ounce can fire-roasted tomatoes

1 cup water

1 generous pinch saffron threads

1½ cups frozen peas or fresh peas blanched in boiling water

½ cup chopped fresh parsley

1. In a Dutch oven over medium-high heat, cook the sausage pieces in the olive oil until lightly browned, about 5 minutes. With a slotted spoon, lift the sausage pieces out of the oil and set them aside (I put them on the upturned lid of the pot).

2. Sprinkle the chicken thighs with the salt and pepper and brown them in the oil left in the pan, turning them once to brown evenly on both sides, about 5 minutes in all.

3. Lift the chicken out of the pan, and in the oil left behind, sauté the onion and pepper until the vegetables are soft and the onion is beginning to brown. Stir in the rice, garlic, and smoked paprika, then pour in the beer, fire-roasted tomatoes, and water, and add the saffron threads. Bring the liquid to a boil.

4. Put the sausage and chicken pieces back in the pot, reduce the heat to low, and cover. Simmer until the rice has absorbed the cooking liquid and the chicken is cooked through, about 35 minutes.

5. Ten minutes before serving, stir in the peas and parsley, cover the pan, and let the finished dish rest undisturbed until the peas are heated through.

★

ORANGE CHICKEN FOR A CROWD

My friend Greg Young is not a professional chef, but he cooks regularly for a crowd of homeless men and women at his church in Oakland, California, which is housed in a beautiful Arts and Crafts building designed by Julia Morgan in 1917. When he asked me once for some new recipes, I thought of Oakland and walking from his home to the church where the streets are dotted with orange trees. The recipe had to be easy and affordable, and it had to be possible to do some of the work ahead. So I settled on a formula for chicken brined in orange juice. The recipe has been scaled down for home use, but it is easily scaled back up for a big event. If you are making this dish on a budget, use chicken legs. If refrigerator space is at a premium, use a cooler to hold them all. Use ice packs to keep the chicken cold. Serve the chicken with "Blasted Broccoli" with Red Chiles and Garlic (page 250) and long-grain rice.

MAKES 8 SERVINGS

½ cup kosher salt

½ cup sugar

2 teaspoons coarsely ground black pepper

2 bay leaves

4 cups boiling water

One 12-ounce can frozen organic orange juice concentrate

4 cups ice water

2 free-range chickens, 3½ to 4 pounds each, cut into 8 pieces each (see page 185)

3 tablespoons cornstarch

1. Several hours or even the night before you plan to serve the chicken, make the brine. Stir the salt, sugar, pepper, and bay leaves into the boiling water and let the mixture steep for 20 minutes. Stir in half of the frozen orange juice concentrate and the ice water and continue stirring until the ice and juice concentrate have melted. Plunge the chicken pieces into the cold brine and refrigerate for several hours or overnight.

2. Preheat the oven to 375°F. Transfer the chicken from the brine to a roasting pan and discard all but 1 cup of the brining solution.

3. Roast the chicken until an instant-read thermometer inserted into the thickest piece registers 165°F and the juices run clear, about 40 minutes.

4. While the chicken is roasting, make the sauce. Put the reserved 1 cup brining liquid and the remaining orange juice concentrate in a saucepan with the cornstarch and whisk the liquid until it thickens and comes to a boil. During the last 10 minutes of roasting time, brush the chicken pieces with some of the sauce.

5. Pour the remaining sauce over the chicken pieces and serve the chicken family style from the baking dish, or distribute the chicken pieces evenly among serving plates and pass the sauce separately.

★

CHICKEN BAKED WITH PLUMS AND OLIVES

The combination of sweet and salty is almost always appealing to me. In this dish, the gentle goodness of plums is slightly intensified in the heat of the oven, and the powerful punch of strong dark Mediterranean olives is toned down a notch or two. Together, the plums and the olives create a playful exchange of flavors around baked chicken pieces. The recipe can easily be doubled for a crowd, but do be sure to use a pan large enough to accommodate all the chicken pieces in a single layer. Serve the chicken with San Francisco–Style Rice Pilaf (pages 141–42) and Broccoli Raab Sauteed with Garlic and Chiles (pages 249–50).

One chicken, 3½ to 4 pounds, cut into 8 pieces (see page 185)

2 teaspoons kosher salt

1 teaspoon freshly ground black pepper

12 ripe Italian prune plums, halved and pitted

¾ cup pitted saracena or niçoise olives

2 cloves garlic, grated on a Microplane grater or finely chopped

1 cup dry white wine, such as chardonnay or sauvignon blanc

1. Preheat the oven to 400°F.

2. Sprinkle the chicken pieces with the salt and pepper and arrange the pieces skin side up in a single layer in a 2-quart, nonreactive (glass or ceramic) baking dish.

3. Tuck the plum halves around the chicken pieces, and scatter the olives and garlic over the chicken and plums. Pour the wine over all.

4. Bake until the pieces are well browned on top and an instant-read thermometer inserted into the thickest piece registers 180°F, about 40 minutes.

5. With tongs or a slotted spoon, transfer the baked chicken pieces with the plums and olives to a platter and pour the pan drippings into a small saucepan. Boil over high heat, stirring with a wire whisk, until slightly thickened. Pour the sauce over the chicken and serve hot.

★
BREASTS OF CHICKEN BAKED WITH FOREST MUSHROOMS

Gunther Eschenbrenner, a wise old German who used to dine regularly at one of the restaurants where I cooked once told me, "If you are going to cook well, you have to have a lot of time or a lot of money. If you have costly ingredients you can cook quickly; if you have only humble ingredients you have to spend some time in the kitchen." This dish derives its goodness from costly forest mushrooms, not from spending a lot of time in the kitchen. In the spring, make this chicken with morels and serve it with oven-roasted asparagus, and in the fall, make it with chanterelles and serve it with Southern-Style Greens (page 246).

MAKES 6 SERVINGS

1 pound morel or chanterelle mushrooms, depending on the season, or 1 ounce dried forest mushrooms (porcini or shiitake)

6 boneless, skinless free-range chicken breast halves, about 3 pounds

1 cup dry white wine, such as chardonnay or semillon

1 cup heavy cream

2 teaspoons kosher salt

1 teaspoon freshly ground black pepper

1. Pick through the mushrooms and remove any debris that may have come in from the forest floor. Also discard any mushrooms that have gone mushy. If using morel mushrooms, cut them into round spokes. If using chanterelles, pull them apart into shards by gently tearing

each one lengthwise. If using dried mushrooms, put them in a small mixing bowl and soak them for a few minutes in I/2 cup boiling water, or just enough to cover.

2. Preheat the oven to 400°F and butter a large (4-quart) baking dish. Line the bottom of the baking dish with the mushrooms. Cut each chicken breast half into thirds lengthwise and arrange the pieces in a single layer on top of the mushrooms. Pour the wine over the chicken pieces, then pour the cream over them, lightly coating each piece, and sprinkle with salt and pepper.

3. Bake the chicken until the meat is lightly browned and cooked through, about 25 minutes. An instant-read thermometer inserted into the thickest part of the meat should register 170°F.

4. With tongs or a slotted spoon, transfer the baked chicken and mushroom pieces to a platter or individual serving plates and pour the pan drippings into a medium sauté pan over high heat. Boil the sauce over high heat, stirring with a wire whisk, until it is slightly thickened and reduced to about half its original volume. Pour the sauce over the chicken and serve at once.

BREASTS OF CHICKEN STUFFED WITH SPINACH AND SUN-DRIED TOMATOES

It's hard to believe that sun-dried tomatoes were once a novelty. But when we first started cooking with dried tomatoes in olive oil, imported from Italy in the early 1980s, we West Coast chefs were excited, for here was indeed a new and wonderful flavor. It wasn't long before California growers started producing the dried tomatoes domestically, simply dried without the expensive olive oil and the shipping costs, and we could afford to use even more of them. Before long, dried tomatoes were every-where, and their novelty faded. But I have never tired of this dish, with sun-dried tomatoes and spinach tucked under the chicken skin. It is one of the first things I ever made with dried tomatoes. These days, I buy presliced dried tomatoes in the bulk section of my local super-market. Note that most stores sell chicken breasts either boneless and skinless or whole, with both skin and bones still attached. Ask your butcher if you can buy "airline breasts," with the bones removed and the skin still intact. If not, buy the bone-in, skin-on type and remove the bones yourself, leaving the skin intact.

MAKES 6 SERVINGS

For the Stuffing

I cup julienne-cut sun-dried tomatoes

½ cup boiling water, or just enough to cover the tomatoes

¼ cup olive oil

2 cloves garlic, grated on a Microplane grater or finely chopped

2 teaspoons kosher salt

1 teaspoon freshly ground black pepper

One 10-ounce bag prewashed baby spinach leaves, or one 10-ounce box frozen spinach, preferably organic

For the Chicken

6 boneless free-range chicken breast halves, skin left on, about 3 pounds

1 cup dry white wine, such as chardonnay or semillon

1 cup heavy cream

1. Prepare the stuffing. In a small mixing bowl, cover the sun-dried tomatoes with the boiling water and allow them to soak for 5 minutes.

2. Meanwhile, in a large sauté pan over medium-high heat, warm the olive oil and garlic with the salt and pepper until the garlic is sizzling and just beginning to color, about 3 minutes. Add the spinach and the sun-dried tomatoes in their soaking liquid and cook until the spinach is wilted and heated through, about 3 minutes more. If you are using frozen spinach, cover and cook until the spinach is thawed, about 5 minutes.

3. Transfer the cooked stuffing mixture to a food processor and pulse the motor on and off until the mixture is chopped into a rough paste. (If no food processor is available, transfer the vegetables from the pan to a cutting board, using a slotted spoon, and chop them, then stir the

vegetables back into their cooking liquid.) The stuffing can be prepared ahead and kept refrigerated until just before the chicken is baked.

4. Preheat the oven to 400°F. Lift up the skin from one side of each chicken breast half and tuck about ¼ cup of the stuffing between the skin and the meat. Arrange the stuffed breasts in a single layer in a large (4-quart) baking dish, and pour the wine and cream over them.

5. Bake the stuffed chicken breasts until the skin is browned and the meat is cooked through, about 25 minutes. An instant-read thermometer inserted into the thickest part of the meat should register 170°F.

6. With tongs or a slotted spoon, transfer the baked chicken breasts to a platter or individual serving plates and pour the pan drippings into a medium sauté pan over high heat. Boil the sauce over high heat, stirring with a whisk, until it is slightly thickened and reduced to about half its original volume. Pour the sauce over the chicken and serve at once.

★

SKILLET FRIED CHICKEN WITH PAN GRAVY

Fried chicken may belong to the Deep South, but so do the hearts and minds of many of the "immigrants" from Dixie, who brought their family recipes along with their cast-iron skillets when they came out West. I think it's interesting that Oprah Winfrey, who spent her early childhood in Mississippi, says the best fried chicken she's ever tasted came from Ezell's Famous Chicken in Seattle's Central District—interesting, but not surprising. Folks on the West Coast know how to fry chicken. This recipe is loosely based on my grandfather's recipe. He soaked his chicken in buttermilk; I use yogurt. The tangy yogurt helps to tenderize the chicken. For best results, buy a whole chicken and cut it up yourself. Rice bran oil makes an exceptional frying medium, but if you can't find it, peanut or canola oil will do. A large cast-iron skillet with a lid makes the best fried chicken; if you don't have one, any covered frying pan will do. If the pan is not large enough to accommodate the chicken pieces in a single layer without crowding, preheat the oven to 250°F and line a baking sheet with a brown paper bag or some paper towels and fry the chicken in two batches, holding the first batch on the baking sheet in a warm oven while you fry the second batch. Serve the fried chicken hot with pan gravy, mashed potatoes, and Southern-Style Greens (page 246).

MAKES 4 SERVINGS

For the Chicken

1 cup plain yogurt

1 teaspoon hot pepper sauce

1 (about 4 pounds) free-range chicken, cut into 8 pieces (see page 185)

Rice bran, peanut, or canola oil, for frying

1 cup unbleached white flour

1 tablespoon kosher salt, or 1½ teaspoons table salt

1 teaspoon baking powder

½ teaspoon baking soda

1 teaspoon freshly ground black pepper

1 teaspoon paprika

1 teaspoon dried thyme

¼ teaspoon ground nutmeg

For the Pan Gravy

2 tablespoons oil from frying the chicken

2 tablespoons flour

2 cups chicken broth, homemade (page 68), or store-bought

1 teaspoon brown sugar

1 teaspoon soy sauce

Salt and freshly ground black pepper, to taste

1. In a medium mixing bowl, whisk the yogurt with the hot pepper sauce. Roll the chicken pieces in the mixture and allow the chicken to marinate in this solution for several hours or overnight.

2. In a large skillet, preferably cast iron, heat 2 inches of oil over medium-high heat until a cube of bread dropped into the oil rises immediately to the surface and becomes golden brown in 1 minute, or until a instant-read thermometer registers 375°F.

3. While the oil is heating, in a large bowl whisk the flour with the salt, baking powder, baking soda, pepper, paprika, thyme, and nutmeg. Lift the chicken pieces out of the marinade and roll them in the flour mixture. Lay the floured chicken carefully in the hot oil, preferably using metal tongs to avoid being splashed.

4. When all the chicken is in the pan—or half the chicken if you are frying it in batches—cover the pan and turn the heat to medium. Allow the chicken to fry, covered, for 10 minutes, then uncover the pan, turn the chicken pieces over, and fry, uncovered, until the chicken is cooked through, or until an instant-read thermometer inserted into the thickest part of the meat registers 165°F, about 10 minutes more.

5. After the chicken is fried, transfer it to platter and make the gravy. Discard all but 2 tablespoons of the oil, and whisk in the flour. When it is sizzling, whisk in the chicken broth, brown sugar, and soy sauce. Season the gravy to taste with salt and pepper, and serve with the chicken.

★

CHINATOWN SWEET-AND-SOUR CHICKEN

While I know that Chinese home cooking bears little resemblance to the food served in most Chinese restaurants, it seems to me that a separate authenticity exists in the Chinese restaurant style of cooking that used to be found in Chinatown eateries up and down the West Coast. In this recipe, which is modeled after the kind of dishes served in those restaurants, batter-fried pieces of boneless chicken are sauced with a sweet and tangy mixture of citrus juices and pineapple. Serve the dish very hot, as soon as it comes together, with hot rice or noodles.

For the Chicken

1 pound boneless, skinless free-range chicken breast halves or thighs

2 teaspoons kosher salt

1 egg

1 cup water

1 cup unbleached white flour

1 teaspoon baking powder

Rice bran, peanut, or canola oil, for frying

For the Sauce

1 navel orange

1 lemon

¼ cup brown sugar

3 tablespoons cornstarch

1-inch piece ginger root, grated on a Microplane grater

2 or 3 garlic cloves, grated on a Microplane grater

1 teaspoon dried red chile flakes, or to taste

To Finish the Dish

1 medium red bell pepper, cut into ½-inch strips

1 medium green bell pepper, cut into ½-inch strips

1 bunch green onions, cut into ½-inch lengths

2 cups cubed fresh pineapple (1-inch cubes), or one 20-ounce can pineapple chunks in pineapple juice, drained

1. Cut the chicken into 1-inch cubes. Toss the chicken pieces with the salt. In a small mixing bowl, whisk together the egg and the water. In a separate large bowl, whisk together the flour and baking powder, then stir the two mixtures together to make a thin batter. Stir the salted chicken pieces into the batter.

2. Prepare the ingredients for the sauce. Grate the zest from the orange and the lemon into a small mixing bowl, then juice the fruits and add the juice to the zest. Whisk in the brown sugar, cornstarch, ginger, garlic, and chile flakes, and keep the mixture near the stove.

3. Put 1 inch of oil into a 14-inch wok or large (12-inch) cast-iron skillet and heat over high heat until a drop of the batter bubbles and rises to the top of the oil almost instantly; an instant-read thermometer will register 350°F. Using a slotted spoon or tongs to avoid getting splashed, transfer the chicken pieces from the batter to the hot oil, distributing the pieces evenly over the surface of the wok or skillet. Fry the chicken, turning the pieces once or twice, until they are crisp and cooked through, about 6 minutes. Transfer the fried chicken to a plate and discard all but about 2 tablespoons of the oil. (Let the chicken rest on the plate while you stir-fry the remaining ingredients.)

4. In the oil left in the pan, stir-fry the red and green peppers and green onion until the vegetables are crisp-tender, about 3 minutes. Stir in the pineapple and its juice. Give the sauce ingredients a quick stir and add the sauce all at once to the hot stir-fry. Cook until the sauce has boiled down to a shiny glaze around the vegetables, about 2 minutes. Quickly stir in the reserved fried chicken pieces, along with any juices that may have accumulated on the plate, and serve immediately.

★

STIR-FRIED CHICKEN WITH RED CURRY SAUCE

With the turn of the twenty-first century, West Coast cooks, like cooks all over North America, started trying to re-create the dishes they enjoyed in Thai restaurants at home. Thai-style curries once baffled me. Then I spent a day preparing curry pastes and cooking Thai food with my friend Sri Owen, who hails from Indonesia and spent several years traveling throughout Southeast Asia studying the food there. Ever since, I have felt increasingly confident with the genre. Once I had made my own red curry paste, I feel entitled to use the packaged stuff from Thailand with some understanding of what's in it. Serve this aromatic chicken with basmati rice and Typhoon-Style Green Beans (pages 252–53).

MAKES 4 SERVINGS

1 pound boneless, skinless chicken thighs or breast halves

2 tablespoons coconut or canola oil

2 tablespoons red curry paste

One 14-ounce can coconut cream or coconut milk (*not* "cream of coconut")

2 tablespoons Thai fish sauce

1 tablespoon palm sugar or light brown sugar

1 bunch green onions, cut on the diagonal into ¼-inch slices

1 small bunch (about 30 leaves) fresh basil leaves, cut into ribbons

¼ cup fresh cilantro leaves

1 lime, cut into wedges, as an accompaniment

1. Cut the chicken against the grain into strips about ¼ inch thick, then cut the strips into 1-inch lengths.

2. Heat a 14-inch wok or large (12-inch) cast-iron skillet over high heat until a drop of water dances immediately and evaporates in 1 or 2 seconds. Add the oil and swirl it in the pan. Add the chicken, distributing it evenly over the surface of the wok or skillet, and let it cook, undisturbed, for a minute to brown. Add the curry paste and coconut cream and cook for 2 minutes, stirring constantly with a metal spatula or tongs.

3. Stir in the fish sauce and palm sugar and cook until the chicken is cooked through, about 4 minutes. Stir in the green onions, basil, and cilantro and serve the curry hot, with wedges of fresh lime passed separately.

★

HONEY-LEMON GRILLED BREASTS OF CHICKEN WITH MANGO SALSA

It could be argued that the basic method for cooking a breast of chicken on the East Coast is to sauté it in a pan; on the West Coast, it would be to grill it. On the East Coast, the chicken would be finished with a sauce made in the pan; on the West Coast, chances are the chicken would be finished with a fresh fruit or vegetable salsa. Time spent in brine, a solution of salt water (flavored here with honey and lemon), makes this chicken moister, more tender, and more flavorful than plain grilled chicken. This is the grilled chicken to prepare for topping a Tijuana Caesar Salad (pages 97–98) or filling an I-5 Grilled Chicken Sandwich (pages 117–18). For dinner, serve it with mango salsa, Coconut Rice (page 139), and Sautéed Greens (pages 245–46).

MAKES 6 SERVINGS

¼ cup kosher salt

¼ cup honey

1 cup boiling water

2 tablespoons freshly squeezed lemon juice

1 cup ice water

6 boneless, skinless free-range chicken breast halves, 8 ounces each

For the Salsa

1 teaspoon crushed red chiles, or to taste

2 tablespoons boiling water

2 medium mangoes, or 2 cups frozen mango chunks

⅓ cup finely diced sweet red pepper

⅓ cup finely diced red onion

2 tablespoons freshly squeezed lime juice

1 tablespoon sugar

1 teaspoon kosher salt

1 tablespoon chopped fresh cilantro

1. Several hours before you grill the chicken, make the brine. Stir the kosher salt and honey into the boiling water until dissolved. Stir in the lemon juice and ice water and continue stirring until the ice has melted.

2. Put the chicken breasts in a zipper-lock bag, pour the cold brine over them, seal the bag, and put it in the refrigerator. Allow the chicken to soak in the cold brine for at least 2 hours or for as long as 4 hours.

3. Make the salsa. In a medium mixing bowl, cover the red chiles with the boiling water and allow them to soften. With a sharp knife, cut the halves from the side of each mango, leaving the central section of the fruit attached to the pit. With a large spoon, scoop out the pulp from the skin of each mango half. Slice each half into 4 or 5 vertical slices, then cut across the slices to yield 1-inch chunks of fruit. Stir the mango chunks, red pepper, red onion, lime juice, sugar, and salt into the softened red chilies. Just before serving, toss in the cilantro.

4. Preheat a gas or charcoal grill until the heat from the grill forces you to move your hand away when you hold it 5 inches above the grate. Charcoal should be burned down to white-hot coals. Rub the cooking surface with oil. Remove the chicken from the brine and discard the brine. Cook the chicken breasts on the grill until they are well marked with brown stripes on one side, 2 to 3 minutes. Give each piece a quarter turn and cook on the same side to get cross-hatch marks, another 2 to 3 minutes more.

5. Turn the breasts and cook on the other side until they are just cooked through, about 3 minutes more. An instant-read thermometer inserted in the thickest part of the meat should register 170°F.

★

RASPBERRY GRILLED CHICKEN

During the last decades of the twentieth century, the combination of grilled meat and fresh fruit became ubiquitous. For a time it seemed that the dictum "protein plus fruit equals New American Cuisine" was a guiding principle behind an irksome fad. But combining raspberries with chicken goes back at least as far as the journals of the late, great James Beard. The flavors work so well together that this partnership will be around for a good, long time. Serve the chicken with basmati rice and Chinese Restaurant–Style Snap Peas (page 258).

For the Chicken

¼ cup kosher salt

¼ cup sugar

1 cup boiling water

¼ cup raspberry vinegar

1 cup ice water

1 chicken, 3½ to 4 pounds, cut into 8 pieces (see page 185)

For the Sauce and Garnish

1 pint fresh raspberries

1 tablespoon sugar

1 tablespoon raspberry vinegar

1 teaspoon kosher salt

1 teaspoon freshly ground black pepper

1. Several hours before you grill the chicken, make the brine. Stir the kosher salt and sugar into the boiling water until dissolved. Stir in the raspberry vinegar and ice water and continue stirring until the ice has melted.

2. Put the chicken pieces in a zipper-lock bag, pour the cold brine over them, seal the bag, and put it in the refrigerator. Allow the chicken to soak in the cold brine for at least 2 hours or for as long as 4 hours.

3. Preheat a gas or charcoal grill until the heat from the grill forces you to move your hand away when you hold it 5 inches above the grate. Charcoal should be burned down to white-hot coals. Rub the cooking surface with oil. Remove the chicken from the brine, and save the brine. Cook the chicken pieces on the grill until they are well marked with brown stripes on one side, about 4 minutes. Turn the pieces and cook to mark that side as well, another 4 minutes. Continue turning and cooking, basting with the brine as needed to keep the pieces from burning, until the chicken is almost cooked through, about 15 minutes more.

4. Make the sauce. Purée half of the raspberries in a blender with the sugar and raspberry vinegar. Force the purée through a strainer to remove the seeds, and season the purée with the salt and pepper. As the chicken approaches doneness, start brushing it with the sauce, and continue brushing with a small amount of the sauce until an instant-read thermometer inserted in the thickest part of the meat registers 170°F.

5. Transfer the chicken to a platter, pour any remaining sauce over the chicken pieces, and scatter the remaining raspberries over the finished dish, or distribute the chicken pieces evenly among 4 serving plates and garnish each one with raspberries.

★
POLLO BOLLITO WITH
LEMON AÏOLI

Served as a main course, a simple poached chicken like this one lends itself to any number of menus. Served with Lemon Aïoli (pages 50–51), it's an easy main dish. The broth could become the foundation for Meatballs in Broth (pages 69–70). Use leftover poached chicken for Chicken Enchiladas (pages 200–1).

MAKES 4 SERVINGS

8 cups water

1 teaspoon salt

1 bay leaf

1 chicken, 3 to 4 pounds

Lemon Aïoli (pages 50–51)

1. In a large kettle or Dutch oven over high heat, combine the water, salt, and bay leaf. Cover and bring the water to a rolling boil.

2. Add the chicken and, when the liquid returns to a boil, reduce the heat to the lowest setting and poach the chicken for 1 hour.

3. Remove the chicken from the broth and serve with Lemon Aïoli. Reserve the broth and use it for soup.

★
CHICKEN ENCHILADAS

Enchilada is the past tense of a Spanish verb for chile; basically, it means "chiled." In practical terms, it refers to a tortilla dipped in chile sauce or lightly fried and then filled with a savory filling and doused in more chile sauce. A good deal of the work in the kitchens of West Coast restaurants is accomplished by immigrants from Mexico, and even when the dining room features contemporary American or French cuisine, the cooks in the kitchen are likely to be experts in Mexican cooking. But when I asked my Mexican co-workers about enchiladas, they shrugged. Oddly enough, enchiladas seem to be more popular at northern latitudes. Serve these hot with Alcelmo's Spanish Rice (page 140) and Refried Pinto Beans (page 143).

MAKES 1 DOZEN ENCHILADAS, SERVING 6

For the Enchiladas

¾ cup canola or corn oil

12 corn tortillas

8 ounces cream cheese

12 ounces (about 3 cups) cooked chicken meat

1 cup grated Monterey Jack cheese

Shredded lettuce as an accompaniment

For the Enchilada Sauce

½ cup corn or canola oil from frying the tortillas

½ cup all-purpose flour

¼ cup chili powder

2 small onions (about 1 cup), finely chopped

2 cups chicken broth, homemade (page 68), or store-bought

2 cups freshly squeezed orange juice

1. Preheat the oven to 375°F. Put the oil in a small frying pan over medium-high heat until it is hot but not smoking. It should be about 375°F—a tortilla dipped into the oil will immediately begin to bubble.

2. Fry the tortillas one at a time in the hot oil, turning them once. Cook each tortilla until it begins to puff up, about 10 seconds. As they are cooked, carefully stack the fried tortillas one on top of the other so they won't dry out as they cool. Allow the stacked fried tortillas to stand at room temperature while you prepare the enchilada sauce. Save the oil used for frying to make the enchilada sauce.

3. Make the sauce. In a medium saucepan over medium-high heat, stir the oil and flour with a wire whisk until bubbling hot. Stir in the chili powder and then the onion and cook for 1 minute. Whisk in the chicken broth and orange juice and stir the sauce continually until it comes to a full, rolling boil. Turn off the heat and keep the sauce covered while you prepare the enchiladas.

4. Put 1 cup of the enchilada sauce and the cream cheese in the bowl of an electric mixer and mix with the paddle attachment on slow speed until the cream cheese is soft and well combined with the sauce, about 2 minutes. Add the chicken meat.

5. Put a piece of baker's parchment down on the counter and lay the fried and cooled tortillas out in a single layer. Distribute the chicken filling evenly among the tortillas, and roll each one into a tight little log.

6. Spread 1 cup of the enchilada sauce in the bottom of a large baking dish, and place the enchiladas in a single layer over the sauce. Pour the remaining sauce over the top of the enchiladas, making sure the edges are covered. Sprinkle the cheese over the sauce. The enchiladas can be prepared ahead, refrigerated, and baked several hours later.

7. Bake the enchiladas until the cheese is molten and the sauce is bubbling hot, 15 to 20 minutes. Transfer enchiladas to plates and serve with shredded lettuce.

★

ROSÉ ROAST CHICKEN WITH HERBS

For a long time, rosé wines had a bad reputation. Many of us associated rosé with the spritzy wines from Portugal that earned us our first real hangovers. Then came the overly sweet white zinfandels that made us wonder why anyone would bother with blush wines at all. But real rosé, like the ones made in the south of France or the Rioja region of Spain, are wonderful wines. And the rosé wines made in the Old World style on the West Coast these days are good enough to inspire great meals.

Start with a plate of vegetables with Lemon Aïoli (pages 50–51), move on to Rosé Roast Chicken served with M. F. K. Fisher's "Shook" Potatoes (pages 238–39), and finish with a Fresh Fig and Almond Gallete (pages 337–38).

MAKES 4 GENEROUS SERVINGS

1 free-range chicken, 4 to 5 pounds

1 tablespoon kosher salt

1 tablespoon dried herbes de Provence or Italian seasoning

1 teaspoon freshly ground black pepper

1½ cups rosé wine

1 tablespoon cornstarch

Herb sprigs, for garnish (optional)

1. Preheat the oven to 450°F and position a rack near the bottom. Place the chicken in a large casserole dish and rub it with the salt, herbs, and pepper. Put the chicken upside down (breast side down) in the dish, and pour in ¾ cup of the wine.

2. Roast the chicken for 35 minutes, then turn it over (breast side up), reduce the heat to 350°F, and roast it for 45 minutes longer. Insert a thermometer into the thickest part of the thigh, and when it registers 160°F, the chicken is done, usually about 1½ hours roasting time in all.

3. Transfer the chicken from the casserole dish to a serving platter and cover it with aluminum foil. Pour most of the fat out of the dish, being careful to retain any juices trapped underneath. Dissolve the cornstarch in the remaining ¾ cup wine, and with a wire whisk swirl this mixture in the casserole dish to free any stuck-on pan juices. Transfer the liquid to a small saucepan and cook, stirring, over medium-high heat until the sauce is boiling and slightly thickened.

4. Garnish the roast chicken with sprigs of fresh herbs, if desired. Serve hot with the sauce.

★

GAME HENS WITH FOREST MUSHROOMS AND AÏOLI

I used to serve this dish frequently at a small café in Friday Harbor in Washington's San Juan Islands. What usually prompted me to make it was a cache of mushrooms delivered to the back door by one of the local foragers who delivered morels in the spring and chanterelles in the fall. It is a one-dish meal in which garlic-stuffed hens are first roasted and then briefly stewed with vegetables and broth that serve as sauce and side dish. At the café, I would roast the hens ahead of time, chill them, and finish them with vegetables and broth just before serving, and you can do the same at home.

MAKES 4 SERVINGS

4 game hens, 1 pound each

2 teaspoons kosher salt

1 teaspoon freshly ground black pepper

24 cloves garlic, peeled

1 tablespoon olive oil

1 large onion, peeled and sliced

4 carrots, cut into large matchsticks

8 ounces chanterelle or morel mushrooms

1 cup white wine

6 cups chicken broth, homemade (page 68), or store-bought

8 ounces (about 2 cups) snap peas or tiny green beans, trimmed

Fennel and Caper Aïoli (page 163)

Sprigs of tarragon or Italian parsley, for garnish

1. Preheat the oven to 400°F. If the hens have a packet of giblets inside, remove it. Sprinkle the hens inside and out with the salt and pepper. Fill the cavity of each bird with 6 garlic cloves.

2. Arrange the birds in a single layer in a deep, heavy skillet or 4-quart Dutch oven that can move from oven to stovetop. Roast the birds until their skins are crisp and golden and the meat is cooked through, about 45 minutes. An instant-read thermometer inserted into the thickest part of the thigh should register 170°F.

3. With an offset spatula, transfer the birds from the pan to a plate or to the inverted lid of the pan. Pour off the fat from the pan and replace it with the olive oil. Put the pan over medium-high heat and sauté the onions and carrots until the onions are soft and just beginning to color.

4. Pick through the mushrooms, removing any debris or slimy bits. If they are chanterelles, pull them apart lengthwise

into shreds. If they are morels, slice them into rings.

5. Add the mushrooms to the pan with the carrots and onions and sauté briefly just to warm the mushrooms through. Pour in the wine and boil until it's almost evaporated, about 3 minutes. Add the chicken broth and bring it to a boil.

6. Put the roasted game hens back in the pan, cover, and reduce the heat to a simmer. Let the hens stew in the simmering broth until they are tender and heated through, 15 to 20 minutes. During the last 10 minutes, add the snap peas or green beans. Put each hen in a very large pasta bowl, and distribute the broth and vegetables evenly among the bowls. Garnish each with a dollop of aïoli and a sprig of tarragon or Italian parsley.

★

APPLE CIDER ROASTED TURKEY

To cure the turkey in its cider brine, you will need a container large enough to hold the turkey and small enough to fit in your refrigerator. I use a 3-gallon food storage container from a restaurant supply store and rearrange the shelves in my refrigerator to accommodate it. If no container is available, find a cooler just large enough to hold the bird. Once you get past the brining and roasting, serve this flavorful bird with Apple Sausage Stuffing (page 205), Roasted Delicata Squash (pages 256–57) and West Coast Green Bean Casserole (pages 253–54).

For the Turkey

1 naturally raised turkey, about 12 pounds

½ cup kosher salt

1 small bunch (about 6 sprigs) fresh rosemary

6 cloves garlic, crushed

12 whole dried cloves

2 tablespoons whole black peppercorns

8 cups boiling water

6 cups ice water

One 12-ounce can frozen apple juice concentrate, preferably organic

1 cup natural apple cider vinegar

For the Gravy

Giblets from the turkey

6 cups water

Canola oil, as needed

¼ cup flour

1. Unwrap the turkey and put it in a food storage container or clean cooler. Remove the giblets from the turkey and refrigerate them until the turkey goes into the oven.

2. Make the brine. Stir the salt, rosemary sprigs, crushed garlic, cloves, and peppercorns into the boiling water and let the mixture steep for 20 minutes. Stir in the ice water, frozen juice concentrate, and apple cider vinegar; continue stirring until the ice has melted.

3. Pour the cold brine over the turkey and cover the container or cooler. Allow the turkey to soak in the cold brine for 12 to 24 hours. Use gel packs if necessary to keep the brine cold.

4. Preheat the oven to 325°F. Transfer the turkey from the container to a roasting pan and discard the brine. Roast the turkey until the thigh meat registers 180°F, 3¾ to 4¼ hours, 15 minutes per pound. During the last hour of roasting, you may need to cover the bird loosely with foil to prevent overbrowning.

5. While the turkey is roasting, make the broth for the gravy. Simmer the giblets in a large saucepan with the water for about 3 hours, adding more water if needed to keep the giblets covered. You should end up with about 4 cups of broth. Save the broth for the gravy.

6. When it is ready, transfer the turkey from the roasting pan to a platter and let it rest for 20 minutes before carving.

7. While the turkey is resting, make the gravy. Pour any fat from the roasting pan into a measuring cup. Reserve ½ cup of the fat and discard the rest. (If there is less than ½ cup fat, add canola oil to make up the difference.) Put the turkey fat in a large saucepan over medium-high heat and whisk in the flour. Strain the broth made from the giblets into the roasting pan and scrape up any flavorful bits left in the pan. Then strain the broth from the roasting pan into the saucepan. Whisk

the gravy until it is smooth and thickened. Transfer the gravy to a gravy boat.

8. Carve the turkey at the table and pass the gravy separately.

★
APPLE SAUSAGE STUFFING

This dressing was made to go with the Apple Cider Roasted Turkey on pages 203–5, but it is so flavorful that it could serve as an entrée in itself. Chicken and apple sausage, once a hard-to-find specialty item, has become increasingly available. Bruce Aidells is the brand I use. If you can't find apple sausage, use whatever sausage you like.

MAKES 12 CUPS, ENOUGH TO
STUFF A 12-POUND TURKEY

1 pound fully cooked chicken and apple sausage, sliced ¼ inch thick

2 tablespoons canola oil

1 medium onion, peeled and finely diced

3 stalks celery, cut into ¼-inch dice

2 medium apples (about 1 pound), peeled and cut into ¼-inch dice

4 cloves garlic, peeled and grated on a Microplane grater or finely chopped

1 turkey liver (or 4 ounces chicken livers), finely chopped

1 day-old loaf artisanal bread (about 6 cups), cut into 1-inch cubes

3 cups apple cider or apple juice

1 tablespoon kosher salt, or to taste

1 teaspoon freshly ground black pepper, or to taste

1. Preheat the oven to 350°F and butter a 4-quart baking dish, preferably a ceramic oval.

2. In a Dutch oven over medium-high heat, cook the sausage pieces in the canola oil until they are lightly browned, about 5 minutes. With a slotted spoon, lift the sausage pieces out of the oil and set them aside (I put them on the upturned lid of the pot).

3. In the oil left behind, sauté the onion, celery, apples, and garlic until soft and just beginning to color, about 3 minutes. Add the chopped turkey liver and sauté until it has lost its bright red color, about 4 minutes.

4. Put the bread cubes in a very large mixing bowl. Pile the sautéed vegetable and apple mixture on top of the bread cubes. Pour the apple cider into the sauté pan and scrape the pan with a wooden spoon or heatproof silicone spatula to remove any flavorful bits. Fold the cider and the sautéed mixture into the bread cubes and transfer the stuffing to the buttered baking dish.

5. Cover the pan with baker's parchment and aluminum foil and bake for 30 minutes. Remove the parchment and foil and bake for 10 minutes longer. Serve hot as a side dish with roast turkey.

★

ROAST TURKEY BREAST

When I worked as a chef at IslandWood, an environmental learning center for school-age children near my home on Bainbridge Island, I wanted to offer the kids natural, "homemade" versions of the fast foods and convenience foods they were used to. For their lunches, I baked all the sandwich bread, and I wanted to offer good cold cuts, but the only roast turkey we could find from our distributors seemed rubbery and insipid. So I developed a technique for roasting our own. Now I use the same technique to roast breasts of turkey at home. One serves as dinner and the other gets chilled for sandwiches. Any extra can be used for Turkey Tetrazzini (page 152) or used in place of chicken in the Enchiladas (pages 200–1).

MAKES ABOUT 12 SERVINGS

½ cup kosher salt

½ cup brown sugar

2 teaspoons coarsely ground black pepper

2 bay leaves

4 cups boiling water

4 cups ice water

2 boneless half breasts of natural turkey, about 3 pounds altogether

1. Four hours before you plan to serve the turkey, make the brine. In a large stock pot, stir the kosher salt, brown sugar, pepper, and bay leaves into the boiling water and let the mixture steep for 20 minutes.

2. Stir in the ice water and continue stirring until the ice has melted. Plunge the turkey breasts into the cold brine and refrigerate for several hours or overnight.

3. Preheat the oven to 375°F. Transfer the breasts from the brine to a roasting pan and discard the brine.

4. Roast the turkey breasts until an instant-read thermometer inserted into the thickest part registers 170°F and the juices run clear, about 40 minutes.

5. To serve hot, let the turkey rest for 10 minutes before slicing. Chill the turkey before slicing for sandwiches.

★

RESTAURANT-STYLE ROAST DUCKLING WITH ORANGE SAUCE

While the following recipe may appear difficult, any competent cook with decent kitchen equipment can manage it. The process is time-consuming but doesn't require any special knowledge or skill. Divided over a span of two days, with less than an hour actually devoted to tending the duck, the process won't leave you frazzled, and the results are worth the time involved. Roast and bone the duck the day before you plan to serve it, and make a stock from the bones and giblets. The next day, make a sauce from the stock, and just before you plan to serve it, crisp the boned duckling in a hot oven. Serve the roast duckling with Roasted Delicata Squash (pages 256–57) and Sautéed Greens (pages 245–46) or Roasted Brussels Sprouts with Red Chile Flakes and Sesame Oil (pages 254–55).

For the Duck

2 whole ducklings with giblets (about 5 to 5½ pounds each)

2 tablespoons kosher salt

1 tablespoon freshly ground black pepper

For the Stock

Bones and giblets from the ducklings

1 onion, sliced but not peeled

1 carrot, chopped

1 stalk celery, chopped

2 bay leaves

3 whole cloves

8 cups water

For the Sauce

1 cup heavy cream

Grated zest and juice of 2 oranges

1. Roast the ducks. Preheat the oven to 400°F. Remove the giblets from the ducks. Discard the liver, and reserve the necks, hearts, and gizzards in the refrigerator while the ducks are roasting. Sprinkle the ducks generously inside and out with the salt and pepper. Place them in a large roasting pan, at least 4 inches deep, and roast for 1 hour. Remove from the oven and allow to cool until they can be easily handled.

2. Bone the ducks. Place a bird breast side up on a stable cutting board, with the legs pointing toward you. Using a sharp chef's knife, cut into the bottom of the breast plate and cut through the cartilage all the way to the top. Spread the split carcass open to gain access to the spine. Placing the blade along one side of the backbone, press firmly and rock until the blade is all the way through. Repeat on the other side of the spine. You should have 2 half-ducks and a spine. Next, on each half-duck, run your thumb between the cartilage and the breast meat. With your thumb, carefully separate the meat from the bone along the rib cage toward the wing. Then, with a sharp twist, remove the rib cage. Remove the pelvic bones in the same manner. The bones of the thighs and legs will remain. Trim the wings down to the first joint. Repeat with the second duck. Reserve the bones for the stock. Wrap and chill the boned duck halves for several hours or overnight.

3. Make the stock. In a heavy stockpot, combine the reserved giblets, bones, onion, carrot, celery, bay leaves, and cloves. Cover with the water and bring the mixture to a boil. Reduce the heat and simmer gently for 4 hours or longer. Strain the liquid, discard the solids, and chill the stock.

4. Make the sauce. Skim the fat from the chilled stock, then boil the stock until it is reduced to 1 cup, about 1 hour. In a small, deep saucepan, combine the reduced stock, cream, and orange zest and juice. Boil

rapidly until the liquid has reduced to a thickened, translucent sauce. Stir often to prevent boiling over.

5. Crisp the ducks. Preheat the oven to 400°F. Lay the boned half-ducks on a sheet pan with a ½-inch rim and bake until the meat is heated through and the skin is crisp, 20 to 25 minutes. Take care when removing the pan from the oven, as there will be a little more fat. Serve hot with the orange sauce.

★

GRILLED BREASTS OF DUCKLING WITH SAVORY CARAMELIZED PEACHES

Like any cut cooked over an open flame, duckling cooked this way does not yield pan juices to make a sauce, so the meat is served with a kind of fresh fruit chutney in typical West Coast style. Ask your butcher for breasts of duckling, or remove them from whole ducklings with a sharp boning knife and save the hindquarters for Quick "Preserved" Duck Legs (page 210). I like to serve this grilled duckling when peaches from Pence Orchards in Washington or Frog Hollow Farm in California are ripe, with San Francisco–Style Rice Pilaf (pages 141–42) and Balsamic Blasted Green Beans (pages 250–51).

MAKES 4 SERVINGS

For the Sauce

2 sweet tree-ripened peaches

2 tablespoons sugar

2 tablespoons white port or sweet white wine

For the Duck

4 half boneless duckling breasts (7½ ounces each), split in half

2 teaspoons kosher salt

1 teaspoon freshly ground black pepper

1. Build a fire in a backyard barbecue, using flavorful hardwood or commercial charcoal. Allow the fire to blaze and then settle into a pile of glowing, white-hot coals. A bed of embers spotted with small, lively flames is your goal. Position the grill rack about 6 inches above the glowing coals, and wipe it with an oily cloth.

2. Make the sauce. Plunge the peaches into boiling water to loosen the skins, then slip the skins off, cut the peaches in half, and remove the pits. Cut the peeled peach halves into wedges. In a large, dry sauté pan or cast-iron skillet over medium-high heat, melt the sugar and, when it is caramel colored, add the sliced peaches. Toss to release the peach juices into the caramelized sugar, which will harden at first and then gradually dissolve again. Add the port and boil to cook off the alcohol. The sauce can be prepared ahead and held at room temperature until serving time.

3. With a sharp knife, score the skin side of the duck breasts with a series of cuts too shallow to reach the meat; this will allow the fat to cook out of the skin as the breasts are grilled. Season the breasts with the salt and pepper and lay them on the rack of

the grill, skin side down. Grill until most of the fat has cooked off and the skin is well browned, about 8 minutes. The top, meaty side of the breasts will cook from the heat rising up from the skin side.

4. Take the duck breasts off the grill, cover them with aluminum foil to hold in the heat, and let them stand for 5 minutes before slicing. Slice each breast on the diagonal into 5 or 6 slices and arrange the slices in a fan on each of 4 serving plates. Distribute the peaches and their juices over the grilled duckling.

★

WINE COUNTRY PAN-SEARED BREASTS OF DUCKLING WITH PEPPERED ZINFANDEL

See the note about duck breasts on pages 207–8. Instead of grilling the breasts and losing the juices, this recipe calls for pan-searing, where the pan drippings are captured to make a rich sauce. I think of the grilled duck as a summer dish and this version as a winter one. Serve the duck breasts with Savory Green Lentils with Aromatic Vegetables (page 144), Sautéed Greens (pages 245–46), and a big red wine.

MAKES 4 SERVINGS

For the Duck

4 half boneless duckling breasts (about 7½ ounces each), split in half

2 teaspoons kosher salt

1 teaspoon freshly ground black pepper

For the Sauce

1 medium shallot, peeled and finely chopped

1 tablespoon cracked black peppercorns

1 cup zinfandel

1 cup chicken broth

2 tablespoons unsalted butter

1. Preheat a large sauté pan over medium-high heat. With a sharp knife, score the skin side of the duck breasts with a series of cuts too shallow to reach the meat; this will allow the fat to cook out of the skin as the breasts are seared. Season the duck breasts with the salt and pepper and lay them skin side down in the hot sauté pan. Cook until most of the fat has cooked off and the skin is well browned, about 8 minutes. The top, meaty side of the breasts will cook from the heat rising up from the skin side.

2. Transfer the breasts from the sauté pan to a small baking sheet, cover them with aluminum foil, and then cover the foil with a kitchen towel soaked in hot tap water and wrung dry. This will hold in the heat while you make the sauce.

3. Make the sauce. Discard all but 1 tablespoon of the duck fat from the sauté pan and sauté the chopped shallot and peppercorns in the fat until the shallot is soft and the peppercorns are fragrant, about 2 minutes. Pour in the wine and chicken broth and turn the heat to high. Boil until the sauce is reduced to half its

original volume and the liquid coats the back of a spoon, about 15 minutes.

4. Slice each breast on the diagonal into 5 or 6 slices and arrange the slices in a fan on each of 4 serving plates. Swirl the butter into the sauce and distribute the sauce evenly over the sliced duck.

★

QUICK "PRESERVED" DUCK LEGS

In the Old World, goose and duck were salted to remove as much moisture as possible, then simmered in enough of their own fat to cover them completely. This ancient method produced a "confit" that would last for months. West Coast cooks equipped with modern refrigeration like to conjure the flavor of the original without the necessity of truly preserving the meat in its own fat. Simply reheated and served with potatoes or salad greens, "preserved" duck legs make a wonderful main dish. They can also be incorporated into salads or soups or cooked with beans or lentils to make a comforting cassoulet. If you have duck fat on hand, use it to start cooking the duck legs; if not, use olive oil.

MAKES 8 PIECES

4 duck leg quarters (about 12 ounces each), from 2 ducks

¾ cup kosher salt

¼ cup sugar

1 tablespoon cracked black pepper

1 teaspoon thyme leaves, fresh or dried

¼ cup rendered duck fat or olive oil

1. Cut each duck leg in two to get a leg and a thigh. Rinse them in cold running water and pat dry with paper towels. Combine the salt, sugar, pepper, and thyme. Sprinkle the mixture on all surfaces of the duck legs and put them on a cooling rack over a baking dish to catch any drippings. Put the whole arrangement in the refrigerator and let it stand for 24 hours or overnight.

2. Put a large Dutch oven or heavy covered skillet over medium heat. Brush all the salt mixture off the duck legs, and brown them in the duck fat or olive oil, turning once, about 15 minutes. Reduce the heat to low, cover the pan, and let the duck legs simmer in their own cooking fat until the meat is so tender that it almost falls from the bone, about 1½ hours.

3. Lift the duck pieces out of the pan and put them in a clean, dry crock or jar just large enough to hold them. Pour the duck fat over the cooked duck pieces and store in the refrigerator for up to 2 weeks before reheating or using in recipes.

★

RAGOÛT OF DUCKLING WITH FRIED SAGE LEAVES

Like chicken adobo, this ragoût derives a lot of its flavor from the surprising amount of vinegar in it. The acid tenderizes the meat and balances the richness of the fatty duckling. To remove most of the fat from the duckling before it goes into the stew, the duck pieces are roasted first. The time in the oven caramelizes some of the natural sugars present in the duck skin. Sage leaves, fried in the rendered duck fat, serve as a garnish for the finished dish. Serve the ragoût with Gold Rush Corn Mush (page 142) and Sautéed Greens (pages 245–46).

MAKES 4 SERVINGS

1 duckling (about 5 pounds), cut into 8 pieces (see pages 206–7)

1 tablespoon kosher salt, or to taste

1 teaspoon freshly ground black pepper, or to taste

Leaves from 1 bunch fresh sage (about 24 leaves)

1 medium onion, peeled and thinly sliced

4 cloves garlic, sliced

¼ cup red wine vinegar

1 tablespoon fresh thyme leaves, or 1 teaspoon dried

One 14.5-ounce can diced tomatoes with their juice

1. Sprinkle the duck pieces with the salt and pepper. Put a cooling rack on top of a rimmed baking sheet and arrange the seasoned duck on the rack. If you have time and space in the refrigerator, allow the meat to stand, refrigerated, on the rack for several hours. (This will draw some of the moisture out of the meat and allow it to brown more readily, but it is not vital.)

2. Preheat the oven to 325°F. Put the duckling, still on the rack over the baking sheet, in the oven and roast until the pieces are browned and crisp, about 35 minutes.

3. Carefully remove the pan from the oven. Lift the rack with the duck pieces off the baking pan and set it aside. Pour the fat from the baking sheet into a large, heavy saucepan or a Dutch oven, and place over medium-high heat. Line the baking sheet with a brown paper bag or some paper towels.

4. Fry the sage leaves in the duck fat, about 8 or 10 at a time, until they are crisp, about 2 minutes. Lift them out of the duck fat with a slotted spoon and drain on the brown paper bag or paper towels; reserve the leaves for garnish. Discard all but a tablespoon of the remaining fat.

5. Sauté the onion in the duck fat left in the pan until it is soft and just beginning to brown, about 5 minutes. Add the garlic, vinegar, thyme, and tomatoes and juice, and when the sauce is boiling, add the pieces of duckling to the pan with the sauce. Cover the pan, reduce the heat to medium-low, and simmer until the duck is tender, about 25 minutes.

MEAT

Meat

Several times each summer, Mark Ramsden fills a couple of big coolers with a few hundred pounds of ground, naturally grown Mountain Beef and drives across the state of Washington from Walla Walla to Seattle. Then he boards a Washington State ferry to sell his beef at the Bainbridge Island farmer's market. Like other small producers up and down the West Coast, he's catering to a niche market in which consumers are looking for cleaner, healthier beef from someone they can trust.

Just a stone's throw from the Bainbridge farmer's market is the swank Town & Country Market, where shoppers pay a premium for all-natural Oregon Country Beef. And in Seattle, at other farmer's markets, folks are lining up for costly "pasture-finished" ground beef from Thundering Hooves or shopping for sustainably raised Niman Ranch ground beef at Puget Consumers' Co-ops or Whole Foods Markets. What's different about all this beef?

By law, any beef labeled "organic" qualifies as all natural and free from antibiotics, steroids, and animal by-products. Cows raised for organic beef or organic dairy production must spend a significant part of their lives grazing on live grass. If the cows are grain fed, the grain must be organically grown. But what about all-natural beef that's not certified organic?

Ramsden's beef comes from a unique breed. "Corriente cattle," says Ramsden, "are descended from cows that were brought here by Spanish settlers in the eighteenth century. They're basically wild, as close as you can get to game." Because they are smaller and more adapted to the natural environment, Ramsden maintains, his cattle are better for the land.

My friend Ramsden's Mountain Beef, beef from Thundering Hooves, and even beef from somewhat larger collectives together constitute a very small percentage of U.S. beef that's "grass fed." Ironically, up until the mid-twentieth century almost all beef was grass fed. But a confluence of social and economic factors, including a surfeit of commodity corn and a taste for costlier, fattier beef in a newly prosperous postwar America, made the old-fashioned grass-fed stuff a rarity. Unfortunately, today's conventional supermarket beef contains about twice as much saturated fat as grass-fed beef, and only a fraction of the heart-healthy omega-3 fatty acids. And conjugated linoleic acid (CLA), a cancer-fighting compound abundant in grass-fed meats (and, incidentally, in the milk of grass-fed cows) is largely absent from grain-fed beef.

Oregon Country Beef and Niman Ranch are brand names applied to meat from multiple ranches that practice standards of animal husbandry established by marketers concerned with making the beef industry more sustainable. Neither of these brands is organic or grass fed because, in order to make the meat more tender and flavorful (and heavier at the time of their sale), the animals are fed grain for a few weeks prior to slaughter. But both brands qualify as "all natural" because this "finishing phase," unlike the routine fattening that goes on at most feedlots, is carefully monitored to ensure that the grain is free from antibiotics, steroids, or animal by-products.

The use of animal by-products, such as ground bones once commonly used as a calcium supplement, are a major concern to many consumers because mad cow disease can be transmitted only through the flesh of another contaminated animal, and the practice has recently been banned. All-natural beef suppliers also make sure that their beef is not weaned on a "milk replacer." Milk replacers typically contain cow's blood. Cattle are naturally vegetarian, and feeding them the ground bones or blood of their kindred is, to many consumers, repugnant.

Not long ago, I spent a day at a cattle ranch in central Texas near where my father grew up. We were with one of his childhood friends, who owns a half-mile "section" of mostly open land. Bluebonnets and Indian paintbrush were blooming, and a little stream meandered between the cottonwoods and mesquite trees. Along the horizon, a small herd of cattle stood in silhouette against the clear blue sky. As we walked, my old man and his friend shared memories of their days spent during the Great Depres-

sion, when their parents worked at the nearby cotton gin.

"Do you remember the burgers?" my father's friend wanted to know. "I used to ride my bike from the cotton gin into town to buy hamburgers for the crew," he said. "They charged a nickel apiece, but if I could get five of the guys to order one, the burger joint would give me six for a quarter and I could keep the sixth one for myself. Those hamburgers were the best-tasting things in the world."

I couldn't help thinking that the cheap hamburgers these guys enjoyed as kids were all natural, grass fed, and free from steroids or antibiotics. They would undoubtedly scoff at the high prices my generation pays for what they call "designer beef," but I bet they would recognize the clean, honest taste. That taste is what motivates West Coast meat producers.

★

BEEF STIR-FRY WITH BROCCOLI AND SHIITAKE

My friend Grace Young, author of Breath of a Wok, *grew up in San Francisco, where she says most of her Chinese relatives had long since stopped cooking in woks. In the interest of assimilation and modernity, they were using Western-style sauté pans. But as an adult, she realized that to capture true "wok hay," the breath or spirit of wok cooking, the higher temperatures and larger cooking areas offered in a wok were essential. Following her advice, I got a 14-inch cast-iron wok, and I love it.*

In a pinch, a large cast-iron skillet or sauté pan can be used. Do not use a nonstick pan.

MAKES 4 SERVINGS

2 tablespoons Chinese soy sauce

2 tablespoons Chinese cooking wine or sherry

1 teaspoon grated ginger

1 clove garlic, grated on a Microplane grater or finely chopped

1 tablespoon cornstarch

1 teaspoon toasted sesame oil

1 pound flank steak

2 tablespoons vegetable oil

1 pound Chinese broccoli, rinsed and cut into 2-inch-long pieces

4 ounces fresh shiitake caps, cut into ½-inch slices

1 bunch green onions, cut on the diagonal into ¼-inch slices

1. Stir the soy sauce, wine, ginger, garlic, cornstarch, and sesame oil together in a small bowl and set aside.

2. Cut the flank steak across the grain into strips about ¼ inch wide, and then cut the strips into 1-inch lengths.

3. Heat a 14-inch wok over high heat until a drop of water dances immediately and evaporates in 1 or 2 seconds. Swirl the oil in the pan. Add the beef, distributing it evenly over the surface of the wok, and let it cook, undisturbed, for a minute to brown. Add the broccoli and shiitake

caps and cook for 2 minutes, stirring constantly with a metal spatula or tongs.

4. Give the soy sauce mixture a quick stir to unsettle the cornstarch, and pour the mixture all at once over the beef and broccoli. Toss and cook the mixture for another minute to form a shiny glaze over the vegetables. Scatter green onions over the hot beef and broccoli just before serving.

STEAK TERIYAKI

As a chef at Canlis restaurant, I learned that the secret to good steak teriyaki is small batches. Cook one or two servings at a time, and keep the first round warm while cooking subsequent batches. The addition of the beef in its marinade drastically reduces the temperature of the hot pan in which the beef is sautéed. If the chunks of beef were to finish cooking in one pan, they would simply boil in their own juices. Moving the beef to a second hot pan reduces the marinade to a shiny, dark brown glaze on the surface while the inside remains a juicy medium-rare.

MAKES 6 SERVINGS

For the Teriyaki Sauce

½ cup Japanese soy sauce

½ cup water

⅓ cup sugar

2 tablespoons grated ginger

1 tablespoon chopped garlic

1 teaspoon cornstarch

For the Beef

2 pounds beef tenderloin, trimmed and cut into bite-sized pieces

4 tablespoons canola oil

Hot steamed rice as an accompaniment

1. In a nonreactive container (glass or stainless steel), whisk together the soy sauce, water, sugar, ginger, garlic, and cornstarch to make the teriyaki sauce. Stir in the beef and allow the mixture to marinate, refrigerated, for at least an hour, or for as long as 8 hours.

2. Just before serving time, preheat the oven to 250°F, have a 9- by 13-inch baking dish near the stove, and heat 2 sauté pans over high heat. Put a tablespoon of oil in one of the pans and add about 8 ounces of the beef (one fourth of the total) with about ¼ cup of the marinade. Cook for about 2 minutes, then transfer the beef to the other hot pan and cook for 1 minute longer, or until marinade is reduced to a shiny glaze. Transfer the beef to a baking dish and keep it in the oven while you cook the remaining beef.

3. Put another tablespoon of oil into the first pan and sauté another fourth of the beef, again moving it from one pan to another. Repeat until all of the beef is cooked. Serve the cooked beef on hot plates, with steamed rice.

STEAK PIERRE

Peter Canlis, the celebrated Washington restaurateur noted for incorporating Mediterranean, Asian, and Pacific influences into mainstream American dining rooms, developed his signature take on steak Diane even before he opened Canlis restaurant in 1950. He used to serve it at the casual Canlis Broiler in Hawaii, which opened in 1948. I learned to make this version, known as steak Pierre, when I went to work at Canlis in Seattle in the 1990s. With a copious amount of Worcestershire sauce that interfered with the subtle nuances of the expensive wines on the restaurant's ever-expanding list, the dish seemed like an anachronism that had to go. But when I took it off the menu, many customers who had been enjoying the dish for decades continued to order it. With Garlic Mashed Potatoes with Cheese (page 240) or San Francisco–Style Rice Pilaf (pages 141–42) and a green vegetable, this is comfort food at its best.

MAKES 2 SERVINGS

12 ounces beef tenderloin

Kosher salt and freshly ground black pepper, to taste

2 tablespoons flour

1 tablespoon olive oil

¼ cup vermouth

3 tablespoons Lea & Perrins Worcestershire sauce

3 tablespoons freshly squeezed lemon juice

1 clove garlic, finely chopped

¼ cup (½ stick) cold unsalted butter, cut into bits

2 tablespoons chopped fresh parsley

1. Cut the beef into 4 rounds, and pound these into ¼-inch-thick fillets. Season the fillets generously with salt and pepper. Sprinkle the flour over one side of the seasoned steaks, and shake off the excess.

2. Put a large cast-iron frying pan over high heat and add the olive oil, swirling the pan to coat the inside. Place the fillets, floured side down, in the hot pan and cook for 3 minutes. Add the vermouth, Worcestershire sauce, lemon juice, and chopped garlic. Turn the fillets and cook for 1 minute longer.

3. Move the fillets to warm plates and let the pan juices boil for a few seconds longer to become concentrated. Whisk in the butter and parsley and pour the sauce over the fillets. Serve at once.

★

BULGOGI OR FIRED BEEF

Korean restaurants all over the West Coast serve this flavorful version of barbecued beef. It has transcended the Korean community to become a part of the mainstream fare. Thick malt syrup, available in Asian groceries, lends the beef a nutty undertone, but dark corn syrup is a reasonable substitute. Serve the beef with lettuce leaves and chile flakes. Each person wraps pieces of grilled beef in the lettuce leaves and seasons them to taste with chile flakes. To make the beef easier to handle, I like to thread each piece onto a bamboo skewer.

MAKES 4 TO 6 SERVINGS

For the Beef

2 pounds lean beef sirloin

For the Marinade

½ cup vermouth or rice wine

½ cup soy sauce

½ cup freshly squeezed orange juice

2 green onions, sliced thin

4 cloves garlic, sliced thin

3 tablespoons malt syrup or dark corn syrup

1 tablespoon sugar

1 tablespoon toasted sesame oil

1 tablespoon sesame seeds

2 teaspoons freshly ground black pepper

Bamboo skewers, pre-soaked in cold water

1. Slice the beef across the grain into strips ⅛ inch thick.

2. In a medium mixing bowl, stir together the vermouth, soy sauce, orange juice, green onions, garlic, malt syrup, sugar, sesame oil, sesame seeds, and black pepper until well combined. Add the beef to the marinade and toss to coat thoroughly. Cover and refrigerate the beef in the marinade for at least 1 hour or for as long as 8 hours.

3. Preheat a gas or charcoal grill until the heat from the grill forces you to move your hand away when you hold it 5 inches above the grate. Charcoal should be burned down to white-hot coals.

4. Thread the beef strips onto bamboo skewers and grill the beef until it is well browned, about 3 minutes on each side.

★

BEEF RAGÙ IN THE WEST COAST STYLE

Strict rules govern the exact proportions and procedures for making the authentic meat sauce of Bologna. (It is important to remember that this sauce is a meat sauce with tomato, not a tomato sauce with meat.) But the West Coast version is less rigid, more forgiving, and slightly lighter in nature. In its home territory, the dairy-rich Emilia-Romagna region of northern Italy, ragù bolognese is always finished with a generous splash of heavy cream. Here, olive oil is the primary enrichment. If you can afford it, use extra virgin California olive oil such as Pasolivo from Willow Creek Olive Ranch in Paso Robles. There is no real substitute for the real Parmigiano-Reggiano that is passed separately with the finished dish. Serve the ragù in small amounts with plenty of hot cooked Homemade Noodles (pages 144–45) or spaghetti. Pass the grated cheese separately.

MAKES 6 SERVINGS

8 ounces pancetta or salt pork, cut into ¼-inch dice

⅓ cup olive oil, plus additional oil as desired

1 large carrot, peeled and cut into ¼-inch dice

2 stalks celery, cut into ¼-inch dice

1 medium onion, peeled and cut into ¼-inch dice

½ cup off-dry red wine, such as lambrusco

1 tablespoon chopped garlic

1 pound chopped stew meat or ground beef

1 tablespoon chopped fresh oregano leaves, or 1 teaspoon dried

1 tablespoon chopped fresh thyme leaves, or 1 teaspoon dried

2 cups chopped tomatoes in their juice

Salt and freshly ground black pepper, to taste

Fresh tagliatelle or fettuccine, cooked al dente (see page 151 for instructions), as an accompaniment

Grated Parmigiano-Reggiano cheese as an accompaniment

1. In a large saucepan over medium-high heat, cook the diced pancetta until most of the fat is rendered. Pour off most of the fat and replace it with the olive oil.

2. Add the carrot, celery, and onion, and sauté until the onion is translucent and just beginning to brown, about 5 minutes. Add the wine and garlic and cook until the wine has boiled away and the vegetables are beginning to fry again, another 5 minutes. You will hear the vegetables sizzle when the liquid is gone.

3. Add the beef and chopped herbs, then cook until the beef is browned, another 5 minutes. Add the tomatoes and reduce the heat to low.

4. Simmer the sauce, stirring occasionally, for at least 2 hours, or until the liquid has almost completely evaporated. Do not allow the sauce to dry out or stick. Just before serving, add salt and pepper and additional olive oil to taste. Serve with the cooked pasta, passing the cheese at the table.

★

PEPPERED NEW YORK STEAKS WITH CARAMEL PEPPERCORN SAUCE

It seems ironic that here on the West Coast we call strip steaks "New York steak" while New Yorkers usually call them "Kansas City steaks." The somewhat shocking amount of peppercorns in this recipe comes from a West Coast steakhouse tradition where, at the customer's request, a steak is completely coated in cracked peppercorns. Since the hot and spicy components of peppercorns are in the form of volatile oils that are not particularly heat stable, the peppercorns mellow considerably while they're on the grill. They soften too, becoming a robust but not overwhelming element of the finished dish. Because the steaks are cooked directly over hot coals, there are no pan juices with which to make a sauce. Instead, the steaks are served with a rich, savory sauce based on caramelized sugar. To round out the meal, serve Garlic Mashed Potatoes with Cheese (page 240) and Jade Green Broccoli (page 252).

MAKES 4 SERVINGS

For the Steaks

4 New York steaks, 12 ounces each

Vegetable oil

Kosher salt, to taste

1 cup cracked Tellicherry or high-grade black peppercorns

For the Sauce

¼ cup sugar

1 cup robust red wine, such as zinfandel

1 tablespoon soy sauce

1. Build a hardwood fire in a backyard barbecue and allow the wood to burn for 45 minutes, or until it settles into a pile of red-hot glowing coals. If using a gas grill, preheat the grill.

2. Coat the steaks lightly with oil and sprinkle generously with salt. Put the cracked peppercorns on a plate and press each side of each steak into the cracked peppercorns to coat. Save any peppercorns left on the plate for the sauce.

3. Make the sauce. Put the sugar in a medium, dry sauté pan over high heat and cook, swirling the pan, until the sugar has melted and become dark brown. Add any peppercorns that did not stick to the steaks, and let them toast for a few seconds in the hot, caramelized sugar. Stand back a little as you pour in the red wine; it will boil furiously when it hits the hot sugar, and the caramel will "seize up" into a solid. Reduce the heat to medium and let the sauce boil until the sugar is liquefied again and the wine is reduced to about half its original volume. Swirl in the soy sauce.

4. Grill the steaks for 3 to 4 minutes in one position and then, without flipping them over, turn them 45 degrees and grill for 3 to 4 minutes longer. Flip the steaks and grill for 5 to 7 minutes for medium-rare. Serve, passing the sauce separately.

★
NAPA VALLEY PAN-SEARED STEAK WITH WINE SELLER'S SAUCE

Even though the grill has been the preferred way to cook a steak for more than half a century, it's not unusual to see a pan-seared steak on a West Coast menu. Catering to an increasingly worldly clientele, the chefs who manned the stoves at the first fancy restaurants in San Francisco tried to re-create the flavors of the Belle Epoque palaces of Paris and New York. Today, when open kitchens with massive grills practically define West Coast cooking, chefs still occasionally use this Old World technique. It's especially important when the menu is designed to highlight an extraordinary wine.

MAKES 4 SERVINGS

4 filet mignons, 8 ounces each

2 teaspoons kosher salt

1 teaspoon freshly ground black pepper

2 tablespoons olive oil

¼ cup finely chopped shallot

½ cup beef broth or brown stock

½ cup red wine

¼ cup finely chopped fresh parsley, or 2 tablespoons dried

¼ cup (½ stick) unsalted butter, cut into ½-inch bits

1. Sprinkle the steaks with the salt and pepper. Put the oil in a large frying pan over medium-high heat, and when it is just beginning to smoke, cook the steaks, turning once, until the surface of each is golden brown, about 7 minutes altogether.

2. Use tongs or a fork to transfer the steaks to a plate. Toss the shallots in the oil left behind in the pan and sauté until soft, about 2 minutes. Pour in the beef broth and red wine and turn the heat to high.

3. When the broth has boiled down to about half its original volume, after about 5 minutes, return the beef to the pan, along with any juices that have collected on the plate. Reheat the steaks in the sauce for a minute, then transfer them to serving plates. Swirl the parsley and butter into the pan juices and pour the sauce over the steaks.

★
ROGUE RIVER RIB-EYE STEAKS WITH OREGON BLUE CHEESE

Oregon blue cheese from the Rogue River Creamery is one of the original artisanal cheeses of North America. It's been made in virtually the same way at the same facility for half a century. Rib-eye steaks from Niman Ranch or Oregon Country Beef are the perfect match.

MAKES 2 GENEROUS SERVINGS

2 sustainably raised rib-eye steaks, 12 ounces each

1 tablespoon cracked peppercorns

2 teaspoons kosher salt

2 tablespoons unsalted butter

2 large shallots, peeled and thinly sliced

½ cup port wine

4 ounces Rogue River blue cheese

I bunch watercress, trimmed, rinsed, and shaken dry

1. Preheat the oven to 225°F and warm 2 large steak plates. Press the steaks with the cracked pepper and salt. Melt the butter in a large frying pan over medium-high heat. When it is sizzling and beginning to brown, cook the steaks, turning once, until both sides are well browned, about 8 minutes altogether.

2. Use tongs or a fork to transfer the steaks to the warm plates. Toss the shallots in the oil left behind in the pan, and sauté until soft, about 2 minutes. Pour in the port wine and turn the heat to high. Take the steaks from the oven and put a large chunk of the blue-veined cheese on top of each steak. Divide the bunch of watercress evenly between the 2 plates, arranging it attractively beside the steaks.

3. When the wine has boiled down to about half its original volume, after about 2 minutes, pour the reduced sauce, shallots and all, over the blue cheese—topped steaks. Serve immediately.

★

ROAST TENDERLOIN OF BEEF

This is a special-occasion roast and worthy of your best efforts, but ironically, it is an extremely easy cut to prepare. Less expensive cuts take considerably more time and effort. Choose beef that was raised without the use of hormones or antibiotics; better still is grass-fed beef. Oregon Country Beef and Niman Ranch beef are two good and widely available choices. If you have doubts about where the beef is from or how it was raised, ask your butcher.

MAKES 12 SERVINGS

I sustainably raised beef tenderloin, 5 to 6 pounds

Kosher salt and freshly ground black pepper, to taste

2 tablespoons olive oil

2 cups chicken or beef broth or a combination of broth and wine

2 tablespoons cornstarch dissolved in ¼ cup water

1. Preheat the oven to 425°F. Put a large roasting pan on top of the stove over a low flame and sprinkle a generous amount of salt and pepper over the entire surface of the roast. Heat the olive oil in the roasting pan and brown the seasoned roast in the pan for 15 minutes, turning it every 4 minutes or so to brown the roast evenly on every side.

2. Move the pan to the oven and roast, uncovered, until the beef reaches an internal temperature of between 125° and 130°F, 40 minutes to an hour. Remove the roast from the pan and allow it to stand at room temperature for 30 minutes before slicing.

3. Pour the fat out of the roasting pan and discard it, then put the roasting pan on top of the stove again and add the broth. Boil the broth with the pan drippings for

about 5 minutes. Use a whisk or spatula to loosen any bits clinging to the bottom of the pan. Whisk in the cornstarch and water mixture, and when the sauce is slightly thickened, pour it through a strainer.

4. Slice the roast and arrange the slices on a platter. Pass the sauce separately.

MOM'S ROAST AND NOODLES

Less-expensive cuts of beef generally call for braising—that is, browning followed by slow simmering in some liquid to soften the tougher proteins. Just before this meal is served, children of a certain age should march around the kitchen singing "Roast and Noodles and Peas, Oh My!" to the tune of "Lions and Tigers and Bears" from The Wizard of Oz. *The peculiar vibrations of that particular sound enhance the dish as much as any seasoning ever could. Serve the roast hot with the noodles and Minted Peas (pages 258–59).*

MAKES 6 TO 8 SERVINGS

1 chuck roast or rump roast of beef, 3½ to 4 pounds

1 tablespoon kosher salt

1 teaspoon freshly ground black pepper

¼ cup olive oil

1 medium onion, peeled and thinly sliced

4 cloves garlic, chopped

2 cups red wine

2 cups beef broth

1 pound dried egg noodles

1. Sprinkle the roast with the salt and pepper. In a Dutch oven, brown the roast in the oil, turning several times.

2. Pull the roast out of the pan, and in the oil left in the pan, sauté the onion until it is soft and slightly browned. Add the garlic, red wine, and beef broth and bring the liquid to a boil.

3. Put the roast back in the pot, reduce the heat to low, and cover. Simmer until tender, about 2½ hours.

4. Pull the roast out of the pan again and add the noodles to the pan. Stir to cover the noodles with the broth, then put the roast back in. Cover and simmer for another 20 minutes, or until the noodles are tender.

TACO BEEF

Ground beef, browned in a pan with onion and seasoned with the seasoning blend commonly marketed as chili powder, becomes the foundation of many great meals. Use store-bought chili powder or make your own. We use the beef in tacos, burritos, and as a topping for simple taco salads.

MAKES ABOUT 2 CUPS

1 medium onion, peeled and chopped

1 tablespoon chili powder, homemade (page 224) or store-bought

1 pound sustainably raised ground beef

1 teaspoon kosher salt, or to taste

1. Put the onion in a large, dry cast-iron skillet over medium heat and cook, stirring intermittently, until it is a little scorched and smells sweet, about 5 minutes. Add the chili powder and cook for a few seconds longer to release some of its essential oils.

2. Add the ground beef, increase the heat to medium-high, and cook until the meat is browned through, 10 to 12 minutes. Serve hot or keep warm until serving time.

★
CHILI POWDER

Like curry powder, the chili powder sold in North America is not a single spice, nor is it a particularly authentic blend. It is, however, a very useful kitchen staple. It is most often a blend of ancho chile pepper, cumin, garlic, and Mexican oregano. Try blending your own with organically grown spices purchased from the bulk section of our local supermarket. The addition of a little smoked paprika gives the blend an extra nuance.

MAKES ABOUT ¾ CUP

¼ cup ground ancho chiles

¼ cup smoked (Spanish) paprika

¼ cup dried oregano

1 tablespoon garlic powder

1 teaspoon ground cumin

Blend all the spices and, if a finer texture is desired, grind them in a coffee mill or spice grinder. Store, tightly covered, in a cool, dark place for up to 3 months.

★
MEAT LOAF

A good homemade meat loaf should be in every cook's repertoire. While many cooks prefer the uniform results achieved by confining the loaf to a loaf pan, I prefer the rustic, "artisanal" look of a freeform loaf. The advantage of this form is that more surface area is exposed to the dry heat of the oven, where it caramelizes to delectable effect. The loaf can be baked with bacon strips on top or finished with a glaze of ketchup.

MAKES 8 SERVINGS

1 tablespoon canola or olive oil

1 pound ground beef

1 pound bulk pork sausage

1 medium onion, peeled and coarsely chopped

2 eggs

1 cup panko (Japanese breadcrumbs) or fresh white breadcrumbs

¼ cup water

¼ cup ketchup, plus another ¼ cup for glaze (optional)

1 tablespoon kosher salt

1 teaspoon freshly ground black pepper

1 teaspoon dried thyme

½ teaspoon freshly ground nutmeg

4 slices bacon, cut in half crosswise (optional)

1. Preheat the oven to 375°F and oil a 2-quart ceramic or glass baking dish. Put the ground beef and sausage in a large mixing bowl.

2. Finely chop the onion or put it in the food processor and process, pulsing the motor on and off, until the onion is virtually puréed. Add the eggs, panko, water, ¼ cup ketchup, salt, pepper, thyme, and nutmeg and whisk or pulse the motor on and off a few times to incorporate all the ingredients.

3. If you are using a food processor, pour the mixture from the food processor into the mixing bowl with the ground beef and pork, and with a wooden spoon or clean hands, work the mixture until all of the ingredients are thoroughly combined.

4. Shape the mixture into an elongated ball or oval shape and place it in the oiled pan. If desired, lay half-slices of bacon over the loaf.

5. If you're using the bacon, bake the meat loaf until a thermometer inserted in the middle of the loaf reads 160°F, about 1 hour. If you're using the ketchup glaze, bake the meat loaf for 50 minutes and then brush it with the optional ¼ cup ketchup. Bake for another 10 minutes, or until the internal temperature is 160°F. Allow the meatloaf to rest for 10 minutes at room temperature before slicing.

ROAST LEG OF LAMB IN THE PROVENÇALE-CALIFORNIA STYLE

Similarities between Northern California and the French countryside are myriad. When we visited the late M. F. K. Fisher at her Last House in Glen Ellen, near Sonoma, California, one February when our oldest boy was still a baby, my wife commented that the place felt more like France than it did like California. There, I cooked lamb for the first lady of food letters, but her diminished appetite made it impossible for her to enjoy more than a few bites. Over dinner, she told us that she loved both California and Provence, in part because each one reminded her of the other. A few years later, when my wife and I had an opportunity to spend a winter in Provence, I discovered exactly what she meant. Serve the lamb with M. F. K. Fisher's "Shook" Potatoes (pages 238–39) and Minted Peas (pages 258–59).

MAKES 8 TO 10 SERVINGS

1 small leg of lamb, 4 to 5 pounds, trimmed and the pelvis bone removed

2 tablespoons olive oil

1 tablespoon kosher salt, or 1½ teaspoons table salt

1 teaspoon freshly ground black pepper

2 cloves garlic, peeled and finely chopped

2 tablespoons dried herbes de Provence

½ cup water

1. Preheat the oven to 425°F. Rub the leg of lamb with the olive oil and then with the salt, pepper, garlic, and herbes de Provence. Place it in on a rack in a roasting pan and put it in the oven.

2. Roast for 30 minutes, reduce the heat to 400°F, and roast until the meat registers 130°F, about 30 minutes more.

3. Transfer the lamb to a platter and keep it warm by covering it first with baker's parchment and then with a tent of aluminum foil. Pour off the most of the fat from the roasting pan, but try to reserve any brown juices trapped under the fat. Pour the water into the roasting pan and stir with a silicone spatula or wooden spoon to loosen the flavorful baked-on bits. Serve the lamb sliced, passing the hot pan juices separately.

★

ROASTED RACK OF LAMB WITH ROSEMARY AND SHALLOTS

The lamb cut familiarly known as the "rack" consists of a thick, meaty band of tenderloin with eight ribs curving off it. It is typically sold "frenched," which means that excess fat has been removed from the rack of lamb and from between the ribs. This elegant cut is quite expensive and deserves careful attention. Before roasting it, I like to sear it in oil in which rosemary has been fried. The crispy leaves of fried rosemary become a garnish for the finished roast. Serve the lamb with Gold Rush Corn Mush (page 142) or with Garlic Mashed Potatoes with Cheese (page 240) and sautéed spinach or Swiss chard.

MAKES 4 SERVINGS

2 racks of lamb, about 1½ pounds each

1 tablespoon kosher salt

1 teaspoon freshly ground black pepper

3 tablespoons olive oil

4 sprigs rosemary

1 medium shallot, peeled and finely chopped

1 cup beef or chicken broth

1. Preheat the oven to 400°F. Cut each lamb rack in half to make 4 portions with 4 ribs each. Season with the salt and pepper.

2. Put the olive oil in a large, oven-safe skillet over medium-high heat, and when it is hot, fry the rosemary sprigs until they are crisp and fragrant. Lift the sprigs out of the oil and set them on paper towels to drain. In the oil left behind, sear the lamb racks, fatty side down, until they are browned, about 3 minutes. Drain off the fat, turn the racks over, and roast until an instant-read thermometer inserted in the middle of the rack registers 135°F for medium-rare, 15 to 20 minutes.

3. Take the lamb out of the pan and let it stand while you make the sauce. Put the pan over medium-high heat and sauté the shallot until soft, about 3 minutes. Add the chicken broth, increase the heat to high, and boil until the broth is reduced to about half its original volume.

4. Carve the lamb racks into individual chops. Distribute the sauce among 4 large serving plates. Place the carved lamb on top of the sauce, and lay the fried rosemary sprigs over the lamb.

★
BRAISED ELLENSBURG LAMB SHANKS

If you drew an "x" or a cross through the rectangular state of Washington, the lines would intersect near the town of Ellensburg. Located just east of the Cascade Mountain range that runs north and south, dividing the state into east and west, the town lies in the heart of the Kittitas Valley, named for a Yakima word meaning "plenty of food." Yakima was originally named for the abundant berries, grains, and game that proliferated here before the introduction of the orchards and ranches that characterize the area today, but while the specific foods produced here have changed, the "plenty" still applies. In the last quarter of the twentieth century, the Ellensburg Lamb Company became synonymous with great lamb, and the name appeared on menus up and down the coast. These days, lamb is likely to be shipped across state lines to be processed at bigger plants in Oregon, but the name still evokes a certain charm. The portion size, 1 pound per person, sounds large, and it is, but almost half the weight is bone and a considerable amount of the rest is fat, which is rendered and discarded before the lamb is served. Shanks prepared this way are meltingly tender. Serve them with Gold Rush Corn Mush (page 142), Fennel Risotto (page 138), or M. F. K. Fisher's "Shook" Potatoes (pages 238–39).

MAKES 6 SERVINGS

6 lamb shanks, about 1 pound each

Kosher salt and freshly ground black pepper, to taste

6 tablespoons olive oil

1 medium onion, peeled and sliced

2 carrots, peeled and sliced

3 stalks celery, cut into ½-inch slices

12 garlic cloves, peeled

2 cups red wine, such as zinfandel or syrah

4 cups beef or chicken broth (page 68)

1 small bundle fresh thyme leaves

6 sprigs thyme, for garnish

1. Preheat the oven to 350°F. Season the shanks generously with salt and pepper. Put a large roasting pan on top of the stove over 2 burners. Over medium-high heat, sear the shanks in 3 tablespoons of the olive oil for about 5 minutes on each side. (If this arrangement will not work on your stove, sear the shanks 3 at a time in a large skillet.)

2. When the shanks are caramel colored, remove them from the pan and set them aside. Pour off about half the fat in the pan (there will be some lamb fat in addition to the olive oil you started with), and add the remaining 3 tablespoons olive oil. Sauté the onion, carrot, and celery until the vegetables begin to caramelize, about 5 minutes. Add the garlic and sauté until the cloves just begin to color; do not let them brown.

3. Add the red wine, broth, and thyme. Return the shanks to the pan. (If you seared the shanks in a large skillet, sauté the vegetables in the same pan and then transfer the vegetables and shanks to the roasting pan and deglaze or "rinse" the pan with the red wine to remove any

flavorful bits.) Cover the roasting pan. If it does not have a snug-fitting lid of its own, cover it first with baker's parchment and then with aluminum foil to make a seal. (The parchment prevents the foil from coming into direct contact with the meat, which would cause it to break down.) Put the covered pan in the oven and bake until the meat is so tender that it almost falls off the bone, about 3½ hours.

4. Remove the shanks from the pan and let them rest while you make the sauce. Strain the pan juices into a saucepan, pressing on the solids, then skim off the fat. You should have about 3 cups of juice. Serve each lamb shank in a large soup or pasta bowl with polenta, risotto, or potatoes then ladle ½ cup of the sauce over each serving and top each one with a grind of black pepper and a sprig of fresh thyme.

★

WINE COUNTRY PORK CHOPS

These chops are finished in a way that would seem familiar to a nineteenth-century homemaker, but the technique of brining the chops before they are browned is decidedly twenty-first century. Modern pork, bred to be leaner than what our grandparents ate, is less juicy and flavorful than the old-fashioned breeds; brining makes these lean cuts more tender and juicy. The addition of wine vinegar serves as an additional tenderizer and flavor booster and accentuates the flavor of the wine in the sauce.

MAKES 6 SERVINGS

2 tablespoons kosher salt

¼ cup sugar

1 teaspoon cracked black peppercorns

4 sprigs thyme

4 cloves garlic, crushed

1 cup boiling water

2 cups crushed ice

¼ cup white wine vinegar

6 thick-cut bone-in pork chops, about 10 ounces each

½ cup olive oil

1 cup white wine

2 tablespoons green peppercorns

1. At least 2 hours before you plan to serve the chops, make the brine. In a large stock pot, stir the kosher salt, sugar, peppercorns, thyme sprigs, and garlic cloves into the boiling water and let the mixture steep for 20 minutes. Stir in the ice and the vinegar. Chill the brine, then add the chops. The chops and brine can be held in a heavy-duty zipper-lock bag or in a nonreactive (glass or enameled) baking dish covered with plastic wrap. Allow the chops to soak in the cold brine for at least 2 hours, or for as long as 8 hours before cooking.

2. Thirty minutes before serving, preheat the oven to 350°F. Remove the chops from the brine and pat them dry. Warm the olive oil in a large sauté pan over

medium-high heat, and when it begins to shimmer, sear the chops, 3 at a time, until they are well browned, about 5 minutes on each side.

3. Transfer the chops as they are browned to a baking dish large enough to hold them in a single layer. When all of the chops have been browned, bake them until an instant-read thermometer inserted in the center of a chop registers between 145° and 150°F, about 10 minutes.

4. While the chops are baking, add the white wine and green peppercorns to the sauté pan in which they were browned, and boil until the wine is reduced to about ⅓ cup. When the chops come out of the oven, transfer them to plates and pour the juices into the pan with the reduced white wine. Distribute the sauce evenly over the chops.

★

PAN-SEARED PORK TENDERLOIN WITH QUICK BING CHERRY PAN SAUCE

Cherries and pork constitute a match made in heaven. Here, the flavors of the savory pork and the sweet cherries are melded in a simple sauce made from pan juices spiked with a little balsamic vinegar and mellowed with a swirl of butter. If it's too late in the summer for cherries, consider making the dish with apricots instead. In the winter, you can follow the same procedure using sliced and peeled apples. Serve the pork with sautéed greens; the fruit serves as a starch.

MAKES 2 SERVINGS

1 pork tenderloin, about 1 pound

1 teaspoon kosher salt

½ teaspoon freshly ground black pepper

2 tablespoons canola oil

1 cup pitted Bing cherries

1 cup chicken broth

1 tablespoon balsamic vinegar

3 tablespoons unsalted butter, cut into ½-inch bits

1. Cut the pork tenderloin into 6 pieces. Put the pieces, one at a time, between layers of plastic wrap and use a meat tenderizer or rolling pin to pound them into rounds about 4 inches across. Sprinkle the rounds with the salt and pepper.

2. Put the oil in a large frying pan over medium-high heat, and when the oil is hot, cook the pork, turning once, until the surface of each piece is golden brown, about 7 minutes altogether.

3. Use tongs or a fork to transfer the pork to a plate. Toss the cherries in the oil left behind in the pan. Pour the chicken broth and balsamic vinegar over the cherries and turn the heat to high.

4. When the broth has boiled down to about half its original volume and the cherries are tender, about 5 minutes, return the pork to the pan, along with any juices that have collected on the plate. Reheat the pork in the sauce for a minute, then transfer it to serving plates. Swirl the

butter into the pan juices and pour the sauce over the pork.

★
CHINESE BARBECUE PORK

Red-tinted Chinese barbecue pork is available in most Asian groceries and in many supermarkets. Before I worked at Canlis restaurant in Seattle, it never occurred to me that this was something people could make at home. But Rocky Toguchi, who served as executive chef at Canlis for almost twenty years, grew up on Oahu, where his own family's Okinawa-Japanese food traditions were enhanced with the myriad cultural influences of the Hawaiian Islands. From time to time, when he was making dinner for the crew, Rocky would break out an old box of "Chinese barbecue spice" that he kept in a dark corner of the dry storage area. According to the ingredient list, it contained dehydrated garlic, artificial coloring, anticaking agents, and "spices." Once, when I was cleaning the storage area, I put it in a pile to be dis-carded. Rocky pulled it out of the pile and said, "You can get rid of it after I retire." I tucked it farther back in the storage room and determined to make Chinese barbecue pork without the dubious seasoning blend. This version lacks the distinctive red hue of the commercial stuff, but it tastes better.

MAKES 4 SERVINGS

1 whole pork tenderloin, about 1 pound

2 tablespoons sherry

2 tablespoons hoisin sauce

1 tablespoon tomato paste

1 tablespoon brown sugar

1 tablespoon honey

2 cloves garlic, grated with a Microplane grater

¼ teaspoon Chinese five-spice powder

Hot Chinese mustard as an accompaniment

1. Cut the pork in half lengthwise, then in half crosswise to make 4 strips approximately 3 inches in diameter by 5 inches long.

2. In a nonreactive (glass or ceramic) baking dish, whisk together the sherry, hoisin sauce, tomato paste, brown sugar, honey, garlic, and five-spice powder. Roll the pork pieces through the mixture to coat, and allow them to marinate in the refrigerator for at least 4 hours or for as long as 12 hours.

3. Preheat the oven to 425°F. Put a half-inch of water in the bottom of a roasting pan, set a rack in the roasting pan, and arrange the marinated pork pieces on the rack above the water. Roast until the pork is golden brown and tender, 25 to 30 minutes. (An instant-read thermometer inserted in the thickest part of the pork should register 160°F.) Serve the pork cold, in thin slices with hot Chinese mustard.

★
SMOKY VANILLA PORK ROAST

A tender, slow-cooked pork roast is the ultimate main dish for a nostalgic supper. This one reveals my own southern roots, but its similarities to Hawaiian-style kalua pig also evoke some of the Pacific flavors that have influenced my adult years at the stove. Serve the pork with Sweet Potato Home Fries (page 244) to enhance the southern influence, or with rice to augment the Pacific flavors.

¼ cup canola oil

1 boneless natural pork shoulder, about 6 pounds

3 tablespoons kosher salt

1 cup water

1 vanilla bean, split lengthwise and scraped

1 teaspoon whole black peppercorns

¼ cup liquid smoke

1. Preheat the oven to 300°F. In a covered casserole that can go from stovetop to oven, warm the oil over medium-high heat. Sprinkle the pork with the salt and cook it in the oil, turning once or twice, until it is browned on each side, about 10 minutes.

2. Pour in the water and add the vanilla bean, the whole black peppercorns, and the liquid smoke. Cover tightly and bake until the pork is very tender and shreds easily, about 3 hours.

3. Remove the pork from the pan and set aside. Strain the liquid left in the pan; discard the solids, and pour the liquid back over the pork. The pork can be served at once or held covered in a warm (200°F) oven for up to an hour.

★

TONKATSU OR BREADED PORK CUTLETS

A conjunction of the Japanese word for pork and the English word "cutlet," tonkatsu is a pork dish that sprang out of Japan in the late nineteenth century, when Japanese cooks began to embrace Western cooking techniques. Today it is a staple of Japanese home cooking and a regular feature on Japanese-American menus. Commercially produced tonkatsu sauce is available in Asian groceries and in many supermarkets. Following instructions found in Japanese-American cookbooks, I tried making homemade tonkatsu sauce using various combinations of bottled sauces—Worcestershire, ketchup, and mustard—but I was not satisfied. When I started from scratch, softening dried plums in a simmering bath of vinegar and water, I got the results I was after.

MAKES 4 SERVINGS

For the Tonkatsu Sosu

½ cup water

1 tablespoon cornstarch

¼ cup rice vinegar

3 tablespoons sugar

1 teaspoon kosher salt

¼ cup (about 6 medium) packed pitted dried plums (prunes)

For the Pork

1 pork tenderloin, about 1 pound

Kosher salt and freshly ground black pepper, to taste

½ cup unbleached white flour

2 eggs

¼ cup water

1½ cups panko (Japanese breadcrumbs)

Rice bran or canola oil, for frying

Steamed rice as an accompaniment

Shredded cabbage as an accompaniment

1. Make the tonkatsu sauce. Put ¼ cup of the water and the cornstarch in a teacup, stir to dissolve, and set aside.

2. In a small saucepan, combine the remaining ¼ cup water with the rice vinegar, sugar, and salt.

3. Cut the dried plums into ½-inch pieces and add them to the saucepan. Cook the mixture over medium-high heat until the plums are slightly softened, about 5 minutes. Stir in the cornstarch mixture and cook until thickened, about 1 minute more.

4. Purée the mixture in a blender until very smooth. If no blender is available, the mixture may be puréed in a food processor, but it will not be as smooth.

5. Preheat the oven to 250°F or to the "warm" setting and line a baking sheet with a brown paper bag.

6. Cut the pork tenderloin into 8 pieces. Put the pieces, one at a time, between layers of plastic wrap and pound them into thin rounds about 5 inches across. Sprinkle the rounds with salt and pepper and set aside.

7. Set up 3 wide-rimmed soup bowls. Put the flour in the first bowl. In the second bowl, beat the eggs with the water until smooth. Put the panko in the third bowl.

8. Working with one piece of the pork at a time, dip them first in the flour, shaking off the excess, and then in the egg mixture, allowing the excess to run off. Finally, lay them in the panko, turning and patting gently to coat both sides.

9. Put 3 inches of oil in a large frying pan over medium-high heat. When the oil is hot enough to brown a cube of bread in 30 seconds, fry the pork, 2 pieces at a time. Cook, turning once, until the crust is golden brown on both sides, about 7 minutes altogether.

10. Hold the first browned cutlets in the warm oven on the paper-lined baking sheet while you cook the remaining cutlets. When all the cutlets are cooked, slice them about ½ inch thick and serve with steamed rice, shredded cabbage, and tonkatsu sosu.

★

BARBECUED SPARERIBS

Spareribs, cut from the lower half of the rib cage along the underbelly of a pig, are the quintessential cut for barbecue. (They are somewhat different from so-called baby back ribs, which are not cut from younger pigs but from the top half of the rib cage at the forward end. They are different from so-called country-style ribs too; those are boneless rib-shaped cuts from the shoulder or butt of the animal.) A full row of spareribs contains 13 ribs and weighs about 3 pounds. Count on about a pound of ribs for each serving. Since the process takes almost three hours, you might as well plan to cook quite a few at one time.

2 full strips spareribs, about 3 pounds each

Barbecue sauce (optional)

For the Spice Rub

¼ cup brown sugar

¼ cup smoked paprika

3 tablespoons dried oregano leaves

2 tablespoons dried thyme leaves

2 tablespoons kosher salt

1 teaspoon cornstarch

1. To make the spice rub, combine all ingredients in a small bowl. Rub the ribs with the spice rub. Allow them to stand for at least 30 minutes, or cover and refrigerate for up to 24 hours.

2. Soak about 3 cups of hardwood chunks in water for at least 15 minutes. Build a fire in a charcoal grill or light a gas grill. Put the soaked wood chips in a disposable foil pan, or craft an impromptu foil pan from a double layer of aluminum foil. Put the pan of wood chunks on the fire and allow them to flame up and burn out.

3. Put the ribs on the grill. If you're using a gas grill, turn it down to the lowest possible setting. If you're using a charcoal grill, push all the coals to one side and put the ribs on the opposite side. Cover the grill.

4. After 10 minutes, turn the ribs over, then check every 10 to 15 minutes over the next 2 hours, turning regularly. Ideally, the barbecue should be kept at 300°F, or "low" on a gas grill. A charcoal grill will gradually slow down to about 250°F.

5. Turn off the gas grill; if you are using charcoal, it will have pretty much burned out by now anyway. Wrap the ribs in baker's parchment, and put them back in the grill. Allow the ribs to stand in the residual heat for at least 30 minutes or for as long as an hour. Serve the ribs warm, with or without barbecue sauce.

★

NOT MY GRANDFATHER'S HAM

Over the years, I have gradually reinvented the ham I remember from childhood. That one was pierced with cloves and studded with pineapple rings and maraschino cherries. This one is sleek and finished with a simple glaze. One thing it shares with my grandfather's ham is the bottle of beer poured into the bottom of the roasting pan to provide braising liquid. For the best flavor, I buy a naturally raised ham like the Applewood Smoked Ham from Niman Ranch. It's expensive, but this is a special occasion dish, perfect for a family gathering.

MAKES 12 SERVINGS, WITH LEFTOVERS

1 fully cooked, bone-in half ham, 7 to 8 pounds

One 12-ounce bottle lager beer

1 cup brown sugar

1. Bring the ham up to room temperature by removing it from the refrigerator at

least an hour before baking. Preheat the oven to 300°F. Score the ham on the fatty side, cutting about ⅛ inch deep in a crisscross pattern.

2. Place the scored ham, fatty side up, in a 9- by 13-inch roasting pan and pour the beer into the pan around the ham. Cover the pan with baker's parchment and then with aluminum foil, tucking the foil in at the edges of the pan to create a seal. Bake the ham until an instant-read thermometer registers 110°F when inserted into the meatiest part of the ham, about 1½ hours.

3. Remove the ham from the oven, take it out of the pan, and pour the juices that have accumulated in the pan into a small saucepan. Ladle off any excess fat and stir in the brown sugar. Cook over medium heat until the sugar is dissolved to make a glaze.

4. Put the ham back in the pan. Pour the glaze over the surface of the ham. Put the ham back in the oven and bake, uncovered, until it is heated through and the glaze is caramelized, about 30 minutes. Allow the ham to rest at room temperature for 10 minutes before slicing.

chapter 11

VEGETABLES

TUBERS AND ROOT VEGETABLES
M. F. K. Fisher's "Shook" Potatoes
Psychedelic Mashed Blue Potatoes
Aligot or Garlic Mashed Potatoes with Cheese
Roasted Balsamic Beets with Greens
Gerald's Beet Purée
Beets for Antipasto
Matchstick Carrots in Browned Butter
Mom's Buttered Carrots
Sweet Potato Home Fries
Parsnip Fritters

LEAFY GREENS
Sautéed Greens
Southern-Style Greens
Sesame Spinach
West Coast Creamed Spinach
Swiss Chard Gratin

VEGETABLE TOPS AND FLOWERING HEADS
Cauliflower Gratin
Broccoli Raab Sautéed with Garlic and Chiles
"Blasted Broccoli" with Red Chiles and Garlic
Balsamic Blasted Green Beans
Baby Bok Choy
Jade Green Broccoli or Green Beans
Typhoon-Style Green Beans
West Coast Green Bean Casserole
Roasted Brussels Sprouts with Red Chile Flakes and Sesame Oil
Roasted Sugar Pumpkin with Cinnamon
Pumpkin or Winter Squash Purée
Roasted Delicata Squash
Twice-Roasted Miniature Pumpkins with Onions and Thyme
Chinese Restaurant–Style Snap Peas
Minted Peas
Stir-Fried Broccoli and Shiitake Mushrooms with Oyster Sauce
Madeira Grilled Portobello Mushrooms

Vegetables

Whenever I shop at a farmer's market, I promise myself that I won't buy more vegetables than I will actually use. But at the height of summer, when the stalls are piled high with so many bright and wonderful things not found in grocery stores, that promise is hard to keep. I come not in search of any particular item; instead I go to the market to find out which foodstuffs are particularly vibrant that day.

Staying in touch with what local growers offer at the market spurs ideas that may lead to new dishes on my menu or on the home dinner table. Tomatoes in twelve shades of yellow, red, and green inspire a colorful salad of several different varieties dressed with little more than a drizzle of olive oil. Twisted fingerling potatoes, which are indeed shaped like pudgy little fingers, prompt a warm potato salad or perhaps a batch of M. F. K. Fisher's "Shook" Potatoes. At farmer's markets, I've discovered vegetables like edible pea vines that have since become favorites.

But even if it weren't for the more unusual items, the standard produce from small farms would draw me in. Very fresh produce, procured from the same hands that grew it, is a world away from factory-farmed vegetables purchased at the supermarket. At a farmer's market I might find myself suddenly enthusiastic about ordinary green beans and cabbage.

So even though I promise myself that I won't buy more than I need, I almost always do. For example, I may already have purchased several pounds of potatoes from one farmer, but if I see a variety I've never tried before, or some particularly nice specimens of an old favorite variety like German Butterballs or Peruvian Purples, I am likely to buy more.

I'm also a sucker for greens. I am easily captivated by ready-to-grab bundles of the three kinds of kale; delectable mustard greens of some obscure variety, crowned with tiny broccoli-shaped buds; bright stalks of rainbow chard in yellow, orange, and red framed by the impossibly dark and shiny green of their leaves; and the crinkled matte-finished gray-green of Tuscan kale.

Some people plan ahead and peruse the market with specific purchases in mind. They might circle the stalls and do some comparison shopping, deciding exactly which items they will purchase before they begin. Not me. Like a bee trying one flower after another, I bounce from stall to stall, stopping wherever I am compelled to stop, tasting cherries and apricots here, asking about bok choy or mizuna there, gathering produce as if it were pollen.

Even as I shop, I am mentally preparing some of the vegetables. I tell myself that on Tuesday night, the beans will be blasted in a very hot oven until their skin begins to blister, then tossed with balsamic vinegar. The carrots might be puréed with caramelized onions or simply cut into tiny matchsticks and sautéed in butter with a hint of freshly grated nutmeg. On Sunday, I promise myself, some of these fine potatoes will be layered in a ceramic baking dish with alternating slices of tomato, drizzled with olive oil and baked directly under a dripping leg of lamb until they come together in a crusty gratin.

Behind all the planning is the nagging fear that some of these vegetables may go to waste. In the clamor and excitement, I sometimes buy vegetables I wouldn't ordinarily buy, and I tend to buy more than I really need. But even if I do come home with what appears to be an overabundance of produce, there are ways to use it before it loses the vitality that attracted me to it.

The first step is to keep the vegetables fresh, in a state as much like life as possible. Even though they may look beautiful in a basket on the kitchen counter, most vegetables should be refrigerated. But different vegetables call for different conditions.

Potatoes and other root vegetables should be stored unwashed in a brown paper bag. Keep root vegetables in the dark because light will turn potatoes green and cause the vitamins in other vegetables to disintegrate. Washing can scrape away the protective skin that keeps the inside of the vegetables fresh, and moisture on root vegetables is an invitation to rot. So leave them dirty and keep them dry.

Leafy greens, on the other hand, should be washed in a sink full of cold water and lifted out, leaving the dirt behind. Soil left on the leaves will damage them, but rough spray could also bruise them and make them more vulnerable to decay. After draining, pack the leaves, still wet, into plastic bags and refrigerate them to keep them crisp. Even leafy greens that have wilted can be rejuvenated after a bath and an hour in the fridge.

Fruiting or seeding vegetables like beans, corn, and artichokes are the most delicate of all. These should be purchased in small amounts and used promptly. Plan to use them within a day or two of bringing them home from the market, and save the roots and leafy greens for later in the week. Tomatoes, incidentally, should not be refrigerated. Inside the fridge, their texture changes and their flavor rapidly wanes.

A note on boiling vegetables: Somewhere along the road to the twenty-first century, West Coast cooks in particular, and North American cooks in general, got the idea that boiling vegetables was a bad idea. In fact, boiling in a large amount of salted water is often the very best way to cook vegetables, especially ones from the top of the plant, like green beans, corn, and asparagus. The vegetables cook quickly and keep their brilliant colors and—I think—most of their nutrients intact. (Make sure the water is well salted, though. If the water is not already saturated with salt, the vegetables are more likely to leach out their nutrients.)

Covered and steamed, green vegetables like green beans, broccoli, asparagus, and baby bok choy turn a dull shade of olive drab long before they become tender. They look and taste rather awful, I think. What seems to be happening chemically is that when they cook, the vegetables release a certain amount of acid that becomes concentrated in the confines of the steamer and denatures the chlorophyll. If they're cooked in an open pot of boiling water, the acid dissipates and evaporates before it affects the color of the vegetables.

I remember once in the mid 1980s, when Julia Child, who was born and raised in Pasadena, California, was sitting on a panel discussion about Pacific Northwest cooking held at Seattle's Pike Place Market, an audience member demanded to know why she recommended boiling, when "everyone knows it's a terrible way to cook vegetables." Julia countered that boiling was the best way to cook them and the audience member argued with her, citing the late Adelle Davis as an authority on healthy food who recommended steaming or braising instead of boiling to "preserve vitamins."

"Adelle died rather young, didn't she?" quipped Julia.

Of course no one knows what caused Ms. Davis' cancer and it would be wrong to dismiss her tireless efforts on behalf of good nutrition, but Julia's biting sense of humor helped drive home a valuable lesson for me. No matter how healthy food is, if it doesn't look and taste wonderful, no one is going to eat it. When they are cooked briefly in plenty of rapidly boiling salted water, green vegetables like broccoli, green beans, and

asparagus are fantastic, and I cook them this way often.

Rather than "shock" the vegetables in ice water after boiling them, I follow the advice of former Stars chef Jeremiah Tower, who recommends scattering the just-cooked vegetables over the surface of a large baking sheet to cool. Green beans, especially, cooked this way come out with a gorgeous green color, snappy-tender texture, and bright, fresh green flavor. Sauté them briefly in butter or finish them as in the recipe for Typhoon-Style Green Beans (pages 252–53).

Tubers and Root Vegetables

★

M. F. K. FISHER'S "SHOOK" POTATOES

Adapted from a technique that Fisher described without much detail in her book With Bold Knife and Fork, *this is a dish that should be in every home cook's repertoire. When the tender cooked potatoes are shaken with butter and seasonings, the starch in the potatoes combined with the butter makes a smooth and creamy "sauce" around the not-quite-mashed chunks of potato.*

MAKES 6 SERVINGS

3 pounds small red or yellow thin-skinned potatoes

8 cups water

1 tablespoon kosher salt

6 tablespoons (¾ stick) unsalted butter, cut into ½-inch bits

½ cup chopped fresh parsley or a mixture of parsley and chives

I teaspoon freshly ground black pepper, or to taste

I. Scrub the potatoes and put them in a large, heavy saucepan with the water and salt. Cover the pot and put it over high heat until the water is boiling; lower the heat to a simmer.

2. When the potatoes are very tender, after about 20 minutes, take the pan off the stove. Drain off most of the water by holding the lid of the pan with a hot pad and tilting the pan over the sink. There is no need to pour the potatoes through a colander; leave a little bit of the cooking liquid in the pan.

3. Add the butter, chopped parsley, and pepper. Shake the pan very vigorously to break up the potatoes and mix them with the other ingredients. Serve hot.

★
PSYCHEDELIC MASHED BLUE POTATOES

Purple or "blue" Peruvian potatoes are smooth textured and excellent for mashing. Peel the potatoes and cut them into uniform small dice, so that they cook rapidly and evenly. Use just enough water to barely cover the potatoes, and when you drain them, just before mash-ing, save the cooking liquid and pour some back into the mash to make a smoother purée. The outrageous color is especially effective with dark or red meats and brilliant green vegetables. It's nice to know that anthocyanins, the pigments that make some vegetables purple, are healthy antioxidants. Use this same technique to make mashed parsnips.

MAKES ABOUT 6 CUPS, SERVING 6

3 pounds purple potatoes

I tablespoon kosher salt

About 6 cups water

6 tablespoons unsalted butter, cut into ½-inch bits

I. Peel the potatoes and cut them into I-inch cubes. Put the cubed potatoes and salt in a heavy, I-gallon stockpot and cover them with the water. Cook the potatoes until they are fork-tender and just beginning to fall apart, about 15 minutes.

2. Drain the potatoes through a colander over a bowl or another pot to save the cooking liquid. Force the cooked potatoes through a ricer, or, if no ricer is available, put the drained potatoes back in the pot in which they were cooked and mash them with a potato masher or a whisk. Whisk in the butter and just enough of the reserved cooking liquid to render the mashed potatoes smooth and creamy.

3. Covered and placed over the lowest possible heat, the potatoes can be held for up to 20 minutes before serving. If they are going to be held for more than a few minutes, make a ring of aluminum foil and put it between the burner and the pot of

potatoes to keep them from burning on the bottom. Serve the mashed potatoes hot.

⭐

ALIGOT OR GARLIC MASHED POTATOES WITH CHEESE

I discovered this dish when I was in Ardèche, a region of France just west of Lyon in the high hills that occupy the heart of the country. I made it first with potatoes I bought at the farmer's market in a tiny village called St. Bonnet le Froid, on a small burner in my hotel room. If Cantal cheese is not available, try fontina or, in a pinch, a simple Monterey Jack. Stirring the mash as the cheese melts makes it super-elastic and stringy. The texture is as much fun as the flavor. This dish is so rich that it is practically a meal in itself. Leftover aligot can be cut, pressed into patties, coated in breadcrumbs, and warmed in butter.

MAKES ABOUT 4 CUPS, SERVING 4

2 pounds Yukon Gold potatoes

1 tablespoon kosher salt

About 6 cups water

12 cloves garlic, peeled

8 ounces imported Cantal cheese, grated

1. Scrub the potatoes thoroughly and cut them into 1-inch cubes. Put the cubed potatoes and salt in a heavy, 4-quart stockpot and cover them with water. Cook the potatoes until they are quite tender and beginning to fall apart, about 15 minutes.

2. Meanwhile, in a separate pot, cook the garlic over medium-high heat with just enough water to cover. As soon as the

garlic is tender, transfer it with its cooking liquid to a blender and purée until very smooth.

3. Drain the potatoes through a colander. Put the drained potatoes back in the stockpot and whisk in the garlic purée, mashing the potatoes in the process. Keep whipping until the mashed potatoes are smooth and creamy.

4. Stir in the grated cheese and continue stirring until the melted cheese forms long strands that stretch away from the spoon as you stir. Serve hot.

⭐

ROASTED BALSAMIC BEETS WITH GREENS

Beets suffer from the erroneous notion that they can be kept for a long, long time. In fact, old beets taste bad; if they have black spots, reject them. The best beets are usually sold with their leaves still attached. The leaves are more than an indication of freshness, though; they are also quite delectable in and of themselves. With the stems removed, beet greens can be thinly sliced crosswise and sautéed to be served with the cooked beet roots.

MAKES 4 SERVINGS

2 bunches small to medium beets with greens (8 beets)

2 tablespoons olive oil

Kosher salt and freshly ground black pepper, to taste

1 tablespoon balsamic vinegar

1. Preheat the oven to 375°F. Snip the leaves from the beets with scissors, and set aside. Trim the stems attached to the roots to 1 inch. Rub each beet with a few drops of olive oil, then wrap each one in a square of baker's parchment, twisting the ends like a candy wrapper.

2. Place the parchment-wrapped beets in a baking dish and bake until tender when poked with a knife, 45 to 50 minutes.

3. Swish the beet greens in a sink full of cool water, then lift them out, leaving any dirt behind. Keep the washed greens in a colander until the roots are tender.

4. When the beets are tender, slip off the skins and stems and discard. Cut the peeled roasted beets into rounds, about ½ inch thick.

5. In a large sauté pan or cast-iron skillet over medium-high heat, warm the olive oil with the salt and pepper, and when the pepper begins to release its aromatic oils into the air, add the beet greens. When the greens wilt and begin to soften, after about 2 minutes, add the roasted beets.

6. Transfer the beets and greens to a serving dish and drizzle the balsamic vinegar over them.

★

GERALD'S BEET PURÉE

Chef Gerald Knight ran the kitchen at a place called Café Bissett in Friday Harbor on San Juan Island, where *I worked in the 1980s. He was a brilliant cook. One of his signature vegetable side dishes was this preparation of puréed beets. Caramelized onions render the purée so incredibly sweet that people often refused to believe that we had not added refined sugar to the purée. Because we used very fresh-tasting organically grown beets, which taste quite different from the sad old specimens found softening in supermarkets or rendered lifeless in cans, many people were surprised upon tasting them to discover that they liked beets. When you trim the beets, leave an inch of stem attached. This will keep the roots from "bleeding" as they cook.*

MAKES 6 SERVINGS

1 pound beets, trimmed to within 1 inch of the root

2 tablespoons unsalted butter

1 medium yellow onion, peeled and thinly sliced

½ cup heavy cream

1 teaspoon kosher salt

1. Cook the beets whole in boiling water until they are tender when poked with a fork. Depending on the size and maturity of the beets, this will take anywhere from 15 to 45 minutes. When they are cooked through, drain them and, holding the beets one at a time under cold running water, slip off their skins. Chop the peeled and cooked beets and pile them into a blender.

2. While the beets are cooking, melt the butter in a medium sauté pan over medium-high heat, add the onion, and

cook, stirring often, until tender and golden brown, about 15 minutes.

3. Add the sautéed onion, cream, and salt to the blender with the beets. Purée until perfectly smooth. Serve as a side dish.

★

BEETS FOR ANTIPASTO

Beets, especially fresh ones, recently pulled quaking with soil from the summer garden, make an excellent addition to the antipasto platter. Prepared as they are here with a simple vinaigrette of red wine and olive oil, they also make a wonderful focal point for a salad.

MAKES 6 APPETIZER-SIZED SERVINGS

2 pounds (about 3 medium to large) beets

¼ cup red wine vinegar

½ cup olive oil

2 teaspoons kosher salt

1 teaspoon freshly ground black pepper

¼ cup chopped fresh Italian parsley

1. Trim the leaves off the beets, leaving about ½ inch of the stem attached. Do not attempt to peel them before they are cooked. (This keeps more of the juice trapped inside the beet so that it doesn't bleed into the cooking water.) Cook the beets whole in boiling water until they are fork-tender. Depending on the size and freshness of the beets, this will take anywhere from 15 to 45 minutes.

2. While the beets are cooking, whisk together the vinegar, oil, salt, and pepper in a medium mixing bowl.

3. Transfer the cooked beets to a colander under cold running water until they are cool enough to handle, and peel them; the skins will slip off easily. Cut the cooked, peeled beets into large matchsticks.

4. Toss the cut and cooled beets in the vinaigrette with the parsley, and serve at room temperature.

★

MATCHSTICK CARROTS IN BROWNED BUTTER

A recipe with as few ingredients as this one can be deceptively simple. Some serious but not too difficult prep work goes on behind the scenes. Cutting the carrots is a lot easier if you have access to a mandoline, one of those guillotine-like contraptions that cuts vegetables into slices or strips. It's important to use clarified butter because the whey in whole butter would burn, but I don't like to clarify butter the old-fashioned way. I render it instead into a golden-brown ghee and keep the lightly browned butter right beside the stove for sautéing carrots or greens. The recipe makes more browned butter than you will need. Save the rest to sauté greens (pages 245– 46) or make Sweet Potato Home Fries (page 244).

MAKES 4 SERVINGS

For the Browned Butter

1 cup (2 sticks) unsalted butter

For the Carrots

1 pound carrots

1 teaspoon kosher salt

½ teaspoon freshly ground black pepper

¼ teaspoon freshly grated nutmeg

1. Make the browned butter. In a large saucepan over medium heat, melt the butter and allow it to simmer steadily. As it foams, stir it down. When all the water has boiled out and the foam on top is beginning to brown, remove from heat and pass the hot fat through a fine strainer.

2. Peel the carrots and cut them crosswise in half or into thirds to make short logs, about 4 inches long. On a mandoline or with a sharp knife, cut the logs into julienne strips, about ⅛ inch square. If you cut the carrots ahead of time, don't put them under water or the water will leach out the natural sugars. It won't matter if they dry out a little; they will perk up when they are sautéed.

3. Put ¼ cup browned butter in a large sauté pan over medium-high heat and add the salt, pepper, and nutmeg. When the spices are sizzling, add the cut carrots. Cook the carrots in the hot browned butter until they are heated through and barely tender, about 2 minutes. Serve at once.

★
MOM'S BUTTERED CARROTS

A quick braise with sugar and salt, followed by a blast of intense heat to boil away any liquid, leaves carrots lightly glazed in a flavorful, shiny coat. The parsley makes them look and taste bright and fresh.

MAKES 4 TO 6 SERVINGS

2 pounds organic carrots

2 tablespoons unsalted butter

1 teaspoon sugar

1 teaspoon kosher salt

½ teaspoon freshly ground black pepper

2 tablespoons water

2 tablespoons finely chopped fresh parsley

1. Peel the carrots and slice them into rounds, about ⅛ inch thick.

2. Melt the butter in a large saucepan over medium-high heat. Stir in the carrots, sugar, salt, and pepper and sauté for about 1 minute. Add the water, cover the pan, reduce the heat to low, and cook until the carrots are fork-tender, about 10 minutes.

3. Just before serving, uncover the pan, turn the heat to high, and cook off any standing moisture. When the water is boiled away and the carrots begin to sizzle in the butter, toss in the parsley and serve piping hot.

⭐ SWEET POTATO HOME FRIES

Some confusion over yams and sweet potatoes is inevitable. True yams are very large vegetables that originated in Asia; they are almost never seen in the United States. What we call yams are really dark red sweet potatoes. Marketers label dark sweet potatoes yams because it helps distinguish them from the lighter varieties. Our favorite sweet potatoes are the very dark ones sold as "ruby red yams." They make a great side dish with chicken or pork, but they can also be the centerpiece of a plate of winter vegetables.

MAKES 4 SERVINGS

4 medium (about 2 pounds) sweet potatoes or "yams"

2 tablespoons browned butter (see pages 242–43) or canola oil

1 tablespoon brown sugar

1 teaspoon kosher salt

½ teaspoon freshly ground black pepper

1. Preheat the oven to 400°F. Prepare a baking sheet by lining it with a nonstick silicone sheet or baker's parchment.

2. Use a sharp knife or a vegetable peeler to peel the sweet potatoes. Cut each one in half lengthwise, then place each half cut side down and cut them into wedges about 1 inch wide at the thickest part.

3. Put the wedges in a large mixing bowl and rub them with the browned butter. Sprinkle the sugar, salt, and pepper over

the slices and toss to coat them evenly on all sides.

4. Arrange the sweet potato wedges on the prepared baking sheet with plenty of space between them. Bake for 8 minutes, then turn the slices over and bake until they are slightly browned and perfectly tender, about 5 minutes more. Serve hot.

⭐ PARSNIP FRITTERS

Parsnips can be thought of as starchy white carrots, but the comparison fails to capture the unique and wonderfully aromatic nature of this old-fashioned root vegetable. Contrary to the intuitive assumption that a large parsnip might be tough or fibrous, big parsnips are actually sweet and tender. Do avoid parsnips that have begun to sprout new leaves; they have been held too long and will have lost their charm. Parsnips can simply be boiled and mashed (follow the technique for Psychedelic Mashed Blue Potatoes on pages 239–40), but they also benefit from a little extra attention in recipes like this one. Serve these fritters with any roast, such as Restaurant-Style Roast Duckling with Orange Sauce (pages 206–8).

MAKES SIX 4-INCH FRITTERS

1 parsnip, about 12 ounces

1 medium egg

½ cup unbleached white flour

½ teaspoon baking powder

1 teaspoon kosher salt

½ teaspoon freshly ground black pepper

2 tablespoons unsalted butter, cut into 6 teaspoon-sized pats

1. Peel and grate the parsnip. You should have about 2 cups, packed.

2. Crack the egg into a medium mixing bowl, beat it lightly, and then stir in the grated parsnip.

3. In a separate, small bowl, whisk together the flour, baking powder, salt, and pepper. Stir the dry ingredients into the parsnip and egg mixture.

4. Preheat a griddle or a large cast-iron skillet over medium-high heat.

5. Arrange the pats of butter on the hot griddle and scoop ⅓ cup of batter on top of each butter pat. Flatten the scoops slightly to form six 4-inch cakes. Allow the fritters to sizzle gently in the butter until they are well browned and crisp on the underside, about 5 minutes. Turn the fritters and fry until they are cooked through, about 3 minutes more.

Leafy Greens

★

SAUTÉED GREENS

Curly green Scotch kale, nearly black Tuscan kale, and the myriad types in between are all varieties of the same species, Brassica oleracea. *My favorite variety is the Tuscan, sometimes marketed as dinosaur kale. Sautéed kale is an excellent accompaniment to grilled or roast meats. It also provides a satisfying and very nourishing element of a vegetarian meal. I use precisely the same technique to sauté Swiss chard; I think the red-veined chard is especially appealing when it's served with Gerald's Beet Purée (pages 241—42) or with roasted red meats.*

MAKES 4 SERVINGS

2 bunches (about 18 large leaves) leafy kale or chard

¼ cup browned butter (see pages 242—43) or olive oil

2 tablespoons garlic, sliced thin (optional)

1 teaspoon kosher salt

½ teaspoon freshly ground black pepper

1. Rinse the greens and shake off the excess water. Cut the stems off the greens and stack the leaves into a bundle. Roll the bundle and cut across the stem line into neat ribbons, about ½ inch wide. The greens can be cut ahead and held, refrigerated, until just before serving time.

2. Put a large saucepan over high heat, and when you are almost ready to serve the greens, put the browned butter in the pan. Add the garlic, if using, salt, pepper, and then the greens. Cook, moving the greens around the pan with tongs, until they are wilted, 1 or 2 minutes. Remove from the heat and serve at once.

SOUTHERN-STYLE GREENS

Traditional southern-style greens were chopped and cooked in fatback or salt pork with a lot of liquid for a very long time, until they were meltingly tender. The liquid in which they were cooked became a flavorful "pot liquor." The tradition may rightfully belong to the Third (Gulf) Coast, but plenty of West Coast folks came here from there, and this updated version captures the spirit of southern greens with a shorter cooking time that preserves a little of their natural texture. This side dish fits beautifully with Skillet Fried Chicken (pages 193–95) or Not My Grandfather's Ham (pages 233–34), but equally well with West Coast foods like Rosé Roast Chicken with Herbs (pages 201–2) or Smoky Vanilla Pork Roast (pages 230–31) and Sweet Potato Home Fries (page 244).

MAKES 4 TO 6 SERVINGS

4 ounces bacon, chopped

1 large bunch collard greens or dark green kale, rinsed

½ teaspoon freshly ground black pepper

2 cups chicken broth, homemade (page 68), or store-bought

1. Put the chopped bacon in a large skillet or sauté pan over medium heat until the bacon is sizzling.

2. Cut the greens into a chiffonade like this: Make stacks of the greens, several leaves at a time, and roll the stacks into bundles. Slice crosswise with a large, sharp knife into thin strips.

3. Add the greens to the sizzling bacon bits and sauté over high heat until hot and glossy, about 3 minutes. Add the pepper and chicken broth and simmer, loosely covered, over medium heat until the greens are tender, 20 to 30 minutes.

SESAME SPINACH

Because spinach cooks down so much, I can never seem to get enough of this vegetable in one pan. This is my all-time favorite way to cook it. To feed a large group (more than four people), it may be necessary to make several batches. Don't try to make one super-sized batch or the spinach will release too much water and it will be ruined. Serve this spinach with the Grilled or Seared Rare Ahi on pages 169–70.

MAKES 4 SERVINGS

1 pound whole spinach, or one 10-ounce bag prewashed baby spinach leaves

2 tablespoons browned butter (see pages 242–43)

1 teaspoon toasted sesame oil

1 tablespoon white or black sesame seeds, or a combination

I teaspoon kosher salt

½ teaspoon freshly ground black pepper

1. If you are using whole spinach, fill a sink with water and pick the leaves from the stems, letting them fall into the water. Discard the stems and roots. Swish the spinach leaves around in the water to free them from any soil, then lift them out of the sink, allowing the soil to sink to the bottom. Spin the spinach leaves dry in a salad spinner or lay them on several layers of paper towels and pat them dry. Keep the washed, dried spinach in a bowl near the stove, ready to cook.

2. In a large sauté pan over medium-high heat, heat the browned butter and the sesame oil until the sesame oil is very fragrant, about 30 seconds. Add the sesame seeds, salt, and pepper and swirl until the sesame seeds are toasted, about 30 seconds more.

3. Stir the spinach into the hot oil mixture and cook just until it is wilted, about 1 minute. Serve hot, as quickly as you can.

★
WEST COAST CREAMED SPINACH

Once a steakhouse standard, old-fashioned creamed spinach involved cooking the spinach first in boiling water or steam and then squeezing out the excess water before combining it—just before serving—with a simple white sauce. This version eliminates the precooking and uses reduced heavy cream in place of the white sauce. When boiling the cream, it's important to use a large pan, *because before it reduces it will foam up and expand to several times its original volume. You can boil the cream ahead of time, but add the spinach just before you plan to serve the dish; if it cooks too long, it will release extra water into the sauce. Also, if you can find it, the thicker crinkly leafed variety of spinach known as savoy works best. Serve this spinach with steaks or roasts.*

MAKES 4 SERVINGS

I pound spinach, or one 6-ounce bag prewashed baby spinach

¾ cup heavy cream

I medium shallot, finely chopped

½ teaspoon salt

¼ teaspoon white pepper

⅛ teaspoon ground nutmeg

1. If you are using whole spinach, fill a sink with water and pick the leaves from the stems, letting them fall into the water. Discard the stems and roots. Swish the spinach leaves around in the water to free them from any soil, then lift them out of the sink, allowing the soil to sink to the bottom. Spin the spinach leaves dry in a salad spinner or lay them on several layers of paper towels and pat them dry. Keep the washed, dried spinach in a bowl near the stove, ready to cook.

2. In a large sauté pan over medium-high heat, boil the cream with the shallot, salt, white pepper, and nutmeg until it foams up and thickens slightly; it should be reduced to slightly less than half of its original volume. (The sauce can be

prepared in advance and reheated just before you add the spinach.)

3. Just before serving time, stir the spinach into the boiling reduced cream mixture, and cook just until it is wilted, about 1 minute. Serve hot, as quickly as you can.

★
SWISS CHARD GRATIN

This recipe takes greens one step further than the process outlined in the recipe for West Coast Creamed Spinach. Here they're creamed, topped with buttered bread-crumbs, and baked until the crumbs are crisp and golden and the greens beneath are meltingly tender. Swiss chard leaves, which contain less water than spinach, are especially well suited to this dish. The advantage of this preparation is that it need not be put off until the last minute. The gratin can be prepared ahead and then finished in the oven minutes before serving.

MAKES 4 SERVINGS

¼ cup (½ stick) unsalted butter, plus 1 tablespoon for the pan

1 cup fresh breadcrumbs

1 bunch Swiss chard

¾ cup heavy cream

1 medium shallot, finely chopped

½ teaspoon salt

¼ teaspoon ground white pepper

⅛ teaspoon nutmeg, preferably freshly ground

1. Preheat the oven to 400°F. Melt the ¼ cup butter in a medium saucepan, then mix in the breadcrumbs and set the mixture aside to be crumbled over the cooked greens later. Use the extra tablespoon of butter to grease an oval baking dish or an 8-inch square baking pan.

2. Trim the base of the stems from the chard. Fill a sink with water and swish the leaves around to free them from any soil, then lift them out of the sink, allowing the soil to sink to the bottom. Shake or pat the leaves to free them from excess water. Roll the leaves into rough cylinders and slice the cylinders crosswise to make thin ribbons. Keep the prepared leaves in a bowl near the stove, ready to cook.

3. In a large sauté pan over medium-high heat, boil the cream with the shallot, salt, white pepper, and nutmeg until it foams up and thickens slightly; it should be reduced to slightly less than half of its original volume.

4. Stir the cut Swiss chard into the boiling reduced cream mixture and cook just until the leaves are wilted, about 2 minutes. Transfer the creamed chard to the buttered dish and top with the buttered breadcrumbs. Bake until the crumbs are brown and the chard is boiling underneath, about 15 minutes.

Vegetable Tops and Flowering Heads

CAULIFLOWER GRATIN

Sometimes called a gratin after the crust that forms under and over the vegetables, and sometimes called a tian after the oval baking dish in which these things are made, this is basically a vegetable casserole. This one follows a technique popularized by the late Richard Olney, who lived most of his life in the south of France but had a profound influence on West Coast cooking. He found devoted fans in many cooks here, including Marion Cunningham and Olney's protégé, Jeremiah Tower. The dish also owes something to M. F. K. Fisher, who offered a brief description of a similar dish in her book The Gastronomical Me.

MAKES 4 SERVINGS

1 small head cauliflower

½ to ¾ cup heavy cream

Kosher salt and freshly ground black pepper, to taste

2 tablespoons unsalted butter

6 ounces Gruyère or other Swiss-style cheese, grated

I. Preheat the oven to 325°F and butter a 1-quart oval baking dish. Cut off the base of the cauliflower and cut or break the head into individual florets. Cut the larger florets in halves or thirds to create bite-sized morsels. Parboil the florets, if you like, in boiling salted water, but do not

cook them for more than 3 to 5 minutes or the cauliflower will be mushy. (I just pile them in raw.)

2. Arrange the cauliflower florets in a single layer in the buttered baking dish and pour in the cream, just enough to reach about halfway up the sides of the florets. Sprinkle generously with salt and pepper. Dot the top of the dish with bits of butter, and spread the grated cheese over the top.

3. Bake the dish until the cheese is brown and the cauliflower is very tender, 45 minutes to 1 hour. Serve at once with crusty bread and a green salad.

BROCCOLI RAAB SAUTÉED WITH GARLIC AND CHILES

According to Elizabeth Schneider in her wonderful book Vegetables from Amaranth to Zucchini, *broccoli raab, which is sometimes called "rapini," was already growing wild all over California in the 1930s, when Italian-American produce growers recognized the vegetable from the Old Country and started a breeding program to select the most flavorful strains to grow for East Coast markets. With a rustic, almost bitter edge, the vegetable tastes like the primordial version of the more familiar and less flavorful broccoli that it is.*

1 large bunch (about 1¼ pounds) broccoli raab

8 cups water

1 tablespoon kosher salt

2 tablespoons extra virgin olive oil

1 clove garlic, grated on a Microplane grater

½ teaspoon dried red chile flakes

1. Trim the stems off the base of the raab and rinse it under cold running water; let it drain in a colander. In a large pot or Dutch oven, bring the water and salt to a full, rolling boil and drop in the broccoli raab. Cook until the vegetable is very bright green and the leaves are wilted, about 2 minutes.

2. Meanwhile, heat the olive oil in a large sauté pan over medium heat and cook the garlic and chile flakes until the garlic is soft and golden, about 2 minutes.

3. Lift the raab out of the boiling water with tongs, shake off any excess water, and carefully transfer it to the sauté pan with the garlic and chile flakes.

4. Sauté briefly, tossing the raab to coat it with the hot olive oil mixture. Serve at once.

★

"BLASTED BROCCOLI" WITH RED CHILES AND GARLIC

Compared with the recipe for Broccoli Raab Sautéed with Garlic and Chiles, this recipe demonstrates how a different technique can be applied to a very similar list of ingredients with profoundly different results. It makes sense to cook broccoli this way when the stovetop is tied up with some other part of a dinner; roasted vegetables require less attention than sautéed vegetables do, and they go very well with grilled or pan-seared meats.

1 large head broccoli

2 tablespoons extra virgin olive oil

1 teaspoon kosher salt

1 clove garlic, grated on a Microplane grater

½ teaspoon dried red chile flakes

1. Preheat the oven to 500°F. Trim the broccoli into florets (you should have about 4 cups). Rinse and drain the broccoli florets.

2. Put the florets in a bowl with the olive oil, salt, garlic, and chile flakes and toss to coat. Spread the seasoned broccoli in a single layer on a baking sheet and put it in the preheated oven. Bake until the edges of the florets are browned and crisp, about 4 minutes. Serve hot.

★

BALSAMIC BLASTED GREEN BEANS

In the 1990s, "blasting" vegetables was seemingly in the wind. Chefs and home cooks alike were popping aspar-agus and green beans into hot ovens all over the coun-try. Food & Wine *editor Tina Ujlaki offered a recipe that followed a technique like this one to a reader who wrote requesting a healthy vegetable side dish. At about that same time, I picked up on the trend from my friend*

Sharon Kramis, an acolyte of the late James Beard, who was experimenting with blasted vegetables on her own. Intense heat assures that the vegetable is irresistibly crisp, and any trace of bitterness from the browning is trumped by the sweet tang of balsamic vinegar. The same technique can be employed with other green vegetables, such as broccoli or asparagus, or with winter squash.

MAKES 4 SERVINGS

1 pound green beans

2 tablespoons olive oil

2 teaspoons kosher salt, plus more if needed

½ teaspoon freshly ground black pepper

1 tablespoon balsamic vinegar

1. Preheat the oven to 500°F. Trim the green beans to remove the tough stem ends, but leave the delicate "tails" intact. Rinse and drain the beans.

2. Toss the beans in a medium bowl with the olive oil, salt, and pepper. Spread the seasoned beans in a single layer on a baking sheet and bake until the edges of the beans are browned and crisp, about 4 minutes.

3. Put the cooked beans back in the bowl and toss with the balsamic vinegar. Taste and add more salt if desired. Serve hot.

★
BABY BOK CHOY

From the first time I saw this vegetable, which is sometimes called Shanghai or green-stemmed bok choy, I have been enamored of its shapely form, which is reminiscent of a fennel bulb. Baby bok choy is refreshingly simple, with none of the bite that other members of the cabbage family have. I have always enjoyed the contrast between its elegant simplicity and the bold flavors of the dishes with which I usually pair it, so I was surprised and a little taken aback when a friend whose good taste I admire told me that I should "jazz it up with a little green curry or something." I didn't follow that advice, and if the vegetable is a side dish neither should you. Keep it simple, and pair it with Pacific Ponzu Salmon (pages 162–63) or Restaurant-Style Roast Duckling with Orange Sauce (pages 206–8).

MAKES 6 SERVINGS

1½ pounds baby bok choy

1 gallon boiling water

2 tablespoons kosher salt

1. Split each head of baby bok choy in half lengthwise and rinse in several changes of cold tap water to remove any soil trapped between the leaves.

2. Put the water and salt in a large saucepan over high heat, and when the water comes to a full, rolling boil, drop in the bok choy. Cook until the leaves turn a brilliant shade of jade green and the bulbs are barely tender, about 3 minutes, then lift them out of the boiling water and serve at once, or scatter them over the surface of a baking sheet so they will cool and stop cooking. The bok choy can be prepared ahead up to this point and reheated in boiling salted water for 15 seconds or so just before serving.

★

JADE GREEN BROCCOLI
OR GREEN BEANS

Green vegetables simply boiled in plenty of salted water become tender without losing their bright green color. My theory about why they retain so much of their delightful green color and flavor has to do with the distribution of particles in water. Because the water is already saturated with salt, I think less of the goodness leaches out from the broccoli. The quantity of water is critical too: There must be enough so that the vegetables don't cool it down too much, so they cook quickly instead of slowly stewing in a warm bath.

SERVES 4

1 pound broccoli crowns or green beans

2 quarts boiling water

1 tablespoon kosher salt

2 tablespoons butter

1. If using broccoli, trim the crowns into individual florets that are all about the same size. If using green beans, trim them to remove the tough stem end but leave the delicate "tails" intact.

2. Put the water and salt in a large saucepan over high heat, and when the water comes to a full, rolling boil, drop in the broccoli. Cook the broccoli until dark green and barely tender, about 3 minutes, then lift the florets out of the boiling water and scatter them over the surface of a baking sheet so they will cool and stop cooking. The vegetables may be prepared

ahead up to this point and finished just before serving.

3. Melt the butter in a large sauté pan over medium-high heat. Add the broccoli and sauté until the florets are coated with the butter and heated through. Serve at once.

★

TYPHOON-STYLE GREEN BEANS

When I learned to cook green beans in the Thai style from my friend Bo Klein, who owns four Typhoon! restaurants in Portland and Seattle, he taught me to deep-fry the beans in hot oil before finishing them in a stir-fry. Unless I'm making doughnuts or something equally decadent, I find deep-frying at home to be too messy a process, so I tried parboiling the beans instead, and the results were fantastic.

MAKES 4 SERVINGS

12 ounces green beans

8 cups boiling water

1 tablespoon kosher salt

1 tablespoon canola oil

1/4 medium onion, peeled and thinly sliced

2 teaspoons grated garlic

1 teaspoon dried red chile flakes

1 teaspoon soy sauce

2 tablespoons Chinese oyster sauce

2 teaspoons brown sugar

⅓ cup chicken broth

1. Trim the green beans to remove the tough stem end, but leave the delicate

"tails" intact. Put the water and salt in a large saucepan over high heat, and when the water comes to a full, rolling boil, drop in the beans. Cook until the beans are dark green and barely tender, about 3 minutes, then lift them out of the boiling water and scatter them over the surface of a baking sheet so they will cool and stop cooking. The beans can be prepared ahead up to this point and finished just before serving.

2. Heat the canola oil in a wok over medium-high heat. Add the onion, garlic, and chile flakes and stir until the garlic begins to turn golden.

3. Add the soy sauce, oyster sauce, and brown sugar. Stir quickly. Add the chicken broth. Boil the sauce for a few seconds to reduce it to about half of its initial volume. Add the beans and sauté until they are heated through and coated with the sauce. Serve at once.

★

WEST COAST GREEN BEAN CASSEROLE

Made with a real, albeit very simple, homemade velouté sauce and fresh or dried mushrooms, this traditional American side dish can be a revelation. For too long, the building blocks of the dish were replaced with canned soup, giving the dish an undeservedly bad reputation. It is overdue, I think, for some rehabilitation. This version, which is really a gratin or tian, presents the beans in a flavorful sauce, topped with golden brown buttered breadcrumbs. Serve these green beans with Apple Cider Roasted Turkey (pages 203–5) at Thanksgiving dinner

or with Rosé Roast Chicken with Herbs (pages 201–2) for a simple Sunday night supper. If you are preparing this dish when green beans are out of season, you can achieve good results with frozen beans; choose the "petite" green beans, which are less likely to develop the unpleasant rubbery texture that frozen vegetables sometimes have.

MAKES 6 SERVINGS

For the Beans

1½ pounds fresh young green beans, or two 10-ounce bags frozen green beans

1 gallon boiling water

2 tablespoons kosher salt

For the Sauce

¼ cup (½ stick) unsalted butter

¼ cup flour

2 cups chicken broth, homemade (page 68) or store-bought

½ cup heavy cream

1 teaspoon kosher salt, or to taste

½ teaspoon freshly ground black pepper, or to taste

For the Topping

1 cup fresh breadcrumbs

½ cup grated Parmesan cheese

¼ cup (½ stick) unsalted butter

1. Preheat the oven to 350°F and butter a 2-quart baking dish. (The casserole looks best in a ceramic oval.)

2. Trim the green beans to remove the tough stem end, but leave the delicate "tails" intact. Put the water and salt in a large saucepan over high heat, and when the water comes to a full, rolling boil, drop in the beans. Cook until they are dark green and barely tender, about 3 minutes, then lift them out of the boiling water and scatter them over the surface of a baking sheet so they will cool and stop cooking. The beans can be prepared ahead up to this point and finished just before serving.

3. Make the sauce. Melt the butter in a large sauté pan over medium-high heat, whisk in the flour, and then whisk in the broth and cream. Cook and stir until the mixture boils and starts to thicken. Stir in the salt and pepper to taste. Combine the sauce with the green beans and transfer the mixture to the buttered baking dish.

4. For the topping, combine the breadcrumbs with the Parmesan cheese and butter and scatter the mixture over the beans. Bake until the topping is golden brown and the filling is bubbling around the edges, 30 to 35 minutes.

★

ROASTED BRUSSELS SPROUTS WITH RED CHILE FLAKES AND SESAME OIL

Brussels sprouts do not appeal to some people, but sometimes I think this is only because they have been exposed to ones that have been very badly cooked. My father-in-law tells of a time when he was in the army during World War II. "I was stationed in France," he says, "and the only vegetable we had to eat all winter was Brussels sprouts. They were always boiling away in a big pot, and they smelled yucky." Lifted out of the boiling water before they are overcooked, the sprouts do not smell yucky at all, and tossed with a mixture of fragrant and savory sesame oil and red chiles, they take on an exotic air that even my father-in-law can appreciate.

MAKES 6 SERVINGS

For the Brussels Sprouts

1 pound (about 36) Brussels sprouts

8 cups water

1 tablespoon kosher salt

For the Seasoning Blend

2 tablespoons peanut or canola oil

1 tablespoon toasted sesame oil

2 tablespoons turbinado sugar or Sugar in the Raw

2 teaspoons kosher salt

1 teaspoon dried red chile flakes

1. Use a paring knife to trim the bottoms from the Brussels sprouts. Pull away

any loose or damaged leaves. In a large saucepan, bring the water and salt to a full, rolling boil, and drop in the trimmed Brussels sprouts. Cook until they are dark green and can be easily pierced with the tip of a knife, about 5 minutes. Drain the sprouts and scatter them in a single layer over the surface of a baking sheet to halt the cooking process. The Brussels sprouts can be prepared ahead up to this point and finished later.

2. Preheat the oven to 400°F. In a medium mixing bowl, whisk together the ingredients for the seasoning blend. Cut the parboiled Brussels sprouts in half lengthwise and toss them with the seasoning blend. Roast until the outside leaves of the sprouts are crisp and translucent, about 5 minutes. Serve hot.

★
ROASTED SUGAR PUMPKIN WITH CINNAMON

The big pumpkins raised specifically for carving jack-o'-lanterns will not be particularly good eating; they're too stringy and watery. But the smaller, denser sugar pumpkins grown for pie making are excellent vegetables. Serve blocks of roast pumpkin with pork or chicken. You may wish to roast the pumpkin right in the pan with the meat, in which case you can omit the oil or butter. Even the firmest pumpkin grows very soft when it's roasted, so handle it carefully after it's baked.

3 pounds red-skinned pumpkin or pie pumpkin

2 tablespoons coconut oil, butter, or pan drippings, melted

1 tablespoon turbinado sugar or Sugar in the Raw

1 teaspoon ground cinnamon

1 teaspoon kosher salt

About ½ teaspoon freshly ground black pepper

1. Preheat the oven to 400°F.

2. Cut the pumpkin into wedges. Scoop out the seeds and any stringy fibers, then cut away the skin. Cut the peeled and seeded pumpkin into short, rectangular pieces about 2 inches square and 4 inches long.

3. Toss the pumpkin pieces with the melted coconut oil and arrange them in a single layer on a baking sheet. Do not allow the pieces to touch. Sprinkle the pumpkin with the sugar, cinnamon, and salt.

4. Roast the pumpkin pieces until they are browned on all sides and tender, about 10 minutes. Just before serving, finish them with grind of black pepper. Use a fish spatula to transfer the roasted pumpkin pieces from the baking sheet to plates.

★
PUMPKIN OR WINTER
SQUASH PURÉE

"Cinderella" pumpkins, so called because one was used as a model for some famous illustrations of the fairy tale, are a good choice for pumpkin purée. Butternut or other winter squash can be prepared this way too. Peeled, seeded, and cubed, the squash cooks quickly in an old-fashioned steamer basket. The butter or oil is a healthy addition because it facilitates absorption of the vitamin A so abundant in this vegetable. A dollop of this purée served with roast or sautéed meat makes a welcome change from potatoes. Omit the salt and pepper and use the purée in Golden Pumpkin Waffles (pages 34–35) or Pumpkin Streusel Breakfast Cake (pages 297–98).

MAKES 6 SERVINGS

1 medium (2-pound) cooking pumpkin or winter squash

1 teaspoon kosher salt

½ teaspoon freshly ground black pepper

2 tablespoons unsalted butter or canola oil

1. Cut the squash into wedges, scrape out the seeds, and then cut away the peel. Cut the peeled and seeded squash into 1-inch dice. You should have about 5 cups of cubed squash.

2. Put a steamer basket into a 4-quart stockpot over high heat and pour in a cup of water. Pile the cubed squash into the steamer basket. Cover and steam the squash until it is tender, about 10 minutes.

3. Put the steamed squash through a food mill over a saucepan, or pile it into a food processor and purée until smooth. Add salt and pepper. Whisk in the butter or oil and serve hot.

★
ROASTED DELICATA SQUASH

I first encountered this squash when I was working as a chef in Friday Harbor, Washington, and a farmer invited me to peruse her seed catalog to see if there was anything in particular that I would like her to grow the next year. I was struck by the beautiful green stripes on the bright yellow background of the squash's skin, and by a note in the catalogue that said that unlike other winter squash, this one had tender, edible skin. I had forgotten about this encounter until nine months later, when she showed up at the back door with a case of Delicata, which was everything I had hoped it would be. I cut the squash into circles and then, with an oyster knife, took out the stringy fibers and seeds and roasted the rings with clarified butter until they were brown on the outside and tender on the inside. I served them every year from then on.

MAKES 6 SERVINGS

2 whole Delicata squash (about 3 pounds)

2 tablespoons browned butter (see pages 242–43)

2 teaspoons kosher salt

Freshly ground black pepper, to taste

1. Preheat the oven to 400°F.

2. Cut the tube-shaped squash into slices. Use an oyster knife or the dull side of a

paring knife to scoop out the seeds and any stringy fibers.

3. Toss the rings with the browned butter and salt and arrange them in a single layer on a baking sheet.

4. When the squash rings have browned on the underside, after about 4 minutes, turn them over and bake until the second side is browned and the flesh is tender, about 4 minutes more. Just before serving, finish them with grind of black pepper.

★

TWICE-ROASTED MINIATURE PUMPKINS WITH ONIONS AND THYME

At Thanksgiving, these filled pumpkins make a nice vegan or vegetarian option for members of the party who don't enjoy turkey. Served with green beans, mashed potatoes, and whatever other side dishes are part of the feast, the miniature pumpkins provide a focal point. For people who do eat meat, they provide a whimsical side dish with turkey, pork, or chicken.

MAKES 6 SERVINGS

6 miniature pumpkins (about 8 ounces each)

I medium onion, peeled and finely chopped

¼ cup (½ stick) unsalted butter, or ¼ cup canola oil

I teaspoon fresh thyme leaves, or ½ teaspoon dried thyme

I teaspoon kosher salt, or to taste

½ teaspoon freshly ground black pepper, or to taste

¼ teaspoon ground nutmeg (optional)

I cup fresh breadcrumbs

I egg

1. Preheat the oven to 375°F. On a baking sheet, roast the miniature pumpkins until fork-tender, about 30 minutes. While the pumpkins are roasting, sauté the chopped onion in the butter or oil until soft and translucent. Stir in the thyme, salt, pepper, and nutmeg. Remove from the heat and let cool to room temperature.

2. When the pumpkins are tender, use a very sharp knife to cut a lid from each one. With a teaspoon, scoop out the seeds and stringy fibers, but leave the thick walls of the little pumpkins intact.

3. In a medium bowl, combine the breadcrumbs with the egg and the cooled sautéed onion. Fill each pumpkin with the prepared stuffing. (The pumpkins can be made ahead up to this point and refrigerated for up to a day.) Bake the filled pumpkins until they are heated through, about 20 minutes; serve hot.

CHINESE RESTAURANT-STYLE SNAP PEAS

No single cultural influence has been greater in shaping West Coast sensibilities than Chinese. But the influence has been so pervasive and so consistent over the years that it feels less like an outside influence than an inherent sensibility. It seems telling that the late James Beard grew up under the gastronomic influence of his mother Elizabeth's Chinese cook, Jue Let, who was trained in both classical French and traditional Chinese cooking. The same technique used here for cooking snap peas can be used to cook broccoli florets or tender young green beans.

MAKES 4 SERVINGS

1 pound snap peas

For the Sauce

½ cup vegetable broth or chicken broth

1 tablespoon soy sauce

1 tablespoon sherry

1 teaspoon cornstarch

1 teaspoon sugar

For the Stir-Fry

2 tablespoons canola oil

1 teaspoon toasted sesame oil

2 cloves garlic

1-inch piece ginger root

1. Trim the snap peas, if necessary, pulling off the stem end with the stringy fiber that runs down the length of the pea pod.

2. In a small bowl, stir the broth with the soy sauce, sherry, cornstarch, and sugar, and keep the bowl near the stove.

3. Preheat a wok or large sauté pan over medium-high heat, pour in the canola oil and sesame oil, and swirl to coat the sides of the pan.

4. Use a rasp-style (Microplane) grater to grate the garlic and ginger directly into the hot oil, and stir until fragrant, about 30 seconds. Add the pea pods and toss to coat them in the hot, fragrant oil. Continue stirring until the peas are heated through, about 2 minutes.

5. Stir the broth mixture in the bowl to bring up the cornstarch, which will have settled to the bottom, and pour the mixture over the hot snap peas. Stir-fry until the sauce is reduced to a shiny glaze that mostly adheres to the peas, about 1 minute. Transfer the peas immediately to a communal platter, or distribute them among individual serving plates and serve hot.

MINTED PEAS

Frozen peas are often sweeter than fresh ones. Since sugars in peas are almost immediately converted into more complex and less-sweet starches, peas that are flash cooked and frozen within hours after harvesting can be more satisfying than the peas we buy fresh. Unless you grow your own peas or buy them at the peak of the season in a farmer's market, you're probably better off buying frozen. To give these peas a little extra zip, heat them with a minimum of water and a generous sprinkling of shredded mint leaves.

MAKES 4 SERVINGS

One 10-ounce package of frozen peas

2 tablespoons water

12 mint leaves

1 teaspoon kosher salt

½ teaspoon freshly ground black pepper

1. Put the peas and the water in a sauté pan over high heat.

2. Roll the mint leaves into a little bundle and cut into thin ribbons.

3. Add the mint, salt, and pepper to the peas and water, which should be boiling. As soon as the water evaporates and the peas are heated through, about 2 minutes, they're ready to serve.

★

STIR-FRIED BROCCOLI AND SHIITAKE MUSHROOMS WITH OYSTER SAUCE

Mushrooms, technically speaking, are not vegetables at all; rather, they are among the fungi, a separate order of living things that are neither plant nor animal. So even though the role of mushrooms in the kitchen is basically that of a vegetable, they are unique. Mushrooms are a good source of protein—especially for people who follow a vegan diet. And mushrooms contain glutamates, a group of protein-based chemicals that enhance the flavors of other foods with which they are served. More than many

other domesticated mushrooms, shiitake mushrooms, grown in controlled conditions on chunks of pressed wood chips, capture the characteristics of wild forest mushrooms. Cooked as they are here with broccoli florets, the mushrooms take on a meaty quality. Vegetarians who prefer not to use oyster sauce can use dark Chinese soy sauce instead.

MAKES 4 SERVINGS

8 ounces fresh shiitake mushrooms

1 head broccoli

For the Sauce

½ cup vegetable broth or chicken broth

2 tablespoons Chinese oyster sauce

1 teaspoon cornstarch

For the Stir-Fry

2 tablespoons canola oil

2 cloves garlic, peeled and thinly sliced

1. Discard the mushroom stems and cut the caps into ½-inch slices. Rinse the broccoli, then break off the tops and cut them into individual 1-inch florets.

2. In a small bowl, stir the broth with the oyster sauce and cornstarch, and keep the bowl near the stove.

3. Preheat a wok or large sauté pan over medium-high heat, pour in the canola oil, and swirl to coat the sides of the pan.

4. Add the sliced garlic to the hot oil and stir until fragrant, about 30 seconds. Add the mushrooms and broccoli florets, and toss quickly to coat them in the hot,

fragrant oil. Continue stirring until the vegetables are heated through, about 2 minutes.

5. Stir the broth mixture in the bowl to bring up the cornstarch, which will have settled to the bottom, and pour the mixture over the hot mushrooms. Stir-fry until the sauce is reduced to a shiny glaze that adheres to the vegetables, about 1 minute. Transfer immediately to a communal platter, or distribute them among individual serving plates and serve hot.

★

MADEIRA GRILLED PORTOBELLO MUSHROOMS

When they are mature and fully opened, the little brown-topped mushrooms otherwise known as cremini become quite large, and they are sold as portobello or portabella mushrooms, depending on the purveyor. The name—which seems to be nothing more than a marketing gimmick—might refer to an Italian town called Portobello, where the mushroom is typically served grilled or pan-seared, just like a steak. In Italy, it's referred to as a capellone, or "big hat." West Coast chefs turn to portobellos for a quick solution to the problem of what to offer a vegetarian when the menu otherwise revolves around grilled steak. Offer the grilled or pan-seared mushrooms with baked potatoes and a salad instead of steak, or serve them over a bed of spinach or arugula with a drizzle of olive oil for a salad course.

4 large portobello mushrooms (about 1 pound)

¼ cup Madeira

2 tablespoons soy sauce

1 tablespoon toasted sesame oil

1 teaspoon grated ginger root

1. Preheat a grill or a griddle. On a grill, check the temperature by placing a hand, palm side down, 2 or 3 inches above the cooking surface. When you can keep your hand there for no more than 3 or 4 seconds, the temperature is right. If you are using an electric griddle, set the temperature to 400°F, or "high."

2. Scrape the black gills from the underside of the mushroom caps, using the edge of a tablespoon. Handle the caps carefully to keep them whole; discard the gills. In a small bowl, whisk together the Madeira, soy sauce, sesame oil, and ginger.

3. Put the mushroom caps, gilled side up, on the surface of the hot grill or griddle. Spoon the Madeira mixture over the caps, pressing down lightly with the back of the spoon so that the mushroom caps soak up the liquid like sponges.

4. Grill or cook the mushrooms for 5 minutes, then turn and grill them for 3 or 4 minutes longer. Transfer the mushrooms to a cutting board and slice them in thick slices. Serve hot or at room temperature.

YEAST BREADS

Yeast Breads

A few years ago, I visited a site in the Fremont neighborhood of Seattle that was undergoing a transformation from a twentieth-century Orowheat bread factory to the twenty-first-century Essential Baking Company, an organic artisan bakery. It was an interesting reversal. The "factory floor," where "workers" had been required to wear hard hats and ear protection to cope with the danger and noise associated with the machines that produced thousands upon thousands of uniform loaves of bread, had been cleared. Bakers were moved in, with their wooden tables and simple tools for hand-forming a smaller number of loaves that were infinitely more flavorful than the ones produced by the machines.

Because bread making is labor intensive and requires the combined efforts of growers, millers, and bakers, certain aspects of bread making have often been fairly centralized community activities. But only in the postindustrial world did bread making become completely divorced from individual creativity. The village bakers of yore were artisans, practicing a craft. The workers at industrial bakeries were something else.

But what was happening at the Essential Baking Company was not unique. For the last quarter of the twentieth century, home bakers and small-scale commercial bakeries have been inching steadily away from the industrial model toward a more human scale of bread baking.

Much of the new American cooking that emerged in the last decades of the twentieth century is not exactly new. Rather, some of the "new foods" represent a return to old ways. Traditional methods that had been abandoned for more than a generation, in favor of swifter modern methods of preparing food, have been revisited in the hope of gaining back some of the flavor and character that many of us felt we were missing. This has been especially true of bread, and nowhere has the revival of traditional methods of bread baking been more readily embraced than on the West Coast.

Tucked under the lofty brick archways of a historic building in Seattle's Pioneer Square, "The Bakery," as Grand Central Bakery was originally known, opened its doors in 1972, the same year Starbucks opened its first coffee store in the Pike Place Market. Possessed of a certain magic that goes hand in hand with its location, the place always prompts a sense of discovery. Just by virtue of being there, regulars and first-time visitors alike can feel as if they have uncovered some kind of hidden treasure. And indeed they have.

Grand Central is among a handful of bakeries that reintroduced hand-formed artisanal breads to the public at a critical juncture when the old ways might easily have been lost. In the mid-twentieth century, bread making had become more of an industry than a craft, and the artistry that had been passed from baker to baker over the centuries was fading away.

Gwen Bassetti, who developed all the recipes for the original breads on which the bakery was founded, started with home-style breads based on commercial yeast. Bassetti grew up in a household in Sudbury, Massachusetts, where she says "making bread was a way of life." Her transformation from New Englander to Northwesterner began with a summer job as a baker on a dude ranch in Wyoming and progressed through a culinary sojourn in the San Juan Islands where she sold jam, bread, and vegetables from a roadside stand staffed by her children.

Four years after she and her partners opened "The Bakery," she left to raise sheep and children in eastern Washington. But in 1989, when the kids were grown, she entered a business partnership with Pioneer Square developer and family friend, Alan Black, and together they purchased the bakery and renamed it "Grand Central Baking Company." By this time, Bassetti had developed a passion for the rustic sourdough bread she had tasted on trips to San Francisco, and she had baked her way through Carol Field's classic *The Italian Baker*.

"Without realizing it," says Bassetti, "I was on the crest of a wave that became the artisan bread-baking movement." Indeed, Grand Central was one of the first bakeries on the West Coast, along with La Brea Breads in Los Angeles and Acme Baking Company in Berkeley, to abandon copious amounts of commercial yeast and rigid loaf pans in favor of slow-rising dough inoculated with wild yeast and hand-formed loaves baked in hearth ovens.

These days, artisan bakers produce remarkable quantities of bread. Grand Central Bakery, for instance, produces about 6,000 loaves of bread every day. (The hearth ovens hold up to 480 loaves, each and the mixing bowls hold 425 pounds of dough.) But for the use of electric mixers, every step of the baking process, including the shaping of each loaf, is still performed by hand, and, because it's based on the original slow-rising starter that launched the Grand Central Baking Company, every loaf takes two days to make.

West Coast starters are built on a heritage that reaches as far back as human history itself. Medieval French bakers perfected the art of maintaining a perpetual supply of yeast well suited to introducing carbon dioxide bubbles into bread dough; they called it *levain*. But the tradition has roots in older cultures; even the ancient Egyptians borrowed the technique from people who came before them. What distinguishes West Coast sourdough starters is the particular combinations of yeast and bacteria that inhabit them. Other starters—French levain in particular—are not particularly sour. West Coast starters, though, boast a certain amount of bacteria that produce both acetic or lactic acids, lending the bread a peculiar tang reminiscent of vinegar or yogurt.

About Sourdough

Maintaining a sourdough starter is more like keeping a pet than following a recipe. Think of the starter as a colony of microscopic yeast and bacteria residing in a habitat consisting of flour and water. Along with traces of chemicals like acetone and various strange-smelling aldehydes, the colonists produce a combination of carbon dioxide, acid, and alcohol. The baker serves more or less as a zookeeper or rancher, making sure that the little critters have everything they need, and occasionally harvesting some of them to make bread.

If you cannot procure a bit of starter from a friend, try one of the commercial sourdough starters sold online or in specialty food stores. In these mixtures, the microbes are dried but ready to be revived with the addition of water, just like active dry yeast. Follow the directions that come with the dehydrated microbes to bring them back to life. Once reanimated, the microbes can be kept alive just like the inhabitants of any other starter.

Some of the best sourdough starters are colonized by wild flora and fauna brought in on the backs of unsprayed grapes. The natural denizens of the vineyard are members of the vast family of microorganisms that we employ to make a lot of foods. If organic grapes are within your reach, follow the instructions outlined here to make your own starter from scratch. This formula is based on one that I learned from Nancy Silverton, founder of La Brea Bakery in Los Angeles.

★

SOURDOUGH STARTER

Since I don't want to sound like a fanatic, I sometimes downplay the importance of selecting organic ingredients, but in this case, the argument for organic cannot be made too strongly. Since the essence of a sourdough starter is a colony of wild yeast, it would be ludicrous to use grapes or flour from a nonorganic source. Conventionally farmed flour and grapes—those grown nonorganically—are routinely exposed to antifungal compounds that kill the wild yeast you're trying to harvest here.

MAKES ABOUT 3 CUPS OF LIVING
SOURDOUGH STARTER

1 cup organic unbleached white flour

1 cup filtered water

1 small cluster (about 4 ounces) organic grapes

1. Put the flour and water in a medium mixing bowl and whisk to make a smooth batter.

2. Wrap the grapes in several layers of cheesecloth and tie up the corners to make a little bundle. Press the bundle of grapes to break them slightly, but don't smash them flat. Submerge the bundle of crushed grapes in the batter and cover the bowl with a clean kitchen towel or a very loosely applied layer of plastic wrap.

3. Allow the batter to stand at room temperature, lightly covered, for 2 or 3 days, or until the surface is covered with bubbles. The batter, when stirred, will release a bouquet that smells peculiar but not unpleasant—something like beer and bread, with the faintest hint of nail polish remover.

4. To maintain the starter, keep it refrigerated for up to 2 weeks at a time. For every ½ cup of starter you remove to make a batch of bread, add a thin batter made from ⅓ cup filtered water and ⅓ cup flour, to replenish the starter.

★
SOURDOUGH BREAD

The tradition of sourdough bread on the West Coast began with the forty-niners, the wave of prospectors who came west in search of gold in 1849, and it continued into Alaska when gold was discovered there a few years later. But the tradition really blossomed in the late twentieth century, when the artisanal bread-baking movement took root. Places like La Brea Breads in Los Angeles, Acme Baking Company in Berkeley, and Grand Central Bakery in Seattle introduced Americans to traditional breads based on natural levain, or wild starters.

MAKES 2 LOAVES, 1½ POUNDS EACH

1 cup sourdough starter

1½ cups lukewarm (70°F) water

1 cup whole wheat flour

1 tablespoon kosher salt

4½ cups unbleached white flour

1. Put the starter, water, and whole wheat flour in the bowl of a stand mixer and whisk to make a smooth batter. Using a paddle attachment for the mixer or a wooden spoon, stir in the salt and 3 cups of the unbleached flour, 1 cup at a time, to make a very soft dough. Use a dough hook or the wooden spoon to add the remaining 1½ cups flour and mix or knead the dough until it is very smooth and elastic, about 5 minutes.

2. Lightly coat a 4-quart mixing bowl with oil and transfer the dough to the oiled bowl. Turn the dough over once so that the top of the dough is lightly coated with oil. Cover the mixing bowl with a very loosely applied layer of plastic wrap and allow the dough to rise at room temperature, lightly covered, until it has doubled in bulk, at least 8 hours, and preferably overnight.

3. Press the air out of the risen dough and gently knead it until it is springy again. The dough will have a smooth, flexible "skin." Divide the dough in half and, working with one half at a time, shape the dough into 2 balls, tucking the cut edges of the dough into the center of the balls and stretching the "skin" over the surface of the dough balls without tearing it.

4. Put the balls of dough on a baking sheet lined with a silicone pan liner or baker's parchment. Loosely cover the loaves with plastic wrap and let them rise until they are doubled in size, about 4 hours.

5. Put a baking sheet on the bottom rack of the oven and put a second rack one position above it. Pour a ½-inch layer of water into the baking sheet on the bottom shelf. Preheat the oven to 450°F, and if there is a convection option, use it. Just before putting the loaves in the oven, use a box cutter or a very sharp knife to cut shallow slashes in a cross over the surface of the loaves, about ⅛ inch deep. Bake the loaves until they are well browned and sound hollow when tapped; an instant-read thermometer inserted into the center of a loaf will register 200°F, about 35 minutes. Transfer the baked loaves to a cooling rack and let them cool to room temperature before slicing.

★

GOLD RUSH SOURDOUGH BISCUITS

MAKES 1 DOZEN BISCUITS

2 cups unbleached white flour

2 tablespoons sugar

1 tablespoon baking powder

1 teaspoon salt

½ teaspoon baking soda

¼ cup (½ stick) unsalted butter

½ cup milk

½ cup sourdough starter

1. Preheat the oven to 425°F and line a baking sheet with baker's parchment or a silicone pan liner.

2. Put 1½ cups of the flour in the work bowl of a food processor or a medium mixing bowl. Pulse or whisk in the sugar, baking powder, salt, and baking soda. Cut in the butter until the mixture is uniformly crumbly.

3. In a separate, small mixing bowl, whisk the remaining ½ cup flour with the milk and sourdough starter to make a thin, pancakelike batter. Add the batter to the first mixture all at once and pulse the motor of the food processor or stir the mixture with a wooden spoon to make a soft ball of dough.

4. Turn the dough out onto a lightly floured board and fold the dough over several times, kneading gently until it is smooth and slightly springy.

5. On a floured countertop, roll the dough out ½ inch thick, and cut it into rounds with a 2-inch cutter. Gather the scraps of dough, press them together, and roll and cut again. Put the biscuits on the lined baking sheet and bake until puffed and golden brown, about 10 minutes.

Sandwich Bread

★

PITA BREADS

One of the simplest sandwich breads is the traditional pita pocket. With plenty of lively commercial bread yeast, this dough is springy and fun to work with. A little vinegar adds structural integrity to the dough and tangy flavor to the finished bread. This is a wonderful recipe for introducing young children to the joys of bread baking. Serve it with Hummus (pages 59–60), or have a "build-your-own" pita pocket supper with bowls of crumbled feta cheese, chopped tomatoes, shredded spinach, and black olives.

MAKES 6 SMALL BREADS

1 cup warm water

1 tablespoon (1 packet) active dry yeast

1 tablespoon sugar

2 cups unbleached white flour

1 tablespoon vinegar (any kind will work)

1 tablespoon salt

1 tablespoon olive oil

1. In a large measuring cup, stir together the warm water, yeast, and sugar. Allow the mixture to stand until the yeast is softened, about 5 minutes, then stir until the yeast is completely dissolved. Put the flour in a food processor, the bowl of an electric mixer, or a medium mixing bowl, and mix in the yeast mixture. Mix in the vinegar, salt, and oil; mix or knead the dough until it is smooth and elastic, about 5 minutes.

2. Cover the dough with a damp towel or plastic wrap and allow it to rise, covered, for 1 hour, or until doubled in bulk.

3. Put a baking sheet on the bottom rack of the oven and preheat the oven to 425°F.

4. Divide the risen dough into 6 pieces and shape them into balls about the size of golf balls. Let the pieces rest for about 5 minutes so they won't be too springy, then roll them out on a floured countertop into circles about 6 inches across.

5. Bake the pita breads on the preheated baking sheet until they are puffed and slightly browned, about 5 minutes.

★

BETTER THAN STORE-BOUGHT WHITE BREAD

This all-American white bread is not unique to the West Coast, but it was, in its day, as prevalent here as it was anywhere else. Commercial yeast in a very soft dough makes for soft bread, reminiscent of the "batter-whipped" factory-made breads that gave American bread a bad name. The difference is that this one has none of the strange-tasting chemical additives that make store-bought white bread so disagreeable. Instead, this bread fills the house with pleasant aromas while it's baking and makes terrific sandwiches.

2 cups warm water

2 tablespoons (2 packets) active dry yeast

2 tablespoons sugar

5 cups unbleached white flour, plus up to ½ cup additional flour as needed

2 tablespoons kosher salt

2 tablespoons wine vinegar

1. In the bowl of an electric mixer or in a large mixing bowl, stir together the warm water, yeast, and sugar. Allow the mixture to stand until the yeast is softened, about 5 minutes, then stir until the yeast is completely dissolved.

2. If you are working with a stand mixer, pile in the flour, along with the salt and vinegar. With the paddle attachment, mix on low speed until everything comes together to make a thick, sticky batter. If you are mixing the dough by hand, whisk in 1 cup of flour at a time until the batter is too thick to whisk, then switch to a wooden spoon and stir in the remaining flour.

3. Use the dough hook on the mixer, or turn the dough out onto a well-floured countertop and knead the dough, pressing and folding it until it is very springy, and sprinkling it with additional flour if needed to keep the dough from sticking to the counter. Be careful not to add more flour than necessary, or the dough will be stiff and the bread will be heavy.

4. Leave the dough in the electric mixer bowl or return it to the regular mixing bowl. Cover the bowl with a damp, lint-free kitchen towel or a piece of plastic wrap and put it in a warm place until the dough is doubled in size, about an hour.

5. Lightly oil two 9- by 5-inch loaf pans with canola oil. Punch the dough down, turn it out onto the counter, and divide it in half. Form each half into a ball. Cover the balls of dough and let them rest for 10 minutes. (This will allow the gluten to relax.) To shape the loaves, roll each piece into a rectangle about 10 inches wide by 15 inches long. Starting at the bottom, roll the dough like a jelly roll, pressing it firmly to form a log. Put the loaves into the oiled pans and allow them to rise until they are light and almost doubled in size, about 35 minutes. While the loaves are rising, preheat the oven to 375°F.

6. Bake until the tops of the loaves are brown and the loaves are baked through. When the bread is ready, after about 35 minutes of baking, it will make a hollow sound when tapped, and an instant-read thermometer inserted in the center of a loaf will register about 195°F. Turn the loaves out of the pans onto a cooling rack and cool to room temperature before slicing.

⭐

OATMEAL SANDWICH BREAD

With a relatively large amount of commercial yeast, this bread is somewhat reminiscent of the factory-made sandwich loaves that were so popular in the twentieth century. It rises up quickly, without a lot of time for the yeast to add anything to the bread other than the carbon dioxide bubbles that lighten the dough. And yet old-fashioned goodness does emanate from these homey-looking sandwich loaves. Dark brown sugar lends the bread a hint of caramel and molasses scents, and the oats provide a hearty texture. Use this bread for weekday sandwiches or toast.

MAKES TWO 9-BY 5-INCH LOAVES

1 cup warm water

2 tablespoons (2 packets) active dry yeast

2 tablespoons dark brown sugar

3 cups unbleached white flour, plus more as needed

¾ cup milk

¼ cup (½ stick) unsalted butter

1 egg

¼ cup molasses

1 tablespoon kosher salt

3 cups quick-cooking oats, plus 2 tablespoons for sprinkling

1. In the bowl of an electric mixer or in a large mixing bowl, stir together the warm water, yeast, and sugar. Allow the mixture to stand until the yeast is softened, about 5 minutes, then stir until the yeast is completely dissolved. Whisk in 1 cup of the flour and let the yeast mixture stand, undisturbed, while you prepare the milk mixture.

2. Warm the milk in a saucepan until it is steaming hot but not boiling. Turn off the heat and stir in the butter, egg, molasses, and salt. The mixture should be warm to the touch, about the temperature of a baby's bottle. Whisk in 1 cup of the flour, then stir the warm milk mixture into the yeast mixture.

3. Stir in the remaining 1 cup flour and the oats. Use the dough hook on the mixer, or turn the dough out onto a well-floured countertop and knead the dough, pressing and folding it until it is very springy, and sprinkling it with additional flour if needed to keep the dough from sticking to the counter. Be careful not to add more flour than necessary, or the dough will be stiff and the bread will be heavy.

4. Clean out the bowl in which the dough was mixed and rub the inside with canola oil. Put the kneaded dough in the bowl and turn it over once so that the whole ball of dough is lightly coated with oil. Cover the bowl with a damp, lint-free kitchen towel or with a piece of plastic wrap and put it in a warm place until it is doubled in size, about an hour.

5. Lightly oil two 9- by 5-inch loaf pans with canola oil. Punch the dough down, turn it out onto the counter, and divide it in half. Form each half into a ball. Cover the balls of dough and let them rest for

10 minutes. (This will allow the gluten to relax.) To shape the loaves, roll each piece into a rectangle about 10 inches wide by 15 inches long. Starting at the bottom, roll the dough like a jelly roll, pressing it firmly to form a log. Put the loaves into the oiled pans and allow them to rise until they are light and almost doubled in size, about 35 minutes. While the loaves are rising, preheat the oven to 375°F. Brush the top of each loaf with water and sprinkle with a tablespoon of oats.

6. Bake the risen loaves until the tops are brown and the loaves are baked through. When the bread is ready, after about 35 minutes of baking, it will make a hollow sound when tapped, and an instant-read thermometer inserted in the center of a loaf will register about 195°F. Turn the loaves out of the pans onto a cooling rack and cool to room temperature before slicing.

★

WHOLE WHEAT SANDWICH BREAD

Adapted from a recipe in Homemade Bread *by the food editors of* Farm Journal, *published in 1969, this recipe recalls the first yeast bread I ever baked. As a 12-year-old baker, I was extremely proud of the big brown loaves this recipe produced. I still feel that way every time I bake this style of bread.*

MAKES TWO 9- BY 5-INCH LOAVES

1 tablespoon (1 packet) active dry yeast

2¾ cups lukewarm water

3½ cups whole wheat flour

½ cup brown sugar

¼ cup canola oil

1 tablespoon salt

4 cups unbleached white flour

1. In the bowl of an electric mixer or in a large mixing bowl, stir together the yeast and warm water. Allow the mixture to stand until the yeast is softened, about 5 minutes, then stir until the yeast is completely dissolved. Whisk in the whole wheat flour, brown sugar, canola oil, and salt.

2. Use the dough hook on the mixer or a strong wooden spoon to stir in 3 cups of the unbleached white flour, 1 cup at a time. Put the remaining 1 cup flour on a clean, dry work surface and turn the dough out of the bowl onto the flour. Gently fold it until most of the flour is incorporated into the dough. Keep working the dough, kneading in the remaining flour, until it is smooth and elastic, about 10 minutes.

3. Clean and dry the bowl in which you mixed the dough, then rub it with canola oil. Put the dough back in the bowl, and turn the dough over to grease the top. Cover the bowl with a damp tea towel or plastic wrap and let it rise in a warm place until doubled in bulk, about 1½ hours.

4. Lightly oil two 9- by 5-inch loaf pans with canola oil. Punch the dough down, turn it out onto the counter, and divide it in half. Form each half into a ball. Cover

the balls of dough and let them rest for 10 minutes. (This will allow the gluten to relax.) To shape the loaves, roll each piece into a rectangle about 10 inches wide by 15 inches long. Starting at the bottom, roll the dough like a jelly roll, pressing it firmly to form a log. Put the loaves into the oiled pans and allow them to rise until they are light and almost doubled in size, about 35 minutes. While the loaves are rising, preheat the oven to 375°F.

5. Bake the risen loaves until they are well browned on top and baked through. When the bread is ready, after about 40 minutes of baking, it will make a hollow sound when tapped, and an instant-read thermometer inserted in the center of a loaf will register about 195°F. If the loaves brown too rapidly, cover them loosely with a sheet of foil during the last 20 minutes. Turn the loaves out of the pans onto a cooling rack and let cool completely before slicing.

Rolls

⭐

GARY'S MOTHER'S ROLLS

My friend Gary Howarth once came to me with a scrap of paper on which his late mother had jotted down a list of ingredients with no measurements, and only a hint or two in the way of directions to make her well-loved potato rolls. The late Mrs. Howarth raised her family in Portland, Oregon. My own father-in-law has a very similar recipe from his mother, who lived first in Indiana and then in Alaska before coming to Seattle. I toyed around with both recipes and finally came up with this formula that delivers rolls anyone's mother would be proud to call her own.

MAKES 2 DOZEN LARGE DINNER ROLLS
OR 3 DOZEN SMALLER ONES

1 pound Yukon Gold or other yellow-fleshed potatoes

2 cups boiling water

½ cup warm water

2 tablespoons (2 packets) active dry yeast

2 tablespoons sugar

5½ cups unbleached white flour

1 cup (2 sticks) unsalted butter, cut into 1-inch bits

3 eggs

2 teaspoons kosher salt

1. Peel the potatoes and cut them into 2-inch pieces. Put the potatoes in a pot and cover them with the boiling water. Cook over medium-high heat until the potatoes are soft enough to mash.

2. While the potatoes are cooking, put the warm water in the bowl of a stand mixer or in a large mixing bowl, and stir in the yeast and sugar. Allow the mixture to stand until the yeast is softened, about 5 minutes, then stir again until the yeast is completely dissolved. Whisk in ½ cup of the flour and let the yeast mixture stand, undisturbed, while you prepare the potato mixture.

3. When the potatoes are tender, push them through a sieve, along with the water in which they were cooked. Mash them with the butter, then whisk in the eggs and salt. The mixture should be warm, not hot, about the temperature of a baby's bottle. Pour the mashed potatoes into the bowl with the yeast mixture and stir until well combined.

4. Add the remaining 5 cups flour, 1 cup at a time, mixing well after each addition. (If you're working without an electric mixer, when the mixture becomes too stiff to stir by hand, mix in the cups of flour with your hands.) When the dough begins to come together and leave the sides of the mixing bowl, transfer it from the bowl to a lightly floured countertop and knead in enough additional flour to make it smooth and elastic. Rinse the mixing bowl in hot water and put the dough back in, cover it with plastic wrap, and let it rise, undisturbed, for 1 hour, or until it is doubled in bulk.

5. When the dough has risen, preheat the oven to 350°F and line 2 baking sheets with baker's parchment or butter some muffin tins. Shape the dough into 24 rolls and put them on the baking sheets, or form 36 smaller rolls and put them in the muffin tins. Let them rise for 15 minutes, then bake until they are golden brown, about 20 minutes.

★

HOMEMADE HAMBURGER BUNS OR KAISER ROLLS

When you go to the trouble to find really great ground beef to make your own hamburgers (pages 116–17), it only makes sense to serve them on the best possible rolls. These rolls take the cake. For traditional Kaiser rolls to serve with lunch or dinner, make the rolls half-sized.

MAKES 1 DOZEN HAMBURGER ROLLS OR 2 DOZEN SMALLER ROLLS

½ cup warm water

2 tablespoons (2 packets) active dry yeast

¼ cup sugar

5 cups unbleached white flour, plus more as needed

1 cup milk

¼ cup canola oil

1 egg plus 1 egg yolk (reserve the extra egg white for the egg wash)

2 tablespoons kosher salt

To Finish the Rolls

1 egg white

1 tablespoon sugar

1 tablespoon water

¼ cup poppy seeds or sesame seeds

1. In the bowl of an electric mixer or in a large mixing bowl, stir together the warm water, yeast, and sugar. Allow the mixture to stand until the yeast is softened, about 5 minutes, then stir until the yeast is completely dissolved. Whisk in 1 cup

of the flour and let the mixture stand, undisturbed, while you prepare the milk mixture.

2. Warm the milk in a saucepan until it is steaming hot but not boiling. Turn off the heat and stir in the oil, egg, egg yolk, and salt. The mixture should be warm to the touch, about the temperature of a baby's bottle. Whisk in 1 cup of the flour, then stir the warm milk mixture into the yeast mixture.

3. Stir in the remaining 3 cups flour, 1 cup at a time, to make a very soft dough. Use the dough hook on the mixer, or turn the dough out onto a well-floured countertop and knead it, pressing and folding the dough until it is very springy, and sprinkling it with additional flour if needed to keep the dough from sticking to the counter. Be careful not to add more flour than necessary, or the dough will be stiff and the bread will be heavy.

4. Clean out the bowl in which the dough was mixed and rub the inside of the bowl with canola oil. Put the kneaded dough in the bowl and turn it over once so that the whole ball of dough is lightly coated with oil. Cover the bowl with a damp, lint-free kitchen towel or a piece of plastic wrap, and put it in a warm place until the dough is doubled in size, about an hour.

5. Turn the dough out onto a lightly floured countertop and divide it into 4 equal portions. Shape each piece of dough into a "rope" about 18 inches long.

Working with one rope at a time, cut each one into 3 pieces (cut each into 6 pieces to make smaller Kaiser rolls). Tie each piece into a knot, then tuck one of the loose ends of the rope into the center of the roll and one underneath. You should have round, crown-shaped rolls.

6. As the rolls are shaped, arrange them on a baking sheet lined with baker's parchment. Allow them to rise until almost doubled in bulk, about 20 minutes.

7. While the rolls are rising, preheat the oven to 350°F. Whisk together the egg white, sugar, and water and brush the risen rolls with the egg wash; then sprinkle them with the poppy seeds. Bake the rolls until golden brown, about 15 minutes. Cool on a rack.

Specialty Breads

FOCACCIA

An easy-to-make Italian flatbread, focaccia has become almost as American as the proverbial apple pie. Like other breads that rely entirely on commercial yeast, this one comes together pretty quickly, but to improve the texture and give it some Old World character, start with a biga, or sponge, which is something like a quick sourdough starter. The slower growth of the yeast in the dough affords time for the development of more character in the finished bread.

For the Sponge

2 cups warm water

1 tablespoon (1 packet) active dry yeast

1 tablespoon sugar

2 cups unbleached white flour

For the Dough

2½ cups unbleached white flour, plus more as needed

1 tablespoon kosher salt

For the Topping

¼ cup olive oil

1 tablespoon fresh rosemary leaves

1 teaspoon dried red chile flakes

1. Make the sponge. Put the warm water in a large mixing bowl or the bowl of an electric mixer, sprinkle the yeast and sugar on top, and stir until the yeast and sugar are dissolved. Stir or mix in the flour, cover the bowl, and allow the sponge to rest for an hour.

2. Finish the dough by adding the remaining 2½ cups of flour and salt. Mix in the mixer until the dough is smooth and springy. Put a little flour on the table and scrape the dough from the bowl onto the pile of flour. Sprinkle some of the flour over the top of the dough and start pressing the dough with your fingers and folding the dough over and over again until it is smooth and springy. Put the dough back in the bowl and let it rise for 1 hour.

3. Put the olive oil onto a 12- by 16-inch baking sheet and turn on the oven to 400°F. Sprinkle some more flour on the table to keep the dough from sticking, and roll the dough out into a piece big enough to cover the bottom of the baking sheet. Put the dough in the oiled pan and then flip it over once so it has oil on top.

4. Scatter the rosemary leaves and chile flakes over the surface of the dough and bake the focaccia until brown and crispy, about 15 to 20 minutes.

★

NEW AMERICAN HARVEST BREAD

Based on a recipe from the Bread Bakers Guild of Amer-ica, this recipe in its original form won a silver medal for the Bread Bakers Guild Team USA 2002. I have "mainstreamed" the recipe somewhat, streamlining the ingredients and simplifying the process to make it more accessible for home cooks. Still, like the original, it "pays tribute to the role of Native Americans in our nation's history by incorporating many of their indigenous ingre-dients" into a delicious home-baked bread.

MAKES 2 LOAVES

½ cup coarsely cracked wheat

½ cup sweetened dried cranberries, chopped

¼ cup cornmeal or polenta, plus additional cornmeal for the pan

¾ cup boiling water

1 cup warm water

3 tablespoons honey

1 scant tablespoon (1 packet) active dry yeast

3 cups unbleached white flour, plus more as needed

1 cup Sourdough Starter (pages 264–65)

1 tablespoon kosher salt

¾ cup cooked wild rice

1. Put the cracked wheat, dried cranberries, and cornmeal in a small mixing bowl and pour the boiling water over them. The grains and fruit will soften up a little and absorb most of the water. Let this mixture soak until it has cooled to room temperature, about 30 minutes.

2. Put the cup of warm water in the bowl of a stand mixer or in a large mixing bowl. Stir in the honey, then sprinkle the yeast over it. Let the mixture stand, undisturbed, until the yeast is softened, about 5 minutes, then stir until the yeast is dissolved.

3. Mix 2 cups of the flour into the yeast and water mixture, then work in the sourdough starter and salt.

4. Mix in the cooked wild rice and the presoaked cracked wheat mixture. Add the remaining cup of flour. If the dough becomes too stiff to stir, work in the flour with your hands.

5. Use the dough hook on the mixer, or turn the dough out onto a well-floured countertop and knead it, pressing and folding it until it is very springy, and sprinkling it with additional flour if needed to keep the dough from sticking to the counter. Be careful not to add more flour than necessary, or the dough will be stiff and the bread will be heavy.

6. Clean out the bowl in which the dough was mixed, and rub the inside of the bowl with canola oil. Put the kneaded dough in the bowl and turn it over once so that the whole ball of dough is lightly coated with oil. Cover the bowl with a damp, lint-free kitchen towel or with a piece of plastic wrap and put it in a warm place until the dough is doubled in size, about an hour.

7. Divide the risen dough into 2 equal parts and form each piece into a football shape. Put the loaves on a baking sheet that has been sprinkled with cornmeal, and let them rise in a warm place until they are doubled in bulk, about 45 minutes. While the loaves are rising, preheat the oven to 425°F.

8. With a very sharp knife, carefully cut a line along the length of each loaf. Bake the bread on the center rack of the oven until it is golden brown and baked through. When the bread is ready, after about 35 minutes of baking, it will make a hollow sound when it's tapped; an instant-read thermometer inserted in the center of a loaf will register about 195°F. Transfer the

loaves from the baking sheet to a cooling rack and let cool to room temperature before slicing.

★

ISLANDWOOD CINNAMON ROLLS

IslandWood is an environmental learning center near my home on Bainbridge Island. When I was planning the menus for the place, where school-age children would spend four days and nights away from home, living in lodges in the woods while they studied environmental sciences, I happened to be reading Ruth Reichl's 1998 culinary memoir, Tender at the Bone. *In the book, she describes a summer spent as a camp counselor in France. "When we woke up in the morning, the smell of baking bread was wafting through the trees." In a flash, I knew that on the first morning of their day at IslandWood, I wanted the kids to smell fresh-baked cinnamon rolls.*

MAKES 2 DOZEN CINNAMON ROLLS

For the Dough

1 cup warm water

2 tablespoons (2 packets) active dry yeast

⅓ cup sugar

5 cups unbleached white flour

1¼ cups milk

¼ cup (½ stick) unsalted butter

2 eggs

2 tablespoons kosher salt, or 1 tablespoon table salt

For the Filling

1 cup (2 sticks) unsalted butter, softened to room temperature

2 cups brown sugar

¼ cup unbleached white flour

3 tablespoons ground cinnamon

For the Topping

2 cups powdered sugar

2 tablespoons milk

1 teaspoon vanilla extract

1. In the bowl of an electric mixer or in a large mixing bowl, stir together the warm water, yeast, and sugar. Allow the mixture to stand until the yeast is softened, about 5 minutes, then stir until the yeast is completely dissolved. Whisk in 1 cup of the flour and let the yeast mixture stand, undisturbed, while you prepare the milk mixture.

2. Warm the milk in a saucepan until it is steaming hot but not boiling. Turn off the heat and stir in the butter, eggs, and salt. The milk mixture should be warm to the touch, about the temperature of a baby's bottle. Whisk in 1 cup of the flour, then stir the warm mixture into the yeast mixture.

3. Mix in 2 cups of the remaining flour, 1 cup at a time, to make a very soft dough. Use the dough hook on the mixer, or turn the dough out onto a well-floured countertop and knead the last cup of flour into the dough, pressing and folding it until it is very smooth and springy, and

sprinkling it with additional flour if needed to keep the dough from sticking to the counter.

4. Clean out the bowl in which the dough was mixed, and rub the inside of the bowl with canola oil. Put the kneaded dough in the bowl and turn it over once so that the whole ball of dough is lightly coated with the oil. Cover the bowl with a damp, lint-free kitchen towel or with a piece of plastic wrap and put it in a warm place until the dough is doubled in size, about an hour. While the dough is rising, combine the ingredients for the filling in a medium bowl, to make a smooth paste.

5. On a lightly floured surface, roll the risen dough into a large rectangle measuring 12 by 24 inches. Cut this rectangle in half to make two 12-inch squares. Spread the filling over each square, leaving a strip about 1 inch wide along one side uncovered. Roll the dough up to make a 12-inch log, finishing at the uncovered edge so the edge will seal and the filling will not leak out. The logs can be covered and refrigerated at this point and held overnight to be baked in the morning, or they can be cut into rolls and baked at once.

6. Preheat the oven to 350°F and line 2 baking sheets with silicone pan liners or baker's parchment. If the dough was refrigerated, allow the logs to warm up and soften at room temperature for about 45 minutes before slicing and baking. Cut each log into 12 slices and put them onto the baking sheets. Let the rolls rise at room temperature for 20 minutes, then bake until they are well browned and the filling is bubbling up in the middle, about 20 minutes.

7. In a medium bowl, mix the topping ingredients together. Frost the cinnamon rolls while they are hot, and serve them warm.

BRUSSEAU'S STICKY BUNS

Brusseau is famous for creating the "Cinnabon," but these are the cinnamon rolls that Jerilyn Brusseau's grandmother, Maude Delaney Spurgeon, taught her to make when she was a girl. Brusseau likes to use strong, spicy-sweet cinnamon from Vietnam, technically known as cassia or Saigon cinnamon. She sometimes replaces up to half of the all-purpose flour with whole wheat flour, and she occasionally adds half a cup of raisins to the dough or ¾ cup walnuts to the filling. "The secret," says Brusseau, "is to pour the syrup that forms in the pan over the finished rolls."

MAKES 16 LARGE BUNS

For the Buns

1 cup warm water

3 tablespoons (3 packets) active dry yeast

½ cup sugar

6½ to 7 cups all-purpose flour

1 cup milk

⅓ cup unsalted butter

3 eggs

1¼ teaspoons salt

For the Filling

2 cups (4 sticks) unsalted butter, softened

3 cups dark brown sugar

6 tablespoons ground cinnamon

1. In the bowl of an electric mixer or in a large mixing bowl, stir together the warm water, yeast, and sugar. Allow the mixture to stand until the yeast is softened, about 5 minutes, then stir until the yeast is completely dissolved. Whisk in 1 cup of the flour and let the yeast mixture stand, undisturbed, while you prepare the milk mixture.

2. Heat the milk in a small saucepan until it is steaming hot but not quite boiling. Take the milk off the heat and stir in the butter and then the eggs, one at a time, whisking well after each addition. Whisk in the salt. The butter and eggs should cool the milk to a warm room temperature, about the temperature of a baby's bottle. Stir the milk mixture into the yeast mixture.

3. Stir in 5 cups of the flour, 1 cup at a time. The first 2 or 3 cups can be stirred in with a wire whisk; the mixture will resemble a smooth cake batter. Subsequent cups should be stirred in with a wooden spoon, and the mixture will become a sticky dough that leaves the sides of the bowl.

4. Sprinkle ½ cup of the remaining flour on a smooth board or countertop and turn the dough out of the bowl onto the flour-covered surface. Knead the dough by folding it over and over itself until it

is smooth, satiny, and resilient, almost springy. Sprinkle it with more of the flour as needed to keep it from sticking to the board or your hands.

5. Shape the dough into a ball and place it in a large, well-buttered bowl, turning it once to coat the top of the ball. Cover the bowl with a damp towel or plastic wrap and let the dough rise in a warm place until it is doubled in bulk, about 45 minutes.

6. In a medium bowl, make the filling by whisking the softened butter, brown sugar, and cinnamon into a smooth paste. After the dough has risen, turn it out of the bowl onto a floured board and roll it out into a rectangle measuring 24 by 20 inches. Spread the entire surface of the dough with the filling and roll it up, starting at a long side and ending with the seam on the bottom.

7. With a sharp knife, cut the roll into 16 equal portions. Place the rolls in 2 well-buttered 9- by 13-inch baking pans. Cover the pans with a damp towel or plastic wrap and allow the rolls to rise in a warm place until they are doubled in size, 30 to 40 minutes. Meanwhile, preheat the oven to 350°F.

8. Bake the buns until they are nicely browned and the filling is bubbly, about 35 minutes. Immediately invert the pans onto serving platters or cookie sheets, allowing the syrup to drip from the pan onto the rolls.

QUICK BREADS

MUFFINS

BISCUITS, SCONES, AND SMALL BREADS

BATTER BREADS AND COFFEE CAKES

TORTILLAS AND CRACKERS

Quick Breads

At first, I thought it was kind of fun. Amish friendship bread. What could be more wholesome? Like Quaker oats, kosher salt, and St. Joseph's aspirin, the name resounded with purity and goodness. My neighbor gave it to us when we moved into our home in Friday Harbor on San Juan Island.

She had a loaf in one hand, wrapped in plastic wrap and tied with a ribbon. In her other hand, she had a yogurt container, and inside were the alien spores, the "starter." I should have heard the threatening music. I should have remembered that Ray Bradbury story called "Boys! Raise Giant Mushrooms in Your Cellar!" (That was a science-fiction piece about Martians coming in the form of a fungus; it was later adapted for an episode of *The Twilight Zone*.) But I didn't heed any of the warning signs. I blithely accepted the housewarming gift, ate the bread, and read the instructions on how to make more.

For the benefit of those who have somehow been spared the gift of Amish friendship bread, here's a brief summary of the 10-day—that's right, 10-day—process.

First day: Do nothing. (This lulls the victim into a false sense of security.) Second day: Stir the starter with a wooden spoon. Third, fourth, and fifth days: Same as the second. But don't believe for an instant that nothing is happening. "It's normal," says the instruction sheet, "for the mixture to raise, bubble, and ferment." Yeah, right; normal.

Certain clandestine, ritualistic orders are given during this stage. "DURING THIS PROCESS, DO NOT USE ANY TYPE OF METAL SPOON OR BOWL. DO NOT REFRIGERATE THE STARTER." Apparently, metal or cold would kill the aliens.

Finally, on day 6, the cook—who by now feels just like one of those boys watching Tom Sawyer paint the fence, just itching to get ahold of the brush and do something— is allowed to feed the starter. Add a cup of flour, a cup of sugar, and a cup of milk, and stir with—you guessed it—a wooden spoon.

Days 7, 8, and 9: Stir with a wooden spoon.

Day 10: Turn on the oven, Betsy, we're about to bake. You add more milk, sugar, and flour, along with eggs, oil, nuts, and pudding mix. (Somehow I can't imagine the real Amish keeping a supply of pudding mix on hand for this sort of thing.) Then you bake it. Frankly, I was disappointed. Maybe I'd blown it by whisking the batter right at the end with a wire whisk. Maybe I just wasn't Amish enough. The bread—cake, really—was heavy and smelled a little off.

But it was edible, and we had invested a lot of nurturing in this pet-bread project, so we ate it, and we dutifully followed the instructions to share the starter and the extra loaf of bread with a friend. The next day, we ate more of it, toasted, with butter.

Then we wrapped what was left and put it in the bread drawer.

Then we did it all again. Ten days later, we shared the starter and the extra loaf with another friend. The remains of the first loaf were still festering in the back of the bread drawer, and as soon as they were dispensed with, they were replaced with another loaf. But somehow, I had been hypnotized into doing it all again. I stirred, added stuff, stirred again, baked again. There were variations: chocolate pudding instead of vanilla, pistachio pudding instead of vanilla. I tried making up a variation with no pudding.

Then we ran out of friends. I thought I saw one neighbor quickly pull the blinds when I went to deliver some of the starter. No one answered the door.

Finally, I threw it all on the compost pile and summarily forgot about it. Then, years later, I came across a great little story by Ann Hodgman called "One Bite Won't Kill You." (The story is included in a collection called *Best Food Writing 2000*, edited by Holly Hughes.) It's about getting kids to eat, and one of her tactics is to have them bake this Amish friendship bread. Her story was so smart and lively that I was tempted to try the stuff again. Her secret is to use a plastic bag to store the starter.

"You've got to love a recipe whose main direction is 'Mush the bag,'" she writes. I guess so. She gives a detailed formula for reproducing the stuff from scratch, even if no one has given you any of the starter.

"Pour/scrape the batter into a 1-gallon zipper-lock bag, which should then be put into another bag, because if the first bag broke, you'd go insane." I say you've got to love a recipe that warns you against side effects like mental illness. "It will begin to fizz and bubble and look ugly."

I'll say.

I also discovered that Amish friendship bread has taken over the Internet. A cursory search uncovered 244,955 sites infected with the formula. One was close to home. The Murphy House Bed and Breakfast in Poulsbo, Washington, offered a recipe for the bread right on its home page, so I called Gordon Buhler, the innkeeper, and asked about his experience with the stuff. Do you serve it? I wanted to know.

"Oh, not any more," he laughed. "I used to, but it went off on me and now I don't even have a recipe for the starter, so I can't make anymore." When I told them that there were dozens of web sites with recipes for the starter, he quickly backpedaled.

"Oh no," he said. "I don't think I'll need any more of that. It's not exactly health food, you know . . . extremely high fat. I'm trying to get away from all that. I should get that recipe off the web site."

So, for Gordon Buhler, and the rest of us who are "trying to get away from all that," I offer alternatives to the friendship bread conundrum. These are old-fashioned "quick breads" that use baking powder instead of yeast. You can assemble a batter or dough in minutes and have hot, fresh, and wholesome—if not exactly Amish—bread in well under an hour.

Even very competent cooks and experienced bakers can be intimidated by the challenge of making yeast breads, but almost any cook feels confident about whipping up a batch of muffins or a loaf of banana bread. Handling yeast breads demands an almost spiritual interaction with the living organisms that inflate the dough. But quick breads are simple chemistry. The same straightforward reaction that makes baking soda bubble when it's hit with vinegar imbues batters and doughs spiked with baking powder with thousands of tiny bubbles that render these breads tender and toothsome.

The key to making light quick breads, especially batter breads and muffins, lies in mixing the dry ingredients separately from the liquids. Piling everything into one bowl would result in overmixing, which would develop the gluten in the flour, making the batter gummy and the finished quick bread tough. If only one mixing bowl is available, transfer the flour mixture to a piece of baker's parchment or a plate.

Once the wet and dry ingredients are combined, there is no need to stir out every lump in the batter; in fact, leaving the batter a little lumpy gives quick breads a looser, more desirable crumb. With biscuits and scones, however, which are more substantial than batter breads, some development of the gluten is okay, and so a little kneading improves the texture of these breads.

Every quick bread falls into one of two styles: batter or dough. In batter-style breads—such as muffins and coffee cakes—oil or melted butter is stirred into the liquid, and then the liquid is combined with premixed dry ingredients. In dough-style quick breads, such as biscuits, the fat is cut into the dry ingredients before the mixture is moistened with the liquids. Batter-style quick breads are always baked in a mold of some sort—a muffin tin, loaf pan, or baking dish. Dough-based quick breads are free-form; after they are shaped by hand they go onto a flat baking sheet. Once you've mastered the basic techniques and formulas for these breads, infinite variations are possible.

Replace some of the flour with whole wheat flour or cornmeal, add dried fruits, spices, or nuts. Replace the milk in a recipe with another liquid. Just keep the general proportions and techniques intact, and if the liquid is high in acid, replace some of the baking powder with baking soda. (See the recipes for Rich Country-Style Muffins [pages 284–85] and Orange Poppy Seed Muffins [pages 285–86].) For added sparkle and crunch, sprinkle the tops of your quick breads before they are baked with coarse sugar, or glaze them after they are baked with a mixture of powdered sugar and freshly squeezed lemon juice. If saturated fats and calories are an issue, replace butter with canola oil—this is especially successful in batter-style breads—and replace whole eggs with egg whites (two egg whites can stand in for one whole egg).

Gauging doneness in quick breads takes a practiced eye. The edges of the finished bread will be browned, the center puffed and golden. Very often, quick breads will develop an appealing series of crackles over the surface or a shiny finish. The crackles come from expansion of the dough inside the bread after a crust has already begun to form; the shiny finish comes from sugars in the batter caramelizing in the dry heat of the oven.

Quick breads of the West Coast differ only slightly from those in other parts of the country. Most of the techniques, in fact, were developed elsewhere and then adapted to local ingredients and tastes. But those local ingredients—abundant citrus fruits, dried fruits, nuts, and wonderful fresh and natural dairy foods and grain—have given West Coast bakers a reputation for producing some of the best baked goods in the world.

One more thought: In general, a convection oven will give quick breads a little more loft than a conventional oven. If your home oven offers the option of adding convection heat, go for it, but watch the breads closely; they will be done more quickly.

Muffins

BASIC MUFFINS AND A BLUEBERRY VARIATION

Along with every other boy in my seventh-grade class, I was forced to take home economics. But unlike most of the other guys, I was happy about this. I really liked to cook and bake, and I wanted to know more about it. One of the first lessons was how to make basic muffins. The recipe imprinted itself on my mind because it brought together my budding understanding of basic chemistry and my creative urge to "make something." The recipe also had an elegant simplicity that I have always appreciated. Most of the recipes for quick breads that I have developed as an adult owe some allegiance to this master recipe for the ultimate quick bread. They are simple enough to serve as a dinner roll at a casual supper, and with a few blueberries thrown in, they make a great breakfast—especially when served with tray full of bacon baked in the same hot oven. If you add blueberries to the muffins, stir them in with the flour to avoid overmixing the batter. If the blueberries are frozen, do not thaw them first or they will collapse; add them directly from the freezer, and allow about 5 minutes extra baking time.

MAKES 1 DOZEN STANDARD MUFFINS

2 cups unbleached white flour, or 1 cup unbleached white flour plus 1 cup whole wheat flour

1 tablespoon baking powder

1 teaspoon kosher salt, or ½ teaspoon table salt

1 egg

⅓ cup sugar

⅓ cup canola oil

1 cup milk

1½ cups fresh or frozen blueberries (optional)

1. Preheat the oven to 375°F and put a rack in the upper third of the oven. Butter the cups of a muffin tin, or spray them with nonstick canola oil spray.

2. Whisk together the flour, baking powder, and salt in a medium mixing bowl and set the dry mixture aside. (If only one mixing bowl is available, transfer the flour mixture to a piece of baker's parchment or a plate.)

3. In a separate, large mixing bowl, whisk the egg with the sugar and oil. Whisk in the milk. Add the flour mixture and blueberries (if desired) all at once to the egg mixture, and stir just until the dry ingredients are moistened.

4. Distribute the muffin batter evenly among the prepared muffin tins, and bake until puffed in the center and brown around the edges, about 12 minutes. An instant-read thermometer inserted in the center of a muffin will read 180°F when the muffins are ready. As soon as the muffins come out of the oven, turn them out of the pan onto a wire rack to cool. (Otherwise, steam trapped in the pan will make the bottoms of the muffins mushy.)

★
RICH COUNTRY-STYLE MUFFINS

Tangy yogurt in place of milk gives muffins extra snap, and brown sugar in place of white adds a golden glow. The butter and a splash of vanilla extract make the muffins extra rich. My kids, who are sometimes reluctant to eat breakfast, don't hesitate to eat these muffins when I add mini chocolate chips. Since the leavening in quick breads depends on the balance of acid and base components, baking soda replaces some of the baking powder here, countering the acid in the yogurt. I like to bake these in mini muffin tins; the cups hold only half as much batter as standard muffin tins, and the smaller muffins bake very quickly, an important consideration on school mornings.

MAKES 24 MINI MUFFINS OR
12 STANDARD MUFFINS

2 cups unbleached white flour, or 1 cup unbleached white flour plus 1 cup whole wheat flour

2 teaspoons baking powder

1 teaspoon baking soda

1 teaspoon kosher salt, or ½ teaspoon table salt

2 large eggs

½ cup brown sugar

½ cup (1 stick) unsalted butter, melted

¾ cup plain low-fat or nonfat yogurt

1 teaspoon vanilla extract

¾ cup miniature semisweet chocolate chips (optional)

1. Preheat the oven to 350°F and put a rack in the upper third of the oven. Butter the cups of a muffin tin, or spray them with nonstick canola oil spray.

2. Whisk together the flour, baking powder, baking soda, and salt in a medium mixing bowl, and set the dry mixture aside.

3. In a separate, large mixing bowl, whisk the eggs with the sugar and melted butter. Whisk in the yogurt and vanilla. Add the flour mixture and the chocolate chips (if desired) all at once to the egg mixture, and stir just until the dry ingredients are moistened.

4. Distribute the muffin batter evenly among the prepared muffin tins, and bake until puffed in the center and brown around the edges, about 12 minutes. An instant-read thermometer inserted in the center of a muffin will read 180°F when the muffins are ready. As soon as the muffins come out of the oven, turn them out of the pan onto a wire rack to cool. (Otherwise, steam trapped in the pan will make the bottoms of the muffins mushy.)

★

ORANGE POPPY SEED MUFFINS

Almost cakelike in texture and flavor, these dreamy-tasting muffins come together quickly to ease the transition from dawn into day. They also make a wonderful pick-me-up with an afternoon cup of tea. For a variation on this muffin, replace the orange zest with lemon zest and use a mixture of ½ cup water and ¼ cup lemon juice instead of the orange juice. Since the outer rind or zest is included in this recipe, it's a good idea to use an organically grown orange.

MAKES 1 DOZEN MUFFINS

2 cups unbleached white flour

¼ cup poppy seeds

1 teaspoon baking powder

1 teaspoon baking soda

½ teaspoon salt

2 large eggs

¾ cup organic light brown sugar

½ cup canola oil

1 tablespoon freshly grated orange zest

¾ cup freshly squeezed orange juice

1. Preheat the oven to 400°F and line a 12-cup muffin tin with paper cup liners or butter and flour the cups.

2. In a medium mixing bowl, whisk together the flour, poppy seeds, baking powder, baking soda, and salt.

3. In a separate, large mixing bowl, whisk the eggs with the brown sugar and canola oil until smooth, then whisk in the orange zest and orange juice.

4. Stir the flour mixture into the egg mixture; stir gently with a silicone or rubber spatula just until the dry ingredients are moistened. Do not overmix.

5. Distribute the batter evenly among the prepared muffin tins and bake until

the muffins are puffed in the center and browned around the edges, about 12 minutes. Turn the muffins out of the pans onto a rack to cool.

★

MACADAMIA NUT–BANANA–MILK CHOCOLATE MUFFINS

Associated in most people's minds with the Hawaiian Islands, macadamia nuts originated in Australia; they also thrive in coastal areas of California, where several popular cultivars were developed. The tender crunch of these nuts is mediated by an oil content hovering around 75 percent, which makes them uniquely rich and buttery. A very hard shell presents challenges in their processing, and so they are fairly expensive. If you must, replace them with toasted walnuts in this recipe; the fragrant cinnamon, vanilla, and chocolate will carry the day. Jumbo muffin tins work especially well with this recipe, but regular muffin tins will also do.

MAKES 6 JUMBO MUFFINS OR 1 DOZEN STANDARD MUFFINS

2 cups unbleached white flour

1 tablespoon baking powder

1 teaspoon kosher salt, or ½ teaspoon table salt

2 medium bananas, mashed (about 1 cup)

1 egg

½ cup brown sugar

½ cup (1 stick) unsalted butter, melted

1 teaspoon vanilla extract

¾ cup dry-roasted macadamia nuts

Two 1½-ounce milk chocolate bars, broken into ½-inch bits

1. Preheat the oven to 350°F and put a rack in the upper third of the oven. Line a 12-cup muffin tin with paper cup liners or spray them with nonstick canola spray.

2. Whisk together the flour, baking powder, and salt in a medium mixing bowl and set the dry mixture aside.

3. In a separate, large mixing bowl, whisk together the mashed bananas, egg, brown sugar, melted butter, and vanilla. Add the flour mixture, macadamia nuts, and chocolate pieces to the egg mixture all at once, and stir just until the dry ingredients are moistened.

4. Distribute the muffin batter evenly among the prepared muffin tins, and bake until puffed in the center and brown around the edges, about 18 minutes. An instant-read thermometer inserted in the center of a muffin will read 180°F when the muffins are ready. As soon as the muffins come out of the oven, turn them out of the pan onto a wire rack to cool. (Otherwise, steam trapped in the pan will make the bottoms of the muffins mushy.)

★

MORNING GLORY MUFFINS

I cannot say with any confidence who created the first morning glory muffin or where it happened. It seems to be one of those recipes that arose more or less simultaneously all over the country. I have been eating muffins like this up and down the West Coast for more than a decade, and I modeled my version on the ones that were served in the early 1990s at the Front Street Café in Friday Harbor, Washington. They are sweeter and moister than most breakfast muffins, but with fruits and carrots and nuts, they are more nourishing, too. Since the muffins are extra moist, they tend to stick, so I like to use old-fashioned paper cupcake liners in the muffin tin.

MAKES 1 DOZEN MUFFINS

1½ cups unbleached white flour

½ cup whole wheat flour

1½ teaspoons baking powder

1 teaspoon baking soda

½ teaspoon salt

3 large eggs

1 cup dark brown sugar

¾ cup canola oil

1 cup grated carrot

½ cup fresh or frozen pineapple chunks, not canned

½ cup raisins

¼ cup toasted coconut

¼ cup toasted walnuts

1. Preheat the oven to 375°F, and line a 12-cup muffin tin with paper cup liners, or butter and flour the cups.

2. In a medium mixing bowl, whisk together the flour, whole wheat flour, baking powder, baking soda, and salt.

3. In a separate, large mixing bowl, whisk the eggs with the brown sugar and canola oil until smooth.

4. Stir the flour mixture along with the carrots, pineapple chunks, raisins, coconut, and walnuts into the egg mixture; stir gently with a silicone or rubber spatula just until the dry ingredients are moistened. Do not overmix.

5. Distribute the batter evenly among the prepared muffin tins and bake until the muffins are puffed in the center and browned around the edges, about 12 minutes. As soon as the muffins come out of the oven, turn them out of the pan onto a wire rack to cool. (Otherwise, steam trapped in the pan will make the bottoms of the muffins mushy.)

★

BEST RAISIN BRAN MUFFINS

The first bran muffins I ever baked were made with raisin bran cereal from a box. They were tasty, but the notion that they were made with an already overprocessed food did not sit well with me. So I sought to develop a raisin bran muffin from scratch.

MAKES 1 DOZEN MUFFINS

1½ cups unbleached white flour

½ cup whole wheat flour

1½ cups wheat bran

1½ teaspoons baking powder

½ teaspoon baking soda

½ teaspoon salt

2 large eggs

¾ cup dark brown sugar

½ cup canola oil

¼ cup unsulfured molasses

1 cup plain yogurt

1 cup raisins

1. Preheat the oven to 400°F, and line a 12-cup muffin tin with paper cup liners, or butter and flour the cups.

2. In a medium mixing bowl, whisk together the white flour, whole wheat flour, wheat bran, baking powder, baking soda, and salt.

3. In a separate, large mixing bowl, whisk the eggs with the brown sugar and canola oil and molasses until smooth, then whisk in the yogurt.

4. Add the flour mixture along with the raisins to the egg mixture; stir gently with a silicone or rubber spatula just until the dry ingredients are moistened. Do not overmix.

5. Distribute the batter evenly among the prepared muffin tins and bake until the muffins are puffed in the center and browned around the edges, about 12 minutes. As soon as the muffins come out of the oven, turn them out of the pan onto a wire rack to cool. (Otherwise, steam trapped in the pan will make the bottoms of the muffins mushy.)

Biscuits, Scones, and Small Breads

★

SWEET BISCUITS OR SHORTCAKES

A little sugar goes a long way in a biscuit. The sweetness here seems more noticeable than a mere 2 tablespoons of powdered sugar would indicate. These biscuits, which are perfectly suited for peach or strawberry shortcakes (see pages 343–44), are made extra tender by the addition of cornstarch to the flour. On a molecular level, the starch interrupts the formation of strong gluten chains, which would make the biscuits tough.

MAKES 8 LARGE BISCUITS

1¾ cups unbleached white flour

¼ cup cornstarch

2 tablespoons powdered sugar

1 tablespoon baking powder

1 teaspoon kosher salt

½ cup (1 stick) cold unsalted butter, cut into 1-inch bits

¾ cup milk

1. Preheat the oven to 400°F. In a food processor, combine the flour, cornstarch, powdered sugar, baking powder, and salt. Line a baking sheet with baker's parchment. Add the butter and pulse the motor on and off until the mixture is uniformly crumbly. Add the milk all at once and stir or process briefly to form a soft dough.

2. Turn the dough out onto a lightly floured surface and knead it very lightly; do not overwork the dough or the biscuits will be tough. Roll the dough out ½ inch thick and cut it into 3-inch circles with a biscuit cutter or the top of a wineglass. Press straight down, resisting the urge to twist the cutter. (A straight cut will make neater biscuits.)

3. Arrange the biscuits a few inches apart on the prepared baking sheet, and bake until the tops are lightly browned, 10 to 12 minutes.

★

WHOLE WHEAT BISCUITS

More closely linked to the Gulf Coast than to the West Coast, buttermilk biscuits are nevertheless right at home on this side of the country, especially when they are made with whole wheat flour and tangy plain yogurt. Since West Coast cooks are a lot more likely to have yogurt in the refrigerator than they are to have buttermilk, plain yogurt often serves the same purpose here that buttermilk serves in other parts of the country, adding zip and richness to baked goods. Some of the baking powder, which combines an acid and a base to create bubbles in the dough, is replaced with baking soda (a base) because the yogurt is acidic.

MAKES 8 LARGE BISCUITS

1 cup whole wheat flour

1 cup unbleached white flour

2 teaspoons baking powder

½ teaspoon baking soda

1 teaspoon kosher salt

½ cup (1 stick) cold unsalted butter, cut into bits

1 cup plain, natural yogurt, such as Nancy's

1. Preheat the oven to 400°F. Line a baking sheet with baker's parchment. In a food processor, combine whole wheat flour, white flour, baking powder, baking soda, and salt. Add the butter and pulse the motor on and off until the mixture is uniformly crumbly. Add the yogurt all at once and stir or process briefly to form a soft dough.

2. Turn the dough out onto a well-floured surface and knead it very lightly, 3 or 4 folds, just until the dough is slightly springy. Do not knead it too much or the biscuits will be tough. Roll the dough out ½ inch thick and cut it into 3-inch circles with a sharp biscuit cutter or the top of a wineglass. Press straight down, resisting the urge to twist the cutter. (A straight cut will make neater biscuits.)

3. Arrange the biscuits a few inches apart on the prepared baking sheet, and bake until the tops are lightly browned, 10 to 12 minutes.

⭐
QUICK CINNAMON ROLLS

Most cinnamon rolls are made with yeast, but a bis-cuit-based facsimile has been the fashion in my house ever since my kids were born. With yeast-based rolls, I have to plan ahead and make the dough the night before. These little hummers come together in a matter of min-utes—no prior planning is required.

MAKES 1 DOZEN ROLLS

For the Dough

2 cups unbleached white flour

1 tablespoon baking powder

1 tablespoon sugar

1 teaspoon kosher salt, or ½ teaspoon table salt

½ cup (1 stick) cold unsalted butter, cut into chunks

¾ cup milk

For the Filling

¼ cup (½ stick) unsalted butter, melted and cooled

½ cup sugar

1 tablespoon ground cinnamon

For the Glaze

1 cup powdered sugar

1 tablespoon milk

1 teaspoon vanilla extract

1. Preheat the oven to 400°F and line a baking sheet with a silicone pan liner or baker's parchment.

2. Make the dough. In a food processor, combine the flour, baking powder, sugar, and salt. Add the cold butter and process until the mixture resembles crumbs. Add the cold milk all at once and process, pulsing the motor on and off, for 1 minute, or until the mixture comes together to form a dough.

3. Sprinkle a clean countertop with flour and knead the dough briefly. Sprinkle more flour on the counter as needed to keep the dough from sticking; pat it out into a rough 6- by 8-inch rectangle.

4. Spread the melted butter over the surface of the dough, and sprinkle the sugar and cinnamon over the dough. Roll the rectangle, jelly-roll style, into a log, and slice it into 12 little pinwheels. Arrange the rolls 2 inches apart on the prepared baking sheet, and bake until puffed and golden, about 10 minutes.

5. Make the glaze. In a small bowl, stir together the glaze ingredients with a fork, and drizzle it over the hot cinnamon rolls.

⭐
QUICK FLAKY CRESCENT ROLLS

Sometimes called butterhorns or German crescents, these crescent-shaped rolls are usually made with yeast dough, but a pleasant and flaky dinner roll can be put together in less than half an hour if you have room on the countertop. The process involves rolling out the flour and butter mixture to press the butter bits into flat pieces that form the "flakes."

MAKES 6 ROLLS

2 cups unbleached white flour

2 tablespoons sugar

2 teaspoons baking powder

1 teaspoon kosher salt, or ½ teaspoon table salt

½ cup (1 stick) cold unsalted butter, cut into 1-inch bits

½ cup milk

1. Preheat the oven to 400°F and line a baking sheet with a silicone pan liner or baker's parchment.

2. Put the flour, sugar, baking powder, and salt in the work bowl of a food processor or in a large mixing bowl. Process or whisk these dry ingredients together and then, pulsing the motor or using a fork, work the butter into the flour just until the butter bits are broken down to the size of large green peas.

3. Turn the mixture out of the bowl onto a clean, dry countertop and roll a rolling pin over the pile to flatten the butter balls. Put the mixture back into the mixing bowl. (If you used a food processor to cut in the butter, switch to a mixing bowl at this point.)

4. Add the milk and stir the mixture until it comes together to form a crumbly dough. (Don't overwork it; there is no need to make the dough smooth.) Roll the dough out into a 12-inch circle.

5. Cut it, like a pie, into 6 wedges. Roll the wedges from the wide side to the small side to make ropes, and curl in the ends to form crescents. Put the crescents on the prepared baking sheet and bake until golden brown, about 12 minutes. Serve warm.

OAT, DATE, AND ALMOND SCONES

With a crisp, shiny glaze of raw sugar on top and a tender, buttery crumb inside, these easy-to-make scones just might constitute the world's best breakfast. When the oats are broken up in a food processor, they give the scones a smoother texture, but if no food processor is available you can make them successfully with a whisk and mixing bowl.

MAKES 1 DOZEN SCONES

2 cups quick-cooking oats

1 cup all-purpose unbleached flour

3 tablespoons turbinado sugar or Sugar in the Raw

2 teaspoons baking powder

1 teaspoon baking soda

1 teaspoon kosher salt, or ½ teaspoon table salt

½ cup (1 stick) unsalted butter, cut into 1-inch bits

1 egg

¾ cup sour cream

½ cup sliced almonds, lightly toasted

½ cup chopped dates

For the Glaze

1 egg

3 tablespoons turbinado sugar or Sugar in the Raw

1. Preheat the oven to 400°F and put a rack in the upper third of the oven. Line a baking sheet with baker's parchment.

2. Put the oats, flour, sugar, baking powder, baking soda, and salt in a food processor. Pulse the motor on and off until these dry ingredients are very well combined and the oats are pulverized. If no food processor is available, simply whisk the dry ingredients together in a medium mixing bowl. Add the butter and pulse the motor on and off, or cut in the butter until the mixture is uniformly crumbly.

3. In a separate, large mixing bowl, whisk the egg with the sour cream. (If you used a mixing bowl to combine the dry ingredients, use a separate bowl for this step.) Add the oat and flour mixture all at once to the egg mixture, along with the almonds and dates, and stir just until the dough comes together in a sticky mass. Transfer the dough to a floured work surface and knead briefly.

4. Divide the dough in half and pat each half into a 5-inch circle. Cut each circle into 6 wedges and arrange the wedges on the prepared baking sheet. Whisk the egg

for the glaze and brush it over the scones. Sprinkle the turbinado sugar over the egg wash and bake the scones until golden brown, about 12 minutes.

★

ORANGE AND DRIED CRANBERRY SCONES

Both the bright zest and the sweet juice of an orange are included in these scones to make them super flavorful. Tangy red cranberries add texture and color. I like to serve these sunny-looking scones on winter mornings when oranges are at the peak of their season and my senses are craving sunshine.

MAKES 6 SCONES

2 cups unbleached white flour

¼ cup sugar

2 teaspoons baking powder

½ teaspoon baking soda

½ teaspoon salt

6 tablespoons (¾ stick) unsalted butter, cut into 1-inch bits

1 large egg

1 tablespoon grated orange zest

¾ cup freshly squeezed orange juice

½ cup dried sweetened cranberries

For the Glaze

1 cup powdered sugar

1 tablespoon freshly squeezed orange juice

1 teaspoon grated orange zest

1. Preheat the oven to 400°F and line a baking sheet with baker's parchment.

2. In a food processor or medium mixing bowl, process or whisk together the flour, sugar, baking powder, baking soda, and salt. Add the butter and pulse the motor on and off, or cut in the butter until the mixture is uniformly crumbly.

3. In a separate, large mixing bowl, whisk the egg with the orange zest and orange juice until smooth.

4. Stir the flour mixture, along with the dried cranberries, into the egg and orange mixture. Knead gently—no more than 2 or 3 turns—just until the dough is smooth.

5. Shape the dough into a ball, flatten it slightly, and cut it into 6 wedges. Put the scones on the prepared baking sheet. Bake until they are puffed in the center, about 12 minutes.

6. Stir together the powdered sugar, orange juice, and orange zest for the glaze, and drizzle the mixture over the warm scones. Cool the scones on a rack.

★

BUTTERMILK BANNOCK, AN IRISH SODA BREAD

Soda bread is traditionally very lean (no butter, no sugar), but not knowing what I was doing, I taught myself to make this bread using a little sugar and butter, as if I were making a big egg-free scone, leavened with baking soda and buttermilk instead of baking powder.

I liked the results and kept right on making it this way, even after I learned that I was "wrong" about the butter and sugar.

MAKES 2 SMALL LOAVES

1 cup whole wheat flour

1 cup all-purpose flour

2 tablespoons sugar

1 teaspoon baking soda

1 teaspoon kosher salt

6 tablespoons (¾ stick) cold unsalted butter, cut into 1-inch bits

½ cup dried currants

⅞ cup buttermilk (¾ cup plus 2 tablespoons)

1. Preheat the oven to 350°F and line a baking sheet with baker's parchment.

2. Put the whole wheat flour in a large mixing bowl or in a food processor with the white flour, sugar, baking soda, and salt. Add the butter and pulse the motor on and off, or cut in the butter until the mixture resembles fine breadcrumbs.

3. If you used a food processor, move the mixture to a large bowl at this point. Stir the currants into the flour mixture and then add the buttermilk and stir until the mixture comes together to form a soft dough.

4. Sprinkle some flour onto the countertop and transfer the dough from the mixing bowl to the floured surface. Knead the dough lightly 2 or 3 turns to

stiffen it up a little, then divide it in half and press each piece into a round ball. Place the balls of dough on the baking sheet, cut a cross in the top of each one, and bake until well browned and cooked through, about 30 minutes. (An instant-read thermometer inserted into a loaf should read about 190°F.)

Batter Breads and Coffee Cakes

★

SKILLET CORNBREAD

The hot skillet causes the batter around the edges of this cornbread to bake more quickly than the center, so you get a crisp, brown crust around tender yellow cornbread. The skillet itself provides a charming old-fashioned presentation, too, that makes me think of the forty-niners and other pioneers who came to the West Coast in the nineteenth century. If you can find whole-grain cornmeal, buy it: It has a more pronounced flavor than the more refined plain yellow stuff. But be sure it's fresh; the bran in the whole grain contains oils that give the meal a shorter shelf life.

MAKES ONE 10-INCH ROUND

1 cup unbleached white flour

1 cup cornmeal, preferably whole grain

1 tablespoon baking powder

1 teaspoon kosher salt, or ½ teaspoon table salt

1 egg

⅓ cup brown sugar

⅓ cup corn or canola oil, plus 2 tablespoons for the pan

1 cup milk

1. Put a 10-inch cast-iron skillet in the oven and preheat the oven to 400°F.

2. In a large mixing bowl, whisk together the flour, cornmeal, baking powder, and salt.

3. In a separate, medium mixing bowl, whisk the egg with the brown sugar and ⅓ cup oil until the mixture is perfectly smooth; then whisk in the milk.

4. Add the egg and milk mixture all at once to the flour and cornmeal mixture and stir just until the dry ingredients are moistened. Do not overmix; there is no need to stir out all the lumps.

5. With a hot pad, take the preheated cast-iron skillet out of the oven and pour in the remaining 2 tablespoons oil. Gently swirl the skillet so that the oil covers the inside surfaces. Transfer the batter to the oiled skillet and bake until the bread is puffed in the center and golden brown, about 15 minutes. Cut into wedges and serve hot.

⭐ WALNUT CREEK BANANA BREAD

It seems bizarre that cooks who live in a region that grows only a few specialty bananas in isolated areas would find themselves with so many bananas, but bananas are imported with such enthusiasm that an overabundance is common. What gives this particular banana bread its extra character is toasting the walnuts before stirring them into the batter. Extra flavor also comes with walnut oil, if you can find it, but canola oil will produce banana bread with good flavor too.

MAKES ONE 4- BY 10-INCH LOAF
OR 9-INCH TUBE CAKE

2 cups unbleached white flour

1 tablespoon baking powder

1 teaspoon ground cinnamon

1 teaspoon kosher salt, or ½ teaspoon table salt

3 medium-ripe to overripe bananas, mashed (about 1½ cups)

2 large eggs

¾ cup brown sugar

½ cup walnut or canola oil

1 teaspoon vanilla extract

1 cup lightly toasted walnuts, chopped

1. Preheat the oven to 350°F and put a rack in the upper third of the oven. Butter and flour a 10-inch tube cake pan or a 4- by 10-inch loaf pan, or spray it with nonstick canola oil spray.

2. Whisk together the flour, baking powder, cinnamon, and salt in a medium mixing bowl and set the dry mixture aside.

3. In a separate, large mixing bowl, whisk together the mashed bananas with the eggs, brown sugar, oil, and vanilla extract. Add the flour mixture and the walnuts all at once to the egg mixture and stir just until the dry ingredients are moistened.

4. Transfer the batter to the prepared pan and bake until puffed in the center and brown around the edges, about 50 minutes. An instant-read thermometer inserted in the center of the loaf will read 180°F when the bread is ready. As soon as the banana bread comes out of the oven, turn it out of the baking pan onto a wire rack to cool.

⭐ APPLESAUCE STREUSEL COFFEE CAKE

Because I have apple trees, I often make applesauce, but in all honesty, we don't eat a lot of applesauce at my house, so I use it in baked goods like this moist and tender breakfast cake. Streusel, German for "scatter," refers to the action of crumbling a mixture of flour, butter, and sugar over the batter. Dividing the streusel among layers of batter gives the cake an interesting variation in textures.

MAKES ONE 9- BY 9-INCH CAKE, SERVING 9

For the Cake

2 cups unbleached white flour

2 teaspoons baking powder

I teaspoon baking soda

I teaspoon kosher salt

I egg

⅔ cup sugar

⅓ cup canola oil

2 cups applesauce

For the Streusel Topping

⅔ cup unbleached white flour

¼ cup brown sugar

2 teaspoons ground cinnamon

½ teaspoon ground nutmeg

¼ teaspoon salt

¼ cup (½ stick) unsalted butter

I. Preheat the oven to 375°F, and butter a 9-inch square baking dish or spray it with nonstick canola oil spray.

2. In a medium mixing bowl, whisk together the flour, baking powder, baking soda, and salt. In a separate, large bowl, whisk the egg with the sugar and oil, and when they are thoroughly combined, whisk in the applesauce.

3. Add the flour mixture all at once to the applesauce mixture and stir just until well combined; do not overmix. Put half the batter in the baking dish.

4. In a food processor or small mixing bowl, combine the ingredients for the streusel topping and process or mix with a fork until the mixture forms crumbs.

(Do not overprocess or the mixture will form a hard-to-handle paste.) Crumble the streusel topping over the cake batter in the pan. Dollop the remaining batter on top of the streusel layer, then crumble the remaining streusel over it.

5. Bake until the cake is browned around the edges and puffed in the center, about 25 minutes. A straw or bamboo pick poked into the center of the cake will come out clean when the cake is baked through, and an instant-read thermometer will register 180°F. Allow the cake to cool for about 10 minutes to firm up, then cut it into nine 3-inch squares, and serve warm.

★

APRICOT ALMOND CRUMB CAKE

Former executive pastry chef of Windows on the World Nick Malgieri directs the baking program at the Institute of Culinary Education. He did not create crumb cake, but his recipes are so good that he might as well have. This recipe is my West Coast version of his traditional crumb cake. I lightened Malgieri's East Coast version slightly by replacing the egg yolks with whole eggs and substituting canola oil for the butter in the cake. I've also added California almonds to the traditional crumb topping.

MAKES ONE 10-INCH CAKE, SERVING 12

For the Cake

1¼ cups all-purpose flour

I teaspoon baking powder

½ teaspoon salt

2 large eggs

¾ cup sugar

½ cup canola oil

1 teaspoon vanilla extract

10 medium apricots (1½ to 2 pounds)

For the Topping

1 cup all-purpose flour

½ cup whole almonds

½ cup brown sugar

¼ teaspoon almond extract

½ cup (1 stick) cold unsalted butter, cut into 1-inch bits

1. Butter a 10-inch springform pan and line it with a disk of parchment or wax paper. Preheat the oven to 350°F.

2. Whisk together the flour, baking powder, and salt in a large mixing bowl and set aside.

3. In a separate, medium bowl, whisk together the eggs and sugar until the mixture is very smooth and creamy. Stream in the oil and vanilla extract, whisking all the while.

4. With a rubber spatula, stir the egg mixture into the flour mixture and transfer the batter to the prepared cake pan.

5. Cut the apricots in half, pluck out the pits, and arrange the apricot halves, cut sides up, on top of the batter.

6. To make the crumb topping, put the flour, almonds, and brown sugar in the bowl of a food processor and process until the almonds are completely ground and the mixture is uniformly crumbly. With the motor running, add the almond extract and butter. Process just until the mixture is crumbly; do not overprocess or it will become pastelike.

7. Distribute the crumb topping evenly over the apricots and bake the cake until the crumbs are well colored and the cake is firm and no longer liquid in the center, about 55 minutes. Cool the cake on a rack for 20 minutes before removing the sides of the pan and transferring the cake to a serving plate.

PUMPKIN STREUSEL BREAKFAST CAKE

Fresh pumpkin purée is very different from canned pumpkin. To make your own, follow the technique described on page 256. Although fresh pumpkin purée is less expensive, if it's too much bother, frozen squash purée (preferably organic) is a close second—in fact, once its baked into this cake you can hardly tell the difference. Green pumpkin seeds give the streusel topping character and crunch. For a memorable brunch, serve this cake with well-browned pork and apple sausages on a Sunday morning in the fall.

For the Cake

1½ cups unbleached white flour

I tablespoon baking powder

I teaspoon salt

I egg

⅔ cup sugar

⅓ cup canola oil

1¼ cups pumpkin purée, or one 10-ounce package frozen winter squash purée

For the Topping

½ cup unbleached white flour

½ cup pumpkin seeds (pepitas)

⅓ cup brown sugar

2 teaspoons ground cinnamon

½ teaspoon salt

¼ cup (½ stick) cold unsalted butter

I. Preheat the oven to 375°F and butter a 9-inch square pan.

2. In a large mixing bowl, whisk together the flour, baking powder, and salt.

3. In a separate, medium bowl, whisk the egg with the sugar and oil. When thoroughly combined, whisk in the pumpkin.

4. Add the pumpkin mixture all at once to the flour mixture and stir until well combined. Do not overmix. Transfer the batter to the prepared pan.

5. In a food processor, combine the ingredients for the topping and process until the mixture forms crumbs. Scatter the topping over the surface of the batter.

6. Bake the cake until the topping is well-browned and the cake is firm and no longer liquid in the center, about 25 minutes. Allow it to cool for about 10 minutes to firm up, then cut it into 9 squares and serve warm.

Tortillas and Crackers

★

HOMEMADE FLOUR TORTILLAS

Since tortillas are very widely available and fairly inexpensive, one might wonder if making them from scratch is worth the effort. It is. Fresh tortillas, hot off the plancha, or griddle, are incredible. The difference between a tortilla fresh from your own kitchen and a store-bought tortilla is like the difference between a waffle fresh from the waffle iron and one that was made the day before. The process is very simple, but do be sure to let the dough rest for a few minutes before trying to roll it out.

MAKES 6 LARGE TORTILLAS

2 cups unbleached white flour

I teaspoon salt

6 tablespoons (¾ stick) unsalted butter, cut into ½-inch bits

⅔ cup water

I. In a mixing bowl, whisk together the flour and salt. Add the butter and work it in with your fingers until the mixture is crumbly. Add the water all at once and stir until the water is absorbed and the mixture comes together to form a soft dough.

2. Knead the dough briefly, then cover it with a damp paper towel or a piece of plastic wrap and let the dough rest for 5 minutes.

3. Cut the dough into 6 equal pieces. Shape each piece into a ball and, on a lightly floured surface, roll each into an 8-inch circle.

4. Cook the tortillas one at a time. On an ungreased griddle or in a dry frying pan over medium heat, cook on one side until the surface bubbles, then turn and cook the other side until the tortilla is cooked through, about a minute longer. The tortillas should be covered with toasty brown spots. Serve hot.

★

HANDMADE RYE CRACKERS

These crackers were developed to serve as a foundation for the chanterelle mushroom appetizer on pages 56–57, but they serve as a perfect foil for other toppings too, like cheese or cold cuts. At the cocktail hour, the crackers can be served plain in one dish with olives in another dish and toasted almonds in a third. The savory little bites make perfectly appetizing nibbles that are not too filling.

MAKES 3 DOZEN CRACKERS

1 cup whole-grain rye flour

1 cup unbleached white flour

1 tablespoon sugar

1 teaspoon baking powder

1 teaspoon salt

½ cup (1 stick) unsalted butter, cut into ½-inch bits

⅔ cup water

1. Preheat the oven to 350°F.

2. Put the rye flour, white flour, sugar, baking powder, and salt in a food processor and pulse the motor on and off to mix. Add the butter and pulse on and off for 10 or 15 seconds to mix.

3. Transfer the mixture to a medium mixing bowl and add the water all at once. Combine, mixing lightly with your hands just until the mixture comes together to form a shaggy mass of dough.

4. Roll the dough out on a floured surface to a rectangle measuring about 9 by 18 inches, and place the rectangle of dough on a sheet of baker's parchment. Use a pizza cutter to cut the dough into eighteen 3-inch squares, then cut the squares in half diagonally to make triangles. Move the sheet of parchment with the pastry rectangles to the baking sheet. Prick the crackers with a fork. (This will keep them from puffing up too much in the oven.)

5. Bake the crackers until brown and crisp, about 12 minutes. Cool completely and serve at room temperature. Keep any leftover crackers in an airtight container for up to 1 week.

⭐

SESAME CRACKERS

In most kitchens where English is spoken, the breads that Americans call crackers are called biscuits. I was inspired to try making my own thin, crisp biscuits to serve with appetizers. From the very first attempt—flaky, buttery, Ritz-like things that melted in my mouth—I knew I was on to something. These crackers are more like the classic Californian–Armenian stone ground wheat and sesame crackers known as Ak-Mak. Baked by the Soojian family in Sanger, California, since 1893, real Ak-Maks are great, but there is something satisfying about baking your own.

MAKES 36 CRACKERS

2½ cups whole wheat flour

1 teaspoon baking powder

½ teaspoon salt

¾ cup (1½ sticks) cold unsalted butter, cut into 1-inch pieces

¾ cup sesame seeds

¾ cup water

¼ cup egg whites

1. Preheat the oven to 400°F. In a food processor, combine the flour, baking powder, and salt. Add the butter and process, pulsing the motor on and off until the mixture is crumbly. Add ½ cup of the sesame seeds and process briefly to incorporate. Add the water all at once to the mixture; pulse the motor on and off just until the mixture comes together to form a ball of dough, about 10 pulses.

2. Roll the dough out on a floured surface to a rectangle measuring about 9 by 18 inches, and place the rectangle of dough on a sheet of baker's parchment. Use a pizza cutter to cut the dough into eighteen 3-inch squares, then cut the squares in half diagonally to make triangles. Move the sheet of parchment with the pastry rectangles to the baking sheet. Prick the crackers with a fork. Brush with the egg white and sprinkle with the remaining ¼ cup sesame seeds.

3. Bake until the crackers are golden, 10 to 12 minutes. Serve warm or at room temperature. The crackers keep, in a tightly covered container, for up to 1 week.

CAKES

LAYER CAKES

SPONGE CAKES

CAKES WITH FRUIT

CUPCAKES

MORE CAKES

FROSTINGS AND GLAZES

Cakes

Cake. The very word evokes comfort, ease, and celebration. "It'll be a piece of cake," we say, meaning that a task will be a breeze, a "cakewalk" if you will. Cakes are synonymous with prizes too. Probably a reference to the award at the end of a cakewalk, the saying "That really takes the cake" means it is worthy of the grand prize. Cakes have a kind of magic in them. Such simple ingredients—flour, sugar, butter, and eggs—are, through the alchemy of the kitchen, transformed into something far greater than the sum of its parts.

"The essence of most cakes," writes Harold McGee, in his definitive work *On Food and Cooking*, "is sweetness and richness. A cake is a web of flour, eggs, sugar, and butter, a delicate structure that readily disintegrates in the mouth and fills it with easeful flavor." A Californian who often pops up at the heart of cutting edge cuisine, working beside Thomas Keller at the French Laundry or making cheese with Soyoung Scanlan in Sonoma County, McGee studied and taught English literature before he launched into a career devoted to the science of food and cooking. His sense of poetry infuses his work and characterizes, I think, the holistic approach to food that distinguishes West Coast cooking.

Cooking, and especially baking, depends on a synergistic relationship between the chemistry of the ingredients that combine and interact to produce the actual, physical cake and an aesthetic approach to the assembly and enjoyment of the thing that borders on the mystic. A cake without its cultural context is not complete. A cake is a thing-in-itself that symbolizes the care and attention we bring to one another by sharing food. Because it is superfluous, something above and beyond what is nutritionally required, it represents and even evokes the mystical bond we share around the hearth and around the table.

Homemade layer cakes used to be stacked up on pedestal plates all over North America. They were on the sideboard at Aunt Millie's house, on the kitchen table at Grandma's house, and down the street at the Pfeiffers' house. They were practically part of the furniture.

My mom could whip one up without batting an eye; even in her seventies and fairly arthritic, she could put together a cake from scratch and have it cooled and halfway frosted before most people could read the instructions on a box of cake mix. But nowadays, homemade layer cakes seem to have gone the way of the spotted owl. If it weren't for birthdays and all the contingent nostalgia, we probably wouldn't have homemade cakes at all.

American cakes as they evolved during the last half of the century became more and more a product of the factory and less a product of the home. And food scientists less poetic than Harold McGee, working in food laboratories in the great mills where flour was produced, sought ways to make cakes lighter and able to maintain structural integrity with higher ratios of inexpensive fat and sugar to flour. They lightened the flour by selecting wheat with less protein, bleaching it and reducing it to simple starch. They replaced the butter with hydrogenated vegetable shortening.

Cake mixes with premeasured ingredients—most of them chemically altered on their way to the box—came to dominate how Americans made cakes. And more than flavor was lost: "Hydrogenated oil does not have the flavor that butter does," writes McGee, "and has the more serious disadvantage of containing high levels of trans fatty acids." So health and vitality were compromised too.

But more than flavor and nutrition are sacrificed when a baker opts for a mix instead of using raw ingredients. The accomplishment that comes from transforming straw into gold is more precious than any time saved by opening a box instead of a flour bin. When the miller's daughter allows Rumpelstiltskin to work the spinning wheel, she buys some time, but she risks losing everything.

A cake truly made from scratch with wholesome ingredients is a fun and healthy way to enrich our lives. Both the baker and her family can take enormous and wholesome pleasure in a homemade cake. But a cake made from bleached flour and hydrogenated oil is of dubious merit at best,

and the loss of personal connection with the assembly of the thing renders it perfunctory, almost dismal behind its pretty façade. Homemade cake is something else. To the degree that it is a link to the farmers who produced the ingredients, it connects us to the earth. And since it connects us to those who taught us to make it, it is a kind of culture carrier, a link to our own traditions.

Aunt Lois' Coconut Cake (page 305) is a prime example. During the final years of her life, my Great-Aunt Lois was ensconced in a nursing home in Eugene, Oregon, where she wandered freely from the past to the present among the living and the dead who inhabited her world. Whenever I visited, she was likely to share details from conversations she had enjoyed earlier in the day with my grandfather (he died in 1962) or with my great-grandmother (she died when I was still in college).

Even though her belongings, like her loved ones, were scattered over time and space, she managed once, when I went to visit her in the nursing home, to find the recipe for her favorite layer cake, handwritten on an ancient, yellowed index card, and she wanted me to bake it for her.

So I wheeled her out of the nursing home and helped her into the car. We swung by the grocery store and took her to my cousin's house, where we turned on the oven and went to work. Unable to find a hammer, I broke open the coconut with a cast-iron frying pan (and broke the pan while I was at it). Aunt Lois wrung her hands and shouted instructions from her wheelchair and wondered how the devil a boy ever learned to cook anyway.

When the cake was ready to eat, majestic in its coat of fluffy white icing and freshly flaked coconut, we paused to admire it. "The first time we baked this cake," she said, "we all liked it so much that we ate the whole thing and baked another one." I think she was hinting that we too might do it all over again. We didn't bake a second cake that day, but I have baked the cake since then, and every time I do, Aunt Lois comes to visit.

Layer Cakes

★

STRAW INTO GOLD CAKE

This is a glorious old-fashioned cake for birthdays and Sunday suppers that could have come from anywhere in North America before cake mixes came into vogue after World War II. Simple ingredients come together as if by magic into something sweet and alluring. Be sure to use real butter. Butterfat is the measure of quality in milk; it reveals how much solar energy the grass was able to capture and how efficiently the cows were able to convert that energy into butter. So I like to think of butter as solid sunshine, and I believe that cows raised on organic farms produce better-tasting butter.

MAKES ONE 9-INCH
2-LAYER CAKE, SERVING 12

1 cup (2 sticks) unsalted butter, preferably organic, softened to room temperature

2 cups sugar

4 eggs

2 teaspoons vanilla extract

3 cups unbleached white flour

1 tablespoon baking powder

½ teaspoon salt

1 cup milk

Vanilla Lover's Frosting (page 321) or Chocolate and Coffee Frosting (page 321)

1. Butter and flour two 9-inch round cake pans, and line the pans with baker's parchment. Preheat the oven to 350°F.

2. In a large bowl or the bowl of an electric mixer, whip the butter until it's smooth, then gradually add the sugar, beating all the while. Beat in the eggs, one at a time, beating well after each addition, then stir in the vanilla extract.

3. Put the flour, baking powder, and salt in a separate bowl and whisk them together. Add half the flour mixture and half the milk to the butter mixture, and whisk until smooth. Then stir in the remaining flour mixture with the rest of the milk and whisk again until the batter is smooth.

4. Distribute the batter evenly between the prepared cake pans and bake until the cakes spring back when pressed lightly in the center, about 30 minutes.

5. When cool, place one cake round on a cake plate and cover with the frosting of your choice. Top with the second cake layer and frost the top and sides.

★

AUNT LOIS' COCONUT CAKE

My Great-Aunt Lois taught me how to make this cake when she was 90 years old and confined to a wheelchair in Eugene, Oregon. "If you're not going to start with a fresh coconut," she said, "don't bother to make this cake. It won't be worth the trouble." The foundation of the cake is the "coconut water," a pearly, almost clear liquid found in the center of a fresh coconut. To extract it, use an ice pick or a screwdriver to poke two holes in the eyes of the coconut and shake the liquid into a measuring cup. Make sure the juice is fresh and sweet; if the water is absent or sour, the coconut will not be a good one. While the cake is baking, break open the coconut with a hammer, extract the meat from the shell, peel off the brown skin with a vegetable peeler, and grate the meat through the largest holes of a cheese grater or with the grater attachment of a food processor.

MAKES ONE 9-INCH
2-LAYER CAKE, SERVING 12

½ cup (1 stick) unsalted butter, softened to room temperature

1½ cups sugar

2 eggs, at room temperature

1 teaspoon vanilla extract

½ teaspoon almond extract

2¼ cups cake flour

2 teaspoons baking powder

1 teaspoon salt

1 cup coconut water or a combination of coconut water and milk

Fluffy White Icing (pages 322–23)

Freshly grated meat from 1 whole coconut (about 3 cups)

1. Preheat the oven to 350°F. Butter the bottom and sides of two 9-inch round cake pans, then sprinkle the pans with flour and shake out the excess.

2. In the bowl of an electric mixer, whip the butter and sugar until light and fluffy. Add the eggs, one at a time, beating well after each addition, then beat in the vanilla and almond extracts.

3. In a separate bowl, whisk together the flour, baking powder, and salt. Add about a third of this mixture to the butter mixture, along with one third of the coconut water, and beat until smooth; scrape down the sides of the bowl with a rubber spatula. Repeat this twice with the remaining thirds of flour and water.

4. Divide the batter evenly between the prepared cake pans. Bake until the cakes are golden brown and spring back when pressed lightly in the center, about 25 minutes. Cool for 5 minutes in the pans, then remove from the pans and cool completely on racks.

5. When cool, place one cake round on a cake plate and cover with Fluffy White Icing. Top with the second cake layer and frost the top and sides. Cover the top and sides with freshly grated coconut.

★

BLUE RIBBON CHOCOLATE CAKE

This cake, which appeared in my first real cookbook, In Season: Culinary Adventures of a San Juan Island Chef, *takes its name from the fact that it took first prize at the San Juan County Fair. One trick that might have helped it win the ribbon may have been the fancy piped-on frosting. But the real secret to this cake is simple ingredients with naturally good flavor.*

MAKES ONE 9-INCH
2-LAYER CAKE, SERVING 12

2½ ounces unsweetened chocolate

¾ cup (1½ sticks) unsalted butter, softened to room temperature

2 cups brown sugar

2 eggs

2¼ cups unbleached white flour

1 teaspoon baking soda

½ teaspoon salt

1⅓ cups brewed coffee

1 teaspoon vanilla extract

Chocolate and Coffee Frosting (page 321)

1. Have all ingredients at room temperature. Preheat the oven to 350°F. Butter the bottom and sides of two 9-inch round cake pans, preferably ones with removable bottoms, then sprinkle the pans with flour and shake out the excess.

2. In a double boiler or a stainless steel bowl set over a pan of barely simmering water, melt the chocolate and set aside. In a large mixing bowl, whisk the butter with the brown sugar until very smooth and fluffy. Add the eggs, one at a time, beating well after each addition. Stir in the melted chocolate.

3. In a separate bowl, whisk together the flour, baking soda, and salt. Whisk about ¾ cup of the flour mixture into the butter mixture, then whisk in ½ cup of the coffee. Add another ¾ cup flour mixture and another ½ cup coffee, stirring well after each addition. Stir in the remaining flour mixture, the remaining coffee, and the vanilla.

4. Transfer the batter to the prepared cake pans. Bake until the cakes spring back when pressed lightly in the center, about 30 minutes. Cool on racks before removing from the pans. Place one cake round on a cake plate and cover with one third of the frosting. Top with the second cake layer.

5. Put half the remaining frosting into a zipper-lock bag and snip off about an inch from one corner. Pipe the frosting onto the sides of the cake in even, overlapping stripes to completely cover the sides. Refill the impromptu pastry bag with the remaining frosting and cover the entire top surface of the cake with fanciful whirls to give it an impressive-looking finish.

★
CARROT CAKE

With just a hint of spice and the deep, warm flavors of brown sugar, browned butter, and toasted walnuts, this recipe for carrot cake is my favorite of the many versions that I have tried. For some reason—maybe because I make it most often in the fall—it always makes me feel a little sentimental, but in a good way. It can be baked either in a rectangular sheet pan or in two 9-inch round pans and layered. If you opt to layer it, frost only the tops of the layers and not the sides.

MAKES ONE 9-INCH 2-LAYER CAKE OR A
9- BY 13-INCH RECTANGLE, SERVING 12

¾ cup (1½ sticks) unsalted butter

1½ cups brown sugar

4 eggs

I teaspoon vanilla extract

2 cups unbleached white flour

I tablespoon baking powder

I teaspoon ground cinnamon

½ teaspoon salt

3 cups grated carrots (about 4 medium carrots)

¾ cup toasted walnuts, chopped

Cream Cheese Frosting (page 322) or Vanilla Lover's Frosting (page 321)

I. Preheat the oven to 350°F. Butter and flour the sides of a 9- by 13-inch cake pan, or butter and flour two 9-inch round cake pans and line the bottom of each one with baker's parchment.

2. Soften the butter: Cut the butter into 1-inch chunks. Put half of the butter in the bowl of a stand mixer. Put the rest of the butter in a saucepan and cook over medium heat until it is melted and beginning to brown. Pour the browned butter over the cold butter and beat until all the butter is smooth and creamy. Add the brown sugar and continue beating until smooth. Beat in the eggs, one at a time, beating well after each addition, then stir in the vanilla extract.

3. In a separate, large mixing bowl, whisk together the flour, baking powder, cinnamon, and salt. Add the whipped butter mixture, grated carrots, and toasted walnuts all at once to the flour mixture. Fold together just until the dry ingredients are moistened; do not overmix.

4. Transfer the batter to the prepared pan or pans and bake until the cake feels firm when pressed lightly in the center, about 20 minutes for rounds, closer to 30 minutes for the 9- by 13-inch rectangle. Cool on a rack.

5. Frost the cake with your choice of frosting when it is completely cool.

⭐
ORANGE LAYER CAKE

People have been making cakes and other desserts flavored with oranges for as long as they have been recording recipes on paper. But orange cake really came into its own during the middle years of the twentieth century, when stand mixers and ample supplies of butter, sugar, eggs, and flour were pretty much standard in American homes. During that golden age of American baking, with fresh oranges just as widely available as dry goods, orange cake in various forms became a favorite. From coast to coast, recipes for orange cakes sprang up in recipe contests and in newspaper columns. This one combines the best elements of all those recipes. A tender butter cake is filled with tangy orange custard sauce and topped with sweet orange frosting. It is made, of course, with the all-American navel orange.

MAKES ONE 9-INCH
2-LAYER CAKE, SERVING 12

For the Cake

½ cup (1 stick) butter, softened to room temperature

1 cup sugar

4 eggs

½ cup freshly squeezed orange juice

2 cups unbleached white flour

2 teaspoons baking powder

½ teaspoon baking soda

½ teaspoon salt

Navel Orange Frosting (page 322)

For the Filling

½ cup sugar

2 tablespoons cornstarch

Grated zest of 1 orange

¼ cup plus 2 tablespoons freshly squeezed orange juice

2 tablespoons freshly squeezed lemon juice

1 egg, lightly beaten

1 tablespoon unsalted butter

1. Butter and flour two 9-inch round cake pans, and line the pans with baker's parchment. Preheat the oven to 350°F.

2. In a large mixing bowl or the bowl of an electric mixer, whip the butter until it's smooth, then gradually add the sugar, beating all the while. Beat in the eggs, one at a time, then whisk in the orange juice.

3. Put the flour, baking powder, baking soda, and salt in a separate medium bowl and whisk them together, then add the dry ingredients all at once to the butter mixture. Stir until the batter is smooth.

4. Distribute the batter evenly between the prepared cake pans, and bake until the cakes spring back when pressed lightly in the center, about 30 minutes.

5. Make the filling. Put the sugar, cornstarch, orange zest, orange juice, lemon juice, and egg in a heavy saucepan over medium-high heat and whisk until smooth. Cook the mixture, whisking constantly, until it is thick and boiling hot. Remove from the heat, whisk in

the butter, and transfer the filling to a glass pie pan or a plate and chill it before spreading it between the cake layers.

6. Cool the cake completely, then spread the filling between the layers. Spread the frosting on the top and around the sides.

★

LEONETTA'S RUM CAKE

Gina Batali, sister of the famous Food Network chef Mario Batali, lives on Bainbridge Island near Seattle, where she makes this cake from her grandmother's recipe. Their father, Armondino, a former Boeing sales executive, launched a very successful artisanal salami factory or salumeria called Salumi in Seattle's Pioneer Square when he retired. Gina runs the shop, just a stone's throw from the place where her great-grandparents once ran an Italian food import business. The cake is made very much like a classic sponge cake, with butter and rum stirred into the beaten egg yolks. More rum goes into a soaking liquid to moisten the layers before they are filled and covered with a rum-flavored filling.

MAKES ONE 9-INCH
2-LAYER CAKE, SERVING 6 TO 8

For the Cake

1¼ cups unbleached white flour

1½ teaspoons baking powder

6 eggs

¼ teaspoon salt

½ teaspoon white balsamic vinegar or lemon juice

1 cup sugar

¼ cup (½ stick) unsalted butter, melted and cooled

¼ cup dark rum

1 teaspoon vanilla extract

¾ cup sugar

For the Rum "Soak"

1¼ cups strong brewed coffee

¾ cup dark rum

For the Filling and Frosting

6 egg yolks

¼ cup sugar

3 tablespoons flour

2 cups (1 pint) heavy cream

2 tablespoons dark rum

1. Grease and flour two 9-inch round cake pans, and line the bottom of each with baker's parchment. Preheat the oven to 350°F. Whisk together the flour and baking powder in a small mixing bowl and set aside.

2. Separate the eggs into whites and yolks, putting the whites in the bowl of a stand mixer and the yolks in a separate large mixing bowl.

3. Add the salt and vinegar (or lemon juice) to the egg whites and whip the whites on high speed until they are light and fluffy. With the motor still running, stream in ½ cup of the sugar and continue whipping until the egg whites hold stiff peaks and are very smooth and glossy.

4. Meanwhile, whisk the remaining ½ cup sugar, melted butter, rum, and vanilla into the egg yolks and beat until smooth.

5. Fold half of the beaten egg whites and half of the flour mixture into the egg yolk mixture, then fold in the remaining egg white mixture and the remaining flour mixture, lifting and stirring the batter gently with a silicone or rubber spatula until it's smooth.

6. Transfer the batter to the prepared cake pans and bake until the cakes are puffed and golden brown and a skewer inserted in the center comes out clean, about 25 minutes (an instant-read thermometer inserted in the deepest part of a cake will register 180°F). Cool the cakes in the pan, then stir together the coffee and rum to make the rum "soak." Soak the cakes before applying the filling.

7. Make the filling. Put the egg yolks, sugar, and flour in a heavy saucepan and whisk until smooth. Stir in the heavy cream and cook over medium-high heat, stirring constantly, until the mixture is thick and boiling hot. Remove from the heat and cool to room temperature. Stir in the rum, and transfer the filling to a glass pie pan or a plate and chill before spreading it on and around the cake layers.

Sponge Cakes

★

CLASSIC SPONGE CAKE

With no butter or oil, sponge cakes are naturally lighter than butter cakes. But the texture of a sponge cake depends on beaten egg whites. This is the type of cake that becomes a vehicle for whatever is served on top. Fresh fruit, whipped cream, frosting—whatever the topping, this cake is the perfect host. Try spreading the cake batter in a thin layer into an 11- by 17-inch rimmed baking sheet lined with baker's parchment and forming the resulting cake into a classic jelly roll. Or fill the roll with whipped cream for a roulade similar to the ones sold in Asian bakeries and supermarkets all over the West Coast.

MAKES ONE 9- BY 13-INCH CAKE
OR AN 11-INCH JELLY ROLL

6 eggs

½ teaspoon salt

½ teaspoon freshly squeezed lemon juice

1 cup sugar

1 teaspoon vanilla extract

¾ cup unbleached white flour

¼ cup cornstarch

1. Grease and flour a 9- by 13-inch cake pan, or butter the sides and line the bottom with baker's parchment. Preheat the oven to 350°F.

2. Separate the eggs into whites and yolks, putting the whites in the bowl of a stand

mixer and the yolks in a separate large mixing bowl.

3. Add the salt and lemon juice to the egg whites and whip the whites on high speed until they are light and fluffy. With the motor still running, stream in ½ cup of the sugar, and continue whipping until the egg whites hold stiff peaks and are very smooth and glossy.

4. Meanwhile, whisk the remaining ½ cup sugar and the vanilla into the egg yolks and beat until smooth. In a separate bowl, whisk together the flour and cornstarch.

5. Fold half of the beaten egg whites and half of the flour mixture into the egg yolk mixture, then fold in the remaining egg white mixture and the remaining flour mixture, lifting and stirring the batter gently with a silicone or rubber spatula until it's smooth.

6. Transfer the batter to the prepared cake pan and bake until it is risen evenly in the pan and a skewer inserted in the center comes out clean, about 25 minutes. Turn the cake out of the pan to cool on a rack before filling or frosting.

★

COCOA SPONGE CAKE

Dress this cake up or down according to the occasion. Dust squares of it with powdered sugar for a picnic. Layer it with raspberry jam for a memorable afternoon coffee or tea. Make a double batch and layer it with Fluffy White Icing (pages 322–23) and it's ready for a casual family birthday party. Topped with ice cream and meringue, it becomes a Baked Alaska (pages 320–21), ready for the most formal occasion.

MAKES ONE 9- BY 9-INCH
CAKE, SERVING 6 TO 8

½ cup unbleached white flour

¼ cup unsweetened cocoa powder

4 eggs

½ teaspoon salt

½ teaspoon balsamic vinegar

¾ cup sugar

1 teaspoon vanilla extract

1. Grease and flour a 9-inch square cake pan, and line it with baker's parchment. Preheat the oven to 350°F.

2. Whisk together the flour and cocoa in a small mixing bowl and set aside.

3. Separate the eggs into whites and yolks, putting the whites in the bowl of a stand mixer and the yolks in a separate large mixing bowl.

4. Add the salt and vinegar to the egg whites and whip the whites on high speed until they are light and fluffy. With the motor still running, stream in half of the sugar (6 tablespoons) and continue whipping until the egg whites hold stiff peaks and are very smooth and glossy.

5. Whisk the remaining 6 tablespoons sugar and the vanilla extract into the egg yolks and beat until smooth.

6. Fold half of the beaten egg whites and half of the flour mixture into the egg yolk mixture, then fold in the remaining egg white mixture and the remaining flour mixture, lifting and stirring the batter gently with a silicone or rubber spatula until it's smooth.

7. Transfer the batter to the prepared pan and bake the cake until it is risen evenly in the pan and a skewer inserted in the center comes out clean, about 35 minutes (an instant-read thermometer inserted in the deepest part of the cake will register 180°F). Cool the cake in the pan.

★

LEMON CHIFFON CAKE

Harry Baker, an insurance salesman living in Los Angeles, started baking his "Secret Recipe" cakes in 1927 and selling them to local residents and restaurants. One of his clients was the famous Brown Derby restaurant in Hollywood, for which he personally baked 32 cakes a day in a spare room of his house. Lighter and more tender than traditional butter cakes but richer than angel food cake, Baker's cake captured the imagination of bakers who tried unsuccessfully to imitate his technique. The secret came out in 1947 when General Mills bought the recipe for an undisclosed sum and published a pamphlet on "Betty Crocker Chiffon" in 1948. The big secret? Vegetable oil instead of butter in an otherwise fairly traditional sponge cake. Nevertheless, the cake tastes like more than the sum of its parts. Whenever I bake it, it disappears almost instantly.

MAKES 1 TUBE CAKE, SERVING 12

6 eggs

¼ cup freshly squeezed lemon juice

I teaspoon salt

I½ cups sugar

¼ cup water

I tablespoon grated lemon zest

I teaspoon vanilla extract

½ cup canola oil

I½ cups unbleached white flour

I teaspoon baking powder

½ teaspoon baking soda

Lemon Glaze (page 323)

I. Preheat the oven to 350°F and position a rack in the center of the oven, with at least 10 inches of clearance to accommodate a large (16-cup) 2-part tube cake pan (the kind used for angel food cakes) with room to spare for rising.

2. Separate the eggs into whites and yolks, putting the whites in the bowl of a stand mixer and the yolks in a separate large mixing bowl.

3. Add I tablespoon of the lemon juice and the salt to the egg whites and whip the whites on high speed until they are light and fluffy. With the motor still running, stream in ¾ cup of the sugar and continue whipping until the egg whites hold stiff peaks and are very smooth and glossy.

4. Meanwhile, whisk the remaining 3 tablespoons lemon juice, the remaining ¾ cup sugar, water, lemon zest, and vanilla extract into the egg yolks and beat until smooth. Whisk in the oil. In a separate, medium bowl, stir the flour, baking powder, and baking soda to combine.

5. Fold half of the beaten egg whites and half of the flour mixture into the egg yolk mixture, then fold in the remaining egg white mixture and the remaining flour mixture, lifting and stirring the batter gently with a silicone or rubber spatula until it's smooth.

6. Transfer the batter to an ungreased 16-cup 2-part tube cake pan. Bake the cake until it is risen evenly in the pan and golden brown on top, about 50 minutes (an instant-read thermometer inserted in the deepest part of the cake will register 180°F). Turn the finished cake upside down over a bottle and let it cool completely to room temperature before turning it out of the pan. Cover the top of the cake with the lemon glaze, allowing the excess glaze to run down the sides of the cake.

Cakes with Fruit

★

DARK ORANGE CAKE

Darigold, the Northwest dairy cooperative, once sponsored a contest to discover the Northwest's "best butter desserts." My wife's Aunt Terry submitted her mother's recipe for this cake, and it took second place. (First place went to a recipe for "Grandmother's Buttery Lemon Light Cake.") Terry was a teacher at a one-room schoolhouse on a remote island in the San Juans between Washington and British Columbia. "When I moved to Waldron Island," says Terry, "I used a hand grinder like Mother's to grind the oranges. Now I use a food processor." This moist and fragrant cake is cut and served directly from the pan.

MAKES ONE 9- BY 13-INCH CAKE, SERVING 12

For the Cake

½ cup (1 stick) unsalted butter

1 cup sugar

2 eggs

1 teaspoon vanilla extract

2 cups unbleached white flour

1 teaspoon baking soda

1 teaspoon baking powder

½ teaspoon salt

1 cup buttermilk or plain yogurt

1 large seedless navel orange, scrubbed and patted dry

1 cup raisins

1 cup walnuts

For the Topping

2 cups powdered sugar

2 tablespoons unsalted butter

1 teaspoon vanilla extract

2 tablespoons sour cream or plain yogurt

2 tablespoons reserved ground orange mixture

1. Have all the ingredients at room temperature. Butter a 9- by 13-inch cake pan, and preheat the oven to 350°F.

2. In a large mixing bowl or the bowl of an electric mixer, beat the butter and sugar until light and fluffy. Beat in the eggs, one at a time, beating well after each addition, then stir in the vanilla extract.

3. In a separate medium mixing bowl, whisk together the flour, baking soda, baking powder, and salt. Add the flour mixture to the butter mixture in 3 parts, alternating with thirds of the buttermilk and beating well after each addition.

4. Cut the unpeeled orange into 6 or 8 rough chunks. Use a food processor or an old-fashioned meat grinder to grind the orange with the raisins and walnuts. Set aside 2 tablespoons of the ground orange mixture for the topping, and fold the rest of the mixture into the cake batter.

5. Transfer the batter to the buttered cake pan and bake until a cake tester comes out clean, about 45 minutes.

6. Cool the cake in the pan on a rack. Stir together the ingredients for the topping in a medium bowl, and when the cake is completely cool, spread the topping over it.

Cupcakes

★

CLASSIC CUPCAKES

These tender vanilla cupcakes are a favorite for the lunch-box set. Bake and frost them on the weekend, wrap each one in plastic wrap and put them in the freezer, then send them off with your loved ones to school or work. They're soft and fresh at noon. Make a double or triple batch to mark important occasions like a schoolchild's birthday party or that sacred holiday, the Last Day of School.

MAKES 1 DOZEN CUPCAKES

½ cup (1 stick) unsalted butter, softened to room temperature

1 cup sugar

2 eggs, at room temperature

1 teaspoon vanilla extract

1¾ cups unbleached white flour

¼ cup cornstarch

1½ teaspoons baking powder

½ teaspoon salt

½ cup milk

Vanilla Lover's Frosting (page 321) or Chocolate and Coffee Frosting (page 321)

Candy sprinkles, for decoration (optional)

1. Preheat the oven to 350°F and line a 12-cup muffin tin with paper cup liners or butter and flour the cups.

2. Cream the butter and sugar in the bowl of an electric mixer or in a large mixing bowl with a whisk. Add the eggs, one at

a time, beating well after each addition, then stir in the vanilla extract.

3. Whisk the flour, cornstarch, baking powder, and salt together in a medium mixing bowl. Add half the flour mixture and half the milk to the butter and sugar mixture, and stir or mix until smooth. Add the remaining flour mixture and the rest of the milk and stir until smooth again.

4. Distribute the batter evenly among the prepared muffin cups, and bake until the cupcakes are puffed up and golden brown, about 20 minutes. When pressed lightly in the center, the cakes should spring back up.

5. Cool the cupcakes completely, then frost them with the frosting of your choice and sprinkles, if desired.

★

COCOA COFFEE CUPCAKES

Tender and delectable, these soft chocolate cupcakes taste like you always wished those packaged cupcakes tasted, only better. The cornstarch in the flour mixture makes the texture of these cupcakes extra smooth and light.

MAKES 1 DOZEN CUPCAKES

½ cup (1 stick) unsalted butter, softened to room temperature

½ cup unsweetened cocoa powder

1 cup brown sugar

1 egg, at room temperature

½ teaspoon vanilla extract

1 cup unbleached white flour

2 tablespoons cornstarch

½ teaspoon baking soda

¼ teaspoon salt

⅔ cup brewed coffee, at room temperature

Chocolate and Coffee Frosting (page 321)

1. Preheat the oven to 350°F and line a 12-cup muffin tin with paper cup liners or butter and flour the cups.

2. Combine the butter, cocoa, and brown sugar in the bowl of an electric mixer or in a large mixing bowl with a whisk until the mixture is smooth and creamy. Add the egg and vanilla and whisk again until smooth.

3. In a separate, small bowl, stir the flour, cornstarch, baking soda, and salt together. Add half the flour mixture and half the coffee to the butter mixture, and stir or mix until smooth. Add the remaining flour mixture and the rest of the coffee and stir until smooth again.

4. Distribute the batter evenly among the prepared muffin cups, and bake until the cupcakes are puffed up and cracked on top, about 20 minutes. When pressed lightly in the center, the cakes should spring back up.

5. Cool the cupcakes completely, then frost them with the frosting.

More Cakes

✦

MANDARIN ORANGE POUND CAKE

Years ago, I came into an 8-cup enameled cast-iron cake pan shaped like the Bundt cake pans or tube cake pans that were so popular in the seventies. It hangs on the wall of my kitchen and occasionally comes down to be called into service for a pound cake. This recipe is based on the old formula for pound cakes: 1 pound each of butter, sugar, eggs, and flour; only here, I use a half pound of each item, perfuming everything with the grated zest of those wonderful satsuma mandarins that come into the market around Thanksgiving. Since the ingredients are so basic, it is important to use the best you can find; I like to make this pound cake with organic butter and off-white organic sugar made from evaporated cane juice, and I use a little more than the traditional formula for a sweeter, moister cake.

MAKES 1 TUBE CAKE, SERVING 8 TO 12

1 cup (2 sticks) unsalted butter

1½ cups organic or light brown sugar

4 eggs

2 tablespoons grated satsuma mandarin zest

2 teaspoons vanilla extract

2 cups unbleached white flour

1 teaspoon baking powder

Orange Glaze (page 323), made with satsuma mandarin juice and zest

1. Have all the ingredients at room temperature. Butter an 8- or 10-cup Bundt cake pan or tube cake pan, and preheat the oven to 350°F.

2. In a large mixing bowl or the bowl of an stand mixer, whip the butter until it's smooth, then gradually add the sugar, beating all the while. Beat in the eggs, one at a time, beating well after each addition, then stir in the orange zest and vanilla.

3. Whisk together the flour and baking powder in a separate, small bowl. Add the flour to the butter mixture in 4 or 5 parts, beating well after each addition.

4. Transfer the batter to the buttered pan, and bake until a cake tester comes out clean, 45 to 55 minutes.

5. Turn the cake out of the pan to cool on a rack, and when it is completely cool, cover the top of the cake with the orange glaze, allowing the excess glaze to run down the sides of the cake.

✦

AUNT ILSE'S SANDTORTE

My friend Jessica Stern, who grew up in San Francisco, gave me this recipe, which she herself received from her Austrian Aunt Ilse. Jessica first tasted the cake when she was 10 years old and Ilse was serving it with tea. "It was this gorgeous structural thing, the kugelhopf," said Jessica. Ever since she saw it amid all the silver and porcelain at her aunt's house, Jessica wanted to make it. Finally, as an adult, she wrote her aunt and asked for the recipe. Ilse sent the recipe, a hand-drawn sketch of how the finished cake should look, and a kugelhopf pan in which to bake it. "The recipe said to sift the flour and measure it again," says Jessica, "which is dumb, because it always measures out exactly the same, but I do it anyway. I follow this recipe to the letter."

MAKES 1 KUGELHOPF, SERVING 12

1 cup (2 sticks) unsalted butter

3 cups sugar

6 eggs

1 cup sour cream

3 cups unbleached white flour, sifted and remeasured

¼ teaspoon baking powder

1½ teaspoons vanilla extract

Powdered sugar, for dusting

1. Have all the ingredients at room temperature. Butter a 10-cup kugelhopf or tube cake pan, and preheat the oven to 350°F.

2. In a large mixing bowl or the bowl of an electric mixer, whip the butter until it's smooth, then gradually add the sugar, beating all the while. Beat in the eggs, one at a time, beating well after each addition, then stir in the sour cream.

3. Sift together the flour and baking powder (I whisk them together in a bowl). Add the flour to the butter mixture in 4 or 5 parts, beating well after each addition. Then stir in the vanilla extract.

4. Transfer the batter to the buttered pan, and bake until a cake tester comes out clean, about 1 hour and 15 minutes.

5. Turn the cake out of the pan to cool on a rack, and when it is completely cool, sprinkle it with powdered sugar.

★

TRES LECHES CAKE

I was training a young pastry chef who hails from the state of Puebla in Mexico to work in the pastry station at Canlis restaurant in Seattle, and we were comparing notes about desserts we had enjoyed as children. The ultimate dessert, he insisted, was galleta de tres leches, *or "three milks cake," and other Mexican cooks in the kitchen immediately starting waxing poetic about the pleasures of this cake. From Oaxaca, from Michoacán, and from Baja California, they all agreed: tres leches was the best. Eventually, I gleaned a recipe.*

MAKES ONE 9- BY 13-INCH CAKE, SERVING 12

Classic Sponge Cake (pages 310–11)

One 14-ounce can sweetened condensed milk

One 5-ounce can evaporated milk

1 cup heavy cream

1 tablespoon light rum

1 teaspoon vanilla extract

½ teaspoon natural almond extract

Fluffy White Icing (pages 322–23)

Fresh fruit as an accompaniment

1. Bake the sponge cake and, while it is cooling, prepare the tres leches. In a large measuring cup or small pitcher, stir together the sweetened condensed milk,

evaporated milk, and heavy cream with the rum, vanilla extract, and almond extract.

2. Pour the tres leches slowly over the cooled sponge cake, pressing lightly with a silicone or rubber spatula so that the cake will absorb the milks. Chill the cake in the refrigerator while you prepare the icing.

3. Spread the icing over the chilled cake and serve with fresh fruit, such as strawberries or diced mangoes.

★
MEXICAN CHOCOLATE CAKE

Chocolate originated in Mexico where it was traditionally used in a spicy beverage, and Mexican chocolate is still spiced and used mostly for a hot drink. The "Mexican" in my Mexican chocolate cake lies not in any authentic foothold in culinary tradition but in a simple allegiance to the taste of Mexican hot chocolate. Take a bite and you'll immediately get it. The cake tastes like Mexican chocolate. A web pattern of white glaze over chocolate gives this cake a distinctive look.

MAKES ONE 9-INCH
1-LAYER CAKE, SERVING 12

½ cup almonds

½ cup semisweet chocolate chips

¼ cup unsweetened cocoa powder

½ cup unbleached white flour

½ teaspoon ground allspice or cinnamon

4 eggs, separated

¾ cup sugar

¼ cup canola oil

I teaspoon vanilla extract

½ teaspoon vinegar

½ teaspoon kosher salt

Chocolate Glaze (pages 324)

Royal Sugar Glaze (page 324)

I. Grease the sides of a 9-inch round cake pan and line the bottom with baker's parchment. Preheat a convection oven to 350°F.

2. In a food processor, grind the almonds and chocolate chips with the cocoa until very, very fine. In a medium bowl, stir the ground chocolate mixture together with the flour and allspice and set aside.

3. In a large mixing bowl, whisk the egg yolks with ½ cup of the sugar until light and fluffy, then whisk in the oil and vanilla. Put the egg whites in the bowl of a stand mixer, add the vinegar and salt, and beat until the whites are very light and fluffy. With the mixer still running, stream in the remaining ¼ cup sugar and continue whipping until the egg whites hold stiff peaks and are very smooth and glossy.

4. Fold one third of the egg whites and half of the ground chocolate mixture into the bowl with the yolks. Fold in another third of the whites with the remaining chocolate mixture, then fold in the last third of the whites to make a light, fluffy batter.

5. Transfer the batter to the prepared cake pan and bake just until the cake springs

back when pressed lightly in the center, about 30 minutes. Allow the cake to cool in the pan for 20 minutes. Turn the cooled cake upside down onto a larger pan or directly onto a serving platter, and peel away the baker's parchment.

6. Coat the cake with the chocolate glaze, then drizzle the sugar glaze over the surface. Run a knife through the glazes to create a web pattern.

★

ORCAS ISLAND WHITE CHOCOLATE CHEESECAKE

My friend Christina Orchid used to serve this cake at her eponymous restaurant on Orcas Island; I learned to make it when my friend Kate Wisniewski left Christina's to work with me at a place called Café Bissett on nearby San Juan Island. Even though it is dense, sweet, and almost impossibly rich, it somehow gives the illusion of lightness, especially when it's served with a handful of fresh-picked blackberries piled on the plate.

MAKES ONE 10-INCH CAKE, SERVING 12 TO 16

For the Cake

2 cups chocolate wafer cookies or chocolate sablés, crushed

¼ cup (½ stick) unsalted butter, melted

¼ teaspoon ground cinnamon

2 pounds (four 8-ounce packages) cream cheese

1 cup sugar

4 whole eggs

1 egg yolk

2 tablespoons flour

1 pound white chocolate, melted

1 tablespoon vanilla extract

For the Topping

1 cup sour cream

2 tablespoons white crème de cacao

3 tablespoons sugar

Fresh blackberries as an accompaniment (optional)

1. Preheat the oven to 325°F. Combine the chocolate cookie crumbs, melted butter, and cinnamon. Press the mixture into the bottom of a 10-inch springform pan and set aside.

2. With an electric mixer, beat the cream cheese and sugar until smooth. Add the eggs and egg yolk, one at a time, mixing well after every addition. Stir in the flour, melted white chocolate, and vanilla extract.

3. Pour the batter over the cookie crumb crust, and wrap the bottom of the cake pan in a piece of aluminum foil. Put the foil-wrapped pan in a larger baking pan or roasting pan and pour boiling water into the larger pan to reach about 1 inch up the side of the foil-wrapped cake pan.

4. Bake the cake in its hot water bath until it is lightly browned and beginning to crack on top, about 1 hour and 15 minutes.

5. Combine the sour cream, crème de cacao, and sugar and pour the mixture over the hot cheesecake. Turn off the oven and return the cake to the oven. Let the cheesecake rest in the oven for 15 minutes or so to allow the topping to set. Refrigerate the cake for several hours or overnight before attempting to slice it. Serve the cake cold, with ripe blackberries on the side, if desired.

★

INDIVIDUAL BAKED ALASKAS

According to Marion Cunningham in The Fannie Farmer Cookbook, *this dessert was invented by a physicist around the year 1800. Because it's insulated by sponge cake below and meringue on top, the center of the dessert stays frozen in the heat of the oven. To further protect the ice cream from melting, place the cake on a sheet of baker's parchment on top of a board before baking. (The wooden board will not conduct heat the way a baking sheet will.) Although the dessert has nothing whatsoever to do with the state of Alaska, it is popular there. On board Holland America Cruise Lines, the thousands of passengers who tour the state each summer are awarded a spectacle of flaming baked Alaska delivered by a parade of smiling waiters in the formal dining room on every cruise.*

MAKES 8 SERVINGS

For the Cakes

Cocoa Sponge Cake (pages 311–12)
Chocolate Ganache (page 323)

1 quart homemade or quality store-bought chocolate ice cream, or any flavor you prefer

For the Meringue

6 egg whites (¾ cup)
½ teaspoon salt
½ teaspoon freshly squeezed lemon juice
¾ cup sugar

1. Bake the sponge cake, turn it out of the pan onto a cooling rack, and cool it completely. Spread the ganache over the cooled cake, and chill.

2. Select a board that will fit in the freezer and in the oven (I use a sawed-off cedar shake), and line it with baker's parchment. Cut the chilled sponge cake into 8 squares. Arrange the squares at least 2 inches apart on the paper-lined board, and top each cake with a ½-cup scoop of chocolate ice cream. Keep the prepared cakes in the freezer until ready to bake.

3. Preheat the oven to 450°F and make the meringue. In the bowl of an electric mixer, whip the egg whites with the salt and lemon juice on high speed until they are light and fluffy. With the motor still running, stream in the sugar and continue beating until the egg whites form a very stiff meringue.

4. Transfer the meringue to a pastry bag (if no pastry bag is available, use a zipper-lock bag with a ½-inch wedge snipped from one corner). Pipe it onto the cakes

and ice cream in a decorative pattern. (I make even stripes of meringue running from the bottom of the cakes to the center of the top.) Take care to cover the ice cream thoroughly.

5. Bake the meringue-covered cakes until they are lightly browned, about 5 minutes. Transfer to serving plates and serve at once, while the ice cream is still frozen inside.

Frostings and Glazes

★
VANILLA LOVER'S FROSTING

I have always been inclined to believe that vanilla is even more romantic than chocolate. This is the quintessential vanilla frosting for a layer cake, for cupcakes, or for sugar cookies. If you can find it, vanilla bean paste is easier to work with than whole vanilla beans.

MAKES ABOUT 3 CUPS, ENOUGH TO FROST A 9-INCH 2-LAYER CAKE

½ cup heavy cream

1 vanilla bean, split lengthwise and scraped to free the seeds, or 1 tablespoon vanilla bean paste

½ cup (1 stick) unsalted butter

5 cups powdered sugar

1. Warm the cream in a saucepan over medium heat and stir in the split vanilla bean or vanilla bean paste. When the cream is very hot, almost boiling, lift out the vanilla pod if using a whole vanilla

bean, and scrape it with the dull side of a knife; stir any pulp and seeds clinging to the knife back into the cream. Remove the pan from the heat and stir in the butter.

2. Measure the powdered sugar into a large mixing bowl and stir in the vanilla cream. Continue stirring until the frosting is smooth and spreadable. Pipe or spread onto the cooled cake.

★
CHOCOLATE AND COFFEE FROSTING

A touch of bitterness in the frosting makes it as compelling for grown-ups as it is for kids.

MAKES ABOUT 3 CUPS, ENOUGH TO FROST A 9-INCH 2-LAYER CAKE

¼ cup (½ stick) unsalted butter

4½ ounces unsweetened chocolate

½ cup plus 1 or 2 tablespoons coffee

5 cups powdered sugar

1. Warm the butter and chocolate with the coffee in a small saucepan over medium heat, stirring constantly until the chocolate is almost melted. Remove the pan from the heat and continue stirring until the chocolate is completely melted.

2. Measure the powdered sugar into a large mixing bowl and stir in the melted butter mixture. Continue stirring until the frosting is smooth and spreadable. Pipe or spread onto the cooled cake.

⭐

NAVEL ORANGE FROSTING

The bright, tart flavor and fragrance of orange zest and orange juice offset the cloying sweetness of the powdered sugar in this frosting.

MAKES ABOUT 3 CUPS, ENOUGH TO
FROST A 9-INCH 2-LAYER CAKE

½ cup (1 stick) unsalted butter

1 tablespoon freshly grated orange zest

½ cup freshly squeezed orange juice

5 cups powdered sugar

1. Melt the butter in a saucepan over medium heat and whisk in the orange zest and orange juice.

2. Measure the powdered sugar into a large mixing bowl and stir in the melted butter mixture. Continue stirring until the frosting is smooth and spreadable. Pipe or spread onto the cooled cake.

⭐

CREAM CHEESE FROSTING

A little whipped cream folded into this cream cheese frosting makes it a bit lighter than more traditional versions, which are made with butter.

MAKES ABOUT 2 CUPS

One 8-ounce package cream cheese

1 ¼ cups powdered sugar

1 teaspoon vanilla extract

⅓ cup heavy cream, whipped to soft peaks

1. Soften the cream cheese by whipping it in an electric mixer with the powdered sugar and vanilla.

2. Stir in half of the whipped cream to lighten it up, then fold in the rest of the whipped cream. Keep cold until serving time.

⭐

FLUFFY WHITE ICING

This frosting is mandatory for Aunt Lois' Coconut Cake (page 305), but it also serves as an excellent topper for Cocoa Sponge Cake (pages 311–12).

MAKES ABOUT 3 CUPS, ENOUGH TO
FROST A 9-INCH 2-LAYER CAKE

1 cup sugar

⅓ cup water

⅓ cup light corn syrup

3 egg whites

1 teaspoon vinegar or freshly squeezed lemon juice

½ teaspoon salt

1 teaspoon vanilla extract

1. In a fairly large saucepan over high heat, stir the sugar, water, and corn syrup until the mixture comes to a vigorous boil. Watch closely so it doesn't boil over. Reduce the heat to the lowest setting and cook, without stirring, for 3 minutes.

2. While the syrup is cooking, whip the egg whites with the vinegar and salt on high speed in the bowl of an electric mixer until they just start to hold soft peaks. With the motor running, stream in the hot syrup and continue whipping until the frosting is very smooth and glossy. Stir in the vanilla extract and spread over the cooled cake layers.

CHOCOLATE GANACHE

Chocolate ganache can be used as a simple glaze or whipped to make a softer frosting. Layered between cakes or cookies and other fillings such as chocolate mousse or ice cream, it becomes a kind of barrier, keeping the cake or cookie dry. It can also be used as the filling for chocolate truffles.

MAKES 2 CUPS

1 cup heavy cream

8 ounces (about 1½ cups) bittersweet chocolate, chopped into ⅛-inch bits

1. In a small saucepan over medium-high heat, warm the cream until it is steaming hot, almost boiling. Remove from the heat.

2. Stir the chocolate into the hot cream and continue stirring until the chocolate is melted and the mixture is smooth.

VANILLA GLAZE

Plain muffins or a cake will soar under an elegant and diaphanous layer of this simple coating of sugar.

MAKES ⅓ CUP

1 cup powdered sugar

1 tablespoon milk

1 teaspoon vanilla extract

Pinch of salt

Whisk all of the ingredients together in a small mixing bowl.

LEMON (OR ORANGE) GLAZE

Use this simple citrus glaze for scones or sugar cookies warm from the oven, or for Lemon Chiffon Cake (pages 312–13).

MAKES 1 CUP

2 cups powdered sugar

1 teaspoon freshly grated lemon (or orange) zest

¼ cup freshly squeezed lemon (or orange) juice

1 teaspoon vanilla extract

In a medium bowl, stir together the powdered sugar, orange zest, orange juice, and vanilla extract. Drizzle the mixture over hot scones or cake and allow to stand for 5 minutes, or until the glaze hardens.

★
CHOCOLATE GLAZE
OR "MAGIC SHELL"

Poured over ice cream, this glaze hardens instantly to make a crisp chocolate shell. Poured over cake, the glaze takes a while to firm up, but a little time in the refrigerator speeds the process.

MAKES 1 CUP

1 cup (6 ounces) semisweet chocolate chips

2 tablespoons canola oil

Put the chocolate chips and oil in a small saucepan over medium heat and stir until the chips are almost melted. Remove the pan from the heat and stir until smooth.

★
ROYAL SUGAR GLAZE

This is a good glaze for cookies. It hardens as it cools and remains shiny. It also works well for piping highlights onto cakes that are covered with a smooth layer of chocolate glaze or other frosting.

MAKES ½ CUP

¾ cup powdered sugar

2 tablespoons egg white, or as needed

Put the powdered sugar and egg white in a small bowl and stir until smooth.

★
SWEET AND SOUR
CREAM TOPPING

At Canlis, a mixture of sweet and sour cream was served with fresh strawberries. As chef, I found other ways to apply this delicious topping. It became an element of one of my signature desserts, Crisp Meringues with Summer Berries (pages 341–42).

MAKES ABOUT 3 CUPS

1 cup sour cream

¼ cup powdered sugar

2 tablespoons triple sec or other orange liqueur

1 teaspoon freshly squeezed lemon juice

1 cup heavy cream, whipped

Stir the sour cream, powdered sugar, triple sec, and lemon juice into the whipped cream until well combined.

chapter 15

CRISPS, COBBLERS, AND BETTIES
Old-Fashioned Apple or Blackberry Crisp
Spring Betty
Easier Than Pie Summer Apple Betty
Brentwood Peach Cobbler

FRUIT PIES
Butter Pastry for a Double-Crust Pie
Blue Ribbon Peach or Blueberry Pie
Banana Cream Pie

TARTS
Pastry Shell for a 10-inch Tart
Orange Sunshine Tart
Elegant Chocolate Tart
Rhubarb and Ginger Meringue Tart
Peak of the Season Strawberry Tart

GALETTES
Pastry for a Galette
Fresh Fig and Almond Galette
Dried Plum and Walnut Galette

MORE FRUIT DESSERTS
Apples Baked in Pastry
Crisp Meringues with Summer Berries
Strawberries Brulée
All-American Shortcake Stars

PIES & TARTS

Pies & Tarts

Once, on a magical summer evening, I ate dinner in a peach orchard at Frog Hollow Farm in Brentwood, California. The long, long table, which was covered in white tablecloths, was set for a hundred people, and it stood in dappled shade under the fluttering leaves of the peach trees. The trees themselves stood in rows that went on as far as the eye could see. The peaches were ripe, and in the 90-degree heat, they gave off a gently intoxicating scent.

My "date" was Marion Cunningham of *Fannie Farmer Cookbook* fame; she sat opposite me at the table, and Alice Waters from Chez Panisse was seated to my right. In spite of the intimidating company, the warm evening was magically relaxed and the smell of peaches permeated the air. Now, whenever I smell ripened peaches, I remember that night.

But too often, I encounter peaches that have no smell whatsoever. Growers generally pluck their fruit while it's still hard, because the rigors of standard packing and shipping operations would destroy fully ripened fruit. Farmer Al Courchesne of Frog Hollow Farm and a few other like-minded farmers up and down the coast take special pains to allow their fruit to ripen on the trees, and while it does command a higher price, it is worth it. Certainly, I have never had better peaches than the ones grown there.

It may sound unnecessary or redundant to point this out, but fruit desserts, from the simplest to the most elaborate ones, depend on the quality of the fruit with which they are made. But this notion is actually fairly revolutionary. An entire generation of cooks grew up believing that a good cook "could make anything taste good." In fact, I once heard Marion Cunningham bestow that very line of praise upon a mutually loved colleague.

When Alice Waters opened Chez Panisse in 1971 and insisted on the very best produce, some people thought she was fighting a losing battle. The approach for so long had been to make do with whatever was available that to actually try to affect the quality of the ingredients themselves seemed almost like cheating. "That's not cooking, Alice," trilled Julia Child in the early 1980s, "it's shopping."

And yet it was an emphasis on quality ingredients, handled with extreme care, that eventually distinguished West Coast cooking and ultimately New American cooking from the old guard. Sure, it's important to have the skills to transform simple ingredients into interesting things to eat, but to some degree those skills are wasted if the ingredients are not as good as they should be.

Summer fruit desserts fall into several categories. One of those categories is "pie." A fruit pie can have one crust or two. If it's a pot pie, the single crust can be baked on top. If a fruit filling is served inside a single crust, the dessert may become a tart. A galette is a fruit tart that is baked free-form, without a pie plate or a tart pan.

Various other baked-in-the-pan fruit desserts occupy a region of deliciously blurred boundaries that encompasses betties, cobblers, and crisps. To the knowledgeable home baker, each of these desserts is unique, and distinctions here are worth making. While all fruit desserts should include bubbling hot, well-cooked fruit beneath a buttered topping, the nature of the topping is different in each case.

The topping for a crisp should indeed be crisp. Crisps have a higher ratio of sugar than other baked dessert toppings. Cobbler toppings have less sugar and a softer texture; they're like biscuits on top and dumplings underneath because the fruit juices poach the dough. A betty is distinguished from the other two by the use of buttered breadcrumbs in place of dough.

Beyond the realm of pies, tarts, and baked-in-the-pan fruit desserts are various other fruit desserts that should not be overlooked. Fruit can be served under a layer of cream and burnt sugar (see Strawberries Brulée, page 342) or in shortcake.

But don't be afraid to present perfectly ripe fruit au naturel. One of the most enjoyable desserts I have ever had was a selection of tiny, sweet clementines and dark, sticky dates served without flourish in a simple copper bowl after lunch at Chez Panisse in Berkeley, California. And some of the most enthusiastic praise I have ever received for any dessert I've prepared was for a bowl of perfectly ripe and well-chilled cherries garnished with nothing more than fresh cherry leaves, presented after an elaborate five-course dinner on a warm summer evening.

Crisps, Cobblers, and Betties

OLD-FASHIONED APPLE OR BLACKBERRY CRISP

Anyone who enjoys homemade crusty fruit desserts but is intimidated by pie making should take heart; this recipe allows one to make a delectable dessert with a minimum of fuss. A food processor does give the topping a better texture, but if no food processor is available, the ingredients can simply be combined in a mixing bowl. The technique owes something to a recipe for Willie's Crisp that I learned from my friend and fellow cookbook author Sharon Kramis. Instead of cutting butter into the dry ingredients, as in a traditional crisp, she drizzles melted butter over the top to make the topping crispier.

MAKES 6 TO 8 SERVINGS

For the Topping

½ cup unbleached white flour

1 cup quick-cooking oatmeal

¾ cup brown sugar

1 teaspoon baking powder

1 teaspoon kosher salt, or ½ teaspoon table salt

I egg

½ cup (I stick) unsalted butter, melted

For the Filling

4 medium apples, peeled, cored, and sliced, or 6 cups fresh or frozen blackberries

½ cup sugar

I or 2 tablespoons cornstarch

I teaspoon ground cinnamon

Heavy cream or plain yogurt as an accompaniment

1. Preheat the oven to 375°F and butter a 2-quart oval baking dish or an 8-inch square baking dish.

2. Put the flour, oatmeal, brown sugar, baking powder, and salt in the work bowl of a food processor or in a large mixing bowl and pulse the motor or whisk to combine the dry ingredients thoroughly. Beat the egg with a fork, then gradually incorporate it into the oatmeal mixture.

3. Pile the apple slices or blackberries into the baking dish and toss with the sugar, cornstarch, and cinnamon. Use I tablespoon cornstarch with apples or 2 tablespoons with blackberries.

4. Scatter the oat mixture evenly over the top of the fruit. Drizzle the melted butter evenly over the top.

5. Bake until the topping is golden brown, about 40 minutes. Serve warm with a pitcher of heavy cream or a bowl of plain yogurt passed separately.

★
SPRING BETTY

This dessert can be baked in a single larger pan, but on a nice spring day—think Easter or Mother's Day—it seems more appropriate to present it in individual serving dishes with a bowl of Sweet and Sour Cream Topping (page 324) passed separately. For an interesting variation, consider using cornbread crumbs made from Skillet Cornbread (page 294) in place of the fresh white breadcrumbs.

MAKES 6 SERVINGS

For the Filling

2 pounds rhubarb, trimmed and cut into I-inch slices

I cup sugar

I pint red ripe strawberries

For the Topping

2½ cups fresh white breadcrumbs or cornbread crumbs

I teaspoon ground cinnamon

½ cup (I stick) unsalted butter

Sweet and Sour Cream Topping (page 324; optional)

1. Preheat the oven to 375°F and butter 6 individual 8-ounce baking dishes or ovenproof bowls.

2. In a large nonreactive (enameled or stainless steel) saucepan, stir the rhubarb with the sugar until the rhubarb releases some of its juice and the sugar dissolves,

about 5 minutes. Continue cooking, without stirring, until the rhubarb is soft, about 5 minutes more.

3. Trim the crowns from the strawberries and cut each trimmed strawberry into 2 or 3 slices from top to bottom. Stir the strawberries into the cooked rhubarb and distribute the mixture evenly among the baking dishes.

4. Pile the breadcrumbs into a large bowl and sprinkle on the cinnamon. Melt the butter in a small saucepan over medium-high heat and when it begins to sizzle and brown, pour it over the crumbs. Distribute the buttered crumb mixture evenly over the rhubarb and strawberry mixture and bake until the crumb layer is well browned and the filling is bubbling through, about 40 minutes. Serve hot with Sweet and Sour Cream Topping.

★

EASIER THAN PIE SUMMER APPLE BETTY

Juicy summer apples, the first ones to ripen, are generally a little less flavorful than later-ripening varieties, and they are not good keepers. They are best gathered and used as soon as they begin to fall from the trees. I like to cook them into applesauce or bake them under breadcrumbs for this easy summer dessert. Look Ma, no pastry!

MAKES 6 SERVINGS

6 medium (about 3 pounds) summer apples

1 cup sugar

¼ cup freshly squeezed lemon juice

2½ cups fresh white breadcrumbs

1 teaspoon ground cinnamon

½ cup (1 stick) unsalted butter

1. Preheat the oven to 350°F. Butter a 1-quart oval baking dish or a pie plate.

2. Peel the apples and cut the sides away from the core to leave the core behind. Cut the apple pieces into thin slices and pile them in a large bowl with the sugar and lemon juice.

3. Pile the breadcrumbs into a medium bowl and sprinkle the cinnamon over them. Melt the butter in a small saucepan over medium-high heat, and when it begins to sizzle and brown, pour it over the crumbs.

4. Put half the buttered breadcrumbs into the buttered baking dish. Spread the prepared apples over them, then top with the rest of the breadcrumbs. Bake until well browned, about 40 minutes. Serve hot.

★

BRENTWOOD PEACH COBBLER

If a picture is worth a thousand words, then the smell of peaches under a browned and buttery layer of dough is a short novel about coming home. I don't like to insert the brassy aroma of cinnamon into this gentle dish, but others might, especially if the peaches are less than fully fragrant. Try serving the cobbler with Rose Petal Sorbet (page 363).

For the Filling

6 cups sliced, peeled peaches

½ cup sugar

3 tablespoons cornstarch

2 tablespoons freshly squeezed lemon juice

For the Topping

1 cup unbleached white flour

¼ cup brown sugar

1 teaspoon baking powder

½ teaspoon salt

6 tablespoons cold unsalted butter, cut into 1-inch pieces

¼ cup milk

Yogurt, ice cream, or whipped cream as an accompaniment

1. Preheat the oven to 400°F. In a 1-quart oval ceramic baking dish or a 9-inch pie plate, combine the peaches with the sugar, cornstarch, and lemon juice.

2. Put the flour, brown sugar, baking powder, and salt in a medium mixing bowl or in the work bowl of a food processor and process or whisk to combine. Add the butter and work it into the flour until the mixture resembles crumbs.

3. Add the milk all at ounce and process or stir just until the mixture comes together to form a soft dough. Do not

overmix. Use a tablespoon or a 1-ounce scoop to dollop the dough over the fruit.

4. Bake until the fruit is boiling under the cobbler topping and the topping is golden brown, about 35 minutes. Serve hot with yogurt, ice cream, or whipped cream.

Fruit Pies

BUTTER PASTRY FOR A DOUBLE-CRUST PIE

The secrets to butter pastry are cool temperatures and light handling. A food processor does a wonderful job of cutting the butter into the flour, but once the butter is cut into fairly uniform bits, about the size of large BBs or very small peas, it's time to take the mixture out of the machine and use your fingers to work in the cold water just until the mixture comes together to make what Marion Cunningham describes as a "scrappy mass." Do not overwork the pastry or it will lose its delicate, flaky texture and become tough. If you need a single crust, make the full recipe and freeze the other half. It will keep beautifully for at least a month.

MAKES ONE 9-INCH LATTICE-TOP PIE CRUST

2 cups unbleached white flour

1 teaspoon salt

1 cup (2 sticks) cold unsalted butter, cut into bits

⅓ cup cold water

1. Combine the flour, salt, and butter in a food processor or medium mixing bowl

and process or work with a fork until the mixture is crumbly; the butter should be about the size of small peas.

2. If you used a food processor to cut in the butter, transfer the mixture to a medium mixing bowl before adding the water. (The processor would overwork the dough.) Add the water all at once and mix lightly with your fingers until the crumbly mixture is moistened and the mixture comes together to form a scrappy mass; it need not be a smooth ball of dough.

3. Without handling the dough any more than is necessary, divide it in half and press each half into a disk. Wrap in plastic and refrigerate until you're ready to roll it out.

★

BLUE RIBBON PEACH OR BLUEBERRY PIE

A pie I baked following this recipe really did win a blue ribbon once at the San Juan County Fair in Friday Harbor, Washington. Part of what made the pie so good was the all-butter crust, which was woven into a lattice pattern on top. But the real secret was the fully ripe peaches I used. I use the exact same formula to make blueberry pie.

MAKES ONE 9-INCH PIE, SERVING 8

Butter pastry for a double-crust pie (pages 330–31)

3 pounds (about 6 medium) ripe peaches, preferably from Frog Hollow Farm, or 3 pints of fresh blueberries or 6 cups frozen blueberries

¾ cup sugar

¼ cup cornstarch

2 tablespoons freshly squeezed lemon juice

1. Prepare the pastry and chill it in the refrigerator while you make the pie filling. Preheat the oven to 400°F.

2. In a large pot over high heat, bring a gallon of water to a full boil. Fill a large mixing bowl with ice water and set aside. Drop the peaches into the boiling water; after 1 minute, use a slotted spoon to lift them out and put them in the ice water. The skins will slip off.

3. Slice the peeled peaches and combine them in a large bowl with the sugar, cornstarch, and lemon juice.

4. Roll one round of the pastry out into a 12-inch circle. Fold the circle into quarters and place the folded pastry in a 9-inch pie pan, with the point of the folds in the center. Unfold the dough and press it into place, letting the excess dough hang over the sides. Put the peach filling into the pastry-lined pie pan.

5. Roll the second piece of dough out into a 12-inch circle and, using a pizza wheel or sharp knife, cut the dough into 1-inch-wide strips. Lay half the strips of dough over the filling and fold every other one back on itself to the left. Starting at

the right edge, lay a strip of dough at a 90-degree angle from the first strips you laid and unfold the strips that were folded back. Fold the strips that were not folded the first time and lay another strip. Repeat this process to create a lattice top over the surface of the pie. Press the edges of the dough around the edges of the pan, and trim off the excess.

6. Put the pie pan on a baking sheet to catch any overflow. Bake until the crust is well browned and the filling is bubbling up between the gaps in the lattice top, 55 to 65 minutes. Cool the pie on a rack for at least an hour before serving, so the juices have time to set.

★

BANANA CREAM PIE

When I was the chef at IslandWood, an environmental learning center near my home on Bainbridge Island, Washington, we fed about a hundred young people three meals a day, every day. The breakfast spread always included fresh bananas, and we inevitably ended up with a superfluity of ripe bananas from time to time. So banana cream pie was featured almost weekly for dessert. If I had not been compelled to make it, I don't think I would have, but once I did, I became a real fan.

MAKES ONE 9-INCH PIE, SERVING 8

Butter pastry for a single-crust pie (pages 330–31) or pastry shell for a 10-inch tart (page 333)

¾ cup sugar

¼ cup cornstarch

½ teaspoon salt

2 eggs

1 cup whole milk

2 tablespoons unsalted butter

2 teaspoons vanilla extract

3 large bananas

1 cup heavy cream

1. Preheat the oven to 400°F. Roll out the pie crust, fit it into the pan, and put a piece of baker's parchment or aluminum foil inside the crust. Fill it with dry beans or rice to keep it from puffing up in the oven, and bake it for 15 minutes, or until golden brown. Cool the crust for 10 minutes before filling.

2. In a large saucepan, whisk together ½ cup of the sugar with the cornstarch and salt. Whisk in the eggs, then the milk. Cook the custard over medium-high heat, stirring constantly, until it begins to boil. Whisk it rapidly once it starts to boil, to prevent the formation of lumps. When the custard has thickened, transfer it quickly out of the pan into a mixing bowl, and stir in the butter and 1 teaspoon of the vanilla. Let the custard cool before filling the pie shell.

3. Put ¾ cup of the custard into the pie shell. Slice the bananas over the surface of the custard, then spread the remaining custard over the bananas and smooth the surface with a pie server.

4. Whip the cream with the remaining ¼ cup sugar and 1 teaspoon vanilla until it holds stiff peaks. Put the whipped cream into a piping bag and pipe 8 big dollops on top of the pie. Keep the pie well chilled until serving time.

Tarts

★

PASTRY SHELL FOR A 10-INCH TART

Tart dough is somewhat more cookielike than pastry for pie. It should be uniformly crumbly, and not necessarily flaky. But it is still important to avoid overworking the dough or the gluten will be developed, rendering the finished pastry tougher than it should be.

MAKES ONE 10-INCH TART SHELL

1 cup unbleached white flour

2 tablespoons powdered sugar

½ teaspoon salt

6 tablespoons (¾ stick) cold, unsalted butter, cut into bits

1 egg, lightly beaten

1. Preheat the oven to 400°F and position one of the racks in the lowest position. In a food processor or a mixing bowl, combine the flour, sugar, and salt. Add the butter and process, or work it into the flour mixture using a fork, until the mixture resembles breadcrumbs.

2. Add the egg to the flour mixture and work the mixture by pulsing the motor of the food processor on and off or by stirring with the fork until the mass just comes together to form a lump of dough.

3. On a smooth floured surface, roll the dough out into a circle about 12 inches in diameter. Fold the circle into quarters, then unfold it into a 2-part 10-inch tart pan and press it into the corners of the pan to make it fit. Line the pastry with a piece of baker's parchment and fill the parchment with rice, beans, or special pie weights so that it will not puff up when it's baked.

4. Bake the tart shell on the bottom rack of the oven until it is golden brown around the edges and almost baked through, about 15 minutes. Remove the parchment and weights.

5. If you plan to bake a filling in the tart shell, pour it directly into the warm, partially baked crust and proceed. If you plan to fill the shell with a precooked filling or with fresh, uncooked fruit, put the partially baked tart shell back in the oven until it is baked through, about 5 minutes more. Cool the fully baked shell before filling.

★

ORANGE SUNSHINE TART

It's hard to believe that two oranges and one lemon add up to eight servings of outrageous citrus flavor, but in this tart they do. *The orange zest and the juice of both fruits are transformed into a smooth, custardlike filling. Serve this tart with Orange and Strawberry Compote (pages 38–39) after a formal dinner or with dollops of whipped Sweet and Sour Cream Topping (page 324) and cups of espresso as an afternoon pick-me-up. Use a rasp-style Microplane grater to take the zest off the citrus fruits.*

MAKES ONE 10-INCH TART, SERVING 8

Pastry shell for a 10-inch tart (page 333), partially baked

4 eggs

1 egg yolk

1 cup sugar

1 tablespoon grated orange zest

1 teaspoon grated lemon zest

¾ cup freshly squeezed orange juice (from 2 medium oranges)

¼ cup freshly squeezed lemon juice (from 1 medium lemon)

1. After partially baking the tart shell, lower the oven temperature to 375°F.

2. While the shell is baking, whisk together the eggs, egg yolk, and sugar in a medium mixing bowl. Then whisk in the orange and lemon zest and juice. Pour the filling into the partially baked shell, put the tart back in the oven, and bake until the filling is barely set, with a slight jiggle in the center, about 25 minutes.

3. Cool the tart completely before attempting to remove it from the pan, at

least 1 hour. Serve at room temperature, or refrigerate and serve chilled.

★

ELEGANT CHOCOLATE TART

This chic and sumptuous dessert looks as if it took considerably more effort and expense than it really did. It is elegant in its simplicity, but this is one of those cases where simple should not be confused with plain. To ensure that the tart has as much chocolate flavor as you want it to have, choose high-quality dark chocolate such as Scharffen Berger Chocolate from Berkeley, California, with at least 70 percent cocoa solids. Be careful not to overbake the tart, or it will lose its velvety smooth texture, and the subtle, volatile compounds that give fine chocolate its charm would evaporate in the oven.

MAKES ONE 10-INCH TART, SERVING 8

Pastry shell for a 10-inch tart (page 333), partially baked

12 ounces high-quality bittersweet chocolate

2 tablespoons unsalted butter

4 eggs

¼ cup brown sugar

2 tablespoons dark rum

1 teaspoon vanilla extract

1. After partially baking the tart shell, lower the oven temperature to 375°F.

2. While the shell is baking, melt the chocolate with the butter in a saucepan over medium heat. (The small amount of water trapped inside the butter may cause the chocolate to seize or bind up into

a dull, fudgelike paste. If this happens, don't worry; just forge ahead.)

3. Meanwhile, put the whole eggs in a bowl full of hot tap water to remove any chill from the refrigerator. (Cold eggs in the filling would cause the chocolate to harden before the eggs could be stirred in.)

4. Break the warm eggs into a large mixing bowl and whisk them with the brown sugar until they are smooth. Whisk in the melted chocolate and butter mixture, then the rum and the vanilla extract. Transfer the filling from the bowl to the partially baked tart shell and bake just until the edges of the filling begin to puff up and the center is barely set, about 12 minutes.

5. Cool the tart completely before attempting to remove it from the pan, at least 1 hour. Serve at room temperature, or refrigerate and serve chilled.

★

RHUBARB AND GINGER MERINGUE TART

The sour-tart flavor of rhubarb is reminiscent of lemon, and over the years, I have tried using it in just about every dish where lemons would be a more conventional choice. One of the most successful experiments was this unbelievably beautiful meringue tart. Although the combination of rhubarb and ginger is an English tradition, the crystallized ginger here seems to bring with it a hint of the Asian kitchen from across the Pacific. Do not use an aluminum saucepan to cook the filling, or the oxalic acid in the rhubarb will react and the filling will

lose its bright color. When piping the meringue onto the tart, make sure it touches the pastry shell on every edge, so it won't shrink inward when it's baked.

MAKES ONE 10-INCH TART, SERVING 8

Pastry shell for a 10-inch tart (page 333), fully baked

For the Filling

1¼ pounds (about 6 stalks) fresh rhubarb, cut into ½-inch slices

¾ cup sugar

¼ cup sliced crystallized ginger

2 tablespoons cornstarch

2 tablespoons water

4 egg yolks

For the Meringue

4 egg whites

1 teaspoon freshly squeezed lemon juice

½ teaspoon salt

½ cup sugar

1. Fully bake the tart shell, following the directions in the recipe. Lower the oven temperature to 375°F.

2. In a large, nonreactive (enameled or stainless steel) saucepan, stir the rhubarb with the sugar and crystallized ginger until the rhubarb releases some of its juice and the sugar dissolves, about 5 minutes. Continue cooking, without stirring, until the rhubarb is soft, about 5 minutes more.

3. In a medium mixing bowl, dissolve the cornstarch in the water, then whisk in the egg yolks. Stir half the cooked rhubarb into the mixing bowl, then transfer the mixture back into the saucepan with the remaining rhubarb and cook until the filling is boiling and thickened, about 3 minutes more.

4. Transfer the cooked filling to the prebaked tart shell.

5. In a clean, dry mixing bowl, preferably the bowl of a stand mixer, whip the egg whites with the lemon juice and salt until they are very light and foamy. Gradually stream in the sugar and continue beating until the meringue is stiff.

6. Pile the meringue into a large plastic food storage bag and cut about ½ inch off one corner of the bag to make an impromptu pastry bag. Pipe the meringue into a shapely and symmetrical pattern over the surface of the rhubarb filling and bake the tart until the meringue is golden brown and set, about 5 minutes.

★

PEAK OF THE SEASON STRAWBERRY TART

A recipe for a tart very similar to this one appeared in my book The Northwest Essentials Cookbook, *but it so perfectly fit the theme of this book that I felt compelled to include it here as well. The secret of this simple dessert lies in the perfection of the ingredients. Wait until the best local strawberries are available, and rush them in from the garden, or home from the farmer's market, and pile them directly onto the tart just before serving. Don't refrigerate the berries or the finished tart unless you have to. The crust can be baked ahead, and the filling can be prepared in advance and kept chilled, but assembly should take place as close to serving time as possible.*

MAKES ONE 10-INCH TART, SERVING 8

Pastry shell for a 10-inch tart (page 333), fully baked

For the Pastry Cream

¾ cup sugar

¼ cup cornstarch

½ teaspoon salt

2 eggs

2 cups half-and-half

2 teaspoons vanilla bean paste, or 1 vanilla bean, split and scraped

2 tablespoons unsalted butter

For the Topping

2 pints strawberries

¼ cup red currant or apple jelly (optional)

1. Fully bake the tart shell, following the directions in the recipe.

2. In a small, heavy saucepan, whisk together the sugar, cornstarch, and salt. Whisk in the eggs and stir until the mixture is perfectly smooth. Stir in the half-and-half and the vanilla bean paste or the scraped vanilla bean.

3. Cook the mixture over medium-high heat, whisking constantly, until the mixture boils. Remove from the heat and stir in the butter. Let the filling cool completely before filling the tart shell.

4. Close to serving time, spread the pasty cream over the bottom of the tart shell. Trim the crowns from the berries and place them, trimmed side down, on the cream. If the berries are not perfectly red and ripe, melt the jelly in a small saucepan over medium heat and brush it over the top of the tart. Serve at once.

Galettes

★

PASTRY FOR A GALETTE

Baked outside the confines of a pie or tart mold, the more casual, free-form galette is somehow more elegant than either of its cousins. It seems at once more rustic but less homey. Perhaps it's simply more modern. The pastry for a galette needs to be flaky like a pie crust but more manageable; a spoonful of sugar and a little more water make the dough easier to work with.

1⅓ cups unbleached white flour

1 tablespoon sugar

½ teaspoon salt

½ cup (1 stick) cold unsalted butter, cut into bits

¼ cup cold water

1. Combine the flour, sugar, salt, and butter in a food processor or large mixing bowl and process or work with a fork until the mixture is crumbly; the butter should be about the size of small peas.

2. Add the water all at once and pulse the food processor on and off or stir with the fork until the mixture comes together to form a ball of dough. Do not overwork the dough.

3. Wrap the dough in plastic and refrigerate until you're ready to prepare the galette.

★

FRESH FIG AND ALMOND GALETTE

When we bought our home on Bainbridge Island, it came with an acre of fruit trees, including three enormous, hundred-year-old fig trees, planted by the people who homesteaded the place at the turn of the last century. The figs are not the familiar brown figs most often seen in farmer's markets and produce sections; they are larger, juicier, and softer. But they do not hold up well, and when they ripen, they must be eaten at once. This tart can be made with any fresh figs.

Pastry for a galette (page 337)

For the Almond Filling

2 cups whole almonds

1 cup sugar

1 egg white

½ teaspoon natural almond extract

½ teaspoon salt

For the Fig Filling

12 fresh figs

½ cup sugar

1 tablespoon freshly squeezed lemon juice

1 teaspoon freshly grated lemon zest

1. Preheat the oven to 400°F. Line a baking sheet with a silicone pan liner or baker's parchment. Prepare the galette pastry, and while it's chilling, prepare the filling.

2. In a food processor, pulverize the almonds with the sugar until they are ground almost as fine as flour. If no food processor is available, grind the nuts through a rotary grater (an old-fashioned cheese grater), then stir in the sugar in a medium mixing bowl. Add the egg white, almond extract, and salt to the almond mixture and pulse the motor on and off or stir in the mixing bowl until the mixture comes together to form a pastelike dough.

3. Sprinkle a countertop with flour and, on the floured surface, roll the galette pastry into a 12-inch circle. Fold the dough into quarters, then unfold it onto the prepared baking sheet.

4. Spread the almond filling in an 8-inch circle in the center of the dough, leaving a 2-inch ring of uncovered dough all around.

5. Trim the stem end off of each fig and cut the figs into quarters lengthwise, then toss the cut figs with the sugar, lemon juice, and lemon zest in a medium mixing bowl. Pile the mixture on top of the almond filling.

6. Fold the uncovered portion of the dough up and over the filling in loose, even pleats, leaving the very center of the filling uncovered.

7. Bake the galette until the fruit is boiling inside the crust and the crust is golden brown, about 30 minutes. Cool on a rack and serve warm or at room temperature.

★

DRIED PLUM AND WALNUT GALETTE

Sometimes when I read a novel I feel compelled to write something myself. And similarly, when I read a cookbook, I am prompted to cook something. As soon as I encountered Paul Bertolli's book, Cooking by Hand, *I was enamored of his insightful essays and meticulous recipes. (Bertolli was a chef who left Chez Panisse to open the acclaimed Olivetto in Berkeley; more* recently, he followed his passion for all things ovine to leave Olivetto and make artisanal salumi.) But as I started cooking from the book, I couldn't help tweaking Bertolli's recipes to make them my own. This gallete was derived from a similar recipe in Bertolli's book, but in my efforts to make it simpler and tailor it to my own family's tastes, I tweaked it so far from the original that it was no longer the same recipe. Still, every time I make it, which is fairly often, I think of Paul Bertolli.

MAKES ONE 9-INCH GALETTE, SERVING 6

Pastry for a galette (page 337)

2 cups walnuts

1 cup sugar

1 egg white

½ teaspoon natural almond extract

½ teaspoon salt

Vanilla Stewed Prunes (page 39)

1. Preheat the oven to 400°F. Line a baking sheet with a silicone pan liner or baker's parchment. Prepare the galette pastry, and while it's chilling, prepare the filling.

2. In a food processor, pulverize the walnuts with the sugar until they are ground almost as fine as flour. If no food processor is available, grind the nuts through a rotary grater (an old-fashioned cheese grater), then stir in the sugar in a medium mixing bowl. Add the egg white, almond extract, and salt; pulse the motor on and off or stir in the mixing bowl until the mixture comes together to form a pastelike dough.

3. Sprinkle a countertop with flour and, on the floured surface, roll the galette pastry into a 12-inch circle. Fold the dough into quarters, then unfold it onto the prepared baking sheet.

4. Spread the walnut filling in an 8-inch circle in the center of the dough, leaving a 2-inch ring of uncovered dough all around.

5. Use a slotted spoon or tongs to lift the cooked prunes out of their syrup and arrange them in a symmetrical pattern on top of the walnut filling. Reserve the syrup in which the prunes were cooked to serve with the galette.

6. Fold the uncovered portion of the dough up and over the filling in loose, even pleats, leaving the very center of the filling uncovered.

7. Bake the galette until the fruit is boiling inside the crust and the crust is golden brown, about 30 minutes. Cool on a rack and serve warm or at room temperature with a drizzle of the reduced vanilla syrup from the prunes.

More Fruit Desserts

⭐

APPLES BAKED IN PASTRY

If I had a signature dessert, this would be it. Apples wrapped in butter pastry used to be called apple dumplings, and they were very popular. But a dumpling to my mind is something else entirely. Dumplings are generally cooked in boiling liquid, and these are baked in a hot oven, where the crust becomes tender on the inside and delicately crisp on the outside.

MAKES 6 SERVINGS

For the Apples and Filling

6 large baking apples

¼ cup (½ stick) unsalted butter, at room temperature

¼ cup brown sugar

1 teaspoon ground cardamom

For the Butter Pastry

2 cups unbleached white flour

1 tablespoon sugar

1 teaspoon salt

6 ounces (¾ cup) cold unsalted butter, cut into 1-inch pieces

⅓ cup cold water

For the Sauce

Peels and cores from 6 apples, chopped

2 cups water, or enough to barely cover the peels and cores

Juice of 1 lemon

1 cup sugar

2 tablespoons vanilla brandy

Apple leaves or mint sprigs, for garnish

1. With a sharp paring knife, peel the apples and remove the cores, leaving the apples whole. Reserve the peels and cores for the jelly sauce.

2. Make the filling. In a small bowl, combine the butter, brown sugar, and cardamom, and fill each cored apple with this mixture.

3. Make the pastry. In a food processor, combine the flour, sugar, and salt. Add the butter and pulse the motor on and off until the mixture resembles crumbs. Add the water all at once and pulse the motor on and off just until the mixture comes together. Transfer the pastry to a well-floured surface and divide into 6 equal parts. Roll each part into a 7-inch circle.

4. Wrap each filled apple with a round of the pastry dough, leaving a small opening at the top. The apples can be wrapped and refrigerated for several hours or overnight before baking and serving.

5. Make the sauce. In a medium saucepan over medium-high heat, cook the apple peels and cores with just enough water to cover until very soft, about 15 minutes. Press the liquid through a strainer into a measuring cup and discard the solids. Pour 1 cup of the liquid into a saucepan and discard the rest. Add the lemon juice,

and over high heat, bring the liquid to a full, rolling boil. Add the sugar to the boiling juice all at once and cook until a small amount of the syrup holds its shape when dropped onto a chilled plate. (A candy thermometer will register 220°F.) Stir in the brandy and keep the sauce at room temperature until serving time. The sauce can be prepared several hours ahead.

6. Preheat the oven to 350°F, and line a baking sheet with baker's parchment. Arrange the apples a few inches apart on the parchment-lined baking sheet and bake until the pastry is golden brown and the apples are fork-tender, 35 to 40 minutes. Serve each apple in a pool of apple jelly sauce with an apple leaf or mint sprig stuck in its top.

★
CRISP MERINGUES WITH SUMMER BERRIES

Topped with a jumble of summer berries, light and delicate meringues become a show-stopping dessert. This recipe is definitely a "restaurant recipe," but with a little advance planning it can be made at home. The crisp meringues need to be baked overnight in a very slow oven. (Some French bakeries actually sell meringues like these already baked and ready to top with anything you like.) Once the meringues are made, you can store them in an airtight container in a cool, dry place for several days. The extra meringues can be served with ice cream, sorbet, or chocolate mousse.

6 large Crisp Meringue Cookies (pages 377–78)
Sweet and Sour Cream Topping (page 324)

For the Fruit Filling

1 pint strawberries
1 pint blueberries
½ pint raspberries
½ pint blackberries
¼ cup plus 6 tablespoons sugar
2 tablespoons freshly squeezed lemon juice
Mint sprigs, for garnish

1. Make the meringues early in the day or several days in advance. Prepare the cream topping and keep it cold until just before serving time.

2. Prepare the fruit filling. Rinse the strawberries, cut off the green tops, and split them in half lengthwise. Remove any stems that may be still attached to the blueberries and rinse. Combine the halved strawberries and rinsed blueberries with the raspberries and blackberries. Gently fold in ¼ cup of the sugar and the lemon juice.

3. Place the meringues on the serving plates and top with a generous ½ cup of the berry mixture. Dollop about ¼ cup of the cream topping on the berries and, with a hot, wet knife, smooth the top to create a flat surface.

4. Light a small butane or propane torch. Working with one plate at a time, sprinkle a tablespoon of sugar over the cream and run the flame of the lit torch over the sugar until it bubbles up and turns brown. Garnish each serving with a sprig of mint, and serve promptly.

★

STRAWBERRIES BRULÉE

This is a berry lover's answer to crème brûlée: Marinated berries are tucked beneath a layer of whipped cream, sealed in turn by a layer of crisp burnt sugar. The best way to make it is to use a tool called a brûlée iron, designed for making crème brûlée. It consists of a metal knob attached to a long handle; you let the knob rest on a hot burner until it's red-hot and then glide the iron over the sugar, burning it without heating the food below. Unfortunately, brulée irons are almost impossible to find. The best alternative is to use a small propane torch, which can be purchased at the hardware store. If neither of these options seems feasible, simply place the dishes under a preheated broiler element and watch them closely. Keep the oven door open so the berries won't heat up underneath the cream.

MAKES 6 SERVINGS

For the Filling

2 pints strawberries, hulled and halved

1 tablespoon freshly squeezed lemon juice

1 tablespoon granulated sugar

For the Topping

½ cup heavy cream

2 tablespoons powdered sugar

1 teaspoon freshly squeezed lemon juice

1 teaspoon vanilla extract

½ cup natural sour cream

About ¼ cup granulated sugar

1. In a small mixing bowl, combine the strawberries, lemon juice, and sugar. Distribute the mixture evenly among six 4-ounce ovenproof dishes.

2. In a separate bowl, whip the cream until it is stiff. Stir in the powdered sugar, lemon juice, and vanilla, then gently fold in the sour cream. Distribute the cream mixture evenly over the berries and, with the straight side of a rubber spatula or a butter knife, flatten the cream on top of the berries.

3. Light a small butane or propane torch. Working with one dish at a time, sprinkle about 2 teaspoons of sugar over the top of the whipped cream mixture and run the flame of the lit torch over the sugar until it bubbles up and turns brown. The sugar will form a thin layer of brown caramel over the surface of the cream. Serve at once.

★
ALL-AMERICAN SHORTCAKE STARS

By a happy coincidence, Independence Day comes at the peak of West Coast berry season. In accordance with the advice of the nation's founding fathers, we like to celebrate by showing the colors of our flag and shooting off fireworks. Red comes from the strawberries, white from whipped cream, and the blue in these star-shaped shortcakes is provided by blueberries. Sparkling big crystals of clear white decorator's sugar on top of the shortcakes before they're baked provide extra fireworks.

MAKES 8 SERVINGS

For the Shortcake Stars

2 cups unbleached flour

2 tablespoons granulated sugar

I tablespoon baking powder

½ teaspoon kosher salt

½ cup (I stick) cold unsalted butter, cut into bits

¾ cup milk

2 tablespoons large-crystal decorating sugar (optional)

For the Berry Filling

3 tablespoons freshly squeezed lemon juice

½ cup granulated sugar

2 pints red, ripe strawberries

2 pints blueberries

For the Topping

2 cups heavy cream

½ cup powdered sugar

I teaspoon vanilla extract

I. Make the shortcake stars. Preheat the oven to 400°F, and line a baking sheet with baker's parchment.

2. In a food processor, combine the flour, sugar, baking powder, and salt. Add the butter and pulse the motor on and off until the mixture is uniformly crumbly. Add the milk all at once and stir or process briefly to form a soft dough.

3. Turn the dough out onto a well-floured surface and knead very lightly; do not overwork the dough or the shortcakes will be tough. Roll the dough out ½ inch thick and, with a star-shaped biscuit cutter, cut the dough into cakes. Press straight down, resisting the urge to twist the cutter. (Twisting the cutter can pinch the edges of the cakes and prevent them from rising freely in the oven.) Arrange the cakes a few inches apart on the prepared baking sheet, sprinkle with decorating sugar, if using, and bake until the tops are lightly browned, 10 to 12 minutes.

4. While the shortcakes are baking, prepare the filling. Put the lemon juice and sugar in a serving bowl. Use a sharp paring knife to trim the crown off each berry, removing as little fruit as possible. Cut the strawberries in half lengthwise, allowing the berries to fall into the bowl as they are cut.

5. Toss the cut strawberries and the blueberries with the lemon juice and

sugar to lightly coat and allow them to stand in the syrup while you whip the cream in a large bowl with the powdered sugar and vanilla. Pile the whipped cream into a zipper-lock bag and then snip off about 1 inch from the corner to create an impromptu piping bag.

6. When the shortcakes are baked, cut each one in half. Put the bottom half of a shortcake on each serving dish. Distribute the berries evenly among the plates, piling them directly onto the warm shortcake halves. Pipe the whipped cream over the berries. Plant the tops of the cakes over the whipped cream at a jaunty angle, and serve at once.

chapter 16

PUDDINGS AND CUSTARDS

A Meaningful Custard
Chocolate Pudding
Flan
West Coast Ambrosia
Chinese Bakery–Style Cream Puffs
Peach or Raspberry Trifle
Four Swallows Tiramisù
Vanilla Crème Brûlée
Panna Cotta
Bread and Butter Pudding
Sticky Toffee Pudding
Persimmon Pudding with Cinnamon Sauce

FROZEN DESSERTS

Real Vanilla Ice Cream
Chocolate Ice Cream
White Chocolate Ice Cream
Pistachio Ice Cream
Raspberry Sorbet
Frozen Yogurt
Coconut Sorbet
Rose Petal Sorbet
Cedar Bough Sorbet
Wild Fennel Sorbet
Frozen Souffléed Oranges
Individual Frozen Strawberry Soufflés

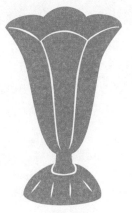

PUDDINGS & FROZEN DESSERTS

Puddings &
Frozen Desserts

In the fall of 1996, I had a peculiar and serendipitous encounter with Chuck Williams, the founder of Williams-Sonoma. I was scheduled to sign copies of my book *In Season: Culinary Adventures of a San Juan Island Chef* at a newly opened Williams Sonoma Cookware store in the University Village shopping center in Seattle. But Williams came to town and offered to sign his books at the store, so my book signing was canceled. On a whim, I decided to go to the store anyway and meet the man who, according to the back flap on the slipcover of one of his books "helped to revolutionize cooking in America."

I am so glad I did. Williams, who must have been 72 or 73 at the time, was charming, erudite, and for the man behind a company with more than two hundred stores and a catalog with a circulation of more than a million, extremely relaxed. He graciously accepted a copy of my book and, after he read it on the plane ride home, sent me a generous note of praise.

Since then, I have paid more attention to the Williams-Sonoma Company, and I have learned a little more about Williams himself. When I asked Thomas Keller, the chef/owner of the French Laundry in Napa Valley and Per Se in New York, who he thought had been the greatest influence on American cooking in our lifetime, Williams' name was the first that came out of his mouth. "I mean, Julia Child told us what to cook," he added quickly, "but Williams gave us the equipment to cook it in."

According to the online encyclopedia Wikipedia, Williams was born in northern Florida in 1915 and moved with his family to California during the Great Depression. The family lived on a date plantation in Palm Springs. When his sister died young as the result of a head injury, his mother moved back to Florida, but Williams stayed to finish school and then moved to Los Angeles.

After World War II, he visited the town of Sonoma, California, was captivated by the town's considerable charm, and moved there in 1947. In 1956, he bought a hardware store in Sonoma and stocked it with the kind of sturdy cookware he had seen on trips to France. Two years later, he moved the store to San Francisco and eventually sold the business to a group of partners, who kept him on as a board member and a creative director.

Not long ago, I was visiting my family in northern Florida, where, like Williams, I was born. Reaching into my mother's cupboard for a coffee cup, I was suddenly and overwhelmingly stricken with the need to possess a custard cup I saw there.

"Mom, can I take this cup home?" I asked impulsively. She looked baffled for a moment and then said yes.

It's a strangely seductive little custard cup. The sole survivor from a set of six or eight, the cup had been a part of my mother's battery of kitchen equipment for as long as I could remember. The inside is white, and the thick white lip of the cup curls out over its plain brown sides in the same way that the pink interior of a conch reveals itself against the brown exterior of that tropical shell.

It was manufactured by the Hall China Company during the 1950s and, according to the family, comes from a little restaurant that my grandfather owned for a short time on Pensacola Bay. My mother must have inherited the custard cups when my grandfather closed the restaurant, about the time I was born. It's intriguing to me that Williams was stocking the shelves in his relocated Williams-Sonoma store in San Francisco, on the other side of the continent, at the same time that my mother was taking these old custard cups home from her father's shuttered restaurant.

The cups seem almost indestructible, and I can't imagine where the rest of them have gone. They couldn't possibly be broken. I imagine one of them being used to rinse out paintbrushes when my sister's kids are working on watercolors, or serving as a manger in a guinea pig cage somewhere, each little cup gone off to find its fortune in the world. In order to see the little cup surrounded by others of its kind, I went to eBay—something I hadn't done before and haven't done since—and ordered a set of similar cups to flesh out the set.

My sister and I used to put chocolate pudding in the cups for after-school snacks. Sometimes, on holidays, we would bake extra pie filling in them for my grandmother, who had for mysterious reasons given up pie but still maintained an appetite for the filling. But their best and highest use—the use for which they were no doubt originally intended—was for baked custard, that most innocent and sublime of all the custard family of desserts.

Properly handled, three simple ingredients—eggs, sugar, and creamy milk—make the silkiest and most satisfying desserts imaginable. Stirred together and cooked on top of the stove, they become a crème anglaise, that most essential of all dessert sauces, which can transform a plain piece of cake or a piece of poached fruit into something memorable—almost meaningful. Baked in the oven, these same ingredients come together to form a thing-in-itself, a whole of such undeniable unity that one wonders how it ever came from separate parts at all.

Because a baked custard is almost too perfect, its simplicity is easily mistaken for plainness, which is, of course, quite a different thing. For this reason, the temptation to doll up a baked custard is almost overwhelming. If the cream were the perfect cream, straight out of a grass-fed Jersey cow stationed in your backyard, if the eggs were the perfect eggs, with glowing yellow yolks standing at attention on top of their whites as soon as the eggs were cracked, and if the sugar were pure maple or perhaps the unrefined, pale straw-colored crystals of turbinado sugar, then these ingredients alone would transcend the ordinariness that threatens a simple dish like this one.

But alas, our cream, even our best organic heavy cream, is sterilized and somewhat insipid compared with what our grandparents enjoyed. Our eggs are too often pale, ghostly reminders of the vibrant things they should be, and our refined white sugar smells sad and sour compared with the caramel and molasses aromas that come from raw sugar. How, then, are we to make a proper baked custard, a custard worthy of the old custard cup I found in my mother's cabinet? We could start by cheating. My mother always added a splash of vanilla extract and a sprinkling of grated nutmeg to the custards. The effect was almost numbing, and I sometimes wondered what it was about baked custard that grown-ups seemed to enjoy.

Then I discovered pots de crème, those baked custards so redolent of chocolate that they render the quality of the cream and eggs moot. In good pots de crème, a velvety texture speaks to the dish's heritage as a variation on basic custard, but the flavor is something altogether different. I had the same epiphany with crème caramel, the baked custard that rides on top of a puddle of melted sugar as long as it bakes and then slips upside down onto the plate in a halo of clear caramel. This is a truly fine dessert, but one that's all about the caramel and hardly about the custard at all. Ditto with crème brûlée. The dishes are good,

but the custard in them is only a component of another kind of experience.

The more I thought about it, the more I wanted to make a straightforward custard that would not have to lean on chocolate or caramel, or anything else to make it flavorful and good. I realized that what I wanted was a custard in which the three simple elements it was made of would shine forth in such a way that I would feel satisfaction with every mouthful. I wanted a custard worthy of the little brown cup. So I sought out the best cream I could get my hands on; some organic, unrefined sugar; and some eggs from my friend Kerrie's happy little flock of chickens. The result was A Meaningful Custard, and the recipe is on page 349.

But the experience of coveting, possessing, and using that custard cup produced more than a good dessert; it launched a series of thoughts not only about custard but about the equipment with which we cook. In the years when my grandfather had his little restaurant, American home cooks had a hard time accessing good kitchen equipment. Following his example, my mother used to shop for certain items at a restaurant supply store.

Then, thanks in no small part to the efforts of Chuck Williams, home cooks had access to sturdy cups, copper pans, and solid mixing bowls, all of the quality that might allow them to survive into another generation, when someone would come along and use them again.

Puddings and Custards

⭐
A MEANINGFUL CUSTARD

The simplicity of baked custard demands that the ingredients be of the very highest quality. Take time to seek out the best cream, eggs, and sugar. Most supermarkets carry organic brands of these basic ingredients, but there are variations between brands. Allow yourself time to compare, and choose the ones you like best.

MAKES 6 SERVINGS

1½ cups organic whole milk

¾ cup organic heavy cream

2 large organic free-range eggs

2 yolks from organic free-range eggs

½ cup organic turbinado sugar or pure maple sugar

¼ teaspoon salt

1 teaspoon vanilla extract (optional)

⅛ teaspoon freshly grated nutmeg, or to taste (optional)

1. Put 6 custard cups in a baking dish, and preheat the oven to 350°F.

2. In a medium saucepan over medium-high heat, stir the milk and cream until the liquid is steaming hot but not boiling.

3. Meanwhile, in a large mixing bowl, whisk together the eggs, egg yolks, sugar, and salt. You may wish to slip in the vanilla and nutmeg as well.

4. Whisk about 2 cups of the steaming hot milk into the egg mixture, then stir all of the egg mixture into the remaining milk in the saucepan. Stir gently until well combined, then transfer the custard to the custard cups.

5. Pour boiling water into the baking dish to reach halfway up the sides of the cups. Cover the cups with aluminum foil and bake just until the custard is set, 25 to 30 minutes. Chill the custard before serving.

⭐
CHOCOLATE PUDDING

If you have never made chocolate pudding from scratch, this will come as a revelation. The smoother the chocolate, the smoother the pudding, so if you can, splurge on high-quality bittersweet chocolate, but a fine casual family dessert can also be made with ordinary semisweet chocolate chips. Extra depth of flavor comes from using brown sugar instead of white and a splash of dark rum along with the vanilla extract.

MAKES 6 SERVINGS

¼ cup cornstarch

½ cup brown sugar

½ teaspoon kosher salt, or ¼ teaspoon table salt

2 eggs

2 cups milk

6 ounces bittersweet chocolate, finely chopped, or 1 cup semisweet chocolate chips

2 tablespoons unsalted butter

I tablespoon dark rum

I teaspoon vanilla extract

Sweetened whipped cream as an accompaniment

I. In a heavy 2-quart saucepan, whisk together the cornstarch, brown sugar, and salt, then whisk in the eggs and beat the mixture until everything is well combined.

2. Stir in the milk and cook the pudding, stirring constantly with a heatproof silicone spatula, over medium-high heat until it is steaming hot and beginning to thicken.

3. Continue cooking, stirring vigorously to prevent the formation of lumps, and when the pudding is thick and beginning to boil, pull it off the heat and stir in the chocolate, butter, rum, and vanilla extract.

4. Distribute the pudding evenly among six 4-ounce custard cups, and chill. Serve cold with a dollop of whipped cream on top of each serving.

★
FLAN

This caramel custard, known in France as crème renversée, might have roots in the Old World, but it has become very well established in the New World as the quintessential Mexican dessert. Caramel poured into the bottom of the dish before the custard goes in becomes sauce when the custard is turned upside down onto a serving plate. A little corn syrup in the cara-

mel sauce prevents the sugar from recrystallizing. It is important to allow the custard to sit for several hours before attempting to turn it out of the dishes, because as it cools, the custard shrinks a tiny bit and releases some of its water into the caramel at the bottom of the dish.

MAKES 6 SERVINGS

For the Caramel Sauce

¾ cup sugar

¼ cup water

I tablespoon corn syrup

For the Custard

2 cups milk

½ cup heavy cream

3 whole eggs

I egg yolk

½ cup sugar

I teaspoon vanilla extract

½ teaspoon kosher salt, or ¼ teaspoon table salt

I. Put 6 custard cups in a baking dish. Preheat the oven to 350°F.

2. Make the caramel sauce. In a small saucepan over high heat, stir the sugar, water, and corn syrup until the mixture comes to a boil. Stop stirring and allow the syrup to cook, swirling the pan occasionally, until the syrup is golden brown.

3. Distribute the sauce evenly among the custard cups. Use extreme caution when doing this; the sauce is very hot.

4. Make the custard. In a medium saucepan over medium-high heat, heat the milk and cream until the mixture is steaming hot, but not boiling.

5. Meanwhile, in a large mixing bowl, whisk together the eggs and egg yolk with the sugar, vanilla, and salt.

6. Whisk about ½ cup of the steaming hot milk into the egg mixture, then stir all of the egg mixture into the remaining milk in the saucepan. Stir gently until the custard ingredients are well combined, then transfer the custard to a large measuring cup with a pouring spout.

7. Pour the custard over the caramel sauce in the custard cups. Pour water into the baking dish to reach halfway up the sides of the cups. Cover the cups with baker's parchment and then with aluminum foil, and bake until the custard is set, 25 to 30 minutes.

8. Cool the custards for several hours or overnight. To remove them from the cups, run a knife around the perimeter of each cup and invert onto a serving plate.

★

WEST COAST AMBROSIA

Ambrosia, the southern kind, can take any number of forms, but every one of them, if it is even remotely authentic, must include coconut and oranges. For the coconut element of this version, we borrowed a coconut custard known as haupia *from a traditional Hawaiian luau and dressed it with fresh, skinless orange segments and bright curls of orange zest.*

MAKES 6 SERVINGS

One 14-ounce can coconut milk

¾ cup sugar

¼ cup cornstarch

½ teaspoon salt

3 large navel oranges

1. In a medium saucepan over medium-high heat, whisk together the coconut milk, sugar, cornstarch, and salt. Cook, stirring constantly, until the mixture boils. Continue stirring and cooking at a boil for 1 minute. Remove from the heat, and transfer the coconut custard to the empty coconut milk can. Chill the custard until set, about 1 hour.

2. With a zester, remove the colorful outer rind from the oranges in long, thin curls, and put them in a bowl. With a sharp knife, cut the top and bottom from each orange, then cut away the white part of the peel or pith and remove any bits of white membrane left behind.

3. Working over the bowl with the zester in order to catch the juice, remove each section by cutting along the membranes on either side. Cut in toward the center and then out. When all the segments have been removed, squeeze the remaining membrane over the bowl to collect any extra juice. (The sections can be prepared several hours in advance.)

4. To serve, dip the can of coconut custard in warm water, then slide the custard out and slice it into 6 portions. Serve each portion in a shallow bowl or on a dessert plate with spoonfuls of the orange mixture.

★

CHINESE BAKERY–STYLE CREAM PUFFS

Cream puffs are much easier than a novice cook might imagine. The dough is boiled and then eggs are stirred in before it's baked. In the oven, the puffs rise majestically, and they can be filled with all sorts of things. In Chinese bakeries, they are often filled with a sweet vanilla–flavored pastry cream, which is essentially a form of pudding.

MAKES 2 DOZEN SMALL PUFFS

For the Puffs

¾ cup water

½ teaspoon salt

¼ cup (½ stick) unsalted butter

¾ cup unbleached white flour

3 eggs

For the Filling

¾ cup sugar

¼ cup cornstarch

½ teaspoon salt

I whole egg

I egg yolk

I cup whole milk

Half a vanilla bean, split and scraped, or I tablespoon vanilla bean paste

2 tablespoons unsalted butter

I teaspoon vanilla extract

1. Line a baking sheet with a silicone pan liner or baker's parchment, and preheat the oven to 375°F. If the oven has a convection option, use it.

2. In a medium saucepan over medium-high heat, bring the water, salt, and butter to a rolling boil. Whisk in the flour and cook, stirring, until the paste leaves the sides of the pan, about I minute.

3. Pull the pan off the heat and beat in the eggs, one at a time, beating well after each addition. Pipe the mixture through a large pastry bag or spoon it onto the parchment-lined baking sheet in I-inch rounds. Bake the rounds until they are puffed and golden brown and fairly dry inside, about 20 minutes.

4. Prepare the filling. Put the sugar, cornstarch, and salt in a medium, heavy saucepan and whisk in the egg and yolk. When the mixture is smooth, whisk in

the milk and vanilla bean or vanilla bean paste.

5. Cook the custard over medium-high heat, stirring constantly, until it begins to boil. Whisk it rapidly once it begins to boil to prevent the formation of lumps.

6. When the custard has thickened, transfer it quickly out of the pot into a clean mixing bowl to halt the cooking process. Stir in the butter and vanilla extract. Chill the custard completely before using it as a filling for cream puffs.

7. Put the custard into a pastry bag fitted with a metal tip and use the tip to poke a hole in the side of each puff. Squeeze a generous tablespoon or so of the custard into each puff. If you do not have a pastry bag with a metal tip, use a paring knife to cut a small opening into each puff and pile the custard into a large plastic food storage bag, snip about ¼ inch off the corner, and squeeze the custard into the puffs.

★
PEACH OR RASPBERRY TRIFLE

Like many other West Coast cooks, I make a lot of jams and preserves. These are great on toast, but one can only eat so much toast. Sometimes it's fun to show off the sparkling fruit in an elegant dessert like this one. Ordinarily, trifle is a layered dessert composed of sponge cake splashed with sweet wine or sherry, fruit, and custard. For a family dessert, I omit the alcohol component and serve it in glasses. The cake in this version is a jelly roll, sliced and pressed against the sides of the trifle dish to show off the colorful fruit filling.

MAKES 8 SERVINGS

For the Jelly Roll

Classic Sponge Cake (pages 310–11), baked in a 11- by 17-inch jelly roll pan

1 cup Perfect Peach Preserves (page 398) or Backyard Raspberry Jam (page 397)

For the Filling

½ cup sugar

¼ cup cornstarch

½ teaspoon kosher salt, or ¼ teaspoon table salt

2 medium eggs

2 cups half-and-half

1 tablespoon vanilla bean paste, or half a vanilla bean, split and scraped

3 tablespoons unsalted butter, cut into 1-inch bits

2 teaspoons vanilla extract

1. Prepare the sponge cake and spread the cooled cake with the peach preserves or raspberry jam. Roll the cake from one short end to the other to make a log and, with a serrated knife, slice the log into 8 rounds.

2. Line a glass trifle dish or a clear glass bowl with the pinwheel rounds cut from the jelly roll, pressing the jam-filled cake against the sides of the dish.

3. Prepare the filling. Put the sugar, cornstarch, and salt in a medium, heavy saucepan and whisk in the eggs. When the mixture is smooth, whisk in the half-and-half and vanilla bean paste or vanilla bean.

4. Cook the custard over medium-high heat, stirring constantly, until it begins to boil. Whisk it rapidly once it begins to boil to prevent the formation of lumps.

5. When the custard has thickened, transfer it quickly out of the pot into a clean mixing bowl to halt the cooking process. Stir in the butter and vanilla. Cool the custard to room temperature and then pour it into the trifle bowl. Chill before serving.

★

FOUR SWALLOWS TIRAMISÙ

When my consulting work landed me in the kitchen of a small Italian restaurant called Four Swallows for six weeks, I developed this recipe for the Italian classic that's traditionally made with lady finger cookies. I made it with a sponge cake instead of the cookies, and I added a small amount of gelatin to the zabaglione filling so that it could be cut into neat portions. I love the smooth texture of this filling; it reminds me of panna cotta.

MAKES 12 SERVINGS

For the Cake

Classic Sponge Cake (pages 310–11), baked in a 9- by 12-inch pan

For the Syrup

¾ cup espresso or strong brewed coffee

¼ cup brandy

¾ cup sugar

I tablespoon vanilla extract

For the Mascarpone Filling

I cup heavy cream

I tablespoon (one ½-ounce packet) unflavored gelatin

I pound (2 cups) fresh mascarpone cheese

4 eggs

¾ cup sugar

For the Garnish

8 ounces bittersweet chocolate, chopped

I tablespoon unsweetened cocoa powder

I. Turn the sponge cake out onto a larger baking sheet lined with baker's parchment, whisk together the ingredients for the syrup, and pour the syrup over the cake. Chill the soaked cake, uncovered, while you prepare the filling.

2. Make the filling. Line a 9- by 12-inch baking dish with plastic wrap. Put the cream in a small saucepan and sprinkle the gelatin over the top. Allow the gelatin to soften undisturbed for a few minutes, then warm the cream over medium heat, stirring gently, until the gelatin is completely dissolved, about 5 minutes. Stir the mascarpone into the warm cream mixture and set aside. In the bowl of an

electric mixer, whip the eggs with the sugar until very light and fluffy, about 5 minutes, then fold the beaten egg mixture into the cream and mascarpone mixture. Transfer the filling to the pan lined with plastic wrap. Chill the filling until it is completely set, at least 1 hour.

3. Make the garnish. Put the chocolate and cocoa in a food processor and grind it until it is uniformly crumbly. If no food processor is available, grind the chocolate in a rotary hand grinder.

4. Assemble the dessert by laying the syrup-soaked sponge cake on top of the chilled filling; invert the cake and the filling onto a serving platter and peel away the plastic wrap. Sprinkle the ground chocolate over the surface of the filling. Serve in squares, or use a biscuit cutter to cut rounds.

★
VANILLA CRÈME BRÛLÉE

French for "burnt cream," crème brûlée is one of those desserts that entered the American lexicon through the restaurant kitchen door. But it happens to be fairly simple to reproduce at home. Choose organic cream, such as Organic Valley brand or heavy cream with a fat content of at least 40 percent. Don't try to cut calories by using half-and-half or anything less than real cream. If you can't risk the heavy cream, opt for a different dessert altogether. It is best made in shallow ramekins instead of deep custard cups.

MAKES 6 SERVINGS

3 cups heavy cream

1 vanilla bean, split and scraped, or 1 tablespoon vanilla bean paste

6 egg yolks

¾ cup sugar

6 tablespoons turbinado sugar or Sugar in the Raw

1. Preheat the oven to 300°F and place six 6-ounce ramekins in a 9- by 13-inch baking pan.

2. In a medium, heavy saucepan over medium heat, stir the heavy cream and the split vanilla bean with a heatproof silicone spatula or a wooden spoon and cook until the mixture is steaming hot and just beginning to boil.

3. Meanwhile, whisk the egg yolks and sugar in a large mixing bowl until the mixture is pale yellow and slightly foamy. Remove the cream mixture from the heat and stir about ½ cup of the hot cream into the egg yolk mixture. Transfer the egg mixture to the pot with the remaining cream and stir gently until smooth. If you used a vanilla bean instead of vanilla bean paste, remove the bean, scrape any clinging pulp or seeds into the custard, and discard the pod.

4. Distribute the custard evenly among the 6 ramekins, and pour enough water into the pan to reach halfway up the sides of the ramekins. Bake the custards in the

hot water bath until the top is set but the custards are still slightly jiggly, about 35 minutes. Remove the custards from the oven and let cool. They can be baked ahead and refrigerated for several hours or, if covered in plastic, overnight.

5. Just before serving, working with one custard at a time, sprinkle I tablespoon of the turbinado sugar over the top and carefully run the flame of a propane torch over it to melt and caramelize the sugar. Serve at once.

★

PANNA COTTA

It's fascinating the way desserts come in and out of fashion. Just as crème brûlée swept restaurants in the 1980s, so panna cotta took us by storm in the '90s. With gelatin as a thickening agent, panna cotta (Italian for "cooked cream") is impossibly smooth. Serve it plain with a pile of fresh berries or with a purée of tart raspberries or strawberries.

MAKES 4 SERVINGS

2 tablespoons cold water

I tablespoon (one ½-ounce packet) unflavored gelatin

2 cups heavy cream

½ cup sugar

½ teaspoon salt

I. Have four 4-ounce ramekins ready to fill. Put them on a small tray that fits in the refrigerator.

2. Put the cold water in a small saucepan and sprinkle the gelatin over it. Allow the gelatin to soften in the water for about 5 minutes, then stir in the heavy cream, sugar, and salt.

3. Cook, stirring constantly, over medium heat until the sugar and gelatin are completely dissolved. Remove from the heat. Distribute the cream mixture evenly among the cups and chill until set, about 2 hours.

4. To serve, dip the cups in hot water, then loosen the custard with the tip of a knife and turn each one out onto a serving plate.

★

BREAD AND BUTTER PUDDING

With the resurgence of artisanal bread baking during the last years of the twentieth century came the return of stale bread. Factory-made breads have additives that keep them soft longer, but traditionally made breads grow hard pretty quickly; hence the need for recipes like this one that render day-old bread delectable. Bread pudding is comfort food at its best. This version, with a crackly coat of cinnamon and sugar on top, is reminiscent of cinnamon toast.

MAKES 8 SERVINGS

½ cup (I stick) unsalted butter

6 cups cubed day-old white bread or rolls (I-inch cubes)

4 eggs

I cup brown sugar

1½ cups milk

1 teaspoon vanilla extract

¼ cup granulated sugar

2 tablespoons ground cinnamon

1. Preheat the oven to 375°F. Melt the butter in a small saucepan over medium heat, then take it off the heat and let it cool down a little. Put the melted butter in an 8-inch square baking dish and pile in the bread cubes. Toss the cubes in the butter to lightly coat them.

2. In a medium mixing bowl, beat the eggs with the brown sugar until smooth. Whisk in the milk and vanilla, and pour the mixture over the buttered bread cubes. Press the bread with the back of a spoon to encourage absorption of the egg mixture; the bread should be barely covered.

3. Stir the granulated sugar and cinnamon together in a small bowl and sprinkle the mixture over the pudding. Bake until the pudding is set, about 30 minutes. Serve warm or cold.

★

STICKY TOFFEE PUDDING

Originally associated with England's Lake District, this warm date pudding with brown sugar (toffee) sauce is right at home on the West Coast, especially in California, where dates are grown extensively. I like to use large, slightly more expensive medjool dates, usually sold in the bulk section of better grocery stores; they are softer and moister than the smaller, drier varieties sold in bags in the baking aisle of most supermarkets.

MAKES 8 SERVINGS

For the Pudding

1 cup (about 8 large) pitted dates

1 cup water

6 tablespoons (¾ stick) unsalted butter

2 cups all-purpose flour

¾ cup granulated sugar

1 teaspoon baking powder

1 teaspoon baking soda

1 scant teaspoon kosher salt

1 egg

1 teaspoon vanilla extract

For the Sauce

6 tablespoons (¾ stick) unsalted butter

¾ cup heavy cream

1½ cups dark brown sugar

1 scant teaspoon kosher salt, or to taste

2 tablespoons dark rum, or to taste

1 teaspoon vanilla extract

Whipped cream as an accompaniment (optional)

1. Preheat the oven to 350°F. Butter eight 6-ounce ramekins and place them in a baking pan.

2. Place the dates in a medium saucepan with the water; bring to a boil, reduce the heat to low, and allow the dates to simmer

until they fall apart, about 2 minutes. Whisk in the butter and let the mixture cool to room temperature.

3. In a large mixing bowl, whisk together the flour, sugar, baking powder, baking soda, and salt.

4. Whisk the egg and vanilla extract into the cooled, cooked date mixture, then add this wet mixture all at once to the dry mixture and stir gently to combine. (Do not overmix.)

5. Distribute the mixture evenly among the buttered ramekins and pour boiling water in the baking pan to reach halfway up the sides of the ramekins. Bake until the puddings are just set, about 15 minutes.

6. While the puddings are in the oven, make the sauce. Stir the butter, cream, brown sugar, and salt in a small saucepan over medium heat until the butter melts and the sauce comes to a boil. Reduce the heat to low and simmer for a few minutes. Stir in the rum and vanilla and keep the sauce warm until the puddings come out of the oven.

7. To serve, invert the puddings onto individual serving plates and ladle the sauce over them. Serve warm, with whipped cream passed separately if desired.

★

PERSIMMON PUDDING WITH CINNAMON SAUCE

Like almost every other fruit under the sun, persimmons thrive in California. I originally developed this recipe for a Thanksgiving dinner, where it did not go over very well; everyone missed the traditional pumpkin pie too much to appreciate the novelty of the persimmon pudding. But I treasure the recipe anyway because it is so peculiar, so old-fashioned, and so homey. When it's served without any prior expectations, any time other than Thanksgiving, shimmering under a translucent layer of cinnamon sauce, it's always a hit. Make sure the persimmons are ripe.

MAKES 6 SERVINGS

For the Pudding

3 large, very ripe, soft persimmons (about 1 pound), stemmed

½ cup (1 stick) unsalted butter, melted

⅔ cup brown sugar

1 large egg, beaten

½ cup milk

1 teaspoon vanilla extract

1 cup sifted unbleached white flour

2 teaspoons baking soda

1 teaspoon ground cinnamon

½ teaspoon kosher salt, or ¼ teaspoon table salt

For the Sauce

¼ cup cornstarch

¼ cup ground cinnamon

1½ cups water

½ cup (1 stick) unsalted butter

1 teaspoon vanilla extract

1. Preheat the oven to 350°F. Butter six 4-ounce ramekins and place them in a baking pan.

2. Peel the persimmons and put them in a food processor or force them through a food mill to purée them. Stir or process in the melted butter, brown sugar, egg, milk, and vanilla extract.

3. In a medium mixing bowl, whisk together the flour, baking soda, cinnamon, and salt.

4. With a silicone spatula or wooden spoon, scrape the persimmon and egg mixture all at once into the mixing bowl with the dry ingredients and stir gently to combine. (Do not overmix.)

5. Distribute the mixture evenly among the buttered ramekins and pour boiling water into the baking pan to reach halfway up the sides of the ramekins. Bake until the puddings are just set, about 15 minutes.

6. While the puddings are in the oven, make the sauce. Whisk together the cornstarch and cinnamon in a medium saucepan, then whisk in the water and cook the mixture over medium heat until the sauce is boiling and thickened. Take the sauce off the stove, stir in the butter and vanilla, and keep the sauce warm until the puddings come out of the oven.

7. To serve, invert the puddings onto individual serving plates and ladle the hot cinnamon sauce over them.

Frozen Desserts

★

REAL VANILLA ICE CREAM

Vanilla is so incredibly nuanced, so ethereal a thing, that it's hard to imagine how it ever became synonymous with "plain." In fact, it's anything but plain; it's quite fancy. The orchid plant from which the vanilla bean pod is gathered is native to Central America, where, in nature, one species of bee is required to pollinate the short-lived flower in order for it to make a bean. The flavoring was enjoyed for centuries in very small amounts before anyone discovered the secret of hand-pollinating the flowers so that a reliable crop could be harvested. Think of this as a master recipe with variations. Instead of a vanilla bean, you can flavor the milk custard on which this ice cream is based with ½ cup of crushed coffee beans, dried rose petals, or lavender flowers, strained out before the hot milk is stirred into the egg yolks.

MAKES ABOUT 6 CUPS

2 cups milk

1 vanilla bean, split and scraped

6 egg yolks

1 cup sugar

2 cups chilled heavy cream

1. Put the milk in a medium saucepan with the split and scraped vanilla bean and heat until it is steaming hot but not boiling, about 180°F. (For the variations, steep the coffee beans or flowers in the hot milk for several minutes until the desired intensity of flavor is achieved, then strain them out before proceeding.)

2. Whip the egg yolks and sugar in a medium mixing bowl until smooth. Stir about a third of the hot milk into the egg yolk and sugar mixture, then stir the mixture into the pot with the remaining milk. Stir with a heatproof silicone spatula or wooden spoon until the custard is steaming hot and slightly thickened.

3. Chill the custard for several hours or overnight.

4. Stir the heavy cream into the custard and freeze in an ice cream maker according to the manufacturer's instructions.

★

CHOCOLATE ICE CREAM

Made with quality bittersweet chocolate, this ice cream reminds me of how Fudgsicles taste in my memory—quite unlike the way they taste in real life. The ice cream is dense and toothsome, the flavor intense and genuine.

MAKES ABOUT 6 CUPS

2 cups milk

6 egg yolks

⅔ cup sugar

6 ounces bittersweet chocolate, chopped

1 teaspoon vanilla extract

⅛ teaspoon salt

2 cups chilled heavy cream

1. Put the milk in a medium saucepan and heat until it is steaming hot but not boiling, about 180°F.

2. Whip the egg yolks and sugar in a medium mixing bowl until smooth. Stir about a third of the hot milk into the egg yolk and sugar mixture, then stir the mixture into the pot with the remaining milk. Stir with a heatproof silicone spatula or wooden spoon until the custard is steaming hot and slightly thickened.

3. Stir the chopped chocolate into the hot custard. Add the vanilla and salt and continue stirring until the mixture is smooth. Chill the custard for several hours or overnight.

4. Stir the heavy cream into the chocolate custard and freeze in an ice cream maker according to the manufacturer's instructions.

WHITE CHOCOLATE ICE CREAM

Technically speaking, white chocolate is not chocolate at all, because it contains no cocoa solids. But quality white chocolate is made with pure cocoa butter, milk, and sugar to form a sublimely decadent confection. Since white chocolate, with its high concentration of cocoa butter, is already incredibly rich, there is no need to add heavy cream to this custard base. The flavor, reminiscent of sweetened condensed milk, is irresistible, and the texture is unbelievable.

MAKES ABOUT 4 CUPS

2 cups milk

6 egg yolks

½ cup plus 2 tablespoons sugar

8 ounces white chocolate, chopped

1. Put the milk in a medium saucepan and heat until it is steaming hot but not boiling, about 180°F on a thermometer.

2. Whip the egg yolks and sugar in a medium mixing bowl until smooth. Stir about a third of the hot milk into the egg yolk and sugar mixture, then stir the mixture into the pot with the remaining milk. Stir with a heatproof silicone spatula or wooden spoon until the custard is steaming hot and slightly thickened.

3. Stir the chopped white chocolate into the hot custard. Chill the custard for several hours or overnight, then freeze in an ice cream maker according to the manufacturer's instructions.

PISTACHIO ICE CREAM

So few things in the world of desserts are green that pistachios are welcomed with considerable enthusiasm by pastry chefs looking for a little fresh spring color. This ice cream would be delicious, though, no matter what color it was.

MAKES ABOUT 6 CUPS

1 cup sugar

1 cup unsalted shelled pistachios

2 cups milk

6 egg yolks

¼ teaspoon almond extract

⅛ teaspoon salt

2 cups chilled heavy cream

1. Put ½ cup of the sugar with the pistachios in the work bowl of a food processor and process until the pistachios are very finely ground. Heat the milk in a medium saucepan until it is steaming hot but not boiling, about 180°F.

2. With the motor running, pour the milk into the food processor over the ground pistachio mixture and run the motor for a few seconds to combine the ingredients. Strain the mixture back into the pan and discard any solids.

3. Put the remaining ½ cup sugar in a medium mixing bowl with the egg yolks and whisk until smooth. Stir about a third of the hot pistachio milk into the egg yolk and sugar mixture, then stir the mixture

into the pot with the remaining pistachio milk. With a heatproof silicone spatula or wooden spoon stir in the almond extract and salt, and continue stirring until the custard is steaming hot and slightly thickened. Chill the custard for several hours or overnight.

4. Stir the heavy cream into the pistachio custard and freeze in an ice cream maker according to the manufacturer's instructions.

★ RASPBERRY SORBET

When I worked at a café in Friday Harbor in the mid-1980s, my friend and coworker Kate Wisniewski and I used to collaborate on the menu. We made our own frozen desserts and kept the little Italian ice cream maker working overtime all summer long. One of our favorite desserts, and one that I can never make without thinking of Kate, was a triple-layered, quiescently frozen confection that we called neo-Neapolitan: a layer of dark chocolate ice cream, a layer of white chocolate ice cream, and a layer of raspberry sorbet stacked in a pan, frozen together, and then unmolded and sliced into 1-inch-thick slabs that were only marginally reminiscent of the relatively insipid blocks of ice cream we ate at birthday parties as children. Made from fragrant local raspberries still warm from the sunshine in which they were picked, the raspberry sorbet went like this. You can make blackberry sorbet in the same way.

4 half-pints fresh raspberries

2 tablespoons raspberry vinegar or freshly squeezed lemon juice

1 cup sugar

1 cup water

1. Put the raspberries, vinegar, sugar, and water in a blender and purée until smooth. Pass the purée through a fine strainer to remove the seeds.

2. Put the purée in an ice cream maker and freeze according to the manufacturer's instructions. If no ice cream maker is available, the sorbet can be partially frozen in a shallow baking dish and then whisked and refrozen until firm.

★ FROZEN YOGURT

With apple pie or berry cobblers, homemade frozen yogurt is a good alternative to ice cream. Nutritional considerations aside, its smooth, light texture and tangy flavor make it more interesting.

MAKES ABOUT 2 CUPS

2 cups homemade or plain, natural yogurt such as Nancy's

½ cup sugar

1. Stir the yogurt and sugar together and freeze in an ice cream maker until firm.

2. Transfer the frozen yogurt to an airtight container and store in the freezer. Serve with fruit desserts.

⭐ COCONUT SORBET

The incredibly smooth texture and the deep, full flavor of this sorbet are a testimony to the late Buckminster Fuller's theory of synergy. Together, the simple ingredients are greater than the sum of their parts. Be sure to choose a high quality coconut milk and do not use pre-sweetened coconut cream. I like to present this sorbet in the lacey coconut cookies I call Coconut Chihuly Cookie Shell (page 373). It also makes a nice accompaniment to cakes and fruit desserts.

MAKES ABOUT 3 CUPS

One 13.5-ounce can coconut milk

¾ cup water

¾ cup sugar

1. Stir the coconut milk, water, and sugar together and freeze in an ice cream freezer until firm.

2. Transfer the sorbet to an airtight container and store in the freezer. Serve with fruit desserts.

⭐ ROSE PETAL SORBET

For this sorbet, choose either dried rose petals, available in the bulk herb section of many supermarkets, or fragrant unsprayed rose petals from your own garden. Dried petals are more concentrated, so if you use fresh petals, you'll need to use about three times as much as you would dried. The sorbet can be served with cookies as a dessert or as an intermezzo between seafood and meat courses to cleanse the palate.

MAKES 4 CUPS

½ cup dried rose petals, or 1½ cups fresh

2 cups boiling water

1 cup sugar

One 2-ounce package powdered pectin

¼ cup freshly squeezed lemon juice

1½ cups cold water

Fresh rose petals, for garnish

1. Put the rose petals in a large, heatproof measuring cup and pour the boiling water over them. Allow the mixture to stand for 5 minutes. Meanwhile, in a medium mixing bowl, stir together the sugar and pectin.

2. Strain the rose petal "tea" into the sugar and pectin, and stir until the pectin and sugar are completely dissolved. Stir in the lemon juice and cold water.

3. Chill the mixture in the refrigerator, then freeze the chilled mixture in an ice cream maker according to the manufacturer's instructions. Serve in chilled glasses with a few fresh rose petals for garnish.

★
CEDAR BOUGH SORBET

Cedar boughs, when crushed, have a very pleasant aroma, a smell that is less like that of other conifers than it is like bay leaves. Walking along one day, enjoying the fragrance of a crushed sprig of cedar, it occurred to me that it might have culinary potential. I love serving this sorbet as a refresher between a fish course and the meat dish at an important dinner.

MAKES 4 CUPS

½ cup fresh green cedar boughs, stemmed and chopped

2 cups boiling water

1 cup sugar

One 2-ounce package powdered pectin

¼ cup freshly squeezed lemon juice

1½ cups cold water

Fresh cedar sprigs, for garnish

1. Put the cedar boughs in a large, heatproof measuring cup and pour the boiling water over them. Allow the mixture to stand for 5 minutes. Meanwhile, in a medium mixing bowl, stir together the sugar and pectin.

2. Strain the cedar bough "tea" into the sugar and pectin, and stir until the pectin and sugar are completely dissolved. Stir in the lemon juice and cold water.

3. Chill the mixture in the refrigerator, then freeze the chilled mixture in an ice cream maker according to the manufacturer's instructions. Serve in chilled glasses with a few fresh cedar sprigs for garnish.

★
WILD FENNEL SORBET

The tall, lacy branches of wild fennel, crowned with umbrella-shaped seed clusters, are a fixture in many Pacific Northwest gardens. Their refreshing scent and delicate licoricelike flavor are perfectly captured in this rejuvenating sorbet.

MAKES 4 CUPS

1 cup fresh fennel leaves, chopped

1 tablespoon dried fennel seeds, crushed

2 cups boiling water

1 cup sugar

One 2-ounce package powdered pectin

¼ cup freshly squeezed lemon juice

2 cups cold water

Fennel blossoms or sprigs, for garnish

1. Put the fennel leaves and seeds in a large, heatproof measuring cup and pour the boiling water over them. Allow the mixture to stand for 5 minutes. Meanwhile, in a medium mixing bowl, stir together the sugar and pectin.

2. Strain the fennel "tea" into the sugar and pectin and stir until the pectin and sugar are completely dissolved. Stir in the lemon juice and cold water.

3. Chill the mixture in the refrigerator, then freeze the chilled mixture in

an ice cream maker according to the manufacturer's instructions. Serve in chilled glasses with fennel blossoms or sprigs for garnish.

★ FROZEN SOUFFLÉED ORANGES

Making these frozen delights is a little time-consuming but not difficult. One of my son's friends, who was only 12 at the time, made them without much adult supervision at all. And all the work can be done in advance, so they make a perfect dessert for company. We like to use all organic ingredients in this dessert because the flavors are more vibrant.

MAKES 6 SERVINGS

3 large navel oranges

1 cup chilled heavy cream, preferably organic

1 cup egg (about 8 large) whites

1 teaspoon freshly squeezed lemon juice

½ teaspoon kosher salt

1 cup sugar

⅓ cup water

Paper leaves, orange leaves, or other nontoxic, bright green leaves

Powdered sugar, for dusting

1. Trim about ⅛ inch from the top and bottom of each orange. Put the trimmings in a food processor and grind until very fine. Cut each orange in half along the equator and carve out the pulp, to form small bowls. Put the pulp in the food processor and process until fairly smooth. Pass the purée through a strainer to remove bits of peel and pith, and chill.

2. Wrap a piece of parchment paper around each half-orange to make a collar rising about 2 inches above the lip of each "bowl," and secure the parchment with freezer tape or masking tape. Freeze the prepared oranges. In a medium chilled bowl, whip the cream until stiff and set aside.

3. In the bowl of an electric mixer, combine the egg whites, lemon juice, and salt and whip until the mixture holds soft peaks. While the egg whites are whipping, stir together the sugar and water in a small saucepan and set over high heat to boil. Cook the syrup for 3 minutes, or until a drop of the syrup holds together to form a soft ball when dropped into cold water. With the mixer motor running, stream the hot syrup into the egg whites and continue beating until the whites are stiff.

4. Chill the egg white mixture by placing the bowl in a larger bowl filled with ice water and stirring occasionally for 10 minutes. Fold the reserved orange pulp into the egg white mixture, then fold in the whipped cream. Pile the mixture into a large pastry bag and pipe it into the frozen orange "bowls." Freeze the oranges for several hours or overnight.

5. To serve, peel away the parchment to expose the filling of each orange. Place the oranges on plates lined with leaves, and sprinkle the tops with powdered sugar.

★
INDIVIDUAL FROZEN STRAWBERRY SOUFFLÉS

Once you grasp the technique of making frozen soufflés, consider the possibilities for variations. Any summer fruit will make a fine frozen soufflé. If you use blackberries or raspberries, strain out the seeds, and if you use peaches, dip them in boiling water first then slip off their skins. In winter, use citrus fruits. A decadent cook might even forgo the fruit altogether and opt instead for a quarter pound of bittersweet chocolate melted in a half a cup of strong coffee. As long as the fruit—or chocolate—you start with is good, the frozen soufflé will be good, and you will have a grand time in the kitchen. Best of all, you will feel like you have really made something.

MAKES 6 SOUFFLÉS

2 pints strawberries

1 cup (about 8 large) egg whites

1 teaspoon freshly squeezed lemon juice

1 teaspoon salt

1 cup sugar

⅓ cup water

1 cup chilled heavy cream

Powdered sugar, for dusting

1. Cut 6 pieces of parchment 3 inches high by 12 inches long. Wrap the parchment around six 4-ounce soufflé dishes. Put the wrapped dishes on a tray in the freezer.

2. Hull and mash the strawberries. Use a blender, food mill, or food processor to make a smooth purée, and then put the purée in a large mixing bowl in the freezer.

3. Put the egg whites, lemon juice, and salt in the bowl of an electric mixer and whisk briefly to combine. Put the sugar and water in a small saucepan over high heat and stir until the mixture is just beginning to boil. While the syrup is boiling, whip the egg whites until they hold stiff peaks. Gradually stream the boiling syrup into the egg whites, whipping all the while. The hot syrup will give the meringue extra loft.

4. Put the bowl of meringue inside a bigger bowl filled with ice. Every few minutes, give the meringue a stir with a rubber spatula to release the heat.

5. While the meringue is cooling, whip the heavy cream until it is stiff.

6. Fold the cooled meringue into the puréed strawberries, and then fold in the whipped cream. Pack the soufflé mixture into the chilled soufflé dishes and freeze for 4 hours, or until completely firm. At serving time, remove the paper collars and sprinkle the soufflés with powdered sugar.

chapter 17

DROP COOKIES
Chocolate Chip Cookies
California Crazin' Cookies
Bainbridge Island Molasses Cookies
Snickerdoodles
Coconut Chihuly Cookie Shell

ROLLED COOKIES
"Sugar in the Raw" Cookie Leaves
Gingerbread People or Snowflakes

HAND-FORMED COOKIES
Biscotti
Chocolate Crinkle Cookies with Cocoa Nibs

FLOURLESS COOKIES
Crisp Meringue Cookies
Chocolate Walnut "Moonscape" Cookies
Walnut Macaroons with Smoked Salt
Almond Macaroons
Basler Brunsli

SHORTBREAD COOKIES
Poppy Seed Dream Cookies
Whole Wheat Shortbread Cookies
Crystallized Ginger Shortbread
Lime and Pecan Shortbread Snowballs

BROWNIES AND BAR COOKIES
Homemade Graham Crackers
Paradise Date Bars
Debbi's Chocolate Brownies
Great Grandma Gonser's Lemon Bars

MORE LITTLE TREATS
Enlightened Baklava

CANDIES
Candied Orange Peel
Chocolate Truffles with Cocoa Nibs
Homemade Marshmallows
Pumpkin Seed Brittle

COOKIES & CANDIES

Cookies & Candies

In these trying times, it would seem natural to crave what we used to call "comfort food," but the whole notion is fraught with challenges. For one thing, what comforts the goose doesn't necessarily comfort the gander. Some like it hot, and all that.

Of course, there are so-called universal comfort foods: those mashed potato, meat loaf, and pudding-driven menus that are supposed to conjure up the good old days. But honestly, how long can anyone put up with all that?

I realize that if food is to pacify or console us, it needs to evoke either childhood, with its attendant charms, or a sense of nostalgia based not necessarily on the nursery but on the era of peace and plenty when America was on top of the world. But to be genuinely comforting, food must be really tempting and good. Unfortunately, nursery foods are uniformly soft, and the great Pax Americana coincided with the 1950s and '60s, decades when the blandest and most highly processed foods imaginable were standard fare. Macaroni and cheese? Please. What's a poor solace-seeking cook to do?

Personally, I bake cookies. It started toward the end of September 2001, when I found myself flipping through the old *Betty Crocker's Cooky Book*, published in 1963 by General Mills.

A little wedge of timeless Americana, the original *Cooky Book* lived within easy reach of the baking cupboard in the house where I grew up. My sister grabbed the family copy when she set up housekeeping, and I latched on to another copy that I found in a used bookstore during my college days. With "more than 450 recipes, dozens of appetizing full-color photographs, and many how-to-do-it sketches," the old spiral-bound classic has been a guilty pleasure for as long as I can remember.

Strangely enough, the *Cooky Book* was also a part of my wife Betsy's childhood, and now her family copy shares shelf space with my copy. I like her copy more than mine because it's authentically stained with what must be remnants of cookie dough from days gone by, and the recipes are annotated in curlicue pencil script by Betsy's sister Kathleen. "Real easy for a quick treat," she wrote above a recipe for Butterscotch Brownies; "Frost with thin chocolate icing, page 141," she scrawled in the margin beside a recipe for Toffee Squares.

In ball-point pen, Molasses Jumbles are dismissed as "Kinda dry," but a pencil was used to scribble in an afterthought. "Look at how dryness can be corrected at beginning of book." These girls took their cookies seriously. I can relate. I learned a lot from the tips in the front of that book: how to measure flour correctly, why to preheat the oven, and the importance of following directions. I wanted my cookies to look exactly like the ones in the book.

These days, I find most of the cookies in the old cookie book more academic than appetizing. I am much more interested in cookies that taste great than in ones that look just like the pictures in any book. But in a way, Betty is still with me—at least as much as she could ever be. I was not very surprised to discover as an adult that Betty Crocker never lived; she was a fabrication conceived by the marketing team at General Mills, and her name and countenance serve as a figurehead for a team of bakers and authors at the company headquarters in Minneapolis.

If Betty Crocker were a real person, I think she would be a lot like Marion Cunningham. It's easy to think of Marion as America's grandmother; when you meet her in person, she radiates a kind of strength that makes others feel safe in her presence. Her sunny Californian disposition and slightly befuddled persona belie a steel trap of a mind and a tough as nails constitution typical of that generation of Americans who weathered the Great Depression, World War II, and the various other calamities that constituted the late, great twentieth century.

"If I had it to do all over," she insists, "I guess I would have been an auto mechanic." She was, in fact, in charge of a garage during World War II, "when all the men were off at war," she told me as I rode with her in her Lexus from her hometown of Walnut Creek to Frog Hollow Peach Farm in nearby Brentwood, California. "I changed oil, changed tires, and filled tanks with gasoline, and I loved it."

"I love cars," she said. "I used to drive only Jaguars; I leased a new one every year. They gave me a lot of trouble—mechanical trouble—but I loved them anyway. I liked the way they looked. I guess it's kind of like falling in love with the wrong man: You don't really pay attention to the faults, you just enjoy them."

Cunningham's husband may or may not have been the wrong man. He did discourage her from pursuing her dream of owning her own garage. Instead, as the dutiful twentieth-century wife and mother, Cunningham stayed at home and cooked. "I baked so many cupcakes for the PTA," she writes in her book *Lost Recipes*, "that if I had sold them instead, I could have retired some time ago a millionaire."

During the 1970s, Cunningham took an excursion to Seaside, Oregon, to take a cooking class from the late James Beard, with whom she immediately established a great rapport. No romance was involved (Beard wasn't interested in women that way), but the two had a definite chemistry, and before long, Beard asked Cunningham to assist him in teaching cooking classes and to travel with him on consulting jobs. When Beard's editor, the legendary Judith Jones at Alfred A. Knopf, was looking for someone to re-create Fannie Merritt Farmer's *Boston Cooking School Cookbook*, Beard suggested Cunningham.

"I had never written a cookbook before," recalls Cunningham, "and I never paid attention in school; I wasn't even sure I

COOKIES & CANDIES

369

could write. But Jim thought I could do it and Judith thought I could, so I just did it." The book was an instant classic. Lists of equipment, a glossary of ingredients, and sensible menu advice bolstered a collection of 1,990 smart, well-tested recipes.

The *Fannie Farmer Baking Book* followed soon after. "I always thought of myself as a baker," confided Cunningham. Then came a little classic called *The Breakfast Book*, the first of five non–Fannie Farmer books that established "Marion Cunningham" as a brand and an icon as significant to the twenty-first century as "Fannie Farmer" was to the twentieth.

Having learned to cook a lot of things by following her terse, perfectly clear instructions, I find it impossible sometimes not to channel her when I write recipes of my own. So this chapter is for you, Marion.

Drop Cookies

★

CHOCOLATE CHIP COOKIES

Since chocolate chip cookies are really at their best when they are very fresh—preferably still warm from the oven— it's a good idea to bake only as many cookies as you plan to serve within the hour. Some of the cookie dough can be formed into balls and frozen, and then baked later. For an elegant twist on the old standard, cookies and milk, I like to make these cookies double sized and serve them with a chilled milk custard. To make, follow the recipe for Panna Cotta on page 356, using milk instead of cream.

MAKES 2 DOZEN COOKIES

1 cup (2 sticks) unsalted butter

1½ cups brown sugar

1 whole egg

1 egg yolk

1 teaspoon vanilla extract

2 cups unbleached white flour

½ teaspoon salt

2 cups bittersweet chocolate chips

1 cup chopped nuts (optional)

1. Preheat the oven to 350°F and line 2 large baking sheets with baker's parchment. Soften the butter: Cut all the butter into 1-inch chunks. Melt half of it in a small saucepan and put the rest in the bowl of a stand mixer. Pour the melted butter over the cold butter and beat until all the butter is smooth and creamy.

2. Add the brown sugar and continue beating until the mixture is light and fluffy. Add the egg, egg yolk, and vanilla, and beat until completely incorporated into the butter and sugar mixture.

3. In a separate, large mixing bowl, whisk together the flour and salt. Scrape the butter, sugar, and egg mixture into the flour mixture, add the chocolate chips and nuts, if desired, and fold gently with a rubber spatula just until the mixture comes together to form a soft dough.

4. Scoop the cookie dough into 1-inch balls and place the cookies on the baking sheets. Chill the cookies on the pans for

10 minutes. The unbaked cookies can be frozen, stored in zipper-lock bags, and baked later. Bake until the cookies spread and begin to brown around the edges, about 10 minutes for chilled dough, 14 minutes for frozen dough. The cookies should be crisp on the outside and chewy on the inside.

★

CALIFORNIA CRAZIN' COOKIES

Based on a recipe from the back of the oatmeal box, these cookies derive extra goodness from dried cranberries and sliced almonds.

MAKES 3 DOZEN COOKIES

2½ cups unbleached white flour

1½ teaspoons baking powder

1 teaspoon baking soda

½ teaspoon salt

2½ cups rolled oats

2 cups sliced almonds, toasted

2 cups dried cranberries

1½ cups (3 sticks) unsalted butter, softened to room temperature

3 cups brown sugar

2 eggs

1 teaspoon vanilla extract

1. Preheat the oven to 350°F. Line 2 baking sheets with baker's parchment and spray the sheets with nonstick spray.

2. In a large mixing bowl, whisk together the flour, baking powder, baking soda, and salt. Stir in the oats, nuts, and dried cranberries.

3. In the bowl of an electric mixer, cream together the butter and brown sugar. Add the eggs and vanilla extract. Stir this mixture into the flour mixture until moistened.

4. Drop tablespoons of the batter onto the prepared baking sheets, leaving 1 inch between them, and bake until the cookies are medium brown and the edges are set but the centers are still soft, about 8 minutes. Halfway through the baking time, switch the pans around to put the bottom pan on top and the top pan on the bottom.

5. Cool the cookies on the pans before attempting to move them.

★

BAINBRIDGE ISLAND MOLASSES COOKIES

Soft and chewy on the inside and slightly crisp on the surface, these dark and spicy cookies evoke the era of cookie jars and grandmothers in the kitchen.

MAKES 2 DOZEN LARGE COOKIES

2 cups unbleached white flour

2 teaspoons baking soda

1 tablespoon ground ginger

1 teaspoon ground cinnamon

½ teaspoon ground allspice

½ teaspoon salt

½ cup (1 stick) unsalted butter, softened to room temperature

1 cup sugar

1 medium whole egg

1 egg yolk

⅓ cup molasses

Turbinado sugar, for rolling

1. Preheat the oven to 350°F and line 2 baking sheets with baker's parchment. In a medium mixing bowl, whisk together the flour, baking soda, ginger, cinnamon, allspice, and salt; set aside.

2. In a medium mixing bowl or the bowl of an electric mixer, cream the butter and sugar, then stir in the egg, egg yolk, and molasses. Add the dry ingredients all at once to the butter mixture, and stir just until combined. Divide the dough into 4 pieces and chill.

3. Roll each piece of chilled dough into 6 balls, and roll the balls in turbinado sugar. Arrange the balls on the baking sheets, allowing plenty of room for the cookies to spread, and bake until the cookies are crackled and lightly browned, about 8 minutes.

★
SNICKERDOODLES

These old-fashioned American cookie-jar favorites are best when they are crisp on the outside and chewy on the inside. An extra egg yolk in the dough and some time spent in the refrigerator before they are baked does the trick. The cold, rich dough inside remains slightly underbaked, while the outside is browned to a crisp.

MAKES 2 DOZEN LARGE COOKIES

1 cup (2 sticks) unsalted butter

1½ cups sugar

1 whole egg

1 egg yolk

1 teaspoon vanilla extract

2 cups all-purpose flour

½ teaspoon baking powder

1 teaspoon kosher salt

½ cup cinnamon sugar

1. Soften the butter: Cut all the butter into 1-inch chunks. Melt half of it in a saucepan and put the rest in the bowl of a stand mixer. Pour the melted butter over the cold butter and beat until all the butter is smooth and creamy.

2. Add the sugar and continue beating until the mixture is light and fluffy. Add the egg and egg yolk and beat until completely incorporated into the butter and sugar mixture. Stir in the vanilla extract.

3. In a separate, large mixing bowl, whisk together the flour, baking powder, and salt. Scrape the butter mixture into the flour mixture and fold gently with a rubber spatula just until the mixture comes together to form a soft dough. Chill the dough.

4. Preheat the oven to 350°F and line 2 baking sheets with baker's parchment. Scoop the chilled cookie dough into 1-inch balls, and roll the balls in cinnamon sugar. Place on the baking sheets and bake until the cookies spread and puff up, about 10 minutes. Do not overbake; they should remain chewy on the inside. Cool the cookies on the pans; they will flatten as they cool.

★
COCONUT CHIHULY
COOKIE SHELL

I named these cookies after glass artist Dale Chihuly, because their free-form shapes recall the Puget Sound Forms he created in the 1980s for the Seattle Aquarium. The wide open cookie bowls with flowing sides are substantial enough to hold any ice cream, sorbet, or custard, but I like them best filled with a perfectly round scoop of Coconut Sorbet (page 363). The cookie dough spreads so make sure to allow plenty of room on the baking sheet.

MAKES ABOUT 2 DOZEN COOKIE CUPS

½ cup coconut oil

1 cup sugar

1 cup unbleached white flour

⅓ cup malt syrup

½ cup shredded coconut

Ice cream, sorbet, or custard, as a filling

1. In a medium, heavy saucepan, melt the coconut oil. Whisk in the sugar, flour, malt syrup, and coconut. Cook, stirring constantly, over medium-high heat until well blended.

2. Transfer the hot batter to a shallow pan and refrigerate until it is stiff.

3. Meanwhile, preheat the oven to 350°F and line several baking sheets with baker's parchment.

4. Using a miniature ice cream scoop or tablespoon, shape the chilled batter into 1-tablespoon balls and place them several inches apart on the prepared baking sheets. Bake no more than 4 or 5 cookies on a sheet. (If a convection oven is used, weight the corners of the paper down with potato pieces.)

5. Bake the cookies until they spread out and turn golden brown, about 10 minutes. Remove from the oven and quickly drape the hot cookies one by one over upside-down glasses or cups to make cup shapes. When cool, place them on a tray and seal in a plastic bag for storage. Store in a warm, dry place.

6. Fill the cookies with ice cream, sorbet, or custard, and serve.

Rolled Cookies

✦

"SUGAR IN THE RAW" COOKIE LEAVES

I like to cut these cookies in the shape of leaves and mark veins in the leaves with the dull side of a paring knife. It is less tedious than it sounds. Served on a tray lined with clean leaves or cedar boughs with chocolate truffles and bite-sized meringue cookies, the leaf shapes evoke the look of an enchanted forest floor where everything is edible.

MAKES 2 DOZEN LARGE COOKIES

1 cups (2 sticks) unsalted butter

¾ cup turbinado sugar or Sugar in the Raw

2 egg yolks

1 teaspoon vanilla extract

2 cups plus 2 tablespoons unbleached white flour

2 teaspoons kosher salt

1. Preheat the oven to 350°F and line 3 large baking sheets with silicone pan liners or baker's parchment.

2. Soften the butter: Cut all the butter into 1-inch chunks. Melt half of it in a small saucepan and put the rest in the bowl of a stand mixer. Pour the melted butter over the cold butter and beat until all the butter is smooth and creamy.

3. Add the sugar and continue beating until the mixture is light and fluffy. Add the egg yolks and vanilla extract, and beat until completely incorporated into the butter and sugar mixture.

4. In a separate, medium bowl, whisk together the flour and salt. Add the flour mixture all at once to the butter mixture and fold gently with a rubber spatula just until the mixture comes together to form a soft dough.

5. Chill the dough briefly until it is firm enough to roll. On a floured surface, roll the dough out ⅛ inch thick and cut into shapes with cookie cutters. Bake until golden brown around the edges and slightly puffed in the center, about 10 minutes. Cool on the pans before removing them. The cookies will crisp as they cool.

✦

GINGERBREAD PEOPLE OR SNOWFLAKES

Half the pleasure of these cookies is derived from their warming aroma. While they bake, the house is filled with a spicy scent that lingers as long as they do. Hang them from the Christmas tree if you like. Before they are baked, use a chopstick to press a hole into each cookie. After the cookies are baked and decorated, slip ribbons or twist ties through the holes. When mixing up the dough, spray the measuring cup with nonstick spray or put a teaspoonful of oil in the bottom of the cup before measuring the molasses, and it will slip right out of the measuring cup with no scraping.

For the Cookies

¾ cup (1½ sticks) unsalted butter or
nonhydrogenated vegetable shortening,
softened to room temperature

¾ cup brown sugar

¾ cup molasses

1 egg yolk

3 cups unbleached white flour

¾ teaspoon baking soda

1 teaspoon ground ginger

1 teaspoon ground cinnamon

½ teaspoon ground cloves

½ teaspoon salt

For the Frosting

3 cups powdered sugar

1 egg white

Decorating sugar (optional)

1. In the bowl of an electric mixer or in a
large mixing bowl with a whisk, combine
the butter, brown sugar, molasses, and egg
yolk.

2. In a separate, medium mixing bowl,
whisk together the flour, baking soda,
ginger, cinnamon, cloves, and salt. Use a
wooden spoon or silicone spatula to stir
the flour mixture into the butter mixture,
and continue stirring until the mixture
comes together to form a dough. Divide

the dough into 2 pieces, wrap the pieces in
plastic, and refrigerate until the dough is
very firm, at least 1 hour.

3. Preheat the oven to 350°F and line
2 baking sheets with baker's parchment.
Working with 1 piece at a time, roll the
dough out on a well-floured surface to ⅛
inch thick and cut it with 5-inch people-
shaped cookie cutters or 4-inch snowflake
cutters. Arrange the cookies on the baking
sheets with 2 inches between them.

4. Bake until the cookies are puffed and
a cookie bounces back when a finger is
pressed lightly into the center, about 8
minutes. As soon as they are baked, use
an offset spatula to transfer the cookies
to a cooling rack, and allow them to cool
completely before decorating.

5. Combine the powdered sugar and egg
white in a small bowl to make the frosting.
Pile the mixture into a zipper-lock food
storage bag. Snip ⅛ inch from a corner
of the bag to make an impromptu pastry
bag, and decorate the cookies with frosting
squeezed from the bag. Sprinkle the frosted
cookies with decorating sugar, if desired.

Hand-Formed Cookies

BISCOTTI

"Her favorite dessert," wrote Angelo Pellegrini *in* The
Unprejudiced Palate, *referring to his five-year-
old daughter, Angela, "is Italian biscotti dipped in*

white wine." I learned to make biscotti from a recipe that Virginia Pellegrini shared with me. "These are not THE biscotti," she confessed. "I promised the kids that I wouldn't share that recipe with anyone but them." At my house, we make biscotti a little more tender than traditional ones, no dipping necessary. But if there is a little vin santo around, we're happy to honor the tradition.

MAKES 2 DOZEN BISCOTTI

2 cups unbleached white flour

½ cup brown sugar

I teaspoon baking powder

I teaspoon kosher salt, or ½ teaspoon table salt

I cup (2 sticks) unsalted butter, cut into bits

I cup whole almonds

2 eggs

½ cup dried currants

I. Preheat the oven to 325°F, and line a baking sheet with baker's parchment.

2. In a food processor, mix the flour, sugar, baking powder, and salt. Add the butter and process until uniformly crumbly. Add the nuts and pulse the motor on and off just until the nuts are chopped.

3. In a medium mixing bowl, beat the eggs and add the mixture from the food processor all at once, with the currants. Mix by hand until everything comes together to form a stiff dough.

4. Knead the dough briefly, then shape it into 2 logs, each one about 8 inches long. Bake the logs until they are cracked on the surface and well browned on the sides, about 25 minutes.

5. Cool the logs completely, then carefully cut them into ½-inch slices (they will be delicate). Bake the slices for 10 minutes, or until crisp.

★

CHOCOLATE CRINKLE COOKIES WITH COCOA NIBS

Based on a cookie that originally appeared in Betty Crocker's 1963 Cooky Book, these cookies take on a whole new life when they are studded with bitter cocoa nibs. Cocoa nibs are simply roasted cocoa beans separated from their husks and broken into bits. With no added sugar, vanilla, or lecithin, the toasty bits are the very essence of chocolate and can be used in place of nuts in sweet or savory dishes. Berkeley, California–based Scharffen Berger Chocolate Maker distributes 6-ounce packages of cocoa nibs to supermarkets all over the West Coast. The cookies should be served warm from the oven; they will be slightly crisp on the outside and still a little soft on the inside. Bake just as many as you plan to eat in a day and keep the rest of the dough refrigerated until you're ready for more.

MAKES 4 DOZEN COOKIES

½ cup canola oil

6 ounces (about I cup) bittersweet chocolate, finely chopped

I½ cups brown sugar

4 eggs

2 teaspoons vanilla extract

2 cups unbleached white flour

2 teaspoons baking powder

½ teaspoon salt

¼ cup cocoa nibs

I cup powdered sugar

I. Put the oil and chocolate in a small, heavy saucepan over medium heat, and stir until the chocolate is almost melted; take the pan off the heat and continue stirring until the chocolate is completely melted and the mixture is smooth.

2. Transfer the melted chocolate mixture to a large mixing bowl and whisk in the brown sugar. Stir in the eggs, one at a time, mixing well after each addition. Stir in the vanilla extract.

3. In a separate, medium mixing bowl, whisk together the flour, baking powder, and salt. With a rubber spatula, stir the flour mixture and cocoa nibs into the chocolate mixture just until the ingredients are all combined. The dough will be soft. Cover the dough securely with plastic wrap and refrigerate for several hours or overnight.

4. Preheat the oven to 350°F and line a baking sheet with baker's parchment. Put the powdered sugar in a small bowl. Shape teaspoonfuls of dough into balls and drop them into the bowl containing the powdered sugar, rolling them in the sugar.

The dough can be shaped into balls, rolled in powdered sugar, and kept refrigerated for several days, or frozen for up to a month.

5. Place the cookies at least 2 inches apart on the prepared baking sheet and bake until the cookies are puffed and crackled on the surface, about 10 minutes. Do not overbake.

Flourless Cookies

★

CRISP MERINGUE COOKIES

These meringues should be very dry and crisp. Serve large ones with custard or ice cream, or stack them with berries and cream. Tiny bite-sized meringues make wonderful flourless cookies. Extra meringues will keep in a cool, dry place for several days, or even weeks.

MAKES ABOUT 1 DOZEN LARGE OR 6 DOZEN BITE-SIZED MERINGUES

I¼ cups granulated sugar

¼ cup powdered sugar

¾ cup (about 6 large) egg whites

I teaspoon freshly squeezed lemon juice

½ teaspoon salt

I. Preheat the oven to 180°F, or to the lowest possible setting. Line 2 baking sheets with baker's parchment. In a large mixing bowl, whisk together the granulated sugar and powdered sugar.

2. In the bowl of a stand mixer, whip the egg whites with the lemon juice and salt until very light and foamy. Very slowly stream in half of the sugar mixture, and continue whipping until the egg whites hold stiff peaks and are very smooth and glossy.

3. With a rubber spatula, fold the whipped egg whites into the remaining sugar, then pile the mixture into a large pastry bag fitted with a straight steel tip with a ½-inch opening. If no pastry bag is available, pile the meringue into a gallon-sized zipper-lock food storage bag and snip ½ inch off one corner to make an impromptu pastry bag.

4. Pipe the meringue onto the lined baking sheets, forming whirled 5-inch circles for desserts or 2-inch dollops for bite-sized cookies. Bake for 6 to 12 hours, or overnight. The meringues should be dry and crisp but still white.

★

CHOCOLATE WALNUT "MOONSCAPE" COOKIES

With no flour, these cookies are almost like a meringue, but the egg whites are not beaten; they're simply stirred in with the other ingredients.

MAKES 3 DOZEN SMALL COOKIES

3 cups powdered sugar

¾ cup unsweetened cocoa powder

3 egg whites (a generous ⅓ cup)

1 teaspoon kosher salt

2 cups walnut pieces, toasted

1. Preheat the oven to 350°F and line 2 baking sheets with baker's parchment.

2. Combine all of the ingredients in a medium mixing bowl. Drop by teaspoonfuls onto the lined baking sheets and bake until crackled on top but still slightly gooey inside, 8 to 10 minutes.

3. Cool and serve or store in a tightly covered container.

★

WALNUT MACAROONS WITH SMOKED SALT

If a food processor is available, these are some of the easiest cookies in the world to make. Even if you don't have a food processor, however, grinding the nuts with an old-fashioned hand-held grinder known as a rotary grater goes pretty quickly. The interesting crisp-chewy texture of these cookies, which contain no butter or flour, comes from the mixture of egg whites and sugar that binds the ground nuts together. The exotic flavor of smoked salt superimposed over the sweet cookies makes them especially compelling, a perfect excuse for lingering at the dinner table while finishing up a fine red wine or sipping coffee.

MAKES 2 DOZEN COOKIES

4 cups chopped walnuts, plus 24 walnut halves for garnish

2 cups powdered sugar, plus more for rolling

1 egg white

1 or 2 teaspoons smoked salt, to taste

1. Preheat the oven to 350°F and line a cookie sheet with a silicone pan liner or baker's parchment.

2. In a food processor, pulverize the walnuts with the powdered sugar until they are ground almost as fine as flour. If no food processor is available, grind the nuts through a rotary grater (an old-fashioned cheese grater) and then stir them into the sugar in a medium mixing bowl.

3. Add the egg white and pulse the motor on and off, or stir in a mixing bowl until the mixture comes together to form a pastelike dough.

4. Sprinkle some extra powdered sugar on the countertop and turn the dough out onto the sugar-covered counter. Divide the dough into 24 pieces and roll each piece into a ball, using additional powdered sugar as needed to keep the dough from sticking.

5. Arrange the balls of dough on the lined cookie sheet and sprinkle each one with a little smoked salt, pressing it in lightly as you go. Top each salted cookie with a half walnut and bake just until the cookies are puffed and beginning to crack on the surface, 8 to 10 minutes. Do not overbake; the cookies should be chewy.

★
ALMOND MACAROONS

Most Americans think of macaroons as coconut cookies, but almond macaroons are more traditional. They are incredibly easy to make. I think they should be in every cook's repertoire.

MAKES 4 DOZEN COOKIES

1 pound almond paste

1½ cups powdered sugar

¼ cup (about 2 large) egg whites

48 whole almonds

1. Preheat the oven to 325°F and line 2 baking sheets with baker's parchment.

2. In a food processor, combine the almond paste, powdered sugar, and egg whites. Divide the dough into 4 equal parts, and shape each piece into a log; cut each log into 12 pieces and roll the pieces into balls.

3. Arrange the balls on the prepared baking sheets and press an almond into the top of each one. Bake until the cookies are puffed and golden, 10 to 12 minutes.

★
BASLER BRUNSLI

The name translates roughly as "brownies from Basel," but these Swiss chocolate almond spice cookies are nothing like American brownies. I learned to make them from my friend Frances Haeberli, whose mother brought the recipe from Switzerland when she moved to the West Coast. You can replace the chopped bittersweet chocolate with semisweet chocolate chips if you must, but these cookies are worth investing in the best chocolate you can find. Traditionalists (including Frances' mother) insist that the nuts and chocolate be ground by hand, but a food processor works for me.

MAKES 4 DOZEN COOKIES

1½ cups whole, natural almonds

1½ cups granulated sugar

1 cup (6 ounces) chopped bittersweet chocolate

1½ teaspoons ground cinnamon

½ teaspoon ground cloves

¼ cup (about 2) egg whites

1 teaspoon kirschwasser (clear cherry brandy)

½ cup powdered sugar, for rolling out the dough

1. Preheat the oven to 300°F and line 2 baking sheets with baker's parchment.

2. In a food processor, combine the almonds and granulated sugar. Pulse the motor on and off until the almonds are coarsely ground, then leave the motor on and grind the almonds fine, about 30 seconds.

3. Add the chopped chocolate, cinnamon, and cloves and pulse the motor on and off to grind the chocolate. (Do not overprocess or the chocolate will melt and the mixture will become pasty; it should be dry and crumbly.)

4. Add the egg whites and kirschwasser and pulse until the mixture comes together to form a stiff dough.

5. On a surface coated with the powdered sugar, roll the dough out ¼ inch thick. (This is thicker than most cookies, so be careful not to roll it out too thin.) Cut the rolled dough into rounds or heart shapes with 2-inch cookie cutters, and transfer the cookies to the lined baking sheets. Reroll any scraps of dough, and cut more cookies in the same manner.

6. Bake the cookies just until they are firm to the touch but still moist inside, 12 to 14 minutes. (Do not overbake or the cookies will harden as they cool; they should be tender and chewy.) Cool the cookies completely and keep in an airtight container for up to 2 weeks.

Shortbread Cookies

★

POPPY SEED DREAM COOKIES

According to Ovid, the god of rest lives in a land where the sun never shines and the still, dusky twilight is disturbed only by the murmur of the gently flowing river Lethe, the river of forgetfulness. Outside the house where the god of sleep rests upon his black, downy cushions, poppies bloom. Poppies bloom in West Coast gardens too: Brilliant red poppies wave their silken petals in the breeze, and in the fall, the hollow skeletons of those flowers shake like maracas in the chill winds. Inside are the poppy seeds of Papaver somniferum, named for

Somnus, the god of sleep. Somnus's son, Morpheus, the god of dreams, lent his name to the drug derived from this plant. The poppy seeds sold for cooking do not contain morphine, but these poppy seed shortbread cookies are so good you will think you are dreaming when you eat one.

MAKES 16 LARGE COOKIES

1 cup (2 sticks) unsalted butter

½ cup powdered sugar

½ teaspoon almond extract

1¾ cups unbleached white flour

¼ cup cornstarch

2 tablespoons poppy seeds

1 teaspoon kosher salt

1. Soften the butter: Melt half of the butter and put the remaining butter in the bowl of an electric mixer. Pour the melted butter over the cold butter and mix on medium speed until all the butter is uniformly smooth and creamy. Add the powdered sugar and almond extract and mix until light and fluffy.

2. Add the flour, cornstarch, poppy seeds, and salt all at once and mix on low speed until the mixture comes together to form a dough. Turn the dough out of the bowl onto a piece of plastic wrap. Shape the dough into a log about 3 inches in diameter, seal it in the plastic wrap, and chill for at least 1 hour, or until it is quite firm.

3. Preheat the oven to 350°F and line 2 baking sheets with baker's parchment. Cut the log of dough into 16 rounds and distribute the cookies, evenly spaced, over the baking sheets. Bake until golden, about 20 minutes. Cool on racks. Serve with tea or coffee. Store extra cookies in an airtight container.

★

WHOLE WHEAT SHORTBREAD COOKIES

These simple "digestives," as the English call them, are the perfect way to round out a holiday meal or say thanks to the host of a family gathering. With only three main ingredients, it is important that each ingredient be of top quality. Don't count on last year's unfinished bag of whole wheat flour to taste fresh anymore, and splurge on some quality designer butter for maximum butter flavor.

MAKES 2 DOZEN COOKIES

2 cups whole wheat flour

½ cup turbinado sugar or Sugar in the Raw

1 teaspoon kosher salt

1 cup (8 ounces) unsalted imported or European-style butter

1. Preheat the oven to 350°F and line a baking sheet with baker's parchment.

2. Put the whole wheat flour, raw sugar, and salt in the work bowl of a food processor and process briefly just to blend. If you don't own a food processor, stir the ingredients together in a large mixing bowl.

3. Cut the butter into ½-inch bits and add them to the flour mixture. Process, pulsing

the motor on and off, until the mixture comes together to form a crumbly dough. If you're working without a food processor, use a pastry cutter or your fingers to work the butter into the flour. Shape the dough into 2 logs, each about 6 inches long, and cut the logs into ½-inch slices.

4. Bake the slices until golden brown, about 20 minutes. Cool completely before storing in airtight containers. The cookies keep for up to 1 week but are best eaten within a day or two after they are baked.

★
CRYSTALLIZED GINGER SHORTBREAD

Crystallized ginger imported from China is available in small 8-ounce boxes in the ethnic food aisle of most supermarkets, but the best crystallized ginger comes from Australia and is sometimes found in tins in the baking aisles of better supermarkets and specialty stores. It is softer and slightly less sugary than the kind in the box. Either kind will make great cookies, but the softer stuff is a little more enjoyable. Serve with tea or coffee. Store extra cookies in an airtight container.

MAKES 2 DOZEN COOKIES

1 cup (2 sticks) unsalted butter, cut into bits

½ cup turbinado sugar or Sugar in the Raw

2 cups unbleached white flour

1 teaspoon kosher salt

½ cup crystallized ginger, cut into bits

1. Soften the butter: Melt half the butter and put the remaining butter in the bowl of an electric mixer. Pour the melted butter over the cold butter and mix on medium speed until all of the butter is uniformly smooth and creamy. Add the sugar and mix until light and fluffy.

2. Add the flour, salt, and crystallized ginger all at once and mix on low speed just until the mixture comes together to form a dough. Turn the dough out of the bowl onto a piece of plastic wrap. Shape the dough into a log about 2 inches in diameter, seal it in the plastic wrap, and chill for at least 1 hour, or until the log is quite firm.

3. Preheat the oven to 350°F and line 2 baking sheets with baker's parchment. Cut the log of dough into 24 rounds and distribute the cookies, evenly spaced, over the baking sheets. Bake until the cookies are golden and darker brown around the edges, about 15 minutes. Cool on racks.

★
LIME AND PECAN SHORTBREAD SNOWBALLS

Mexican wedding cakes and Russian teacakes are two names for powdered sugar–covered shortbread rounds with almost universal appeal. This cookie belongs to that same family of buttery goodness. Here, pungent lime zest and toasted pecans lend the cookies extra character, and cornstarch replaces some of the flour to make the cookies extra tender.

1 cup (2 sticks) unsalted butter, softened to room temperature

1½ cups powdered sugar

1 tablespoon grated lime zest

1 teaspoon vanilla extract

1¾ cups unbleached white flour

¼ cup cornstarch

½ teaspoon salt

1 cup lightly toasted pecans, cooled and chopped

1. Preheat the oven to 350°F and line 2 baking sheets with baker's parchment.

2. In a medium mixing bowl, stir together the butter, ½ cup of the powdered sugar, lime zest, and vanilla. In a separate medium bowl, whisk together the flour, cornstarch, and salt. Add the flour mixture and pecans all at once to the butter mixture, and stir just until the mixture comes together to form a dough.

3. Divide the dough into 4 parts and cut each part into 12 pieces; roll the pieces into balls. Arrange the balls of dough 1 inch apart on the baking sheets, and bake until golden brown, about 10 minutes.

4. As soon as the cookies come out of the oven, sprinkle them with some of the remaining 1 cup powdered sugar. Allow the cookies to cool completely, then roll them in powdered sugar again.

Brownies and Bar Cookies

HOMEMADE GRAHAM CRACKERS

One might wonder why anyone would ever bother to make graham crackers. The boxed variety is very widely available and, when judged by that store-bought yardstick, they would not seem worth the bother. But one of the conceits of West Coast cooking is the dictum "Homemade is always better." Named for Victorian-era vegetarian and health food advocate Sylvester Graham, the cookies seem way ahead of their time. A lecturer on the relationship between diet and health, Graham railed against bakers who used "refined" flour stripped of its husk and germ and "whitened with chemical agents." He would have found kindred spirits in the health food aficionados of our own time. Had he lived to see trans fat–laden hydrogenated shortening, he never would have allowed it to be used in a cookie that bore his name.

1¼ cups whole wheat flour

1 cup unbleached white flour

½ cup brown sugar

1 teaspoon baking powder

½ teaspoon baking soda

½ teaspoon salt

½ cup (1 stick) cold unsalted butter, cut into bits

¼ cup honey

¼ cup cold water

1. Put the whole wheat and white flours, sugar, baking powder, baking soda, and salt in a large mixing bowl or food processor. Add the cold butter and mix with a wire whisk or process on and off until the mixture resembles coarse meal.

2. Stir the honey and water together in a small bowl, then add the liquid to the dry ingredients. Mix just until the dough comes together in a ball.

3. Between 2 sheets of baker's parchment or waxed paper, roll the dough out to a thickness of ½ inch. Chill the dough until it's firm, about 1 hour.

4. Preheat the oven to 350°F and line an 11- by 17-inch baking sheet with baker's parchment. Lightly flour the dough and roll it into a rectangle the same size as the baking sheet. With the dough on top of a piece of parchment, use a pizza cutter or a sharp knife to trim any rough edges off the dough and cut it into 48 rectangles.

5. Lift the parchment with the cut crackers to the baking sheet and, with a fork, prick several holes in each cracker. Bake until lightly browned at the edges, about 15 minutes. Remove from the oven and let cool on the sheet.

★
PARADISE DATE BARS

With a deep, understated sweetness that is never cloying, date bars provide the perfect finish to a casual lunch or dinner. They look rustic and countrified, but creating the

three layers that afford these bars their sublime texture requires a certain amount of skill from the baker. A layer of cooked dates is carefully spread over a layer of delicate shortbread, and then a mixture of more shortbread dough crumbled with oats and nuts is baked on top. To enhance the fruit flavor, I've added a splash of lemon juice to the date filling.

A note on dates: Very often, chopped dates are rolled in oat flour to keep the sticky dried fruit from clumping together. This is not a problem, but when the dates are cooked in liquid, the oat flour makes a slurry around the fruit that is easily scorched, so when cooking the filling for these bars, stir it frequently.

MAKES 2 DOZEN BARS

For the Filling

12 ounces (about 3 cups) chopped dates

¾ cup water

¼ cup freshly squeezed lemon juice

For the Crust

2 cups unbleached white flour

½ cup sugar

1 teaspoon kosher salt, or ½ teaspoon table salt

1 cup (2 sticks) unsalted butter

To Complete the Topping

1 cup quick-cooking oats

¼ cup brown sugar

½ cup chopped pecans

¼ cup (½ stick) unsalted butter

1. Preheat the oven to 350°F. If the oven has a convection option, use it. Spray a 9- by 13-inch baking pan with nonstick spray, then line it with baker's parchment and spray the parchment as well.

2. Stir the dates in a 2-quart saucepan with the water and lemon juice over medium-high heat until the mixture is boiling. Turn off the burner, cover the pan, and allow the dates to cook in the residual heat.

3. In a food processor or large mixing bowl, process or whisk the flour with the sugar and salt to combine. Cut in the 1 cup butter until the mixture is uniformly crumbly. Set half of the mixture aside to make the topping. Press the other half of the dough into the baking dish to make an even layer covering the bottom of the pan. Bake the crust until it is golden brown and lightly puffed, about 10 minutes in a convection oven, 12 to 14 minutes in a conventional oven. Allow the crust to cool to room temperature, then gently spread the cooked date filling over it, being careful not to tear the crust.

4. Combine the reserved crust dough with the oats, brown sugar, and pecans, and with a food processor or your fingers, work in the remaining ¼ cup butter. The mixture should be crumbly, but if it's overprocessed it may become pastelike. If this happens, you will need to roll it out instead of crumbling it over the filling.

5. Bake until the topping is browned, 20 to 25 minutes, a little longer in a conventional oven. Let cool to room temperature, then cut into 24 squares.

★

DEBBI'S CHOCOLATE BROWNIES

I was catering a Christmas party for my friend Debbi Brainerd, and she wanted to know if I would be willing to include her brownies on the menu. "I know you like to use your own recipes," she said, "but these are really good brownies." I said I would be happy to make her brownies, but when I saw that the recipe called for a box of brownie mix, I couldn't bring myself to use it. Instead, I developed this recipe that mirrors the good qualities of packaged brownie mix but is blissfully free of any over-refined or artificial ingredients.

MAKES 4 DOZEN BROWNIES

¾ cup (1½ sticks) unsalted butter

4 cups (24 ounces) semisweet chocolate chips

1½ cups brown sugar

3 eggs

1 teaspoons vanilla extract

¾ cup unbleached white flour

½ cup unsweetened cocoa powder

¾ teaspoon salt

1 cup lightly toasted walnuts, chopped

1. Grease a 9- by 13-inch baking pan, then line the pan with aluminum foil, leaving a 2-inch overhang on both ends. Preheat the oven to 350°F.

2. Melt the butter and half of the chocolate chips in a heavy saucepan over medium heat, stirring regularly until smooth. Remove from the heat, then stir in the brown sugar, eggs, and vanilla. In a separate medium bowl, stir together the flour, cocoa, and salt and add this mixture all at once to the chocolate mixture. Fold in the remaining chocolate chips and the walnuts.

3. Spread the batter in the prepared pan and bake until set, about 20 minutes. Cool the brownies in the pan before slicing. Cut into 48 squares.

★

GREAT GRANDMA GONSER'S LEMON BARS

California citrus fruits are at their absolute best in the winter, and I always like to incorporate them into as many dishes as I can. When one of the cooks at Canlis restaurant agreed to share this recipe for his grandmother's lemon bars, I knew it would become one of my favorites, and it has. A shortbread crust is topped with bright lemon filling that hits just the right notes of sweet and tart.

MAKES SIXTEEN 2-INCH SQUARES

For the Crust

½ cup (1 stick) unsalted butter, softened to room temperature

¼ cup powdered sugar

1 cup unbleached white flour

For the Lemon Filling

2 eggs

1 cup granulated sugar

2 tablespoons freshly squeezed lemon juice

Grated zest of 1 lemon

2 tablespoons flour

½ teaspoon baking powder

¼ teaspoon salt

Powdered sugar, for dusting

1. Preheat the oven to 350°F. Using an electric mixer, cream the butter and powdered sugar. Stir in the flour and spread the mixture over the bottom of an 8-inch square cake pan. Bake until lightly browned, 10 to 12 minutes.

2. While the crust is baking, prepare the lemon filling. In a medium mixing bowl, lightly beat the eggs, then stir in the sugar, lemon juice, and lemon zest. In a small bowl, stir together the flour, baking powder, and salt, and stir into the egg mixture.

3. Spread the filling mixture over the crust. Return to the oven and bake until set, 20 to 25 minutes longer.

4. When the filling has completely cooled, sprinkle with powdered sugar and cut into bars.

More Little Treats

★
ENLIGHTENED BAKLAVA

This traditional Middle Eastern pastry takes on new life when it is brightened with fresh California citrus fruits. It is important to make the pastry long before you plan to serve it. Ideally, it should settle for at least 24 hours. The syrup will set and the pastry will become almost candylike. This might just be the best baklava ever.

MAKES 4 DOZEN PIECES

For the Pastry

1½ cups (3 sticks) unsalted butter, melted

1 pound walnuts

½ cup pine nuts

½ cup sugar

1 teaspoon ground cardamom

One 16-ounce package phyllo dough, thawed

For the Syrup

¾ cup sugar

⅓ cup freshly squeezed lemon juice

⅓ cup freshly squeezed orange juice

¾ cup honey

1 tablespoon grated orange zest

1 teaspoon vanilla extract

1. Preheat the oven to 300°F. Using a pastry brush, lightly brush the bottom and sides of a jelly roll pan (11 by 16 inches, with a ½-inch rim) with some of the melted butter.

2. Combine the walnuts, pine nuts, ½ cup sugar, and cardamom in a food processor and pulse on and off until the ingredients are chopped. If no food processor is available, use a rolling pin to crush the nuts on the countertop, then stir in the sugar and cardamom.

3. Unwrap the phyllo dough and layer 6 whole sheets in the pan, brushing each layer with melted butter as you go.

4. Spread 1 cup of the walnut mixture over the surface of the layered phyllo.

5. Lay another 6 sheets of phyllo over the walnuts, again buttering each layer. Spread with another 1 cup of the walnut mixture.

6. Repeat the layering of phyllo and walnut mixture 2 more times to create a total of 4 layers of nuts, each one sandwiched between 6 sheets of buttered phyllo.

7. Score the layers of pastry halfway through to mark where the baklava will be cut after it's baked. Bake until golden brown, about 1 hour.

8. When the baklava has been in the oven for 45 minutes, combine the sugar, lemon juice, and orange juice in a small saucepan and cook, stirring, over medium heat for 15 minutes. Take the pan off the heat and stir in the honey, orange zest, and vanilla extract.

9. Remove the baklava from the oven and finish cutting through the layers. Pour the syrup over the hot baklava. Cool completely before serving.

Candies

★

CANDIED ORANGE PEEL

If ever something could be greater than the sum of its parts, candied orange peel would certainly be a contender. Somehow the simple ingredients become exotic and wonderful when they are carefully cooked and combined into this sparkling confection. If no organic oranges are available, scrub the oranges well to remove any residual spray on the fruit. You might also consider using organic sugar, also known as evaporated cane juice, but the cost might be prohibitive.

MAKES ABOUT 2 CUPS

2 navel oranges, preferably organically grown

2 cups sugar

I. Line a baking sheet or tray with baker's parchment and set it aside. Cut the oranges into quarters lengthwise, then cut the peel, including about half of the white pith, away from the quarters. Save the pulp for another use. Cut the peelings into ¼-inch-wide strips.

2. Put the strips of peel in a medium saucepan, cover with water, and bring slowly to a boil. Drain off the boiling water. Cover with fresh water and bring slowly to a boil once again.

3. Put I cup of the sugar in a saucepan with ½ cup water and bring to a boil. Add the drained orange peel to the syrup and cook until the syrup is mostly absorbed or boiled away, about 12 minutes. Stir to prevent the peels from sticking and burning. When it appears that the syrup is gone, transfer the candied peel to the parchment-lined tray and, using tongs or a pair of forks, spread it out. Work quickly to prevent the peel from hardening into one massive lump.

4. Let the candied peel air-dry until completely cooled and slightly sticky, at least 2 hours. Toss with the remaining I cup sugar. Store in an airtight jar.

★

CHOCOLATE TRUFFLES WITH COCOA NIBS

Scharffen Berger Chocolates in Berkeley, California, is housed in a venerable-looking century-old building, and the chocolate makers follow artisanal chocolate-making techniques from bean to bar that make the chocolate seem profoundly traditional. But the business is relatively new. Founders Dr. Robert Steinberg and John Scharffenberger did not make their first significant batch of chocolate until the year 2000. When they started selling "cocoa nibs," bakers and cooks were presented with a whole new way to enjoy chocolate. Toasted and crushed cocoa beans that have undergone none of the usual processing that renders chocolate into candy, nibs are chocolate in its purest edible form. They are not sweet, but neither are they particularly bitter; they are simply and deeply flavored of chocolate.

MAKES 48 TRUFFLES

For the Filling

1 vanilla bean

¾ cup heavy cream

4 medium egg yolks

1 tablespoon brandy

1 pound bittersweet chocolate, chopped into bits

For the Coating

4 ounces (about ⅔ cup) bittersweet chocolate, chopped into bits

½ cup cocoa nibs

1. Line a baking sheet with baker's parchment and set aside. Fill a shallow pan or bowl with ice water and set aide.

2. Split the vanilla bean in half lengthwise and scrape it to release the seeds. In a small saucepan over medium heat, heat the cream with the vanilla bean pod and the seeds scraped from inside it. Just before the mixture boils, remove it from the heat. Take out the large part of the bean and scrape it again to get all the seeds and some of the pulp into the cream.

3. In a small bowl, whisk the egg yolks with the brandy and stir in some of the hot vanilla cream. With a rubber spatula,

transfer the egg yolk mixture to the saucepan with the remaining cream and stir gently over medium heat until the cream is slightly thickened and steaming hot.

4. Take the pan off the heat. Stir the chopped chocolate into the hot cream and continue stirring until the chocolate is melted.

5. Place the bowl containing the chocolate mixture in the pan of ice water, and with a wire whisk stir the mixture for 5 minutes, or until it is cooled and slightly thickened.

6. Transfer the mixture to a zipper-lock bag, snip ¼ inch off a corner to form an impromptu pastry bag, and pipe the mixture into cones about 1 inch across onto the parchment-lined sheet. Chill.

7. For the coating, put the chocolate bits and cocoa nibs in the work bowl of a food processor and process until the mixture is uniformly crumbly, about the texture of coarse sand.

8. Roll the cones into balls, and roll the balls in the ground chocolate. Store in tightly sealed containers. Truffles keep, refrigerated in a sealed container, for up to 1 week, or frozen for 1 month.

★

HOMEMADE MARSHMALLOWS

One of the conceits of West Coast cooking is making everything, even items closely linked with mass production, from scratch. Homemade marshmallows are worth the effort. This recipe is derived from an amalgam of several recipes from various sources, but it owes some allegiance to an older edition of Joy of Cooking. *Most marshmallow recipes call for cooling the mixture in a cake pan and then cutting it into cubes. These marshmallows are piped into cloud-shaped puffs.*

MAKES 3 DOZEN PUFFS

2 tablespoons (about 2 packets) unflavored gelatin

⅓ cup cold water

1½ cups sugar

½ cup hot water

½ cup corn syrup

2 teaspoons vanilla extract

1 cup powdered sugar

1 tablespoon cornstarch

1. In the bowl of a stand mixer, sprinkle the gelatin over the cold water and let the mixture stand for at least 5 minutes. The gelatin will soften but will not dissolve at this point.

2. Stir the sugar, hot water, and corn syrup together in a large saucepan over high heat until the sugar has dissolved and the mixture is boiling. When the syrup registers 240°F on a candy thermometer, or as soon as a spoonful dropped into a cup of cold water forms a soft ball, it's ready.

3. With a whisk attachment, beat the gelatin and cold water mixture as you stream in the boiling syrup. The hot syrup will dissolve the gelatin. Stir in the vanilla extract. Continue beating until the mixture is whipped into a puffy, white meringuelike froth that holds stiff peaks.

4. While the marshmallows are whipping in the mixer, whisk together the powdered sugar and cornstarch in a small bowl and sift half the mixture over the surface of a baking sheet.

5. Pile the fluff into a gallon-size zipper-lock bag, snip 1 inch off one corner, and pipe it onto the powdered sugar–lined baking sheet. Sift the remaining sugar-cornstarch mixture over the finished marshmallows.

★

PUMPKIN SEED BRITTLE

In this old-fashioned home-style candy, the hard caramel structure of pure sugar crystals is interrupted by microscopic butter balls and bubbles of air introduced by a reaction from a bit of baking soda added at the end of the cooking time. The result is a more toothsome treat, easier to eat than pure praline.

MAKES ABOUT 1 POUND

1 cup sugar

½ cup light corn syrup

1 cup green pumpkin seeds (pepitas)

1 tablespoon butter or oil

⅛ teaspoon baking soda dissolved in 1 tablespoon water

1. Line a baking sheet with a heatproof silicone pan liner or, if a pan liner is unavailable, a sheet of baker's parchment rubbed lightly with canola oil. Also lightly oil a rolling pin, preferably one made of marble.

2. Put the sugar and corn syrup in a deep saucepan over medium-high heat and stir until the sugar is completely melted. Cook the syrup without stirring until a drop of the stuff forms a hard ball when it's dropped into a cup of cold water, or until it registers 250°F on a candy thermometer. Stir in the seeds and continue to cook until a ribbon of the syrup instantly hardens when it's spun off the tip of a spoon; it will register 295°F on the candy thermometer. Quickly stir in the butter and the baking soda mixture.

3. Pour the candy immediately onto the lined baking sheet and roll it with the oiled rolling pin to a uniform thickness of about ⅛ inch. When it is cool, break the candy into pieces.

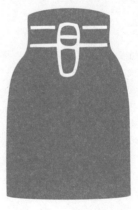

PICKLES & PRESERVES

Pickles & Preserves

"Standing over her stove in a sweltering-hot July kitchen, my grandmother, surrounded by buckets of fruit and dozens and dozens of empty glass jars, stirred cauldrons of chopped fruit for jam and simmered huge kettles of fruit to serve whole," recalls Californian Georgeanne Brennan in *The Glass Pantry*. The scene is archetypal.

My own family had its star preserver in the form of my Great-Aunt Millie. Late in life, she and my Great-Uncle John settled into a house by a lake. Between the house and Uncle John's chair by the lake stood a series of makeshift sheds. Inside one of the sheds they stored furniture and various objects from their old home that never found a spot in the lake house. Inside another was my Uncle John's boating gear, his lawnmower, and a wheelbarrow. In the third was Aunt Millie's larder.

A testament to her hard work, the larder was a somber temple of home economy. Oddly shaped bottles and jars filled with things from the garden shone like stained glass windows in the dim light reflected off the lake. They were oddly shaped because, against the advice found in all the books I've ever seen on home canning, Aunt Millie used only recycled jars. Of course, no one used the word "recycled" then; they just called them old.

"I just use old mayonnaise and pickle jars," she once said. "I can't see puttin' out good money for fancy canning jars and throwin' these away." She took no uncertain pride in "making do" and "getting by on next to nothing."

Sometimes I imagine that what I saw in Aunt Millie's larder was the passing of an era. Home canning, once a vital part of homemaking, has been reduced to a craft practiced only by a few odd souls living on the edges of modern towns and cities. Once many tons of produce went into jars to ensure that winter tables would be brightened with some of summer's bounty. Now only a trickle of produce gets into jars.

The older adults who had to perform the daunting task of processing those jars were probably happy to see the old era end. For them, the very words "canning" and "preserving" conjure images of hard labor.

Our parents' generation, liberated by modern supermarkets, swore they'd never go the way their grandmothers went. Canning might have died. Instead, it has been romanticized into a treasured handicraft— widely practiced, but in a whole new way. "After my grandmother's death," writes Brennan, "the only canning I witnessed was my mother's yearly half-dozen jars of clove-pierced pickled peaches."

So the days of serious canning are over; but for a new generation of homemakers, the age of leisure canning has just begun. Most people who practice home preserving today put up only small amounts of food from their backyard gardens and local farmer's markets, largely out of nostalgia and a lingering hunger for the taste for homemade pickles and preserves.

As for me, I never got ahold of Aunt Millie's recipes for pickles and jams, but I think of her every time I wash out a jar to be used for pickling or canning. Surrounded by an almost incredible abundance of fresh produce as we often are, I suppose it is only natural that West Coast cooks would feel compelled to put some of that bounty into jars to preserve it.

Certainly every West Coast cook I know has dabbled with preserving and pickling things. Take Kathy Casey, the bright young chef who, with her camera-ready smile, her dazzling plate presentations, and her really innovative flavor combinations, became a media darling in the mid-1980s as the spokeswoman for Pacific Northwest cooking. These days she works as a restaurant consultant and runs Dish D'lish, a group of grab-and-go restaurants, but her real passion is putting things up in bottles.

"When I realized that this obsession was more than just a hobby, I took courses from the state and became a master food preserver," she says. Now Dish D'lish includes a line of chutneys, preserves, and even cocktail mixes that have a distinctive West Coast flair.

Once, over a serving of lavender jelly with lamb, I confessed to M. F. K. Fisher that most of what I knew about pickling and preserving I owed to a weird little book called *Fine Preserving*, by Catherine Plagemann. I had found the book in the dark recesses of a used bookstore and knew of no one else who had ever heard of it. To my utter astonishment, the old muse nodded knowingly and said that she knew the book well, that it was in fact "hers" now.

She pointed dramatically to a closet, where I found a neat stack of fifteen or twenty copies of a new paperback version of *Fine Preserving*. Just inside the cover was a line drawing of Mrs. Fisher, seated in a large cane-back chair. The title page bore Plagemann's and Fisher's names, side by side. M. F. K. Fisher's annotated edition of Catherine Plagemann's cookbook was published in 1986. Originally published in 1967, *Fine Preserving* might otherwise have slipped into oblivion.

From artisanal and elegant to simply homey and handcrafted, preserves, pickles, and jams are a satisfying way to enjoy and extend the bounty of West Coast produce.

I always cook jams, jellies, and even most preserves in small batches over high heat, because I like to get them up to jelling temperature before they develop a slow-simmered, cooked taste. The risk is that they will boil over, so it's important to use a large enough preserving kettle or Dutch oven, and to stir the mixture steadily as it cooks; the moment you stop stirring, the mixture boils up.

★

AUNT MILLIE'S APRICOTS
WITH VANILLA BEANS

While I never actually secured any of my Great-Aunt Millie's recipes for preserves and home-canned foods, I think of her when I make this sort of thing. She was, like many women of her generation, a canner extraordinaire, but unlike other women who abandoned the craft when it was no longer a necessary part of her domestic duties, Aunt Millie kept it up because she enjoyed it. In a cool, dark place, the canned apricots will keep for a year.

MAKES 4 QUARTS

6 cups water

4 cups sugar

36 apricots

4 vanilla beans

1. In a stockpot or canning kettle filled with boiling water, sterilize 4 wide-mouth, quart-sized canning jars by submerging them completely; allow them to simmer over low heat for at least 10 minutes, or as long as it takes to prepare the fruit and syrup.

2. In a large saucepan, combine the water and sugar and bring the syrup to a boil. Cut each apricot in half, and remove the pits. Place 18 apricot halves and a vanilla bean in each sterilized jar. Pour the boiling syrup over the fruit, leaving ½-inch headspace at the top of the jars; then seal each jar with a new lid.

3. Place the filled jars in the canning kettle, and when the water is boiling, begin timing. Allow the apricots to boil in the jars for 30 minutes, then lift the jars out of the boiling water bath and allow them to cool, undisturbed, for several hours or overnight.

★

NEW BANANA JAM

Catherine Plagemann's little book Fine Preserving *is the only place I have ever seen a recipe for banana jam. Plagemann's formula was spiked with cloves and contained thin slices of lemon; it was almost like a marmalade. I wanted a jam that could be spread over bread for peanut butter sandwiches, so my version uses powdered pectin and lemon juice. The starchy bananas, especially underripe ones, are inclined to stick, so it is important to stir the jam constantly while it cooks. Serve the jam with bread, or use it in peanut butter sandwiches.*

MAKES 6 HALF-PINT JARS

4 cups mashed ripe bananas

½ cup freshly squeezed lemon juice

One 2-ounce package powdered pectin

1 thumb-sized piece ginger root, finely grated on a Microplane grater

6 cups sugar

1. In a stockpot or canning kettle, cover 6 clean half-pint canning jars with boiling water. Simmer the jars, covered, over low heat to sterilize while you make the jam.

2. Put the mashed bananas in a heavy-bottomed 6-quart saucepan with the lemon juice, pectin, and ginger. Stir the mixture with a spatula, scraping the bottom of the pan regularly over medium-high heat, until the pectin is dissolved and the mixture is boiling. Be careful; it will splatter.

3. Stir in the sugar, and when the mixture returns to a boil, continue to stir and cook for exactly 2 minutes. Transfer the mixture to the sterilized jars, seal the jars with new lids, and process the sealed jars in a boiling water bath for 10 minutes. Any jars that don't seal can be kept in the refrigerator; sealed jars will keep in a cool, dark cabinet for a year.

★

BACKYARD RASPBERRY JAM

This straightforward formula for putting up a few jars of jam works best when the fruit is just ripe—not overripe—and very, very fresh. Once berries are picked, the pectin in them starts to break down. Ideally, the fruit would be picked and preserved all in a matter of minutes. When blackberries come into season, use the same formula to make blackberry jam.

MAKES 5 HALF-PINT JARS

4 cups (tightly packed) raspberries

½ cup freshly squeezed lemon juice

4 cups sugar

1. In a stockpot or canning kettle, cover 5 clean half-pint canning jars with boiling water. Simmer, covered, for at least 10 minutes over low heat to sterilize while you make the jam.

2. In a heavy, 4-quart soup pot or Dutch oven over high heat, mash the berries with the lemon juice. When the fruit has come to a full, rolling boil, stir in the sugar. Continue stirring until the mixture returns to a boil, then stop stirring and insert a candy thermometer. When the thermometer registers 220°F, take the pot off the heat.

3. With tongs, lift the sterilized jars from their simmering water bath and arrange them right side up on a clean kitchen towel.

4. Ladle the jam into the sterilized jars. Dip one corner of a clean, lint-free towel into the boiling water and wipe the lips of the jars to remove any jam.

5. Put on the lids and seal according to the manufacturer's instructions, then put the jam-filled jars back in the boiling water and boil for 5 minutes. Allow the jam to cool in the jars undisturbed for several hours or overnight. Any jars that don't seal can be kept in the refrigerator; sealed jars will keep in a cool, dark place for at least a year.

⋆ PERFECT PEACH PRESERVES

While fully soft, ripened fruit is best for eating out of hand, the complex starch known as pectin is gradually converted into simple sugars as the fruit ripens. So for preserves and jams, barely ripened fruit is best. The key is to get fruit that is already fully fragrant but not yet completely soft. The preserves, if they are not fully set, will still be wonderful spooned over ice cream or made into a trifle (see pages 353–54).

MAKES 6 HALF-PINT JARS

5 medium, barely ripe peaches

½ cup freshly squeezed lemon juice

4 cups sugar

1. In a stockpot or canning kettle, cover 6 clean half-pint canning jars with boiling water. Simmer, covered, over low heat to sterilize while you make the preserves.

2. Peel the peaches. In a large pot over high heat, bring a gallon of water to a full boil. Fill a large mixing bowl with ice water and set aside. Drop the peaches into the boiling water; after 1 minute, use a slotted spoon to lift them out and put them in the ice water. The skins will slip off. Peel the parboiled peaches, then cut each one into 8 wedges. Discard the pits.

3. In a heavy, 4-quart soup pot or Dutch oven over high heat, mash the peach slices with the lemon juice. When the fruit has come to a full, rolling boil, stir in the sugar. Continue stirring until the mixture returns to a boil. Still stirring intermittently to prevent the preserves from sticking, cook the preserves until the fruit is translucent and a spoonful stands upright on a chilled plate; a candy thermometer will register 220°F. As soon as the preserves are ready, take the pot off the heat.

4. With tongs, lift the sterilized jars from their simmering water bath and arrange them right side up on a clean kitchen towel.

5. Ladle the preserves into the sterilized jars. Dip one corner of a clean, lint-free towel into the boiling water and wipe the lips of the jars to remove any jam.

6. Put on the lids and seal according to the manufacturer's instructions, then put the jam-filled jars back in the boiling water and boil for 5 minutes. Allow the jam to cool in the jars undisturbed for several hours or overnight. Any jars that don't seal can be kept in the refrigerator; sealed jars will keep in a cool, dark cabinet for a year.

MANDARIN ORANGE MARMALADE

I always smile when the new crop of satsuma mandarin oranges comes into the market in early November. My favorites are the ones with the green leaves still attached, and sometimes a bowl of them presented after dinner makes the perfect dessert. The fruits are so wonderfully fragrant and sweet, and they brighten the darkening days of early winter. I like to transform some of the bounty into this cheerful preserve to give out as Christmas presents, or to hoard in my own pantry cupboard.

9 medium (about 5 pounds) satsuma mandarin oranges

2 cups water

½ cup freshly squeezed lemon juice

4 cups sugar

1. In a stockpot or canning kettle, cover 6 clean half-pint canning jars with boiling water. Simmer the jars, covered, over low heat to sterilize while you make the marmalade.

2. Peel the oranges, and put the peels in one pile and the innards in another. Stack the peels, a few at a time, on a cutting board and cut them into very thin strips, less than ⅛ inch wide. You will need 2 cups (packed) sliced orange peel; discard the rest.

3. In a large kettle over high heat, cook the sliced peels in the water for 5 minutes. If you want marmalade that's less bitter, pour off the water in which the peels were boiled and replace it with fresh water.

4. Put the insides of the oranges (the segments) in a food processor and purée with the lemon juice. Add the purée to the cooked mixture of peels and water. When the whole mixture has reached a lively boil, add the sugar and boil it, stirring occasionally, for 15 minutes, or until the marmalade has thickened slightly. (A candy thermometer—if you have one—will register 220°F.)

5. Transfer the hot marmalade to the sterilized canning jars, then seal the jars with new two-part lids. Put the jars back into the pot where they were sterilized and let the filled jars simmer under the water for 5 minutes. Any jars that don't seal can be kept in the refrigerator; sealed jars will keep in a cool, dark cabinet for a year.

★

WALLA WALLA SWEET ONION RELISH

Sweet onions do not contain more sugar than stronger, hotter "keeper" onions; they contain more water, which makes them milder. The water makes them more perishable too, so they are perfect candidates for this relish. This is a great condiment for anything from a hamburger to a pot roast.

MAKES 6 HALF-PINT JARS

12 large sweet onions, such as Walla Walla Sweets

½ cup kosher salt

2 cups cider vinegar

1 cup sugar

1 tablespoon mixed pickling spice

1. With a very sharp knife, slice the onions in half vertically, then remove their skins and thinly slice each half to produce thin, even slices. In a large mixing bowl, sprinkle the sliced onions with the salt. After 2 hours, drain the onions in a colander and rinse under running water.

2. In a stockpot or canning kettle over medium-high heat, combine the vinegar and sugar. Secure the pickling spice in a piece of cheesecloth, tied at the corners, or pack it into a tea ball. This will keep the spices from mingling with the onions, which would make it very difficult to fish them out later. Add the secured spices and sliced onions to the cider-sugar mixture and bring the mixture to a rolling boil. Reduce the heat to low and simmer, stirring occasionally, for 45 minutes to an hour, or until the relish is thick.

3. While the relish is simmering, arrange 6 half-pint jars in a kettle and cover with water. Bring the water to a boil, then reduce heat to a simmer. When the relish reaches the desired thickness, remove the spices and transfer the relish to the sterilized jars. Seal the jars with new lids and process in a boiling water bath for 10 minutes. Any jars that don't seal can be kept in the refrigerator; sealed jars will keep in a cool, dark cabinet for a year.

★

PEAR GINGER CHUTNEY

Of course, it goes very well with curried dishes, but this chutney is also the perfect condiment for a turkey sand- wich and a great addition to a cheese tray; a jar of it offered discreetly to the hostess who has everything makes a welcome gift.

MAKES 6 HALF-PINT JARS

1 small red onion, peeled and thinly sliced

1½ cups apple cider vinegar

1½ cups sugar

1 tablespoon salt

6 pounds (about 12 medium) pears

1 lemon

1 tablespoon grated ginger root

1. In a stockpot or canning kettle, cover 6 clean half-pint canning jars with boiling water. Simmer the jars, covered, over low heat to sterilize while you make the chutney.

2. Put the onion, vinegar, sugar, and salt in a heavy 4-quart stockpot or Dutch oven over medium-high heat and boil until the onion is soft and the syrup is reduced to a thick glaze, about 10 minutes.

3. While the onion is boiling in the cider and sugar mixture, peel the pears, core them, and cut the flesh into 1-inch chunks.

4. Add the diced pears to the onion mixture and cook, stirring gently, until the pears are soft and beginning to break down, about 10 minutes.

5. Grate the colorful outer zest from the lemon and add this zest to the chutney. Juice the lemon and add the juice. Add the grated ginger. Continue stirring and boiling for about 5 minutes more.

6. With tongs, lift the jars out of their simmering water bath and stand them empty and upright on a clean kitchen towel. Ladle the chutney into the sterilized

jars and seal the jars. Any bits that dribble onto the lips of the jars can be removed with a clean paper towel dipped into the boiling water.

7. Put on the lids and seal the jars according to the manufacturer's instructions, then put the filled jars back in the boiling water and boil for 5 minutes. Allow the chutney to cool in the jars undisturbed for several hours or overnight. Any jars that don't seal can be kept in the refrigerator; sealed jars will keep in a cool, dark cabinet for a year.

⭐

RHUBARB AND GINGER CHUTNEY

The combination of rhubarb and ginger works so well that rhubarb with almost anything else makes one wish that ginger were involved. This simple condiment is humble enough to garnish a pork chop, but it's swank enough to dress up a serving of pan-seared foie gras. Crystallized ginger can be found along with other Asian ingredients in most supermarkets; the best comes from Australia where it is usually made into small dice. The chutney can be cooked and used at once, refrigerated for several days, or put up in canning jars to be used months later.

MAKES 6 HALF-PINT JARS

8 cups (6 to 8 stalks) chopped rhubarb

¾ cup crystallized ginger, cut into julienne strips or ¼-inch dice

¾ cup sugar

¾ cup raspberry vinegar

1 tablespoon salt

1. In a stockpot or canning kettle, cover 6 clean half-pint canning jars with boiling water. Simmer the jars, covered, over low heat to sterilize while you make the chutney.

2. In a 6-quart nonreactive (enamel or stainless steel) saucepan over medium-high heat, stir together the rhubarb, crystallized ginger, sugar, raspberry vinegar, and salt. Cook, stirring, until the sugar is dissolved and the mixture is beginning to boil. Cover, reduce the heat to low, and cook until the rhubarb is very tender and beginning to disintegrate, 6 to 8 minutes.

3. With tongs, lift the jars out of their simmering water bath and stand them empty and upright on a clean kitchen towel. Spoon the chutney into the sterilized jars. Any bits that dribble onto the lips of the jars can be removed with a clean paper towel dipped into the boiling water.

4. Seal the jars with new lids, then put the filled jars back in the boiling water and boil for 5 minutes. Allow the chutney to cool in the jars undisturbed for several hours or overnight. Any jars that don't seal can be kept in the refrigerator; sealed jars will keep in a cool, dark cabinet for a year.

⭐

SPICY PICKLED GREEN BEANS

I started making these one year when I lived in Belling-
ham and had more green beans than I knew what to do
with. They are crisp, and their zippy flavor is welcome in
winter when good green beans are hard to come by.

MAKES FOUR 24-OUNCE JARS OR 6 PINTS

6 tablespoons canning salt or kosher salt

3¾ cups vinegar

3¾ cups water

3 pounds green beans

4 teaspoons dried red chile flakes

8 cloves garlic, sliced (not chopped)

4 or 6 dill or fennel tops

1. In a stockpot or canning kettle, cover 4 clean 24-ounce canning jars with boiling water. (If you don't have the tall 24-ounce jars, use 6 pint-size jars.) Simmer the jars, covered, over low heat to sterilize while you make the pickles.

2. Put the salt, vinegar, and water in a 4-quart soup pot over high heat and bring the liquid to a boil. While the liquid is heating up, trim the ends off the green beans. Remove the stem ends, but leave the pointed "tails" intact.

3. With tongs, lift the jars out of their simmering water bath and stand them empty and upright on a clean kitchen towel. Pack the jars with the trimmed green beans, standing them upright. Distribute the pepper flakes, sliced garlic,

and dill or fennel tops among the jars and pour the boiling liquid into them, allowing ½ inch of headspace at the top. Tap the jars on the countertop to remove any air bubbles.

4. Put two-piece lids on the jars, then put the filled jars back in the boiling water and boil for 15 minutes. Allow the jars to cool at room temperature. The lids will make a popping noise when they seal as they are cooling. Any jars that do not seal should be stored in the refrigerator. Sealed jars will keep in a cool, dry place for a year.

⭐

PICKLED CARROT STICKS

Pickled carrots make a colorful garnish for everything
from tuna sandwiches to country pâté.

MAKES 4 PINTS

4 pounds carrots

2½ cups apple cider vinegar

1½ cups water

½ cup sugar

1 teaspoon kosher salt

4 bay leaves, broken into 4 pieces

1 teaspoon peppercorns

1. Peel the carrots and cut them into ½- by 4-inch matchsticks; set aside. In a preserving kettle or stockpot, sterilize 4 wide-mouth, pint-size canning jars and allow the jars to simmer, undisturbed, while you prepare the pickles.

2. In a saucepan over medium-high heat, combine the vinegar, water, sugar, and salt and bring the liquid to a boil; reduce the heat to a simmer, and cover.

3. With tongs, lift the jars out of their simmering water bath and stand them empty and upright on a clean kitchen towel. Distribute the carrots evenly among the jars. Put the pieces of 1 bay leaf and ¼ teaspoon peppercorns in each jar. Pour the vinegar mixture into the jars, allowing ½ inch of headspace at the top. Seal with new, sterilized two-piece canning jar lids and return the sealed jars to the boiling water. Simmer the filled jars for 15 minutes, then remove and allow them to cool at room temperature for several hours or overnight. Any jars that fail to seal can be kept in the refrigerator, where they will keep for several months. Sealed jars will keep in a cool, dark place for a year.

★ SWEET PICKLED BEETS

When I first moved to the West Coast in my early twenties, a wild-haired refugee from suburbia, I discovered almost overnight the joys of keeping a vegetable garden. I discovered pickling and preserving at about the same time. The flavor—even the sight—of pickled beets always evokes memories of that chapter in my life. My friend Jeff Showman who taught me a lot about canning said that the most important thing about the whole craft was to use only produce that came directly from the garden to the kitchen. *"Never mess around with old stuff from the grocery store."*

MAKES 4 PINTS

4 pounds very fresh beets

2½ cups apple cider vinegar

1½ cups water

½ cup brown sugar

1 teaspoon kosher salt

1 medium onion, peeled and sliced

1 thumb-sized piece ginger root

4 small cinnamon sticks

1 teaspoon black peppercorns

1 teaspoon whole cloves

1. Cook the beets in boiling water until fork-tender. (Depending on the size and freshness of the beets, this will take anywhere from 25 to 45 minutes.)

2. While the beets are cooking, sterilize 4 wide-mouth, pint-size canning jars in a preserving kettle or stockpot full of boiling water, and allow the jars to simmer, undisturbed, while you make the pickles.

3. Stir together the vinegar, water, brown sugar, and salt in a saucepan over medium-high heat until the sugar is dissolved. When the liquid boils, reduce the heat to a simmer and cover.

4. Peel the cooked beets under cold running water and slice them into ½-inch rounds. If they are very small, leave them whole. With tongs, lift the jars out

of their simmering water bath and stand them empty and upright on a clean kitchen towel. Fill the jars with the beets, layering them with slices of onion. Scrape the skin off the ginger root with the edge of a spoon and slice it into 4 "coins." Distribute the ginger, cinnamon sticks, peppercorns, and cloves evenly among the jars and pour the vinegar mixture into the jars, allowing ½ inch of headspace at the top.

5. Seal the jars with new, sterilized two-piece canning jar lids and return the sealed jars to the boiling water. Simmer the filled jars for 15 minutes, then remove them and allow to cool at room temperature for several hours or overnight. Any jars that don't seal can be kept in the refrigerator; sealed jars will keep in a cool, dark cabinet for a year.

★

HOMEMADE SAUERKRAUT

Making sauerkraut or pickled cabbage is a little messy, but it is not difficult and the results are downright thrilling. Fresh sauerkraut has a sparkle, a vitality that cannot be found in the commercial stuff. It's more than a relish for hot dogs; it is the foundation of a good meal. If you don't have a suitable crock, the big glass food storage jars sold in most big department stores are a good option. The finished pickle can be refrigerated or packed into canning jars and processed.

6 pounds (2 or 3 heads) green cabbage

¾ cup kosher salt

1. Remove any damaged outer leaves from the cabbages and cut the heads into quarters. Cut out the core section from each quarter cabbage and slice the sections into thin ribbons, less than ⅛ inch thick. You should have about 2 gallons loosely packed, shredded cabbage.

2. In a very large mixing bowl, toss the shredded cabbage with the kosher salt and allow the mixture to stand until the cabbage releases some of its juice, about an hour. Rinse a clean 2-gallon stoneware crock or glass jar with boiling water and select a plate the same diameter as the crock. Pack the cabbage into the crock and use the plate to press the cabbage down so that it is completely submerged in its juices. (If you need a little extra liquid, dissolve 3 tablespoons of kosher salt in 2 cups of purified water and pour it over the cabbage.) Fill a zipper-lock gallon bag with water to act as a weight on top of the plate. This will keep the cabbage submerged.

3. Every day, use a spoon to skim off any scum that forms on the surface of the brine. Rinse the plate and the weight in clean water and replace them. When the liquid around the cabbage is no longer bubbly, after 16 to 20 days, the pickle is ready.

4. Transfer the finished sauerkraut to clean, pint-sized jars and keep refrigerated. If you want to can the sauerkraut, sterilize the jars in a kettle of boiling water, pack the sauerkraut into the sterilized jars, seal them with new lids, and process the filled jars in boiling water for 15 minutes.

★
HOME-CANNED TOMATO SALSA

In order to be preserved in jars, salsa must be cooked and, once it's cooked, salsa takes on a different character. But that is not necessarily a bad thing. This salsa, based on a recipe from the Washington State University extension service, combines fresh tomatoes and tomato paste to make a thick, rich salsa that's good with chips or on tacos. It also serves as good sauce for Huevos Rancheros (page 30). Organic tomatoes tend to have higher brix ratings; that is, they have a higher sugar content so they make a more flavorful salsa.

MAKES 7 HALF-PINT JARS

2 pounds (about 4 large) tomatoes, preferably organic, peeled and cut into 1-inch dice

1½ cups onion, peeled and cut into ½-inch dice

4 jalapeño peppers, seeded and cut into ⅛-inch dice

2 Poblano or Anaheim chiles, seeded and cut into ⅛-inch dice

4 cloves garlic, grated on a Microplane grater

Two 6-ounce cans tomato paste, preferably organic

1 cup freshly squeezed lime or lemon juice

1 tablespoon kosher salt

2 tablespoons dried oregano, crumbled

1½ teaspoons sugar

1½ teaspoons ground cumin

¼ teaspoon cayenne pepper

1. In a stockpot or canning kettle, submerge 7 half-pint jars in boiling water and keep the jars simmering while you prepare the salsa.

2. Pile the tomatoes, onion, jalapeño peppers, chiles and garlic into a large heavy-bottomed soup pot over medium-high heat. Stir in the tomato paste, lime juice, salt, oregano, sugar, cumin, and cayenne pepper.

3. Stir the salsa until it comes to a boil, reduce heat to low, and simmer, uncovered, stirring often until all the vegetables are tender and cooked through, about 20 minutes.

4. Ladle the hot salsa into sterilized half-pint canning jars, leaving ½ inch of headspace at the top. Wipe jar rims with clean paper towels. Top with hot, sterilized lids and bands.

5. Return the filled jars to the boiling water bath, and when the water returns to a boil, time for 15 minutes. With canning tongs, transfer the jars from the boiling water to a towel-covered countertop or a cooling rack and let them stand undisturbed until they are cooled to room temperature, about 8 hours.

A–B

T–W

About the Author

GREG ATKINSON has been an active chef for more than 20 years and is currently director of Culinary Consulting in Seattle, Washington. He's been called upon many times to breathe new life into restaurants with his refreshing menu ideas. News editors, restaurant owners, and aspiring cooks all look to Greg for inspiration, which comes readily with sincerity and passion. After launching the nationally acclaimed Friday Harbor House on San Juan Island, Greg was drafted to revitalize the menu at Seattle's venerable Canlis restaurant in conjunction with a major renovation in 1996.

The author of *In Season: Culinary Adventures of a San Juan Island Chef* (1997), *The Northwest Essentials Cookbook* (2000), and *Entertaining in the Northwest Style* (2005), Greg is a prolific writer. He started with a weekly column for the *Journal of the San Juan Islands*. This evolved into a series of "Taste" columns for *Pacific Northwest*, the Sunday newsmagazine of *The Seattle Times*, where his lively works have appeared regularly since 1989. Greg is also a contributing editor to *Food Arts* magazine. In 2001, he won the M. F. K. Fisher Distinguished Writing Award (best food story of the year) from the James Beard Foundation. Also a friendly voice on culinary trends, Greg appears weekly on "The Beat" on KUOW radio, Seattle's NPR affiliate. A Certified Culinary Professional (CCP), Greg is active in the International Association of Culinary Professionals (IACP), and serves as Convivium Leader for Slow Food Seattle. He is a guest chef on the award-winning PBS series *Chef's A'field*. Greg's affection for all things food is eclipsed only by his love of his wife, Betsy, and their two sons, Henry and Erich. Their home is on a peaceful acre with a casual orchard of century-old apple trees and an organic vegetable garden.